The Medieval Fortress

Castles, Forts and Walled Cities of the Middle Ages

The Medieval Fortress

Castles, Forts and Walled Cities of the Middle Ages

J. E. Kaufmann & H. W. Kaufmann

Illustrated by Robert M. Jurga

Combined Publishing
Pennsylvania

PUBLISHER'S NOTE

The headquarters of Combined Publishing are located midway between Valley Forge and the Germantown battlefield, on the outskirts of Philadelphia. From its beginnings, our company has been steeped in the oldest traditions of American history and publishing. Our historic surroundings help maintain our focus on history and our books strive to uphold the standards of style, quality and durability first established by the earliest bookmakers of Germantown and Philadelphia so many years ago. Our famous monk-and-console logo reflects our commitment to the modern and yet historic enterprise of publishing.

We call ourselves Combined Publishing because we have always felt that our goals could only be achieved through a "combined" effort by authors, publishers and readers. We have always tried to maintain maximum communication between these three key players in the reading experience.

We are always interested in hearing from prospective authors about new books in our field. We also like to hear from our readers and invite you to contact us at our offices in Pennsylvania with any questions, comments or suggestions, or if you have difficulty finding our books at a local bookseller.

For information, address:
Combined Publishing
P.O. Box 307
Conshohocken, PA 19428
E-mail: combined@combinedpublishing.com
Web: www.combinedpublishing.com
Orders: 1-800-418-6065

Photo and Art Credits:
All drawings and plans are by Robert M. Jurga unless otherwise noted.
All photos are from the authors' collection unless otherwise noted.

First edition, first printing.

Cataloging-in-Publication Data is available from the Library of Congress.

ISBN 1-58097-062-1

Printed and bound in the United States of America.

To our Parents and Wojciech, Rea and Leo

Contents

Illustrations and Plans

Chapter 5

Sidebars

Acknowledgements

We would like to thank the following people for their contributions and help: Markku Airila* (Finnish castles), Ismael Barba* (Spanish castles), John Bray (English castles), Jaroslaw Chorzepa (Polish castles), Pierre Etcheto* (French, Greek, Arab and Central Asian fortifications), Paul J. Gans (medieval populations), Juan Vasquez Garcia* (Spanish castles), Paddy Griffith (Vikings), Francois Hoff (French castles), Inger E. Johansson (early Swedish fortifications), Kenneth von Kartaschew* (Swedish castles), Patrice Lang (French castles), Alain Lecomte (European castles), Bernard Lowry (Welsh & English castles), Wayne Neel (trebuchet), Dave Parker (medieval populations), Frank Philippart* (Belgian castles), Paolo Ramponi * (Italian fortifications), David Read (statistics on feudal armies), Aleks Reinhardt (Slovenian castles), Lt. Colonel Nuno Rubim* (Portuguese fortifications), John Sloan (Russian and Central Asian fortifications), Christopher Szabo (Hungarian castles), Yuri Tulupenko (early Russian fortifications), Serge Verevka (Kiev and Russian fortifications), Lee Unterborn (providing reference materials), Jo Vermeullen (castles), Stephen Wyley (Constantinople). Also, we would like to thank the agencies at the castles of Beersel and Agile, and Monika Repinc at Bled for providing information and materials.

We would also like to thank Jaroslaw Chorzepa , Pierre Etcheto, Bernard Lowry, John Sloan, Christopher Szabo and Stephen Wyley for providing photographs. Also, several drawings were provided by Pierre Etcheto. We would like to thank Wojciech Ostrowski for preparing drawings and plans of castles needed to finish the illustrations. Also, thanks to Barbara Keane-Pigeon at Combined Publishing for her help in completing this project. We would also like to thank all the other members of SiteO who may have helped and whose names we may have inadvertently omitted.

Denotes those who provided a great deal of information and material to this project. Everyone's contribution was important and we hope we have not forgotten anyone's name.

For those who have questions or comments you may contact the author or others involved in the study of fortifications through the Forum on SiteO at http://www.siteo.net/.

*I*ntroduction

The European Middle Ages are associated with the feudal system, a warrior caste of knights, general stagnation, and, of course, the castle. These generalities are misleading. Although the feudal system was dominant for most of the period, it did not exist at all times and in all places. In feudal Europe the knight was supreme, but his fighting methods and equipment varied throughout the period and from region to region. Castles and other fortifications evolved together with society and technology. Medieval men did not see themselves as backward barbarians, as they were later labeled by Renaissance historians. In most of Europe, culture and technology made prodigious advances instead of stagnating for almost a thousand years. This evolution in society and technology is clearly reflected in the construction and use of castles and other defenses.

There are no simple defining cut-off dates for beginning and ending the Middle Ages. Traditionally, the removal of the last Latin Roman Emperor in the West in 476 A.D. has been set as the beginning of the era. The end of the Middle Ages, on the other hand, is marked by various momentous events such as the fall of Constantinople in 1453, the end of the Hundred Years War, the discovery of America, and the expulsion of the Moors from Iberia in 1492. The beginnings of the Reformation can also be considered a watershed event as far as social change is concerned. The battle of Agincourt, on the other hand, ended the dominance of the armored knight and marked the beginning of a new era in military history. The Middle Ages of course overlap with the Classical Age of Ancient History that preceded them, and the Renaissance that followed. And changes in fortifications did not strictly coincide with the 5th and 15th centuries, so it is necessary to go beyond those centuries in order to understand the evolution of the medieval fortifications.

If there is little consensus about the beginning and ending dates of the Middle Ages, there is even less on the way the period is to be subdivided. According to the more traditional views, the Middle Ages are divided into the Early Middle Ages, whose first couple of hundred years are referred to as the "Barbarian Invasions," the High Middle Ages, ranging from the 10th century to the 13th century, and the Late Middle Ages, which ended in the 15th century. In this book, a simpler, but equally traditional, division is used, which splits the Middle Ages into two parts: The Dark Ages and the High Middle Ages. The first half, referred to as the Dark Ages, extends from the 5th to 10th century. Although the term "Dark Ages" is no longer accepted by most medievalists as a proper designation, it will serve our purposes in the present work. The second half of the Middle Ages went from the 10th century to the 15th century. Although this period is usually further subdivided, we will simplify matters by referring to it as the High Middle Ages.

During the Dark Ages, remains of Roman fortified cities comprised many of the stone fortifications in use throughout Western Europe. In the Eastern Roman Empire, known as the Byzantine Empire, and the remnants of the old Western Roman Empire, some of the strongest masonry fortifications that remained faced the onslaught of the so-called "barbarians." Beyond territories of the old Roman Empire, wooden structures predominated. In most cases, except in Byzantium, new defenses were also made of wood. This was the case in the empire of the Franks where fortifications dwindled in importance. In the dryer regions of the Mediterranean, where wood was hard to come by, stone continued to be the material of choice even after the Arab invaders took over North Africa and the Middle East. There construction methods played an important role in influencing the development of European fortifications.

Photo Left: *The gate of Bodiam Castle, England.*

Meung-sur-Loire, France.

In Northern Europe the Norsemen, also referred to as Vikings, spread a technique of earth and wood fortifications which bore a close similarity to those in the Slavic lands of the East. In the British Isles this type of fortification appears to have been present before the arrival of the Norse and, as in the East, continued to dominate until the end of the Dark Ages. The Norsemen who settled in Normandy at the end of this era began spreading a new type of earth and wood fortifications known as the "motte and bailey," which were eventually replaced with stone.

During the High Middle Ages, the stone castle became a prominent feature of the European landscape, only overshadowed by the great cathedrals. This truly became the "Age of Castles." Whereas the Dark Ages had been dominated by fortified cities, the High Middle Ages were characterized by castles, a solid symptom of the fragmentation and decentralization resulting from the expansion of feudalism. The castle became the symbol of status for many powerful nobles who could then challenge the authority of their king. As the castle's role and function changed, so did its size and shape. In the West the stone castle emerged as the dominant fortification along with the fortified city with its masonry defenses. Meanwhile in the East the more ancient type of earthen and timber fortification known as the gród continued to dominate in the forms of small strongpoints and fortified towns. Masonry works did not begin to replace them until later in the period when techniques for brick making and stone working from the West were introduced. Meanwhile, in the Iberian Peninsula, as a result of the centuries long struggle to drive out the Moors known as the Reconquista, East clashed with West, resulting in sophisticated styles of castle construction. The Christian Crusades in the Holy Lands also yielded similar results.

In the 13th century, even the most advanced and modern fortified sites failed to stop the Mongol hordes from the East, which threatened the very existence of Christian Europe. Dominated by weak feudal kingdoms with powerful lords operating from their fortified sites with small forces, eastern Europe was simply overwhelmed by the Mongol masses.

Understanding the distribution of population and its relationship to the size of armies is quite important not only in understanding warfare in the Middle Ages, but also the role and significance of fortifications. The role of feudalism and the influence of external threats such as the Arabs and Mongols exerted a strong influence on the course of events and development of fortifications.

The cannon has long been credited for bringing about the end to the Age of Castles, the decline of high walls, and the creation of the first Renaissance fortifications. However, this theory accounts only partially for the reduction in the size of walls. The ability of the cannon to batter down castle walls is questionable in many cases. In reality the cannon may have caused a reduction in the height of walls not only to reduce their vulnerability, but also to increase the range and effectiveness of the defenders' artillery.

We examine the various elements of the medieval fortifications and their use in the first chapter and give a brief survey of castles throughout the medieval world in the last. The selection of a limited number of representative castles is very difficult simply because of their sheer numbers and extraordinary variety and diversity. Few authors have succeeded in presenting a comprehensive text on castles. As a result, the reader is usually misled into thinking that there are only two or three important castles in certain regions as for example in Alsace or Flanders, when in reality there are dozens of castles in these areas. Usually, attention focuses on castles with long and important histories or, in some cases, on those in an excellent state of preservation. There is no dearth on guidebooks to castles dealing extensively with individual regions. In our volume we have tried to give the reader a taste of the variety and diversity of building styles across the European continent and the Middle East rather than concentrating only on those castles usually covered by traditional Western literature. We hope we have succeeded.

Elements of a Castle

High castle and upper bailey
1. Shield wall
2. Defensive tower
3. Keep
4. Main hall or palace
5. Kitchens and servants' quarters
6. Well
7. Courtyard
8. Blacksmith
9. Chapel
10. Dovecote
11. Powder tower
12. Arsenal
13. Sanitary tower
14. Garderobe
15. Secret exit
16. Breteche
17. Covered allure
18. Bartizan or watchtower
19. Lists
20. Gate tower
21. Main gate to the upper bailey
22. Double drawbridge

Lower bailey
23. Gate tower
24. Armory
25. Knights' hall
26. Lists
27. Sally port

28. Corner tower with spur
29. Blacksmith
30. Living quarters for the servants
31. Well
32. Wet moat
33. Curtain wall
34. Barn
35. Stables
36. Crenelations
37. Gardens
38. Ramp
39. Granary
40. Lower courtyard
41. Bastion
42. Bastion for guns
43. Loops with oilets for firearms
44. Machicoulis
45. Hoardings
46. Drawbridge

Administrative bailey
47. Barbican
48. Palisade
49. Earth rampart
50. Stockade
51. Wooden gate in curtain wall
52. Obstacles
53. Abatis
54. Church
55. Abatis

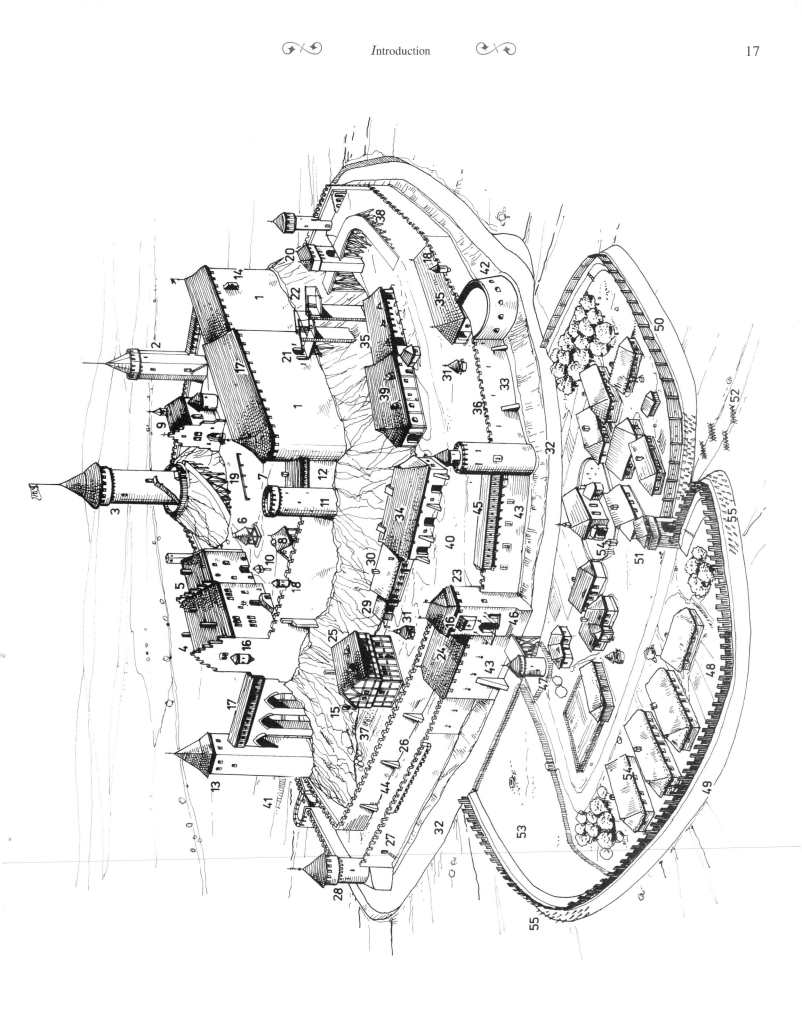

Elements of a Fortified City

1. Castle dominating the city
2. Enceinte
3. Defended bridge
4. Gate tower
5. Lists
6. Wet moat
7. River
8. Chain obstacle across river
9. Arsenal
10. Round bastion
11. Enclosure
12. Drum tower
13. Chatelet
14. Circular bastion
15. Defensive mill
16. Flanking towers
17. City hall
18. Parish church
19. Magazines
20. Central Plaza or market place
21. Fortified monastery
22. Undefended monastery
23. Residence
24. Military road going around the wall
25. Docks
26. Water gate
27. **Suburb of the city**
27. Chatelet
28. Wooden Palisade
29. Curtain
30. Gate tower
31. Bridge
32. Barbican
33. Gate tower
34. Dry moat
35. Church
36. Monastery
37. City Hall of the suburbs
Positions located beyond the city walls
38. Fortified Church
39. Isolated watchtower
40. Hospital and chapel
41. Leper colony
42. Site of executions—"Hangman's Hill"

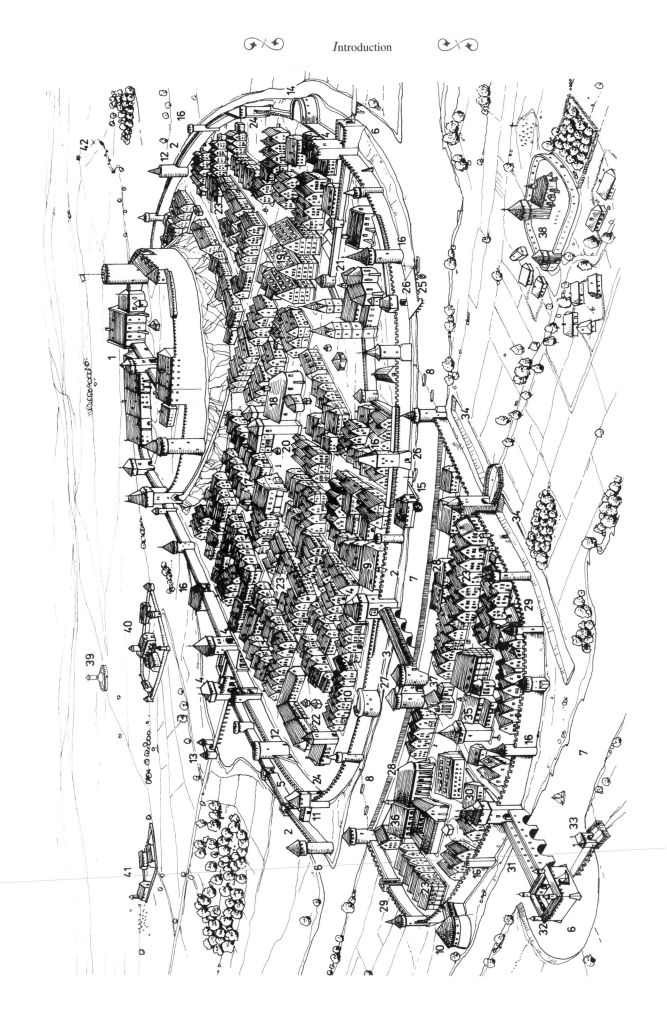

Carcassonne, France.

1

Elements of Medieval Fortifications

The terms castle, citadel, fort, and fortress have been used synonymously with stronghold, which has led to much confusion over time. Each, however, should have its own meaning in military architecture. Although the castle is considered a private fortified residence in northwest Europe, the term is not used in the same way in other regions or in that context with royal castles. The most accurate definition of a castle would be a fortification of the High Middle Ages that was characterized by high walls, usually a moat, and towers, regardless of whether it was a private residence or not. The term fort does not strictly apply to most medieval fortifications since it refers to a small strongpoint usually occupied by military personnel. The typical medieval castle, on the other hand, had not only a military function but also a residential and/or administrative function. The word citadel applies to any strongpoint and can be used to refer to a castle or a section of city that has a fortified position similar to a castle in size.

Although fortress is a term that is usually reserved for large non-medieval fortifications, sometimes it refers to a very large castle-like fortification or a heavily fortified city (town). The fortified city or town usually has many features in common with the castle, but it is larger and may also include a castle, especially if it is a city rather than a town. Many features such as gatehouses, special roofs, crenelations, and moats, which were initially developed for the castle, were eventually incorporated in urban fortifications as well.

Other types of fortified positions of the Middle Ages included tower houses, observation posts, and coastal fortifications, as well as fortified churches, cathedrals, and monasteries. Often these positions incorporated the defensive features found in castles and fortified town. The tower house was simply a residential structure attached to or part of a tower and was somewhat similar to a keep. Tower houses were common in the northern half of the Italian Peninsula and were found as far north as the British Isles and Ireland. Individual observation posts, including those used along the coast, were similar to the bergfrieds or keeps but were usually a solitary tower from which a watchman could sound the alarm as soon as he spotted intruders. Fortified religious structures looked like their unfortified counterparts, but comprised defensive positions like turrets, crenelations, and even murder holes. The fortified monasteries sometimes looked like a small fortified town.

BODIAM CASTLE, ENGLAND

Richard I's unusual keep at Château Gaillard, Normandy.

Gród, Motte and Bailey, Bergfried, and Keep

The origins of the castle in Europe north of the Pyrenees and the Alps are lost in the mists of time, but can be traced to three main types of early fortifications: the gród, the bergfried, and the motte and bailey. The most ancient of them, the gród, was essentially a ring fortification that varied in size and consisted of an earthen rampart, wooden walls, a fortified gate, and a moat.

The bergfrieds are tall towers associated with the Limes built on the frontier of the Roman Empire with the Germanic nations. During the period extending from the Dark Ages to the 11th century they were mostly made of wood and were tall and narrow. It is generally believed that they served as little more than lookout towers at least initially, but some may have been used as residences, although the matter is still a subject of debate. Bergfrieds built of masonry became more common by the 13th century and many were incorporated into castles.

The motte and bailey castle, which may have evolved from earlier ring works akin to the Eastern grody, appeared during the 10th century. It consisted of a wooden tower or donjon standing atop a manmade mound or motte. The motte was located within a courtyard or bailey encircled by a timber palisade with a fortified gate. Whenever the terrain allowed it, the bailey, also known as the ward, was circular. More complicated versions of the motte and bailey included two or more baileys. By the 11th century stone began to replace the timber as a building material. At first, only the donjon was made of stone. Later the gatehouse and finally the walls were also made of masonry. The donjon, which later became known as the keep, was not only a defensive position, but also served as the residence of the local lord or castellan. The keep was square until late in the 12th century, when Richard I introduced the polygonal, almost circular, shape at Chateau Gaillard in Normandy. After that, circular keeps became increasingly popular. It is very likely that the shape of the bergfrieds evolved in a similar manner after masonry was used.

The entrances to the keep and the bergfried were placed on the floor above the ground floor (the European 1st floor). The wooden keeps were built on manmade mounds or mottes for defensive reasons and served as the point of last resistance in the motte and bailey castle. As they became larger and heavier when stone was used, the motte became less practical and was eventually eliminated. During the 12th century, many of the larger keeps were incorporated in the main line of defense, after which they were eliminated altogether. The bergfried too lost its significance in German fortifications during the 13th century as other features grew larger and more dominant.

Bergfried in Otzburg, Germany.

Top left: *Square keep, Portchester, England.*
Top right: *Tour Solidor, Saint Servan near St. Malo, Brittany.*
Bottom right: *Tower of Philip, Villeneuve-les-Avignon, France.*
Bottom left: *12th-century circular donjon, Houdan, France.*
Middle: *Drum tower, Falaise, Normandy.*

Towers

In the gród and the motte and bailey castle, towers were at first made of wood and were either attached to or part of the timber stockade atop an earthen rampart. The rampart was made of soil excavated from the moat. After stone and brick were adopted as building materials for the keeps and gatehouses, the towers too were made of masonry. The towers could be an integral part of the wall or separate entities to which the walls were attached. In some cases, they projected out from the wall, allowing the defenders to cover the curtain walls with flanking fire (and were commonly known as flanking towers). When built of stone or brick they usually had several floors, which were not always connected internally. In some cases, the back of the tower was left open to make it easier to haul up supplies and projectiles from ground level to the fighting platforms above. In addition, the open back prevented the enemy from taking the tower and using it against the defenders. In some cases, access to the tower from the wall walk or allure was only possible over a small drawbridge. Since timber structures no longer survive, it is difficult to know how complex the wooden towers may have been.

The square shape created dead angles on the outside, making towers vulnerable to mining. So during the 12th century, a circular or semicircular pattern was adopted to remedy this problem. Although round towers are attributed to the Crusaders who had seen them in the Orient, it must be pointed out that they were not a new discovery. The Romans had already known that round towers were more efficient than square ones, and had incorporated them in their own fortifications. The city walls of Carcassonne, France, for instance, include semicircular or D-shaped Roman towers.

The spacing of towers along the walls of a castle or a city depended on various factors such as terrain and resources available to the builder. In most cases, towers were placed at the corners but sometimes were also added at regular or irregular intervals along the perimeter. In the Middle East, the Crusaders apparently discovered that regularly spaced mural towers presented many defensive advantages. So, by the 13th century, this principle was increasingly applied in the construction of new castles in Europe. The construction of towers did not follow any standard pattern in medieval Europe though. The size and shape of towers varied considerably, depending on the designer's vision and financial means. However, there are many examples of fortifications where towers followed a uniform design, especially in places where they were regularly spaced.

Another important Middle Eastern feature adopted in Europe at the same time as the round tower was the plinth or thickening and outward sloping of the walls at the base of the tower. The function of the plinth or battered plinth was to add stability to the tower wall and make it more resistant to mining. Eventually the plinth was also adapted to walls.

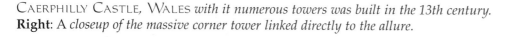

Caerphilly Castle, Wales *with it numerous towers was built in the 13th century.*
Right: A *closeup of the massive corner tower linked directly to the allure.*

Towers

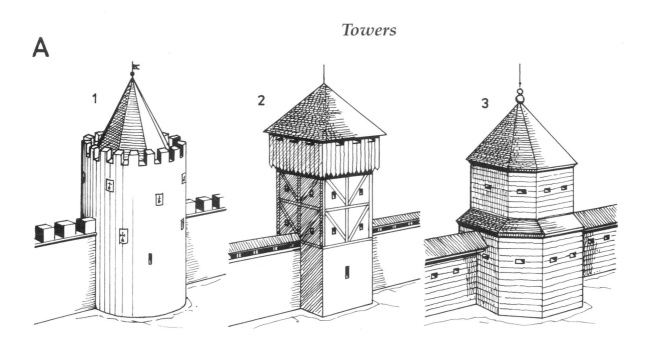

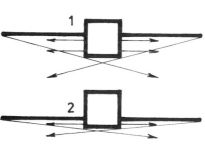

A. Tower Typology
1. Masonry towers
2. Stone and wood towers
3. Wood towers

B. Fields of fire for towers
1. Square tower forward of wall for flanking fire.
2. Square tower flush with wall.
3. Semicircular tower forward of the walls with increased flanking fire.

C. Location of the towers in the curtain walls.
1. Corner tower
2. Mural tower
3. Recessed mural tower
4. Projecting or flanking tower

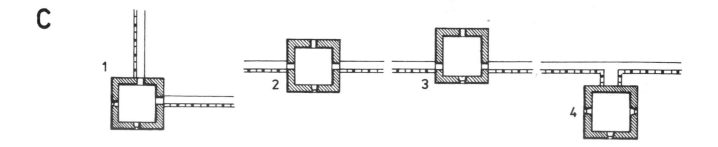

D

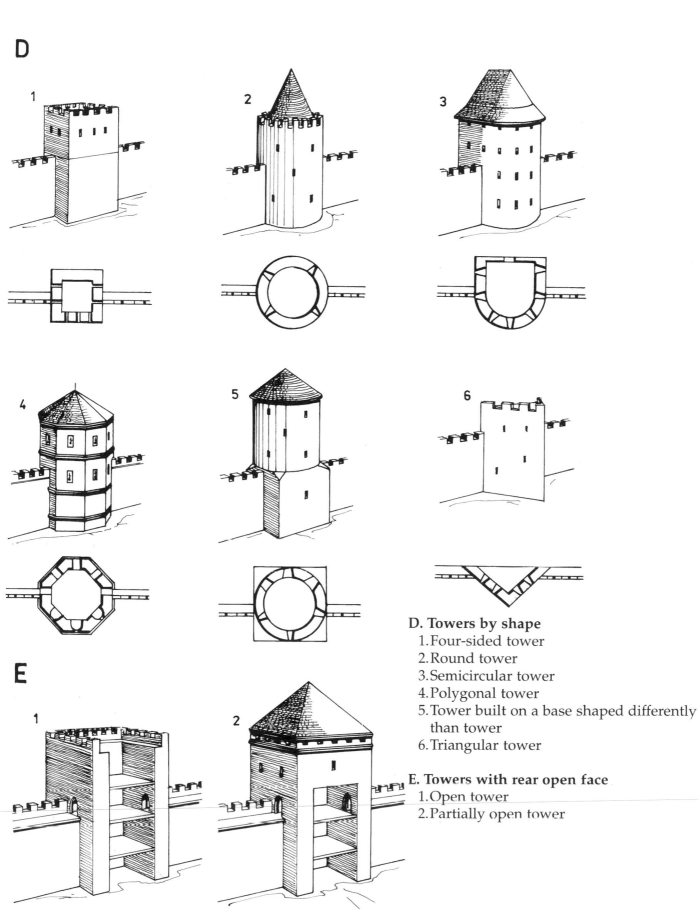

D. Towers by shape
1. Four-sided tower
2. Round tower
3. Semicircular tower
4. Polygonal tower
5. Tower built on a base shaped differently than tower
6. Triangular tower

E

E. Towers with rear open face
1. Open tower
2. Partially open tower

Towers and Keeps

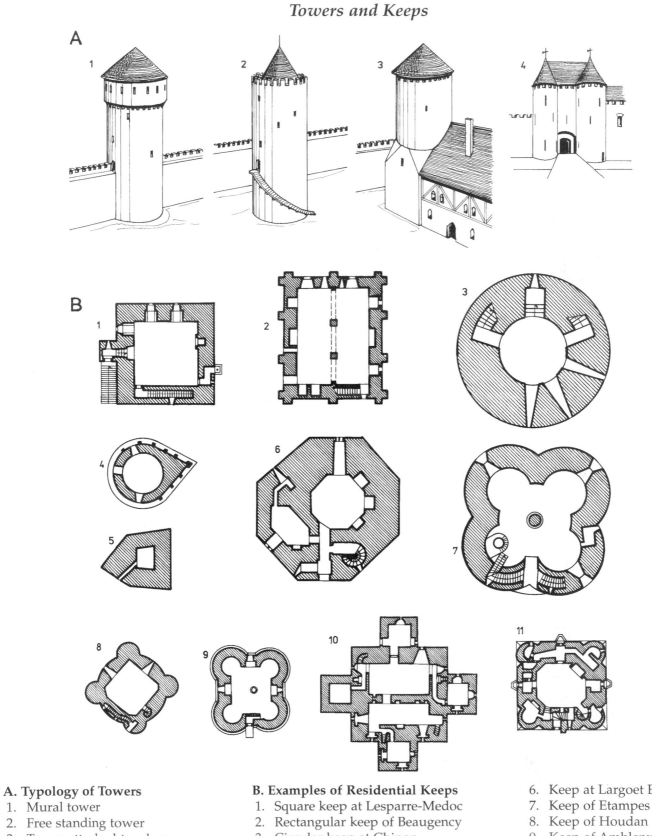

A. Typology of Towers
1. Mural tower
2. Free standing tower
3. Tower attached to a house
4. Gate towers

B. Examples of Residential Keeps
1. Square keep at Lesparre-Medoc
2. Rectangular keep of Beaugency
3. Circular keep at Chinon
4. Beak shaped keep at Chateau Gaillard
5. Keep at Ortenberg

6. Keep at Largoet Eleven
7. Keep of Etampes
8. Keep of Houdan
9. Keep of Ambleny
10. Keep of Trim
11. Keep of Provins

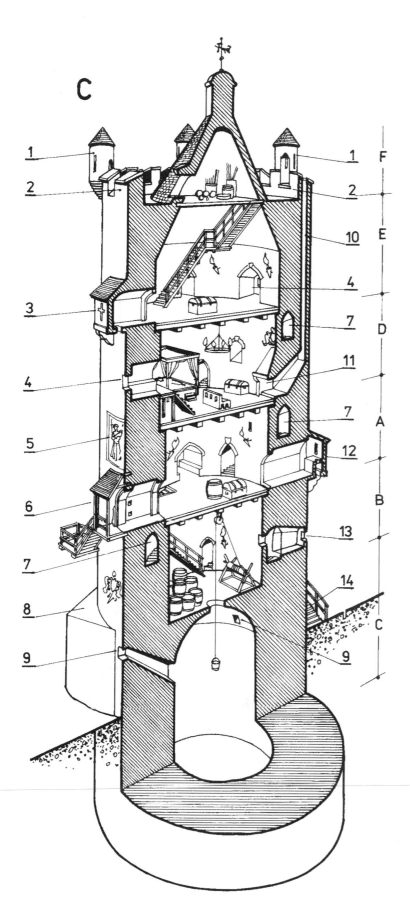

C. Keep cross section

A. Main floor—Great Hall
B. Administrative level
C. Basement or "dungeons"
D. Residential level
E. Arsenal or defensive level
F. Terrace or fighting platform
1. Bartizan
2. Crenelations
3. Bretèche
4. Narrow window for light
5. Coat of arms in bas-relief
6. Entrance with wooden interior stairs
7. Stairs
8. Beak
9. Window
10. Chimney flue
11. Fireplace
12. Garderobe
13. Loopholes for light
14. Entrance stairs

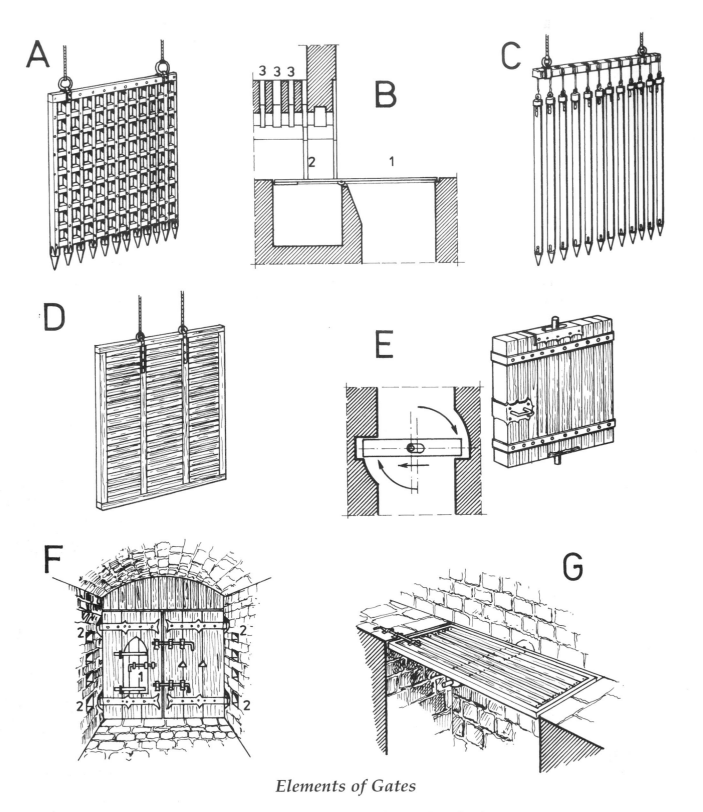

Elements of Gates

A. Portcullis
B. Cross Section
  1. Drawbridge
  2. Portcullis
  3. Murder holes

C. "Organs" (Similar to a portcullis and made popular by Vauban well after the Middle Ages.)
D. Solid portcullis
E. Gate on a central pivot

F. Standard gate
  1. Small door known as "Pedestrian Gate"
  2. Recess for mounting bars to reinforce door
G. Trap door

Gatehouses and Drawbridges

The gate was one of the most critical parts of the defenses of a castle or fortified city since it was theoretically the easiest point of entry which allowed access to the interior. Special attention was therefore devoted to its defense and additional obstacles were placed in front of it.

Not unexpectedly, the first type of towers built into walls were gatehouses. In the motte and bailey castle, the gatehouse and the keep were the first positions to be made of masonry. The gatehouse normally consisted of battlements from which the defenders could keep the enemy away from the gate. As the gatehouses became more sophisticated, various additional defenses such as moats and drawbridges were added. However, where there was no moat, there was no drawbridge. This was mostly the case for interior gatehouses. Drawbridges usually were simple structures that were raised by means of chains and winches. Later, there appeared a more refined version, sometimes called a turning bridge, which was raised by means of a counterweight attached to the end of the bridge. When the weighted end was released, it dropped into a pit moving the other end of the bridge to a 90 degree angle. This mechanism was not only faster to operate, but required less effort. Whether they had a drawbridge or not, the gatehouses included a set of heavy wooden and metal reinforced doors and a portcullis, a wood, iron, or, more commonly, iron-shod wood grating. The portcullis was positioned in grooves in the wall and lowered or dropped down from above with the help of a winch. Most of these gatehouse features date back to the Classical Age where they appear as early as the late 3rd century B.C.

As gatehouses became more sophisticated, they also grew in size, becoming the dominant position in the castle in some cases. One of the best examples of medieval gatehouses is found at Harlech, Wales, where it completely replaced the keep and served as the residence of the castellan. Harlech's gatehouse consisted of four towers. The passage leading into Harlech Castle was flanked by two huge D-shaped towers with a smaller tower behind each. This large gatehouse included three portcullises and three doors, which was not uncommon in gatehouses of this size. Anyone attempting to force entry could be trapped between two of the portcullises. The walls of the tunnel between the portcullises was pierced with arrow loops from which the defenders could fire at the trapped intruders. There were also several openings in the ceiling between the portcullises, known as murder holes, through which the defending archers could fire arrows, drop rocks, or pour hot liquids into the crowd of men trapped below.

Often, the approaches and entrance to the gatehouse were placed at an angle so as not to face outward, thus making it more difficult for attackers to maneuver their weapons directly against the drawbridge or gate. This type of arrangement was particularly effective against the ram. Eventually, an outwork or barbican was added in front of the gatehouse for extra protection. As in the case of other defensive features of the medieval period, the barbican had no standard shape. Some barbicans were directly linked to the gatehouse by walls, forcing the attacker into a narrow, easily defended passage before he could reach the gate. In many cases barbicans were linked to the gatehouse only by a bridge. Most barbicans displayed the defensive features typical of the gatehouse.

In some places like Carcassonne, the barbicans were

MARIENBURG CASTLE (MALBORK), POLAND.
The inner gate complex showing the large portcullis.

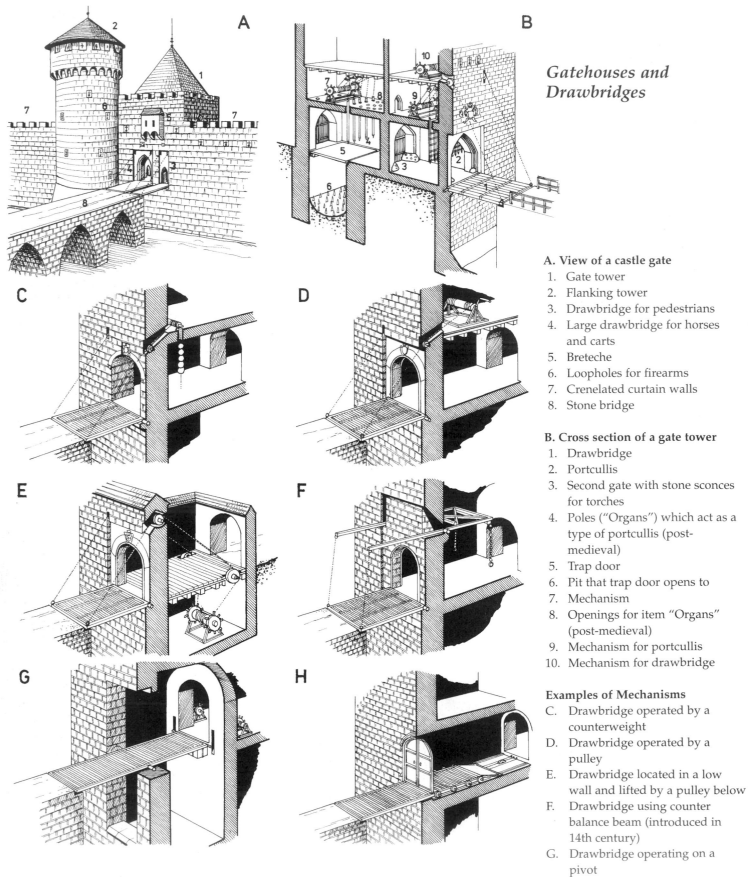

Gatehouses and Drawbridges

A. View of a castle gate
1. Gate tower
2. Flanking tower
3. Drawbridge for pedestrians
4. Large drawbridge for horses and carts
5. Breteche
6. Loopholes for firearms
7. Crenelated curtain walls
8. Stone bridge

B. Cross section of a gate tower
1. Drawbridge
2. Portcullis
3. Second gate with stone sconces for torches
4. Poles ("Organs") which act as a type of portcullis (post-medieval)
5. Trap door
6. Pit that trap door opens to
7. Mechanism
8. Openings for item "Organs" (post-medieval)
9. Mechanism for portcullis
10. Mechanism for drawbridge

Examples of Mechanisms
C. Drawbridge operated by a counterweight
D. Drawbridge operated by a pulley
E. Drawbridge located in a low wall and lifted by a pulley below
F. Drawbridge using counter balance beam (introduced in 14th century)
G. Drawbridge operating on a pivot
H. Rolling bridge

placed well forward of the gatehouse. At Carcassonne, the great barbican, a large circular position located at the bottom of the hill, was linked to the castle and the city walls by a small set of walls that ran up the hill. The castle itself, located inside the city walls, had its own barbican which stood in front of the moat and protected the approaches to the bridge leading to the castle's main gate. The castle's barbican was a large semicircular wall with a defended gate but was not linked to the castle by any fortifications.

In addition to a gatehouse it was quite common for fortified cities and castles to have posterns. These were relatively small entrances only large enough for a knight and his horse to pass through. Posterns served as exits from which the garrison could launch a sortie, as escape routes for the defenders, or as places from which to dispatch messengers. The postern is also known as a sally port. Some posterns were heavily defended and placed in a mural tower. The postern was usually, but not always, located beyond the reach of siege weapons.

Above: Sirmione Castle, Italy.
A view inside the gate tower looking across the moat with the drawbridge down.
Below: Carcassonne, France.
The barbican and fortified bridge over the moat leading to the Narbonne Gate.

Enceintes

The term enceinte refers to the walls and towers that encircled a fortified position, be it a castle, fortified city, or fortified monastery. The curtain refers to sections of wall between towers or the walls of the enceinte. It is quite possible that the early stockades that surrounded a stronghold were not equipped with fighting positions and that they may have relied on the towers for their defense. However, before long, they became an active part of the defense of the castle. The walls were the last elements of the medieval fortified positions to be converted to masonry.

There is no systematic study on the thickness of curtain walls, however, it is a fact that their thickness varied from one fortification to another. The techniques used in the construction of the earth and wood fortifications of the Dark Ages produced exceptionally thick walls. The timber palisades, on the other hand, were rather thin and vulnerable to fire and decay. The first stone or brick walls that replaced the timber palisades, though more durable, were rather thin.

Although Western Europeans of the 12th century were not unfamiliar with the thick Roman walls that still survived in their cities, they did not copy the double wall with rubble fill technique. In some cities the Roman walls were not quarried out of existence but new walls had to be erected between the 11th and 12th centuries because the settlement had grown beyond the old city boundaries. Florence, for instance, expanded across the River Arno and this new settlement area had to be enclosed by new walls during the Romanesque era. By the Gothic period, Florence had to build a new system of walls, which covered more than twice the circumference of the Romanesque walls. Even non-Roman fortified cities, such as Paris, experienced a similar expansion. While larger cities expanded their walls to protect their populations, smaller ones, especially if they were townships, were not always able to afford new walls and went without, unless the sovereign believed it necessary to fortify them for strategic reasons.

The height and thickness of curtain walls, towers, and keeps varied considerably from place to place. In addition, rebuilding, modification, and restoration work that was done over the centuries in the castles changed the structures to such an extent that precise measurements are difficult to come by. No accurate building records were maintained until late in the Middle Ages, so that no accurate information can be obtained on the subject from medieval manuscripts.

Thus much of the data on medieval castle walls has to be based on archaeological excavation and conjecture. Pierre Sailhan in *La fortification* (Paris, 1991), Claude Wenzler in *Architecture du Chateau Fort* (Rennes, 1997), and André Châtelain in *Chateaux Forts* (Cahors, France, 1983) were able to study some trends that apply to France, but other regions of Europe developed differently and have a different history. In the areas occupied by the Romans, four different periods can be established for the development of pre-modern military architecture: the Classical Age, the Dark Ages, the Romanesque period, and the Gothic period.

During the Classical Age, most Roman walls were built on a standard of .25 meters of width for each 1 meter of height. Thus an 8 meter high wall would be 2 meters thick. Normally, no wall would be less than 2.5 meters high. The Servian Walls of ancient Rome were up to 3.6 meters wide at the base. The Aurelian Walls of 3rd century A.D. were 4 meters thick and 6.5 meters high. The towers of the Aurelian Walls were thin in the chambers, but the tower was solid below that and had a height of about 10 meters. These types of towers can be observed in Byzantine fortifications. At Carcassonne, the Roman walls were about 2.6 meters thick and the Visigothic towers were up to 12.5 meters high. The 3rd-century Roman walls of Bordeaux rose to about 10 meters in height.

During the Dark Ages in France, most fortifications were made of wood and usually circular, but the Byzantines continued the Roman tradition of the Classical Age but with some modifications. During the Romanesque period (11th-12th centuries), enceinte wall thickness at the base varied from 1.5 to 4.5 meters. In France buttresses, typical of Romanesque architecture and known as *contreforts* in French, were used to reinforce the walls. The walls of the keeps and the enceinte were built to accommodate the installation of wooden hoardings from which the defenders were able to cover the foot of the wall. The thickness of curtain walls varied according to need. Thus the more vulnerable wall sections were thickest, while those protected by natural features of the terrain were thinner. By the 12th century, most city and castle walls included towers. In the motte and bailey type of fortifications, the motte was 6 to 10 meters high and the surrounding moat was about 3 meters deep. The French donjons or keeps ranged from 20 to 30 meters in height on the average. However, the tallest reached a height of 35 or even 37 meters. The largest keeps were 20 to 30 meters by 15 to 25 meters. The walls of the keep varied between

PROVINS CASTLE, FRANCE. *The enceinte and moat.*

1.5 and 2 meters in thickness, although some were as thick as 4 meters.

The late 12th century witnessed the appearance of innovations in military architecture in the Levant, whence they spread to Europe in the 13th century. These innovations included the machicoulis (French term), the plinth, and the regular spacing of towers. The art of building stone machicoulis or machicolations onto masonry walls made it possible to replace the wooden hoardings, which were very vulnerable to fire. The plinth, an outward splaying of the base of the walls, served as an effective defense against mining. The plinth also maximized the effects of the projectiles dropped from the hoardings or machicoulis. The regular spacing of the towers on the enceinte increased the effectiveness of the defenses.

The Gothic era (13th-15th centuries) represents the zenith of the age of the castle. During the 13th century, the walls of the enceintes became thicker, and the plinth became more common throughout Europe. In France, moats grew to 12 to 20 meters in width and 10 meters in depth. Vaulted towers ranged from 7 to 12 meters in diameter. Castles reached unprecedented sizes, especially at Coucy in France, which had one of the largest keeps in the country, and at Angers, France, which had massive drum towers and plinths.

In France and England when round keeps gained popularity, their walls grew to 3.8 to 4.9 meters in thickness, their diameter to 11.5 to 16 meters, and their height to 25 to 32 meters. In Eastern Europe masonry began to replace earth and timber fortifications after the year 1250.

The trends begun in the 13th century continued in the 14th century. The gród of the Duke of Mazovia at Czersk, was converted to masonry. Its brick walls were 1.8 meters thick and over 6 meters high and may have been up to 15 meters high. Its gatehouse reached 22 meters in height. In France the height of the curtain walls was raised to the level of the towers, a trend that continued into the next century. Machicolations that extended beyond the walls became more widespread and varied.

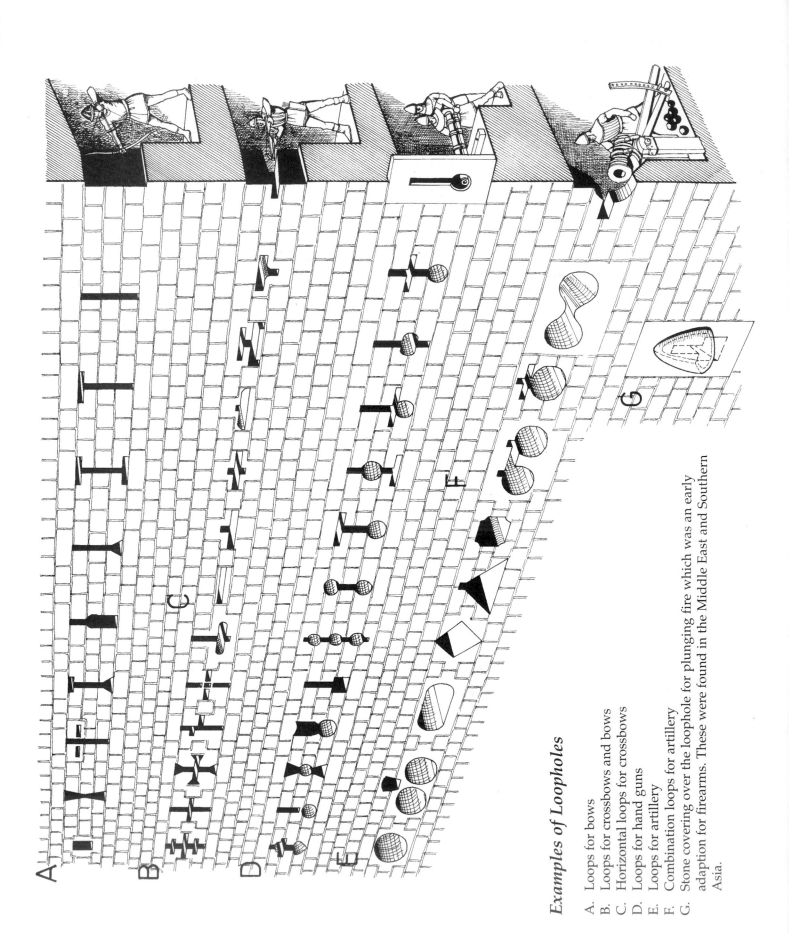

Examples of Loopholes

A. Loops for bows
B. Loops for crossbows and bows
C. Horizontal loops for crossbows
D. Loops for hand guns
E. Loops for artillery
F. Combination loops for artillery
G. Stone covering over the loophole for plunging fire which was an early adaption for firearms. These were found in the Middle East and Southern Asia.

Battlements, Firing Embrasures, and Roofs

The battlements refer to the upper part of a fortified position. They were usually crenelated to protect the defenders from enemy missiles. During the High Middle Ages in some countries like England, special permission from the king was required to build crenelations to fortify a position. The crenelations consisted of a succession of openings called embrasures and small sections of wall called merlons. The simplest, and earliest merlons and embrasures were rectangular in shape. However, many variations soon appeared, reflecting regional and ethnic tastes, converting the crenelations into a decorative feature that long outlasted its military function. Thus, it is not uncommon to see unusually high or curved merlons. In Arab territories the merlons took on a distinctive Islamic shape. Today most of the merlons seen on fortifications are reconstructions and in many cases they do not represent the original style.

Although crenelations go back to antiquity, their degree of sophistication increased in the High Middle Ages. It can only be assumed that the crenelations on the wooden fortifications of the Dark Ages were rectangular in shape since little evidence remains of them. The embrasures between merlons sometimes included shutters to give the defenders added protection. From the 12th century onward, when the trend was toward building masonry fortifications and the skill of the masons became more refined, the crenelations became more complex. In some regions a firing slit, known as an arrow loop, was added to the merlons. These arrow loops afforded the archer increased protection because he did not have to step out into the open embrasure to fire his arrows. The inner section of the arrow loop had to be wide enough for the archer to be able to hold his weapon and fire downward and still give him some degree of coverage. To accomplish this, the position was wedge shaped and the loop itself was cut low enough to give a downward view. At Caernarvon Castle, Wales, more sophisticated arrow loops in the merlons and the walls were formed as wedge-shaped recesses with two loops, which gave the archer two firing directions, thus increasing his angle of fire. At the castle of Boullion in Belgium there were similar openings with three loops, giving the archer an even greater area of coverage.

Along the top of the wall, behind the crenelations, was the wall walk or allure, which allowed the defenders to serve the battlements. In many cases, towers also had allures. Access to the allure and battlements could be by ladder or stairway, although the latter was preferred in masonry fortifications. In some cases the access stairways were located exclusively in the wall towers, which meant that if the attackers managed to reach the allure, they would be trapped there, exposed to the fire from the courtyard and the towers, with no way down from the wall unless they captured a tower.

During the 12th century both tower and wall battlements were equipped with additional defensive devices known as hoardings. These wooden structures formed positions that projected from the wall in front of the crenelations and were normally covered by a wooden roof to protect the defenders. During the construction of the masonry fortifications, slots and supports were set into their walls and towers to accommodate the wooden corbels or beams and supports for the hoardings. The hoardings created an overhanging gallery that ran along the wall or around a tower. However, they did not always cover the

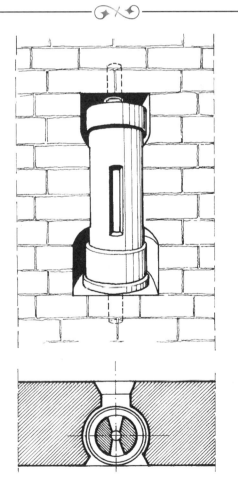

A loop with a wooden rotating embrasure

FROMBORK CASTLE, POLAND, *showing wooden wall walk or allure from which the defenders could man the battlements.*

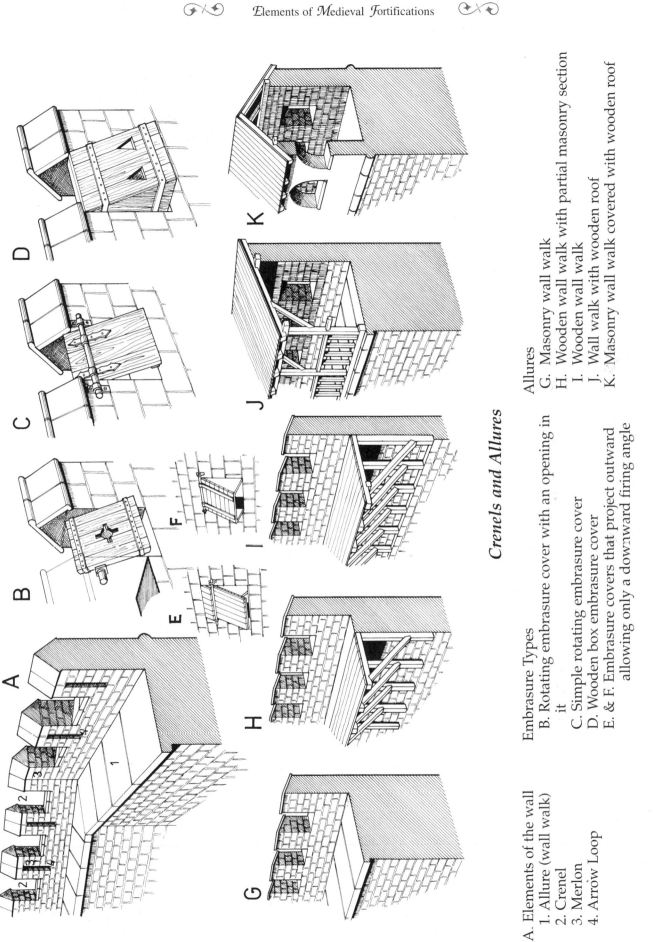

Crenels and Allures

A. Elements of the wall
1. Allure (wall walk)
2. Crenel
3. Merlon
4. Arrow Loop

Embrasure Types
B. Rotating embrasure cover with an opening in it
C. Simple rotating embrasure cover
D. Wooden box embrasure cover
E. & F. Embrasure covers that project outward allowing only a downward firing angle

Allures
G. Masonry wall walk
H. Wooden wall walk with partial masonry section
I. Wooden wall walk
J. Wall walk with wooden roof
K. Masonry wall walk covered with wooden roof

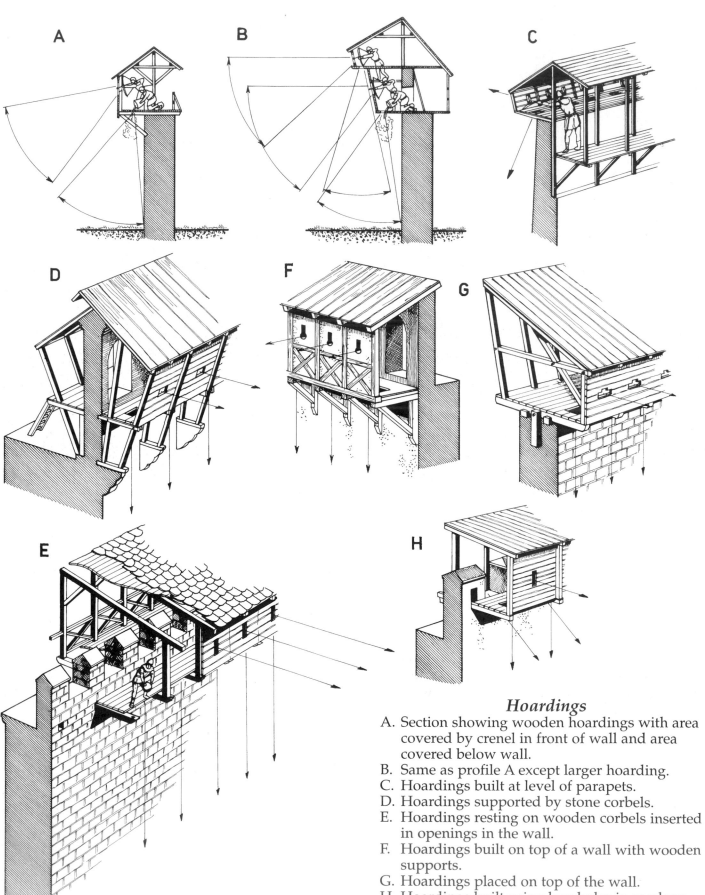

Hoardings

A. Section showing wooden hoardings with area covered by crenel in front of wall and area covered below wall.

B. Same as profile A except larger hoarding.

C. Hoardings built at level of parapets.

D. Hoardings supported by stone corbels.

E. Hoardings resting on wooden corbels inserted in openings in the wall.

F. Hoardings built on top of a wall with wooden supports.

G. Hoardings placed on top of the wall.

H. Hoardings built using loopholes in merlons.

CARCASSONNE, FRANCE. *The hoardings projecting from the wall of the castle created an overhanging gallery. The floors of the hoardings had openings from which the defenders could protect the walls from enemy assault.*

entire length of a wall or go all the way around a tower. The hoardings had embrasures similar to those of the crenelations, which may also have included shutters. The hoardings not only protected the defenders from the elements and from enemy fire, but, most importantly, they also served to protect the foot of the walls from the enemy. The wooden floors of the hoardings had openings from which the defenders could drop rocks or hot liquids on the attackers swarming below. When the base of the wall had a plinth, the projectiles bounced outward and could inflict casualties even on troops standing near the wall but not directly underneath the hoardings. The archers could also fire directly upon anyone below the hoardings. If a section of the hoardings was destroyed, the battlements of the walls still remained behind them. It is commonly believed that the hoardings were only temporary and setup when a site was under threat of attack. When the threat no longer existed, or the war was over, they were usually

removed. It is not known how long the hoardings could be maintained in place, but wooden fortifications lasted for years and even decades, and there is no reason to believe that the hoardings could not last as long. The hoardings were temporary only in the sense that they were not intended as a permanent fixture. However, this is mere speculation since there is no indication that, at least in some places, they were not intended to be permanent.

The wooden hoardings were later replaced by two types of machicolations known in French as machicoulis and bretèche (neither of which has an English equivalent). Stone corbels were used to support these stone projections, which had the same role as the hoardings. In addition to merlons and embrasures, the stone machicolations included openings in the floor between the battlements and the wall from which the bottom of the wall could be covered. In general, the machicoulis covered a long section or the entire length of a curtain wall or a tower. A second

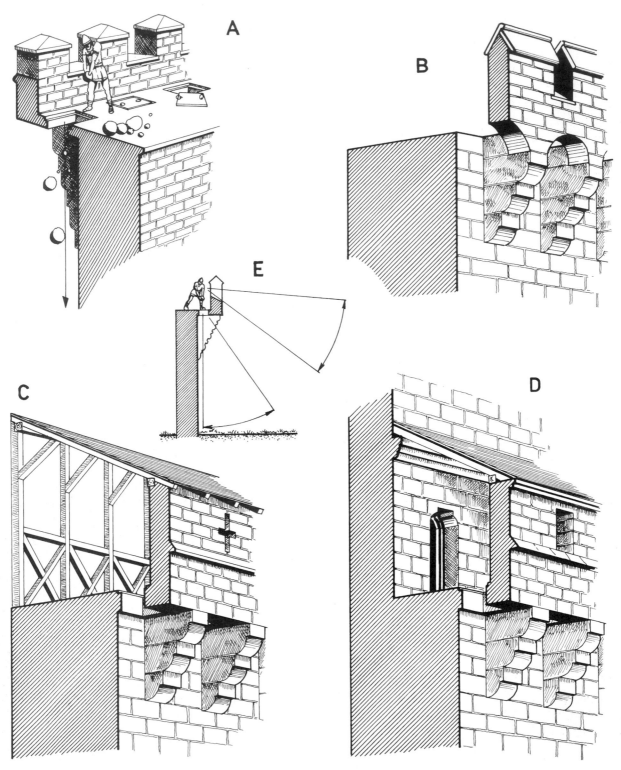

Machicoulis

A. Machicoulis–View from interior.
B. Machicoulis–View of corbells supporting the battlements to form machicoulis.
C. Machicoulis–Wooden frame supporting roof over machicoulis.
D. Machicoulis–Located on lower section of the wall.
E. Cross section showing the area covered by the machicoulis and the embrasures.

type of machicoulis, known as a machicoulis sur arche, consisted of arches that supported the battlements. In this case, the openings were located between the top of the arch and the wall. However, this type of machicoulis prevented the foot of the arch from being covered. To counteract this disadvantage, the foot of the arch was usually very narrow compared to its upper section. This type of machicolations can be found in the keep at Château Gaillard and the Palace of the Popes at Avignon and a number of other fortifications in France and other countries. Most machicoulis were open at the top, but occasionally they were covered by a roof, especially when they encircled all or part of a tower or spanned a section of curtain and were situated below the battlements. Some examples of covered machicoulis can be observed at the French castle of Pierrefonds, whose quality of restoration is questionable.

The bretèche covered only a small portion of wall and looks like a box projecting from the wall or tower. Some bretèches were open on top, others were completely enclosed, but most contained a firing embrasure or a small opening for defending and observing the environs of the castle and an opening in the floor large enough to throw projectiles on the area directly below. They were normally placed either above a window or doorway to protect it. The first bretèches were of wood, but later they were made of masonry.

A feature that is very similar to the covered bretèche and can easily be mistaken for it is the garderobe, which was not a defensive position but a latrine. In theory, it could be used to cover the base of a wall from its opening, but it was never placed above a window or doorway for obvious reasons.

Additional firing embrasures for weapons like the bow and crossbow could also be found in towers at different levels. Windows, however, were a liability, and were not likely to be found outside the residential areas. Towers were virtually windowless because windows created weak points, jeopardizing the security of the entire castle. Only residential towers, like the keep, actually had windows. The most important windows had glass and the chapel windows were usually made of stained glass, while the others were small and often secured with iron bars. Glass was expensive and very uncommon for general use until the later centuries of the Middle Ages. Windows generally opened on the courtyard or on a section of the wall that was well-sheltered from enemy fire. In most towers, narrow slit-like openings shed natural light on the stairways. If many keeps and towers have

normal-sized windows today, it is because they acquired them during renovations at much later dates.

Embrasures for weapons were long and narrow with space on the inside for the bow or crossbow, similar to those found in the merlons of the battlements. There was a wide variety of slits, depending on the purpose they served. Some were cross-shaped to improve the field of vision and later many had an oillet, a small circular opening to give a better view. Later, a large round opening was added to the bottom of some slits to accommodate early cannons.

Towers usually included some type of roof often composed of slate or lead. The roofs were generally tall and conical, giving the castle an even more impos-

LA MOTA, MEDINA DEL CAMPO, CASTILE. *This keep has machicoulis and double bartizans on each corner. The pigeon holes in the structure were common in most Islamic architecture and were used for scaffolding.*

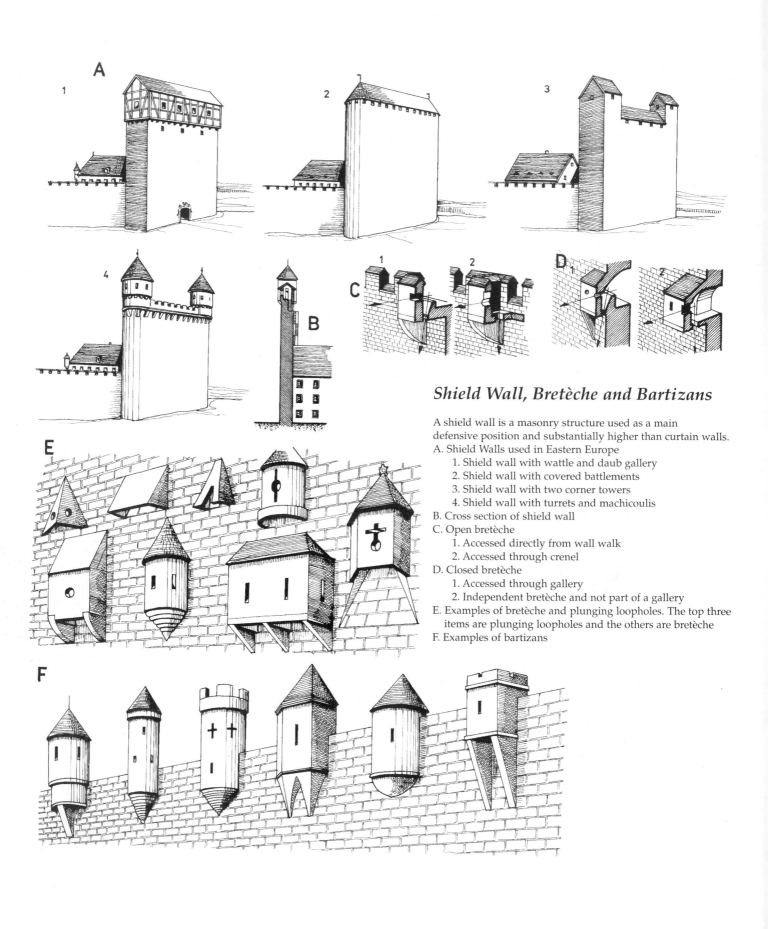

Shield Wall, Bretèche and Bartizans

A shield wall is a masonry structure used as a main defensive position and substantially higher than curtain walls.
A. Shield Walls used in Eastern Europe
    1. Shield wall with wattle and daub gallery
    2. Shield wall with covered battlements
    3. Shield wall with two corner towers
    4. Shield wall with turrets and machicoulis
B. Cross section of shield wall
C. Open bretèche
    1. Accessed directly from wall walk
    2. Accessed through crenel
D. Closed bretèche
    1. Accessed through gallery
    2. Independent bretèche and not part of a gallery
E. Examples of bretèche and plunging loopholes. The top three items are plunging loopholes and the others are bretèche
F. Examples of bartizans

ing air, particularly after the masonry walls were painted. One advantage of the conical roof was that it protected the defenders from the weather when it was extended over the merlons. In many cases, however, the roof did not extend over the towers battlements and not all towers had roofs. A roof damaged by the enemy's pre-gunpowder artillery could also interfere with and endanger the defenders.

Staircases in large towers were often made of wood and served as access to all the floors. Circular stone staircases were found in towers or in corner turrets of the larger towers. Usually, the staircase turned upward in a clockwise direction in order to allow a man to fight with his sword in his right hand, while retreating up the tower.

AIGLE, SWITZERLAND. *Example of a bretéche covering a castle entrance.*

OTZBERG, GERMANY. *The stairway in the bergfried.*

BEAUMARIS CASTLE, WALES.

(© Corel)

The Moat

The moat is undoubtedly one of the oldest features of fortifications. In its simplest form it was a ditch that served as an obstacle meant to check the enemy's momentum. In its more complex forms it presented a serious barrier even to modern armies. The moat was an integral part of fortifications throughout the Middle Ages, beginning with the motte and bailey castle. Indeed, few fortified positions of the Middle Ages are found without a moat, unless they are located on high and rough terrain where a precipice precludes its need. However, even in rugged terrain, an effort was often made to include some kind of moat, as is the case in Sayhun (Saone), Syria. At times, natural water obstacles, such as a river, a lake or a pond, took the place of the moat.

The moat did not always encircle the entire fortification, especially if there were other obstacles. In some cases there was a moat both outside and inside a fortification. This happened mostly in fortified cities where an exterior moat protected the enceinte and an interior one covered the citadel inside the walls. The same arrangement was occasionally found in exceptionally large castles. The moat had to be deep enough to prevent a man from wading through it and wide enough to prevent him from leaping over it. The moat of the early motte and bailey may not have adhered to this principle, since its size depended largely upon the amount of material excavated to create the earthen and timber walls of the bailey and the motte. Generally, a depth of about 3 meters appears to have been sufficient, but after the 11th century, moats were often deeper.

In Western Europe moats were rarely water filled because it was rather difficult to direct water into it, especially if no natural source was available. In addition, water that could be diverted into a moat could also be diverted out. In Eastern Europe, on the other hand, moats were almost invariably filled with water because the fortifications were built near natural water obstacles like rivers, lakes, ponds, or swamps, which abounded in the area. Often, when the earth was dug to build the walls, the resulting ditch would automatically fill with water from the underlying water table. However, in Western Europe, wet moats became increasingly popular late in the Middle Ages. Although water-filled moats are considered very romantic, they were in fact rather unpleasant since garbage from the kitchens and human waste from the garderobes ended up in them, turning them into giant cesspools.

Whether dry or wet, shallow or deep, moats were further reinforced with obstructions such as sharpened stakes at the bottom and along the inner wall. Deep moats also presented a serious obstacle to mining under the walls. Also without filling in the moat, the attacker was not able to assault the enceinte with siege towers or exploit any breach created by his missile-throwing artillery.

SALSES, FRANCE. *The moats of late medieval fortifications were usually much wider and deeper than those of the earlier castles.*

CHEPSTOW CASTLE, WALES.

(© Corel)

Inside the Walls

A fortified site always needed one or more wells to provide water for the garrison, especially during protracted sieges. It was also important to have a well within the keep. In addition, rainwater was usually collected in cisterns located in some of the towers of the fortifications. Water was not only essential to sustain the garrison, but also to put out fires set by incendiary projectiles launched by the besiegers. Hoardings and other wooden components of the fortifications were particularly vulnerable to fire and were often covered with wet hides or other fire-resistant materials. A reliable water supply was absolutely necessary not only to put out the fire, but to keep the wooden components wet and as impervious to fire as possible.

The residence of the owner of the castle was usually located in a keep or some other tower-like position and usually occupied the upper levels. The great hall was usually the largest building in the inner ward or a large room in a great keep which could be used for banquets and entertainment for the noble and his entourage. It was the center of social life for the nobility serving in the castle and the population surrounding it. It was here that the lord of the castle held court and adjucated legal disputes between his tenants.

The great hall was heated by a fireplace, which, until the 15th century, consisted of a round or octagonal shallow depression located in the middle of the chamber where logs burned, giving off warmth and smoke in equal measure, and presenting a constant danger to the occupants. Sometime between the 14th and the 15th centuries, when the chimney flue was invented, the fireplace was moved to the side of the room and placed against the walls. In many cases the fireplaces on each floor were linked to the same chimney stack. Because of the hazard from the fire, kitchens were located in a separate building and the food was carried into the great hall for consumption. Tapestries decorated the walls and also provided some degree of insulation. Artificial light, provided by torches or candles, was necessary to make the dark chambers livable. In some cases a room with windows, known as a solar, served as the family's work room.

A few larger masonry keeps had some type of sewage system. Even though the technology was available since Roman times, plumbing was rarer.

Cleanliness was not a priority, and even the most powerful lords bathed no more than once or twice a year. Bath water was usually heated in the kitchens before it was carried in jars to the lord's chambers where it was poured into a wooden tub. Garderobes were found in different locations and usually projected over a blind wall, like a window box. The garderobe was outfitted with a small bench with a round opening on the seat, which, more often than not, opened directly over the moat. Wherever a primitive sewage system had been installed, the waste was born down to the lowest level of the tower, which acted as a large cesspool and obviously could not be used as the dungeons of 19th century romance. About twice a year the peasants would have to clean out the cesspool.

Depending on the size and type of fortification there were stone or wooden buildings for the garrison. The barracks for a large castle usually consisted of a two-story building with the stables on the lower level. Other structures included storage rooms, dairies, still-rooms, and so on. These were usually attached to the walls of the castle or in detached buildings in the courtyard.

The courtyard or bailey was the main open area within a castle. A castle could have one or more courtyards, separated by additional walls. In the case of castles with concentric walls, the narrow space between the walls was called list rather than bailey. Often the lists were used for medieval jousts. When a castle had one or more baileys, they were usually referred to as the inner and outer ward or the upper and lower or even middle wards, depending on the layout.

Castles also had one or more chapels for the lord and the garrison where Mass was said on Sundays and holy days if the lord was rich enough to have a chaplain. If not, a priest or monk would stop there on his rounds, which could take weeks or months. Often, couples took advantage of the priest's visit to get married. Contrary to popular belief, the lower levels of the castle did not serve as prisons or dungeons. Prisoners were usually held in the highest room of a tower, from which it would be difficult to escape. The highest point usually was the keep or donjon as it was called in France, so the term dungeon became synonymous with prison. When later, in the Renaissance, the prison cells were moved underground, that part of the castle became known as the dungeon.

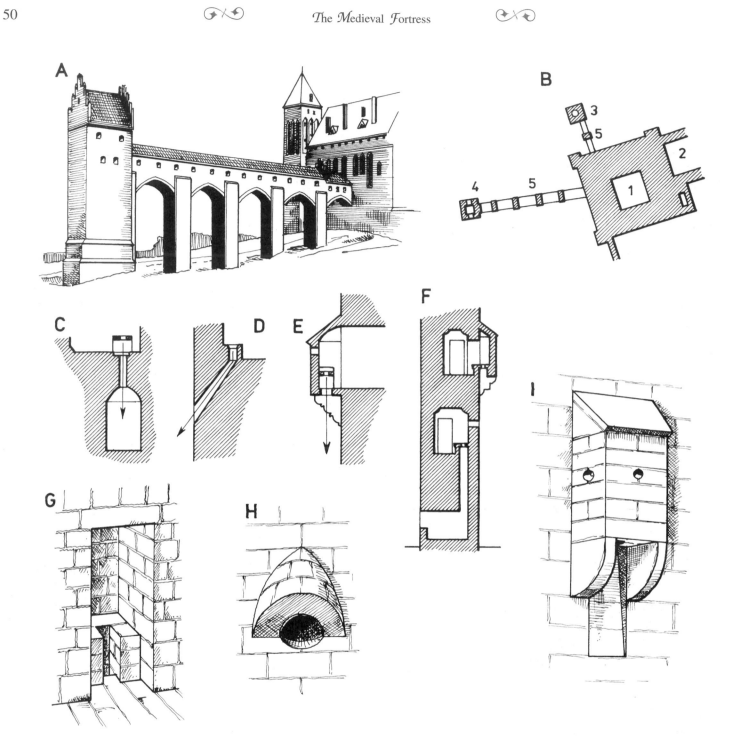

Garderobes

A. Sanitary tower, also known as Danish tower. They are located away from the castle. This type was used on fortifications of the Teutonic Knights.

B. Section of plan of Teutonic Knight castle at Kwidzwn, Poland
   1. Main castle
   2. Church
   3. Small sanitary tower
   4. Large sanitary tower
   5. Covered walk way linking sanitary tower to castle

C. Garderobe with cesspit

D. Garderobe with a sewer taking excrement into moat.

E. Bretèche style garderobe

F. Cross section of garderobe

G. View of a stone latrine

H. View of exit of sewer from the garderobe in face of wall

I. Exterior view of a garderobe

Hygiene during the Middle Ages

Life in a castle was quite luxurious and comfortable compared to life in the nearby village and farms, even though, by modern standards hygiene conditions were quite appalling. The first latrines or garderobes appeared in castles around the 11th century. They consisted of a wooden or stone seat with a round hole through which the waste fell directly at the foot of the castle wall, into the moat, river or lake below the castle. In later periods pipes connecting the garderobe to a cesspit or the moat were installed. In addition to the garderobe, the inhabitants also used chamber pots, which they emptied over the walls. Although plumbing had been known since Roman times, few castles had bathrooms. If the lord or his lady needed to take a bath, their servants carried hot water from the

kitchens, located at the lowest levels, to the bed chambers on the third or fourth level of the castle. The lord and his lady bathed in a padded hip bath, while their servants poured warm water over them. Fortunately for the servants, their masters bathed only a few times a year for major holidays like Christmas, Easter, and Pentecost and for special occasions like weddings. Their attendants and servants bathed even less often.

Parasites plagued everyone in the castles, from the lowliest scullery maid to the masters. The lady of the castle or one of her daughters removed the lice from the lord's and his sons' head and beards. In the absence of the ladies, one of the maids was called into service. In the nearby villages and towns, professional delousers, usually women, plied their trade.

The floors of the castles were covered with rushes, and swept only every few months for major feast days, they were an ideal breeding ground for fleas. The lord's hounds, who were allowed not only into the great hall but also on his bed, were excellent carriers for the pests. Books of etiquette and manners compiled in the Middle Ages often admonished the young to scratch discreetly at the banquet table, for vigorous scratching was unseemly.

Bedbugs were not uncommon in the bedding, which was washed or aired only once a month. Often aromatic herbs, such as lavender, were used not to perfume bedding and clothing, but to repel little pests.

During the hot summer days, flies buzzed around the food in the kitchens, the refuse collected on the rush covered floors, and the waste collected under the garderobes, spreading germs. However, since the connection between parasites and disease had not yet been made during the Middle Ages, parasites were tolerated and treated as a big joke rather than a health threat.

An example of a garderobe in the castle at Fougères, France.

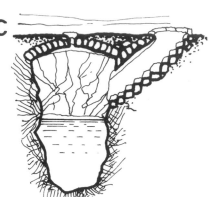

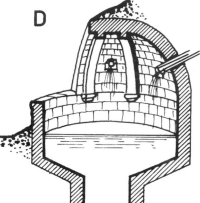

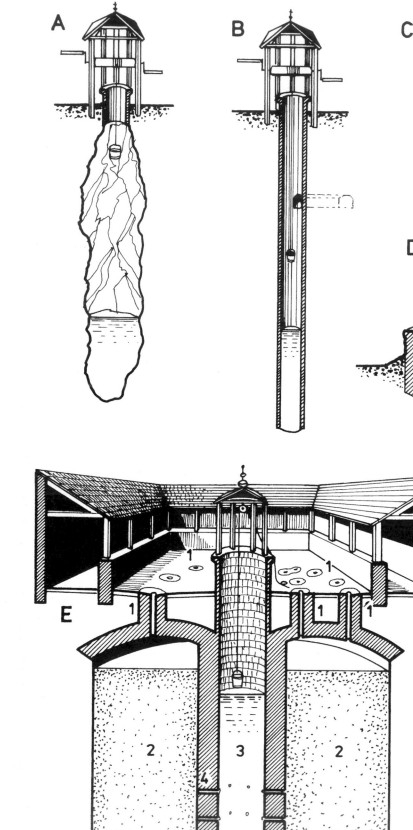

Wells and Cisterns

A. Simple well without walls
B. Well lined with masonry
C. Simple cistern with access corridor
D. Open cistern allowing direct access
E. Profile of cistern
   1. Channels to evacuate excess water
   2. Filtering layer
   3. Well
   4. Drain pipes

Food in Medieval Europe

The staple crops in the Middle Ages were cereal grains such as wheat, barley, rye, and oats. In the northernmost regions of Europe, barley was at least as important as wheat, because it was better adapted to the colder climate and was important in the production of beer and ale. Further south, where the favored alcoholic beverage was wine, emphasis was placed on wheat. Oats were generally reserved for the livestock, especially for the lord's horses, but in times of famine they were included in the diet as well. In some areas, such as the Celtic and Slavic regions, oats formed part of the regular diet and were consumed mainly as gruels, porridges and additives to soups and stews.

Meat supplemented the basic diet of bread only in very rich households. It was served almost every day except during Lent. Beef, mutton, lamb, venison, and poultry were roasted in the huge fireplaces in the kitchens of the castles, which could accommodate a whole ox. Meat was also cut up to be served in stews. In more modest households though, meat was a rare treat. For the peasants hunting was generally prohibited as game was reserved for the lord and his entourage. The peasants had to content themselves with the discards of the hunt, which consisted of the internal organs of the deer. In the cities, meat consumption increased over time as the burghers became more prosperous. Meat, especially pork, was preserved by salting. Smoking was also popular in the heavily wooded regions of northern, central, and eastern Europe. Other meat by-products, such as blood, liver, kidneys, etc. were used in the production of sausages, which also could be preserved for relatively long periods of time.

Fowl (chicken, ducks, geese, and peafowl), rabbits, and pigs were other sources of meat. They were usually kept in the lower bailey of a castle. The association of small livestock with the lower bailey became so firmly established in France that these animals are called *animaux de bassecour* or animals of the lower bailey, to this very day. Cows were also kept near the castle to provide milk and milk by-product, which were processed in the castle buttery. In times of siege, livestock on the hoof were driven into the bailey as well so it could be slaughtered as needed. Dead livestock was sometimes used as ammunition against the besiegers, particularly if it was in an advanced state of decay. Sometimes, however, the besieged did not wait for the carcass to rot, and fired it fresh over the castle walls in order to show the enemy that food supplies were plentiful and the siege was having no effect.

During Lent, large quantities of fish were consumed throughout Europe. Since it was not readily available everywhere, it had to be imported from coastal regions, where it was salted and stored in barrels before it was shipped into the interior. Fish trade was a very lucrative business, especially for the lords and municipalities who collected tolls for its transportation and taxes on its sale.

The popularity of vegetables varied according to geographic region. The most common vegetable, and the most despised, was cabbage, which was served in hovel and castle alike and was known from Italy to Scandinavia. In Central and Eastern Europe it was preserved in barrels in the form of sauerkraut. Legumes such as chick peas, lentils, and fava beans (the only variety of beans native to the Old World), constituted an important source of protein for the poor. They could be cooked fresh or dried and preserved for the winter months. Cauliflower, kale, and turnip greens were less common. Root crops included carrots, turnips, and beets. Most vegetables were cooked and served in soups and stews. Salads made of raw vegetables did not enter the European diet until the Renaissance.

Fruit was raised in orchards and considered a delicacy. It was mostly served cooked in compotes, dried and preserved for the winter months, or used in the production of fruit wines and liqueurs. The most popular fruit for this was, without a doubt, the grape, which was cultivated as far north as the climate allowed it. Wine was the major source of wealth for France, Italy, and Spain. Most varieties of apples, pears, peaches, and cherries known today were developed during the Middle Ages. Citrus was only known in the Mediterranean regions where it was highly prized.

The main sources of fat were olive oil in the Mediterranean, and lard everywhere else. Butter was a luxury, to be enjoyed infrequently outside the castle walls. Food was flavored with onions, leeks, garlic, mustard seeds, and, in the more prosperous households, with spices imported from the Orient.

Above: VERONA, ITALY. *Fortified bridge.*
Below: VILLENEUVE LÉS AVIGNON. *This counter-castle was a large fort built by King Philippe le Hardi to watch over Avignon on the far side of the Rhone River.*

Bastides and Other Fortifications

A special type of fortification was the bastide, which first appeared in southwestern France. It was originally a town founded during the 13th century by the French to occupy a border region. A similar type of settlement was also used by the English as they fought to conquer Wales. The kings of France and England financed the construction of these towns and granted special privileges to those who were willing to settle in them. The typical bastide was laid out in a rectangular shape, ranging in length from 200 to 500 meters and had a grid-like street plan which included the main road that passed through the center. Some of the larger bastides, like the lower town of Carcassonne, had irregular shapes. The funds provided for these towns covered the construction of a set of walls, which were neither very thick nor very high. The bastides usually had no towers other than the two at the main gates. When feasible the entire settlement was surrounded by a moat. The settlers were expected to form a militia to defend the town and maintain the king's hold on the region, in a manner reminiscent of the militia towns founded by the Spanish kings in their campaigns against the Moors.

A true bastide had no strongpoint in the form of a noble's keep or castle, however, some noblemen built towns similar to the bastide next to their castles. During the Hundred Years War, the meaning of the term bastide was widened to encompass several types of fortifications, including wood or stone works built outside of the main defenses of a fortified city, or some types of field fortification or even small forts.

Another type of fortification used during the Middle Ages was the counter-castle, a temporary or permanent fortification erected by the besiegers in order to isolate the castle of the city under siege. Counter-castles were sometimes identified as towers or castles when they became permanent structures and their original purpose was forgotten. Often the besiegers surrounded their objectives with wooden and earth fortifications called bastilles, not to be confused with another type of French fortification by that name.

In the mid-14th century fortified houses or maisons fortes became popular among the minor nobility, who needed to protect themselves against bandits. These fortified houses usually sported one or two towers. In northern England more Pele Towers, simple rectangular towers or keeps first built over a century earlier, were erected by the minor nobility as protection against border raids from the Scots.

Fortified bridges were common in the Middle Ages since they were used either to control river crossings or served as gates into fortified sites bordering a river. Some of the better known bridges used to control river crossings include the bridge at Avignon over the Rhone and the London bridge over the Thames. The London bridge was originally a wooden structure rebuilt from Roman times until the early Middle Ages. In 1176 it was replaced with a stone structure. Over time towers and other structures were added to it.

At Cahors, the Pont Valentré is all that remains of the three fortified bridges built in the 14th century. This stone bridge was begun in 1308 and finished 50 years later. It was well defended by machicolated towers at each end, one at the center, and a barbican on the south side. At Tournai, in Flanders, the city defenses were interrupted by the Scheldt (Escaut) River that passed through the city. In order to link the defenses, two fortified bridges were erected. The only surviving bridge, the Pont des Trous, was reinforced with towers at each of its ends. The tower near the cathedral on the left bank was built in 1281 and the tower on the right bank was begun in 1302. The bridge took about 25 years to complete.

Fortified bridge at Tournai, Belgium. The Pont des Trous was reinforced with towers at each end. The entrance includes a porticullis and murder holes.

Siege Techniques

To fully understand the development of the castle and its various features, it is also important to comprehend siege methods and their evolution. Siege methods are practically as old as fortifications themselves, since as soon as the first defensive walls went up there was someone desirous to tear them down.

Before tackling the enceinte of the fortification, the besiegers usually had to cross the moat. Small ditches serving as a moat could be quickly negotiated either with a good leap or with the help of a log or plank thrown across. If the moat was too deep or wide to be easily crossed or if it blocked the advance of the siege machines, it had to be filled in. If it was water filled, it sometimes had to be drained first. Filling in sections of the moat with dirt, rock, wood, huge bundles of sticks, and other materials was hazardous since it had to be done under a rain of projectiles coming from the castle walls.

Once the moat was filled, the walls and gates had to be tackled next. The oldest type of siege equipment for this kind of operation was the ram. A heavy log carried by a small contingent of men was sufficient to bash in the gate of a smaller fortification. To deal with larger gates and sections of wall, the ram was usually mounted on a carriage. The most sophisticated rams consisted of a tree trunk or large log slung from a framework mounted on wheels. The log was equipped with an iron head that prevented it from shattering as it smashed into the gate or wall. The contraption was covered with a roof of wet hides to protect its operators from the flammable materials raining down from the battlements. These mobile shelters with or without the ram were known as cats and when not mounting a ram they could be used to protect engineers engaged in other activities like working at the base of the wall or filling in moats. A smaller cat with a pointed iron pole instead of a ram was used to chisel away at the joints between stone blocks near the base of a wall. These cats also had other colorful names such as mouse, weasel, and sow, which was one of the most popular. The cat mounted ram seems to have been a key siege weapon until the end of the 13th century. The besieged defended themselves from the rams by smashing them to pieces with heavy projectiles or with beams swinging from above. The Moslems in the Levant developed an efficient method of dealing with the ram—they used a hook on a pole to catch it and overturn it. This stratagem was so efficient that the Crusaders wasted no time in adopting it and implementing it themselves when they returned to Europe.

The simplest method of assault against a castle was the escalade, which involved the scaling of the walls and towers by means of ladders. The ladders had to be of sufficient length to reach the battlements. The attackers found themselves in an extremely vulnerable position while climbing the ladders since they had no other protection than their armor and had to depend on covering fire from friendly archers. If the wall to be attacked had hoardings, they had to be destroyed at the point of entry before the escalade could take place, otherwise the attackers would find themselves standing on the roof of the hoardings, presenting easy targets for the archers in the adjacent towers. In general, the escalade was faster than the ramming, and could be used in conjunction with other stratagems.

However, well-defended high walls made escalades impractical or even suicidal. The solution to the problem was the siege tower or belfry. This ancient device, depicted on Assyrian bas-reliefs, was a wooden tower built on wheels. It consisted of several levels that could be ascended by the besiegers. The number of levels depended on the belfry's height, which in turn depended on the height of the castle walls. At the top, or near the top of the belfry was a wooden drawbridge, which was dropped on the battlements as soon as the tower was moved within reach. The occupants of the belfry were then able to storm over the enemy battlements. More complex siege towers included an additional floor from which archers could fire down into the enemy positions. Some siege towers were even equipped with a battering ram on their lower level. Like the cats, they were hung with wet hides for protection. The building and transportation of these structures was no simple task. Richard the Lionhearted, for instance, had sections of belfries built on Cyprus and transported to the mainland where their assembly was completed before the siege of Acre. The greatest problem was moving these large structures across the moat and up to the walls in preparation for the assault. First, a solid causeway had to be laid down across the moat so the siege tower did not tip over under its great height and weight. The slightest unevenness could spell disaster for the besiegers. Once past the moat, the tower had to be carefully moved into position without toppling over in the uneven terrain surrounding the castle walls. Even the slightest incline could render the whole operation quite arduous if not impossible. All

Methods of Assaulting a Fortification

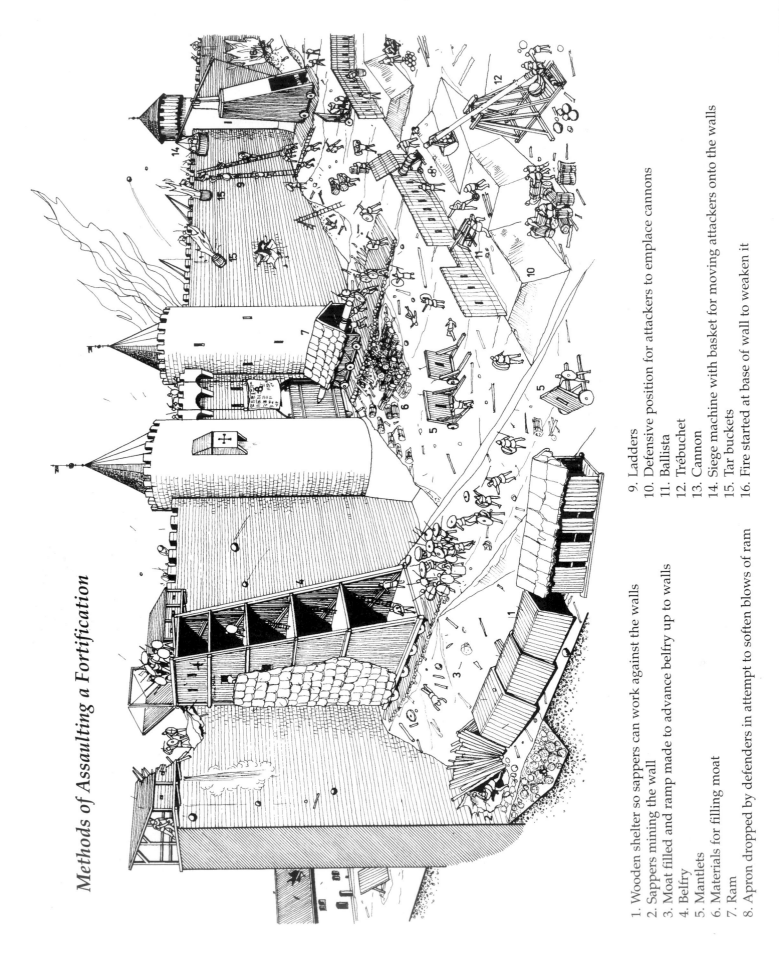

1. Wooden shelter so sappers can work against the walls
2. Sappers mining the wall
3. Moat filled and ramp made to advance belfry up to walls
4. Belfry
5. Mantlets
6. Materials for filling moat
7. Ram
8. Apron dropped by defenders in attempt to soften blows of ram
9. Ladders
10. Defensive position for attackers to emplace cannons
11. Ballista
12. Trébuchet
13. Cannon
14. Siege machine with basket for moving attackers onto the walls
15. Tar buckets
16. Fire started at base of wall to weaken it

Mobile shields or mantlets.

large that they could go right through several men. However, the ballista had almost no effect on the walls themselves. The catapult, also known as the mangonel, was another torsion weapon of great antiquity. It consisted of a beam with a cup for the projectile at one extremity attached to a frame, usually with wheels. The beam was winched down into a horizontal position, and, when released, sprang up to a vertical position where it was stopped by a crossbar. The momentum catapulted forward the projectile resting in the cup. There is evidence that in the 12th century, catapults were used in groups to lay down an effective barrage against sections of walls. These batteries of catapults achieved mixed results since they were low velocity and were not able to fire extremely large and heavy projectiles. Their maximum range

these painstaking maneuvers had to be accomplished under a steady rain of projectiles from the walls of the castle unless the defenders could be kept pinned down to prevent them from interfering.

It was the task of bowmen, crossbowmen, as well as missile-throwing artillery to keep the defenders pinned down off the walls. Wooden or wicker shields on wooden frames known as mantlets, usually about 2 meters high and up to 2 meters wide, held upright by wooden supports offered enough protection to the archers to enable them to get close enough to lay down a barrage of arrows on a chosen spot. The missile-throwing artillery included machines in use since ancient times. The ballista, a giant crossbow from the Roman Era, was a torsion weapon that fired arrows called bolts on a crossbow, which had a devastating effect on the soldiers. Some of these bolts were so

Trébuchet.

Catapult.

though was about 500 meters, which kept them beyond the range of enemy archers.

The trébuchet was a missile-firing weapon that gained prominence in the 13th century. Its origins may also go back into ancient times, but its history is not clear. It consisted of a long beam with a sling for the projectile on one end and a heavy counterweight on the other. The weapon varied in size and could hurl projectiles varying from 40 to well over 150 kilograms (85 to over 300 lbs), depending on the length of the beam and the weight of the counterweight. Trébuchets apparently fired at a high trajectory and

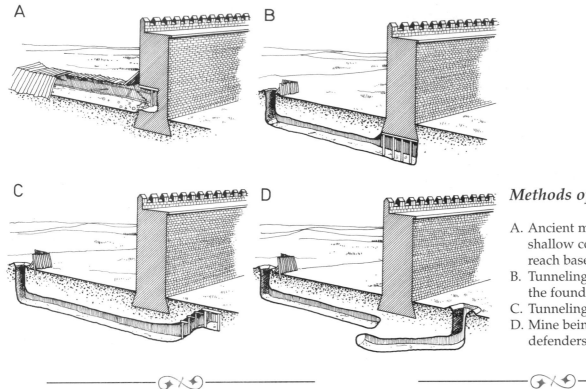

Methods of Destroying Walls

A. Ancient method of making a shallow covered ditch to reach base of wall
B. Tunneling or mining under the foundation of the wall
C. Tunneling into the castle
D. Mine being intercepted by defenders countermine

had effects similar to those of a howitzer or mortar. Reportedly, it was such an accurate and destructive weapon that it remained in service as late as the 16th century in some regions. When used in batteries, or combined with the catapults they could place a devastating fire upon the enemy walls. Despite their low velocity, the heavy projectiles of a trébuchet descended from a high trajectory crashing down with devastating effect on masonry or wood. With a range probably slightly greater than the catapult, it was also safe from enemy archers.

A simpler weapon, sometimes confused with the trébuchet, was the perrier, which was initially used by the Arabs in the Levant. It too consisted of a beam with a sling, looking much like a trébuchet. However, instead of being set into motion by a counterweight, it relied on man- or animal-power to provide the force necessary to launch the projectile. Trébuchets came in many different designs and this may be why they were given a variety of different names by medieval chroniclers. The defenders' response to these weapons was to build higher walls, which, unfortunately, remained vulnerable to the trébuchet and to mining. As a result, walls became thicker in the 13th century. The same happened in the Middle East, where sieges on a grand scale had taken place a century earlier.

In addition to projectile-firing weapons, the aggressors also resorted to mining to bring down fortifica-

tion walls. In its simplest form mining consisted of attacking the foot of a wall with picks and other tools under the protection of cats and large shields. The objective was to cut into the base of the wall in order to weaken its structure. Although the miners often dug from the shelter of a covered trench to protect themselves from the defenders, the operation was extremely hazardous. A more involved mining method required a great expenditure of pure physical labor. The miners began their tunnel from a covered position somewhere behind the moat and preferably out of the range of enemy missile fire and proceeded to dig their way right under the moat to the foundations of the walls. Once they reached their goal, the miners propped up the end of their tunnel with wooden timbers, filled it with flammable material, and set it on fire. When the supports burned through, the mine collapsed bringing down the portion of wall above it. However, this operation did not always meet with success. This type of mining was only practical in ground that was neither marshy nor rocky.

The miners' main fear was that the defenders might detect them and dig a countermine. The way to detect the miners' presence was to set a small bowl of water on the walls or in a previously prepared countermine and watch for the water to ripple. Once the miners were detected, a countermine was dug to intercept them. The object of the defenders was to drive off the

Early example of a bombard found at Bodiam Castle, England

miners by smoking them out or by sending a small armed contingent after them. The mine was then destroyed. An architectural response to the mining was the plinth, which rendered the base too thick to undermine or ram down. Curiously enough, the miners, whose job was not only arduous but also fraught with dangers such as cave-ins and countermining, were among the least respected contingents of the besieging force.

Defenders were not completely helpless against the besiegers, because they too had missile-throwing machines at their disposal. Ballistas were usually placed on towers and ramparts and were quite lethal to the besiegers, who were usually only protected by hide and wood contraptions. Catapults were normally placed in courtyards and were used with great effect against the enemy siege machines. Last but not least, the defenders had at their disposal Greek Fire, an incendiary weapon invented by a Byzantine Greek during the Dark Ages. Although the exact chemical composition of Greek Fire is now lost, its effects were reportedly similar to modern day napalm. The chemical was so effective that it burned even on water and could set fire to ships that had not received a direct hit. It was, therefore, used in naval warfare as well. During sieges, it was infinitely more effective in repelling the enemy than flaming arrows. In addition to Greek Fire, the besieged also poured hot liquids— though oil was too expensive to pour— over the battlements or through openings in hoardings or machicolations to stop attackers.

To counteract incendiary weapons, besieged and besiegers alike relied heavily on wet hides to protect flammable structures such as castle hoardings or siege towers and cats. In addition, since aged human or animal urine was quite effective in dousing or retarding flames, large amounts of the liquid were collected and stored within the castle walls before a siege. Once the battle started the urine was poured over the protective hides.

The final siege weapon to join the medieval arsenal was the cannon. In the 14th century it was too small to have any significant effects on fortifications. However, they became increasingly effective against weaker fortifications during the 15th century when several extremely large guns had a decisive influence on the outcome of the siege. Nonetheless, the cannon did not come into its own until the 16th century.

It must also be noted that in the 13th century, as castle and city fortifications improved to meet the challenges of siege weapons, especially the massed batteries of siege artillery, armies became ever better organized and equipped to deal with the more complex fortifications. Thus development in one area fed on the growth in the other in an ever rising spiral.

Early type of cannon found at Castel Sant' Angelo, Italy

Methods of Defending a Fortification

1. Temporary advanced defensive positions
2. Pushing away the ladders
3. Suspended woven carpets to soften hits from the ram
4. Lowering a hook on a rope to overturn the ram
5. Mining under the walls
6. Countermining of defenders
7. Barrel of flaming material
8. Attempts to raise the height of walls against the enemy belfry
9. Repairing damage to the wall by filling in the breach
10. Knights use sally port to attack enemy outside the walls
11. Digging an additional well
12. New earth and timber wall built to close breach in main wall
13. Defenders' catapults mounted in tower
14. Keep serves as last line of defense.

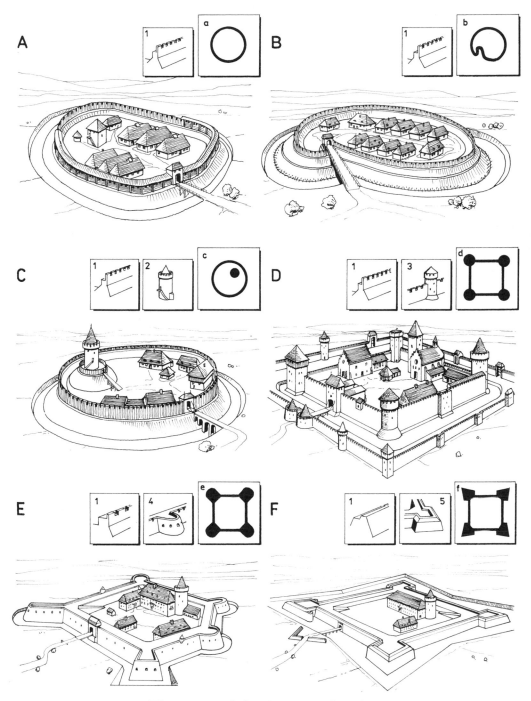

Elements of the System of Defense

From ancient grod to medieval castle to Renaissance fort

A. Simple gród consisting of an enceinte made of earth and timber walls surrounded by a moat
B. Gród with recessed entrance gate
C. Gród with an independent tower
D. Castle with projecting mural and corner towers, and concentric walls
E. Castle in period of transformation with bastions in late Middle Ages
F. Fort of post-medieval era with high walls of Middle Ages gone and modifications made for mounting artillery along the walls. The angular bastions serve to cover the length of walls

Defensive elements
   1. Walls with battlements
   2. Circular tower
   3. Flanking tower
   4. Round bastion
   5. Bastion
Defensive systems
   a. Circular wall system
   b. Sinous wall system
   c. Circular wall systems with interior defensive tower
   d. Square or rectangular wall system with flanking towers
   e. Square or rectangular wall system with round bastions
   f. Post-medieval rectangular wall system with angular bastions

This 13th-century castle with its wet moat is considered almost a classic. The bridge leading to the entrance crosses a small manmade island (barbican). (The present bridge is not in the correct location—the original bridge between the barbican and shore was parallel to the right front of the castle.)

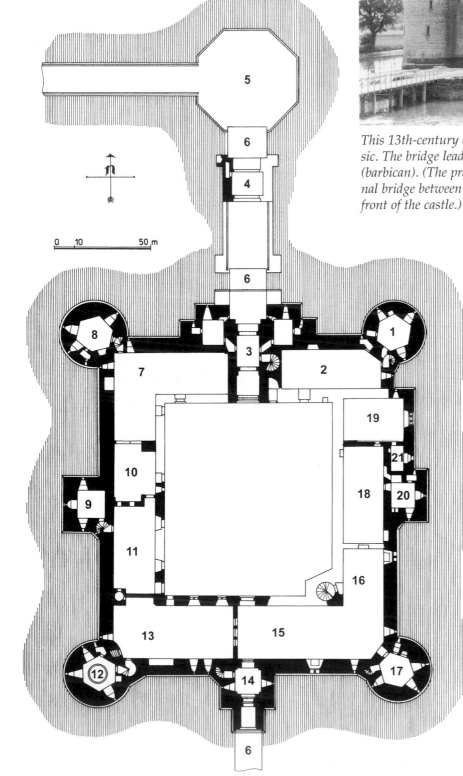

Bodiam Castle, England

1. NE Tower
2. Steward & household offices
3. Gatehouse
4. Barbican
5. Octagon
6. Bridge
7. Garrison & stables
8. NW Tower
9. W Tower
10. Servants kitchen
11. Servants hall
12. SW Tower – Tank
13. Kitchen and pantry
14. Postern
15. Great Hall
16. Great Chamber
17. SE Tower
18. Lady's Chambers
19. Chapel
20. E Tower
21. Sacristy

Provins Castle, France

1. Wall extends down motte and forms a gate
2. Curtains
3. Wall walk
4. Mound (motte)
5. Well
6. Drawbridge
7. 12th century keep

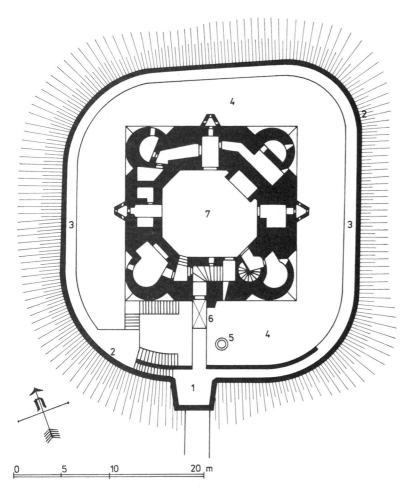

A cutaway section of the keep at Provins. (Illustration is from Military Architecture, *courtesy of Greenhill Books.)*

Tower of Caesar at Provins, France, a mid-12th century castle. It had an unusually shaped keep on a square base with four semicircular corner turrets. It consists of two levels. The crenelated wall that surrounds it is called a chemise.

ANGERS, FRANCE. *This castle was built in the 1230s with a huge enceinte that included 17 tall drum towers. One side ran along the Loire River and the other sides included the formidable moat seen here. The plinth of the towers helped deter mining.*

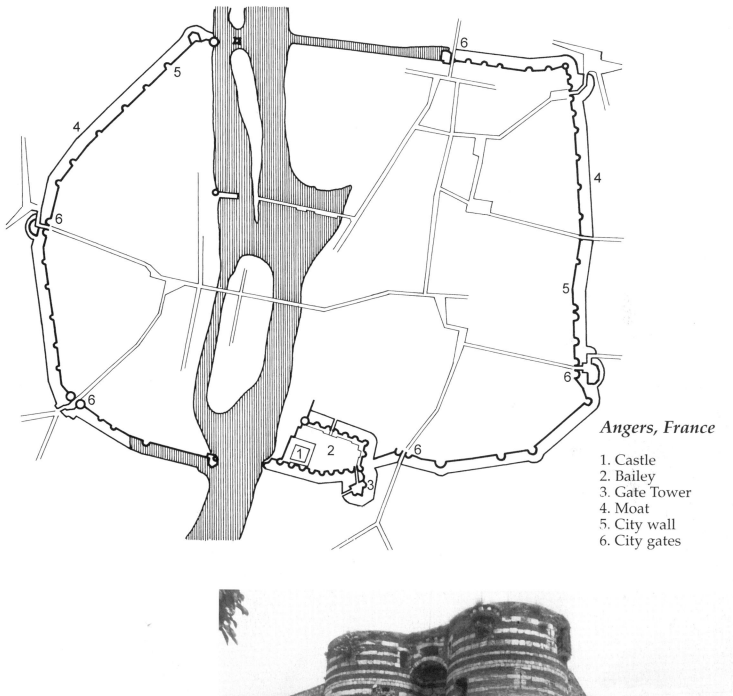

Angers, France

1. Castle
2. Bailey
3. Gate Tower
4. Moat
5. City wall
6. City gates

Angers was built in the early 13th century and served through the Wars of Religion of the 17th century when it was modified by cutting the towers down to the level of the curtains.

BISKUPIN, POLAND.

Early Medieval Fortifications

The popular image of the medieval castle with its high walls and towering turrets overlooking a formidable moat propagated by movies and Walt Disney films stems from a rather late phase in the art of castle building. In fact, the castle evolved over a period of centuries before it reached its classical appearance and many of its features can be traced back to the early centuries of the first millennium B.C.

The medieval castle made its appearance in the latter part of the Dark Ages. Traditional scholarship traces its origins and those of the walled city to Western Europe (which includes part of Central Europe, i.e. Holy Roman Empire). Orientalists, however, believe that the idea of castle building originated in the Near East, and maybe even the Far East, and gradually spread westward, arriving in Europe during the Classical Age. However, some archaeological finds such as the fortified village of Biskupin in Poland seem to point to the fact that the direct roots of the European castle may well be found in Eastern Europe. There is also the possibility of parallel and independent development rather than cultural diffusion. For example, the Mayas built dry moats in Meso-America long before any Europeans set foot on their shores. In this case the dry moats could not be the product of cultural diffusion since there were no contacts with the Old World at the time of their construction.

Fortifications in the Dark Ages

During the Dark Ages, a period extending from the 5th through the 10th centuries A.D. in Europe, many old fortifications remained in use throughout the territories of the former Western Roman Empire. The city of Rome itself was surrounded by an impressive set of walls and included a most unusual and interesting stronghold: the Mausoleum of Publius Aelius Hadrian, known today as Castel Sant'Angelo. It stands on the right bank of the Tiber and is linked to the left bank by a key bridge. It was joined to the Aurelian walls of Rome early in the 5th century A.D. The Aurelian Walls, the first major fortifications built around imperial Rome, had not been erected until the 3rd century A.D. By the 5th century A.D., they reached an impressive thickness of 4 meters at the base and rose to 20 meters. They were reinforced with 381 rectangular towers projecting out of the walls, spaced about 30 meters apart. The towers were able to accommodate artillery such as ballista. Early in the 4th century A.D., the height of the walls had been increased to 8 to 13 meters and in some places up to 20 meters. A considerable improvement over the 6 meters of the original walls. These 4th-century additions included the galleries above the old walls in many sectors. The Aurelian Walls covered 18 kilometers and included 18 well-defended gates. The gates on the major roads included double entrances, while the others had single ones. These walls are some of the most impressive left from the Ancient World. Some of the arched galleries and a concrete wall walk above them still survive today. In addition to the merlons that formed the battlements, there were firing slits within the gallery sections of the walls. These formidable walls included a concrete core that allowed them to survive through the ages, mute witnesses to the engineering skills of the ancient Roman architects. In 537 A.D., the Ostrogoth king, Vitiges, took Rome, only to be driven out by the great Byzantine general Belisarius. According to Hans Delbrück, an author of a series of books on warfare, Belisarius took up defensive positions in Rome rather than face the superior numbers of Vitiges's armies, and from that point on "the war was conducted and decided simply by sieges and capitulations of cities." The last Ostrogoth

Plan of Ancient Rome

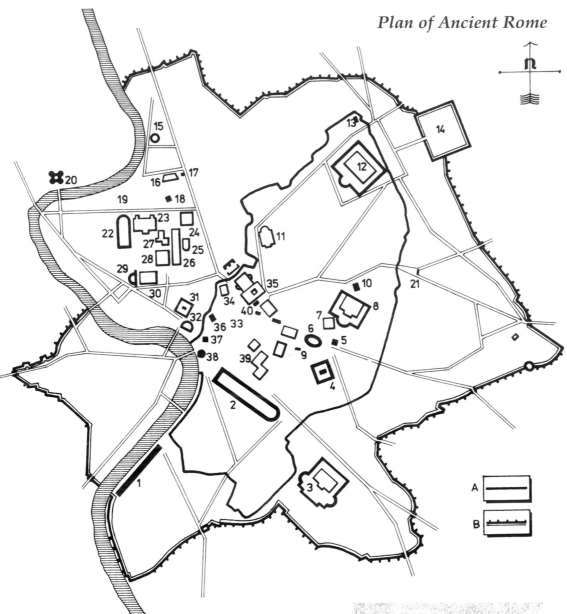

A. Servian Wall
B. Aurelian Wall
2. Circus Maximus
14. Castra Praetoria
20. Hadrian's Mausoleum (later became Castel Sant Angelo

The Ostia Gate in the Aurelian Wall of Rome.

CARCASSONNE, FRANCE. *Gallo-Roman tower of first wall. One of the finest examples of Roman military architecture in Western Europe.*

king in Italy, Totila, had many city walls leveled, a strategy later adopted by the Vandals in Roman Africa. In the case of Rome, Totila attempted to demolish parts of the walls that Belisarius had earlier repaired and reinforced with ditches, making Rome's defenses even more formidable. After Belisarius finally drove Totila out, he made the last major repairs on the walls of Rome in 547 A.D.

After Vitiges was driven from Rome, the city convulsed with ten years of inner turmoil. Castel Sant'Angelo, serving as a fortified bridgehead consisting of a fort built around Hadrian's Mausoleum, was besieged one last time and Totila was forced from Rome by the Byzantine general Narses. By the end of the century Pope Gregory the Great established Rome as the capital of his Papal States. Later, in the 9th century A.D., after the Lombard threat to the Papal States and the Franks' intervention, Pope Leo decided to extend the city walls around the Vatican, enclosing Castel Sant'Angelo, which was to serve as a refuge for him in time of attack.

In the rest of Western Europe and the Mediterranean world, the Romans left behind an impressive set of fortifications that included walled cities with towers and crenelations. These fortified cities of the Late Roman Empire were usually built on defensible terrain and probably did not look much different from those of the High Middle Ages, although there is evidence they included more hygienic features such as

baths, water lines and sewers and the architectural style of their buildings might have been different.

The Roman fortification building methods were described by Flavius Vegetius Renatus, a 4th-century Roman, who wrote a treatise on the art of war based on a number of other Roman sources. This treatise served as a major source for *Military Architecture*, a work compiled by the leading 19th-century authority, E. E. Viollet-le-Duc. According to these sources, the Roman city walls normally consisted of two masonry walls spaced about seven meters apart. The gap was filled with earth excavated from the defense ditches and well-packed rock. A wall walk was formed above and the outer wall was crenelated. This double wall thus became a single structure. This method of construction can be observed today at Carcassonne, France, where the walls and some of the towers constitute some of the finest examples of Roman military architecture in Western Europe. The Roman fortifications at Carcassonne are referred to as Gallic or Gallo-Roman because they are located in Gaul. Construction materials used in Roman fortifications varied according to the location. Thus at Carcassonne, the inner core (or the space between the two masonry walls) was filled with rubble and lime. The towers of the walls are D-shaped, the curved section bulging beyond the wall in a typical Roman fashion. Access to the allure (wall walk) on either side of the towers was through the towers. Each door

Vegetius: *Epitome of Military Science*

Little is known of the life of Publius Flavius Vegetius Renatus, save that he held some type of bureaucratic position in the government of Byzantium at the end of the 4th century. However, he can be considered the Clauswitz of Late Antiquity. Despite some flawed descriptions, his *Epitoma Rei Militaris* became the most read Latin work among the military elite of the Middle Ages. This compendium consists of four books and, like so many works of Late Antiquity, condensed and summarized many other works of the Classical Age. Vegetius's fourth book was mainly devoted to fortifications and siege warfare and discussed techniques used during the Roman era. This volume served as a guide for medieval military leaders.

In his fourth book Vegetius discussed, among other topics, such things as the importance of avoiding straight lines in the construction of walls, the role of towers in the protection of angles, and the benefits of a fossé or moat as an important defensive obstacle. Vegetius also emphasized the protection of gates and recommended such features as murder holes in the passageway and a portcullis to control access. He even mentioned the use of a barbican to protect gates. All these elements would eventually become standard features in many major medieval fortifications. In addition, Vegetius recommended the use of fireproof materials to protect walls and entrances as well as other items to cushion the walls from battering and enemy projectiles. These measures also eventually became common in the Middle Ages.

In his chapters on the siege, Vegetius advised that the besieged must keep adequate supplies of food to prevent starvation and sufficient materials to repair and increase the size of walls in the face of enemy war machines. He also considered essential the presence of a protected water supply to resist a siege. One of Vegetius's less popular propositions was that the besieger must rely on skill rather than terror if he fails in the first assault to take a fortified place. Many medieval leaders disregarded this suggestion, resorting to terror whenever they thought it would expedite matters.

In his fourth volume, Vegetius also described numerous siege machines such as mobile screens, the "tortoise" with its battering ram, huge siege towers with their own attached battering ram and a bridge near the top for crossing onto the enemy walls, and catapult-type weapons. Virtually all of these weapons were put into service during the Middle Ages.

Vegetius also suggested sorties for destroying siege towers and the hanging of blankets or other materials over targeted walls to cushion them from enemy blows. He warned the besieger to protect his own positions with defensive works such as stockades and recommended tunneling to undermine walls or simply penetrate behind the walls. Needless to say, all of these techniques were put to use during many medieval sieges. It is clear that Vegetius's writings had a heavy influence on medieval fortifications and sieges.

Source: Vegetius: *Epitome of Military Science.* Translated by N.P. Milner. Liverpool: Liverpool University Press, 1993.

accessing the tower from the allure included a trap in front of it which had to be spanned by some form of removable foot bridge or drawbridge. The rear of the upper portion of the tower was open (no back wall or embrasures) and could be used for hauling up ammunition for artillery such as ballista and catapults.

Round towers did not come into widespread use in Western Europe until the High Middle Ages although they had been in use elsewhere long before that. The first round towers (or those in a semicircular form) appeared with the Greeks in the Classical Age and were copied by the Romans, who raised their height in order to extend the range of their missile throwing machines. Until the High Middle Ages, height seems to have remained an important factor in the construction of towers, even though the medieval builders returned to a more simple square or rectangular design.

According to Viollet-le-Duc, several French cities were fortified in the classical Roman style. This means that they had a river on one side, a fortified bridgehead across the river that protected a bridge leading into the city, and an escarpment on the side opposite the river side, forming another barrier. The cities of Autun, Cahors, Auxerre, Poitiers, Bordeaux, and Langres were laid out in this manner and remained fortified through the Dark Ages, their Roman defensive systems undergoing little change until the 10th century. Hans Delbrück and other military historians point out that the works of Roman writers such as Flavius Vegetius Renatus were well-known to the Carolingian nobility during the Dark Ages and they continued to be studied and used as guides throughout the Middle Ages.

The walls of the Roman fort at Portchester, England, included 20 bastions and 2 large Roman gates in the center of the east and west walls designed as a double entrance to trap an invader in the courtyard with enfilading fires. Each of the other two walls had a centrally placed postern. A ditch surrounded most of the walls, although it is not certain if there was enough space for it where the walls run along the shoreline, which has eroded in the past millennium. The walls included a wall walk for defense. It must be noted that not all of the Roman forts were rectangular like Portchester. The Saxon Shore Forts were built by the Romans to ward off Saxon raiders and were occupied by Roman ground and naval troops in the 3rd century A.D. After they were abandoned by the Romans, many of them were taken over by the Anglo-Saxon invaders early in the Dark Ages.

One of the most impressive features of Roman fortification are the Limes built along the borders of the Roman Empire during its waning years. The Limes consisted of many forts built in a defensive line. Along the German frontier, the Limes of Germanicus consisted of a western section made of a mound and ditch and an eastern portion made of a stone wall over a meter thick known as the Devil's Wall. These Limes were supported by watchtowers and camps. At first, these Roman camps consisted of a square with a gate in each of its four sides and observation towers along the walls. They were intended only for quartering the troops, protecting them from surprise attack, and possibly serving as a final fallback position. Later, in the 3rd century A.D., these camps evolved into defended gates with numerous towers that could give enfilading defensive fires. The encircling ditches became more difficult to ford. In the 4th century A.D. the Romans situated their forts on high ground, mainly plateaus, for the best defensive advantages. As time went on, these new Roman forts became more refuge than defensive barrier. Delbrück notes that archaeologists had difficulty distinguishing the late Roman forts from earlier Iron Age and later Frankish Carolingian forts. The Romans, no longer able to provide a large reserve force to defend the frontier, found it necessary to build these strongpoints to maintain their control over the region. The Franks, under similar circumstances, followed the Roman example, building similar types of forts and possibly even reusing older Roman hilltop positions, in order to hold their own frontiers.

During this time fortifications were not only known to the inhabitants of the former Roman Empire, but also to the "barbarians" surrounding them. The Germanic tribes were civilized enough to organize towns and create their own fortifications. They relied heavily on wooden fortifications, and probably ditches in many cases, to defend their towns. Even the Asiatic Huns, feared by most of the more "civilized" people, employed fortifications. In 451 A.D. at the battle of Chalons, where their westward advance was checked, Attila the Hun fell back upon a hilltop position which he had previously fortified with his wagons.

The Slavic people, who moved westward to the borders of the Germanic kingdoms on the Polish Plain, and as far south as the Byzantine frontier in the Balkans, had long used sophisticated fortifications. Even the Bulgars, before they were Slavicized, tried to improve some of the abandoned Roman defenses

Portchester, England

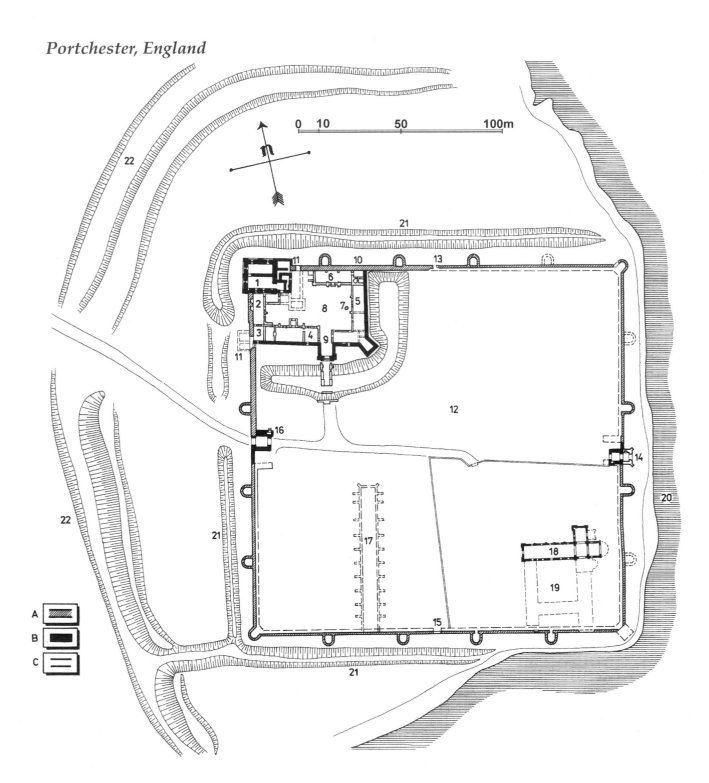

0 10   50   100m

A. Roman constructions
B. Norman constructions
C. 14th century constructions
1. Keep
2. Great Chamber in Palace of Richard II
3. Inner Chamber of Palace of Richard II
4. Kitchen
6. Constable's house

7. Well
8. Inner bailey
9. Gatehouse
10. Assehton's Tower
11. Sally port
12. Outer bailey
13. Posterns
14. Water gate

15. Posterns
16. Land gate
17. Barns
18. Church
19. Cloister
20. Harbor
21. Roman ditch

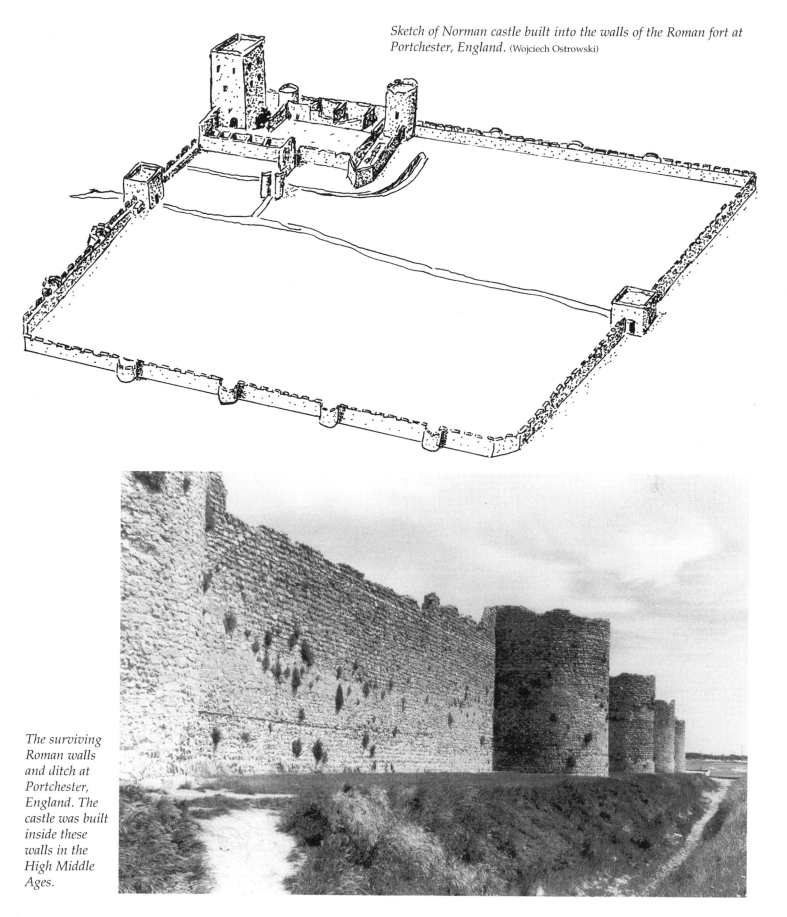

Sketch of Norman castle built into the walls of the Roman fort at Portchester, England. (Wojciech Ostrowski)

The surviving Roman walls and ditch at Portchester, England. The castle was built inside these walls in the High Middle Ages.

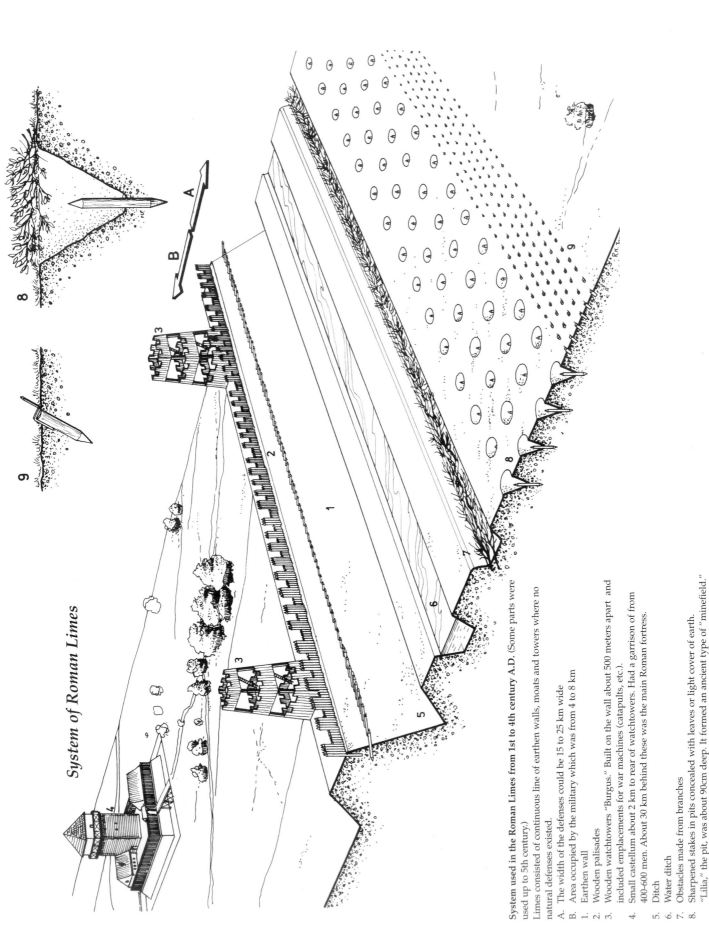

System of Roman Limes

System used in the Roman Limes from 1st to 4th century A.D. (Some parts were used up to 5th century.)

Limes consisted of continuous line of earthen walls, moats and towers where no natural defenses existed.

A.   The width of the defenses could be 15 to 25 km wide

B.   Area occupied by the military which was from 4 to 8 km

1.   Earthen wall

2.   Wooden palisades

3.   Wooden watchtowers "Burgus." Built on the wall about 500 meters apart and included emplacements for war machines (catapults, etc.).

4.   Small castellum about 2 km to rear of watchtowers. Had a garrison of from 400-600 men. About 30 km behind these was the main Roman fortress.

5.   Ditch

6.   Water ditch

7.   Obstacles made from branches

8.   Sharpened stakes in pits concealed with leaves or light cover of earth. "Lilia," the pit, was about 90cm deep. It formed an ancient type of "minefield."

9.   "Stimulus." Sharpened stakes about 30cm long with a metal point.

they came across. However, many of the "barbarian" groups that moved into the Balkans built fortifications strong enough to withstand the more sophisticated siege methods employed by the Byzantine army. The migrating Avars moved into the Balkans and soon proved themselves masters of siege warfare, even against the more formidable Byzantine defenses, before they moved on to the north toward the Danube.

The Celtic people also created numerous fortifications that ranged from older Iron Age "hill forts" consisting of concentric rings of earthen fortifications to towns with defensive wooden and stone walls, which, in some cases successfully repulsed Roman advances. In Ireland and Scotland, the Celtic Picts built simple ring forts before the 2nd century A.D. to protect local populations. At this time in Scotland some of the ancient enclosed compounds were made of stone walls and included a large stone tower known as a broch that was built with no mortar. The broch's entrance was usually so small that access was only possible at a crawl. The broch is believed to have evolved from the strong, round, undefended stone houses built in the area before the Christian era. The brochs were up to 15 meters high and consisted of a courtyard with wooden galleries accessed by ladders. Above the first or second level the broch wall consisted of two thinner walls, an inner and outer wall, which created additional galleries between them. It seems that there were no exterior defenses and that the broch served as a final refuge. Any intruders that succeeded in breaching the broch would find themselves surrounded by the occupants on the galleries above. The broch were so well built that some remained in use throughout the Dark Ages as protection against the Norse raiders. Others provided construction material for newer buildings. In Scotland alone there are the ruins of about 500 brochs. By 200 B.C., the broch became the center of the village. In the Lowlands they remained in use during the early part of the era of Viking invasions in the Dark Age.

In other regions, the Picts reoccupied old hilltop forts and continued to use them until the 8th century. Some of these forts included wooden ramparts. The timber was fired to create a slag-like core for these walls. These forts were still serviceable after centuries of disuse. A typical fort of this type is Burghead in Moray, Scotland, which was built on a promontory as late as the 4th century A.D. It included iron dowels connecting the timber sections of the ramparts and an upper and lower enclosed area. Archaeological evi-

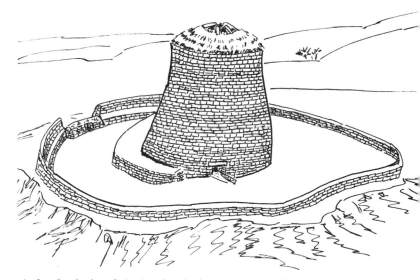

A sketch of a broch in Scotland, showing its small entrance and the surrounding wall. (Wojciech Ostrowski)

dence indicates that this fort was still in use in the 9th century.

Another Pictish fort from the Dark Ages is Dundurn, Perthshire. It had a citadel and a high terrace in the center, which were surrounded by four lower terraces with ramparts. The timber ramparts of the high terrace date from the 5th through 7th centuries, when they were replaced by a stone wall. This fort went though several building phases before it became a formidable Dark Age fort consisting of timber, stone, and earth. Other Dark Age forts of this type occupying a high point and surrounded by a group of enclosed areas are found in Britain and Ireland. When the Scots occupied the Pictish lands of Scotland in the 8th century they began building their own fortifications, but never achieved the degree of sophistication of the Picts.

As the Germanic tribes settled in the old Roman empire, many of the larger Roman fortifications fell into disuse. The armies of the Germanic kings were not large enough to occupy all the cities in the territories of the Western Roman Empire that fell under their control. Since the conquered citizenry could not be trusted to remain loyal, many of these Germanic leaders, following Totila's example in Rome, resorted to destroying the defenses of the places they could not hold effectively. As a result, few key cities retained their Roman fortifications, while other places had to rely on smaller fortifications for their defense.

The Celtic people on the British Isles, on the other

A re-creation of Roman defensive fortifications based on Caesar's description of the walls he built to surround the Gauls in Alesia. The Limes may have been similar and had a comparable array of obstacles in front of them, including the covered pits with sharpened stakes in the foreground.

hand, took over many of the old Roman fortifications and continued to maintain and use them. Thus in England, the Roman Saxon Shore Forts remained in use through the Dark Ages. These forts, some of the largest the Romans ever built, were enclosed by a stone wall that was almost twice as high as in other Roman forts of this type. The walls of many of these coastal forts rose up to 5 meters and had walls over 3.5 meters thick. However, these figures varied from fort to fort. In southeast England, the best representatives of the Saxon Shore Forts are Portchester, Reculver, Burgh Castle, Lympne, Dover, and Richborough. There were a number of other such forts not only in England but across the channel on the continental coast. Portchester, one of the best preserved Saxon Shore Forts, was one of the few that remained in use during much of the Middle Ages. Unlike the others, whose numerous solid circular or semicircular bastions projected from the wall for mounting catapults, Portchester's were hollow with wooden floors.

Sometime during the 9th century, the Saxons began building fortified towns known as "burhs," incorporating, in many cases, the old Roman walls in their defenses. The burhs were placed at strategic points such as crossings and hilltop positions where they could also serve as a refuge for the local populace. When Roman walls were not available, the Saxons resorted to timber palisades and ditches, most of which have been obliterated by the ravages of time, especially since towns later sprang up in and around them.

Offa, the Anglo-Saxon King of Mercia, in the last half of the 8th century constructed Offa's Dike to seal the Welsh border. This was the longest of the defensive dikes built in England and may have even been built in cooperation with the neighboring Welsh prince and may not have been designed as a military obstacle. To this days it remains one of the unsolved historical mysteries.

Fortifications in the Islamic, Byzantine, and Frankish Empires

In 7th century A.D., during the European Dark Ages, a fury spread from the Arabian Desert and overran the Middle East, soon engulfing the Christian world and bringing it close to destruction. This was the rise of the Arab world which brought with it the Islamic faith. The desert warriors swarmed upon the ancient Fertile Crescent, conquering both Byzantine and Persian territories. Before the 7th century A.D. ended, much of the Middle East was absorbed into the Islamic World. By 711 A.D. Islamic warriors stood at the gates of Europe. The great fortified city of Constantinople lay under siege from 717 to 718 A.D. The Wall of Theodosius, built in the reign of Theodosius II extended the city's defenses west of the old Wall of Constantine, and stymied the Arab invaders, who failed to breach it and take the city.

Theodosius' Wall, 4.6 meters thick, had been erected in 413 A.D. across the peninsula which Constantinople occupied. It included massive high towers rising over 20 meters no further than 55 meters apart. These huge towers projected up to 10 meters beyond the front of the wall. Some were square and others were multi-sided but none were round. The upper level of the great towers could only be accessed from the wall walk, while the middle level was entered from the lower floor through an entrance outside the main wall. These walls, about 13 meters high, had successfully repelled the Bulgar and Avar long before the arrival of the Arabs. The only force that was able to weaken these walls was nature itself, when a series of earthquakes inflicted considerable damage upon them. Sidney Toy, who wrote the classic book *Castles: Their Construction and History*, notes that a major earthquake in 447 A.D. destroyed 57 towers. When the Byzantines repaired the damages, they also decided to include some improvements and a new wall was built in front of the old one. Called the outer wall, it was about 2 meters thick, and not as high at about 7.5 meters. The towers of the new wall were square and spaced about 45 to 90 meters apart, and, unlike those of the old wall (known as the inner wall) had no lower level for the most part. A terrace was formed between the level of the entrances to the great towers of the old wall and the upper part of the new wall. The reconstruction and new walls resulted in 192 new towers. The outside of the outer wall with square towers dropped about 5 meters to form another ter-

race that led to a moat 18 meters wide and 6.5 meters deep designed to be flooded in parts. Arches were used in the new walls and the old towers. The inner wall completely dominated the newer one, while the new addition served to protect the older inner wall from direct enemy attack. In addition, a low crenelated wall, sometimes referred to as the scarp wall, ran along the moat. Between the scarp wall and the new wall there was a terrace about 12 meters wide. Another higher terrace about 18 meters wide was formed between the inner and outer walls. The walls stretched about 6 kilometers and included many well-defended gates. In the 8th century, the Byzantine engineers expanded the walls. This whole system of triple walls sealed the peninsula. In addition, a single wall extending about a kilometer to the Golden Horn enclosed a palace and a suburb of the city known as the Blachernae on the northern end. The Blachernae section was considered the weakest part of the land walls, especially where it met the triple walls and included the Imperial Palace. The Lycus River passed through the walls between the Civil Gate of St. Romanus and the Military Gate of St. Romanus, and emptied into the sea in the harbor of Eleutherisus. Thus the river played no significant role in the defenses except to provide a source of water for flooding parts of the moat. The valley of the Lycus stretched from the Civil Gate of St. Romanus towards the Golden Horn. This section of the triple walls was known as the Mesoteichion and considered the easiest to breach. The remainder of the triple walls occupied more rolling, hilly terrain southward to the sea. The remainder of the peninsula was protected by a sea wall from the Golden Horn to the Sea of Marmora.

The sea walls had been the main line of defense, until Theodosius II found it necessary to seal the peninsula with his own wall in the 5th century A.D. The sea walls never lost their importance however, and just like the land walls, they were continually repaired and improved throughout the Middle Ages. During the 7th and 8th centuries the walls not only received some important improvements, but a chain was also put across the Golden Horn. The sea walls later included two fortified ports on the Sea of Marmora to shelter a fleet which was intended to prevent an assault from the sea.

Slavic forces penetrated the first line of defense of the Byzantine Empire in 559 A.D. but were outmaneuvered by the great general Belisarius. In 673 A.D. the Arabs reached the walls of Constantinople for the

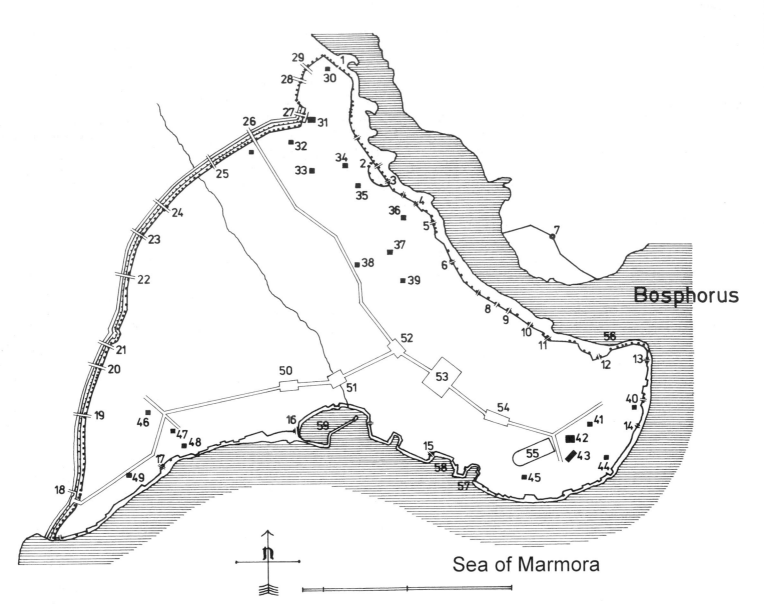

Constantinople

1. Xyloporta Gate
2. Gate of Phanar
3. Gate of Petrion
4. Gate of Theodosia
5-14. Gates
15. Gate of the Contoscation
16-17. Gates
18. Golden Gate
19. 2nd Military Gate
20. Pegae Gate
21. 3rd Military Gate
22. Gate of Rhegium

23. 4th Military Gate
24. Civil Gate of St. Romanus
25. 5th Military Gate
26. Gate of Charislus
27. Gate of Xylokerkon and
    Kerkoporta Postern
28. Gate of the Caligaria
29. Gate of Blachernae
30. Church of St. Mary (in Blachernae)
31. Imperial Palace
32-35. Church
36. Church of St. Theodosia

40. Church of St. George Mangana
41. Church of St. Irene
42. St. Sophia
45-49. Church
50. Forum of Arcadius
51. Forum of the Bull
53. Forum of Theodosius
54. Forum of Constantine
55. Hippodrome

first time, but, faced with the strong defenses and Greek Fire, they withdrew after a five-year siege. In 717 A.D. Islamic forces again were repelled before the great defenses and were also smashed at sea. Constantinople's reputation as the most strongly defended city in Christendom in the Middle Ages was established thanks to its massive fortifications built early in the Dark Ages.

In Asia Minor, the Byzantine city of Nicaea had walls similar to those of Constantinople, also erected in the 5th century. Because of Nicaea's location inland, these formidable walls completely encircled the city. Both Nicaea and Constantinople had many key elements that would be found in later defenses which may support the theory of the Oriental origin of the castle. One important characteristic of Byzantine fortifications noted by T. E. Lawrence (Lawrence of Arabia) was that, from the time of Emperor Justinian through the Middle Ages, their walls were thin. Although this was not a serious disadvantage during the Dark Ages, improving siege methods in the High Middle Ages rendered them more vulnerable as time went by.

While Byzantium withstood the Islamic onslaught, the situation in the West reached a critical point. As Moslem armies marched through Asia Minor to the gates of Constantinople, other Islamic forces reached the Straits of Gibraltar under the leadership of Musa Ibn Nusayr. General Tarik Ibn-Ziyad's reconnaissance mission into Iberia in 711 A.D. to investigate the strength of the Visigothic kingdom quickly turned into a conquest. Tarik engaged the army of King Roderick in a decisive battle on the Guadalete River and routed the Visigoth army, destroying the Visigothic kingdom in the process. The only serious resistance the Arabs faced came from a few fortified cities from the late Roman period such as Ceuta, Merida, and Seville. Soon the Islamic forces overran most of the Iberian Peninsula, forcing the remnants of the Christian forces into the mountain region of Asturias. The Moslem armies crossed the Pyrenees meeting no resistance until 732 A.D. at Poitiers where they were stopped by an army led by Charles Martel. The battle of Poitiers saved the Frankish kingdom and probably the rest of Christian Europe from the Islamic onslaught. Charles Martel later put an end to the Frankish Merovingian Dynasty by seizing the throne and his grandson, Charlemagne, saw the need for fortifications as he attempted to consolidate his power.

One interesting footnote to the Islamic conquest of Iberia is that in northern Spain, in the high valleys of the Ebro River, the Visigoths had built a series of small fortifications of adobe bricks to prevent Bardulians, a Basque group, from raiding their territories. Eventually, these fortifications were occupied by the Bardulians, who used them to repel the Arabs. Early in the 7th century, the Visigoth King Suintila subdued the Basques and used them to build a fortress city called Ologicus, the present-day city of Olite south of Pamplona. Late in the Middle Ages, Olite became one of Christian Spain's most formidable castles.

Slowly, Charlemagne established firm control over the Frankish lands, driving the Moslems beyond the Pyrenees. The Lombards, before they were defeated by the Franks, were checked by the old Roman fortifications in the Italian peninsula, eventually overcoming many of them, but twice failing to take Rome. The Roman defenses of Pavia withstood a three year siege by the Lombards until it was starved into submission in 572 A.D. In 774 A.D., after besieging Pavia for nine months, Charlemagne finally took the town and the iron crown of the Lombards. Charlemagne was rewarded for his service to the faith when Pope Leo III bestowed on him the title of Holy Roman Emperor (this is not the exact title used) on Christmas Day, 800 A.D. His empire consisted of little more than the Frankish kingdom he had already created. Charlemagne defended his borders with forts which, according to Jim Bradbury, author of *Medieval Siege*, were little more than "fortified posts" made mostly of earth and wood, sited on easily defended positions such as a hilltop, and quite effective, since few of them ever surrendered. In 801 A.D. Charlemagne's Frankish forces took Barcelona after a seven month siege which began in 800 A.D. in a campaign in the Spanish March. During the course of this campaign, the Franks erected their own lines of fortifications to contain the Moors. Charlemagne completed the reconquest of Catalonia up to the borders of the Ummayad Caliphate along the Ebro River. This was as far as the empire of the Franks would expand its influence in the Iberian Peninsula.

Before Charlemagne died in 814 A.D., the Vikings launched their first coastal raids. Charlemagne had created the Marches (frontiers) where he attempted to protect his borders with a system of forts. These included the Marches of the Avars (later Ostmark or Austria), Brittany, the Spanish March, and those in modern-day Germany. In the Spanish March, the term Catalonia is supposedly derived from the Latin

The Triple Walls of Constantinople

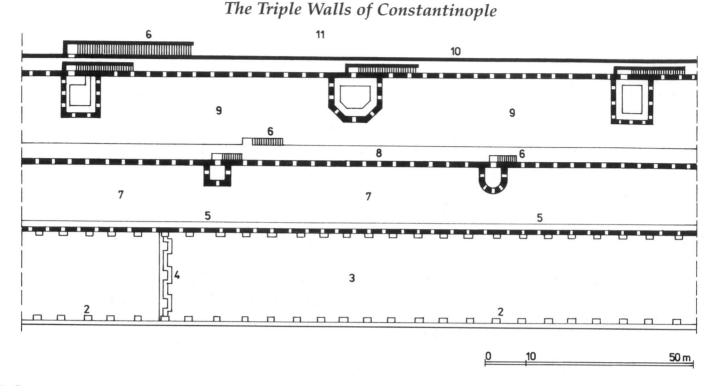

2. Counterscarp
3. Foss – water filled and about 20 meters wide.
4. Dam
5. Scarp with low wall forming first of triple walls.
6. Stairs

7. Peribolos – area between scarp wall and outer wall
8. Outer Wall
9. Parateichion – area between outer and inner wall
10. Inner wall
11. The city

word for castle, indicating their dominance over this land. The emperor had resorted to the feudal system to consolidate his power, using margraves (the count of the march) to maintain his borders. In a land where monasteries became more important as trading centers than the declining cities, his empire teetered on the verge of collapse.

Little evidence remains within the heart of Charlemagne's empire of any significant fortifications between 500 and 800 A.D. with the exception of a few Roman fortified towns such as Cahors (restored in 630 A.D.), Autun (restored 660 A.D.), and Strasbourg (former Roman city of Argentoratum, restored 722 A.D.). The Franks had taken the once important trading center of Cahors in southwest France from the Visigoths in 507 A.D. The bishop of Cahors, Saint Didier, who had also served in the court of the Merovingian kings in the first half of the 7th century, ordered the old town walls rebuilt. The new stone walls were made without mortar and towers were placed for flanking coverage. The town's

location on a bend in the river helped turn it into one of the strongest towns facing the Islamic invaders. Its fortifications served it well over the years as the dukes of Aquitaine, attempting to break away from the Franks, contested control over it in the 8th century. Autun, with its Roman walls, 62 towers, and 4 gates, was larger than most of the Saxon Shore Forts. Strasbourg was taken by the Carolingian dynasty and turned into the major trading center on the Rhine as well as the gateway to modern-day Germany. Thus, the need arose to protect this major center. The defenses of some other Roman fortified towns such as Carcassonne also continued to be maintained and strengthened, first by the Visigoths, then by the Franks after Charles Martel drove the Islamic forces back toward the Pyrenees.

The fact that Charlemagne's Frankish army was able to place many fortified towns under siege, including two major efforts against Pavia and Barcelona, was only possible because of good discipline and organization, and the creation of an effective siege train.

Remains of the triple walls of Constantinople can be seen in this photo of Theodosius's Wall. (Photo courtesy of Steven Wyley)

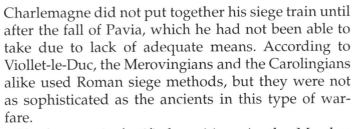

Charlemagne did not put together his siege train until after the fall of Pavia, which he had not been able to take due to lack of adequate means. According to Viollet-le-Duc, the Merovingians and the Carolingians alike used Roman siege methods, but they were not as sophisticated as the ancients in this type of warfare.

Charlemagne's fortified positions in the Marches were linked by roads and served as bases from which his cavalry could operate against invaders. The increased reliance on a new and stronger Frankish cavalry led to the further decline of the infantry. As in other places in Europe where cavalry predominated, the infantry was mainly relegated to garrisoning the fortified positions. The same thing had happened in the former Western Roman empire and the Byzantine empire where reliance on a heavy cavalry force led to smaller armies and the construction of more fortified positions to hold and maintain control over the empire. Like their Roman predecessors, the Merovingians built fortified positions throughout the kingdom that served as way stations for the army. The Franks, on the other hand, were better known for their palaces, like Charlemagne's residence at his capital of Aix-la-Chapel (Aachen), which also included room for a military garrison.

From the time of Charlemagne until the demise of the Carolingian empire, the Franks erected wooden field fortifications that served as encampments for large armies. It is not clear if this idea was original or inspired by Roman military practices. When Charlemagne and his successors attempted to consolidate their control over the Saxons and force their conversion to Christianity, they found that the establishment of forts was necessary to maintain their power. However, these Carolingian positions were by no means impregnable, for the Saxons succeeded several times in taking some of them in Saxony.

During the Dark Ages, as feudalism established a stronger hold in the west, the size of field armies became smaller. These small armies centered on a noble warrior class were inadequate to maintain control over the western Christian kingdoms. The need for strong defenses became increasingly obvious when the Vikings began to threaten the rest of Europe. In addition, the feudal system led to increasing rivalries between noblemen and territorial squabbles. Every feudal lord began to see the need to defend his own counties from rival counts, dukes, and barons, and even his own king. These lords seldom could muster armies of significant size and came to rely heavily on fortifications for their defense.

Fortifications in the British Isles

After the collapse of the Western Roman Empire the Celtic Britons found their lands invaded by the Germanic Angles, Saxons, and Jutes. No longer content with raiding Roman Britain, these tribes occupied outright the former Roman territories and took over the largely unoccupied Saxon Shore Forts. Eventually, the Britons were driven out of what is modern-day England into Celtic Wales, Scotland, and across the sea to Brittany. The Britons' resistance to the Anglo-Saxon occupation was immortalized in the legend of King Arthur and his Camelot. Although the exact location of Camelot is not known, it is suspected that it may have been an Iron Age fort known today as Cadbury Castle in Somerset. This Iron Age hill fort had been abandoned for many years before it was reoccupied in the struggle against Roman occupation. Its ditches had been restored late in the 1st century A.D. It was abandoned again for almost five centuries before it was put back into service at the time of the Anglo-Saxon invasions. The unmortared stone walls were topped with wooden battlements, which were replaced with walls made completely with stone in the High Middle Ages. It was encircled by three ditches, a common defensive feature of the early hilltop forts. The wooden gate was also a tower and was built along the lines of the simpler Roman structures.

Cadbury, however, is not the only place that has claims to being Camelot. In the summer of 1998 a tablet with the Latin inscription of what may well be Arthur's name was found at the castle of Tintagel on the northern coast of Cornwall. Several other Cornish castles, a couple in southern Wales, two more in Northumberland, and even one in Scotland have also been claimed as the home of Arthur. Although Cadbury and the others may no longer be considered as the site of Arthur's court, they were all centers of Celtic resistance and provide information about the development of fortifications in that early part of the Dark Ages. Tintagel was once a formidable hill fort located on an isle of black slate surrounded by cliffs with a narrow spine-like link to the mainland. Unfortunately, it has been ravaged by time and provides little information about its occupation predating the High Middle Ages.

CADBURY CASTLE. *The ruins of the castle many claimed to belong to the legendary King Arthur.* (© *Richard T. Nowitz/CORBIS*)

Fortifications Of and Against the Norse

After the Germanic tribes laid waste to the Roman Empire and established themselves in its former territories, they themselves were terrorized by the specter of barbarian invasions. This time the threat came from the northernmost reaches of Europe: the Scandinavian homeland of the Vikings. The inhabitants of Norway, Denmark, and Sweden were also Germanic people, but they had been neither Romanized nor Christianized and adhered to the old Germanic religion and way of life, which were considered quite barbaric by their Christian neighbors to the south. To the Vikings, on the other hand, the Christian lands seemed to be a feeble, backward region ripe for the picking. Like their other Germanic brethren, the Vikings would eventually convert to Christianity and become part of Western Civilization, which owed so much to the Romans. Their descendants became a dominant force in the West at the end of the Dark Ages and eventually contributed to the birth of modern-day England.

In their Nordic homeland, the Vikings built a number of defensive refuges early in the Dark Ages when the region was in a state of flux. Most of these forts were ring forts placed in terrain with limited access where the local villagers could seek safety. Two of the most important examples of Viking forts were on the Swedish island of Üland. One was located at Ismanstrop and was 125 meters in diameter. The other one was near the southern end of the island at Eketrop. The archaeological evidence at Eketrop indicates that the buildings here were only temporary and show a second construction phase in the 5th century A.D. when its diameter was enlarged and it became a permanent settlement only to be abandoned in 700 A.D. These two forts are fairly representative of Dark Age Scandinavia.

From the 8th century, as they began to emerge as a military power and take the offensive against other peoples, the Vikings stopped building new forts in their own homeland. Instead of erecting fortifications, they only built simple earthen and stone embankments to defend their villages. The major exception was the "Danewirke," or Danish Work, which extended across the base of the Jutland Peninsula. Recent dendrochronology tests done on the timber of this large earthwork indicate that the first ramparts went up in the 730s, rather than in the 9th century, as previously believed. It appears, therefore, that this may be one of the few continuous lines of defenses of any significance erected in Europe after the fortified Roman Limes. The Danish Vikings of Jutland apparently built the Danewirke to keep both Saxons and Franks out of this region to protect a vital portage between the town of Hedeby on the Slien Estuary leading to the Baltic and Hollingsted on the North Sea. The earth embankment with wooden palisades and the ditch covered a distance of about 25 kilometers, but actually occupied only about 14 kilometers. It is estimated that the embankment was about 10 meters wide and 2 meters high, but it may have been as high as 7 meters in certain places. The marshy areas to the west of the town of Hedeby constituted a major obstacle while the woodlands to the south formed another barrier. The strongpoint of the line was Hedeby with its wooden stockade. A single gate pierced the Danewirke just west of Hedeby to allow passage to the north-south military road that gave the only access into Jutland. Early in the 9th century, King Godfred, the first known strong Danish ruler, strengthened the defenses and, over the years, Hedeby received further truly impressive earthworks which reached up to 10 meters in height. Godfred had formed such a strong defensive line across the isthmus that he was able to harass Charlemagne continually and maintain his kingdom. In *The Viking Art of War* (London, 1995), Paddy Griffith estimated that 7,000 to 10,000 men would have been necessary to defend the line, which, he claims, was not an unreasonable number for the Danish ruler to raise. Spread over the distance of the Danewirke, these troops could not have been extremely effective in the face of a mass assault concentrated at a single point. In fact, in 815, the Frankish emperor Louis the Pious did break through the line. The Danewirke continued to be maintained until the 12th century, when King Weldemar I added a brick wall to it. However, several smaller, but more impressive Danish fortified positions had already replaced it by the 10th century. Earthworks like the Danewirke appear in Poland and Russia as well and, in some cases, covered much greater distances.

Norwegian and Danish Vikings mounted a campaign of raids and conquest against the British Isles and raided the Frankish lands. The Swedish Vikings struck out in an easterly direction, raiding Slavic lands and founded the first Russian kingdom at Novgorod with their Slavic subjects. Their raids reached as far as Byzantium and the lands of the Caliph. At Constantinople the old Roman empire was ready to resist the new invaders, while the West frantically improved its fortification to ward off the Norsemen.

The Vikings based in Norway struck at the Scottish and Irish coasts late in the 8th and early in the 9th century, while their Danish cousins raided both sides of the Channel. Initially, many tall towers were used by the locals as refuges from the invaders. Early in the Dark Ages, the Irish had built many ring forts known as raths that consisted of an embankment with a ditch in front of it. Stronger raths occupied a mound and were accessed by a ramp. In Ireland the Norwegians took Dublin, and throughout the first half of the 9th century the Vikings and Irish engaged in warfare involving a number of sieges.

By 840 A.D., the Viking raids took on a new character in Western Europe. The Norsemen began to establish operational bases in Ireland, Scotland, and the Frankish kingdom to serve as winter quarters and bridgeheads. They preferred to locate these settlements at the mouths of key rivers and, in some cases, they used old Roman fortifications. The Vikings also set up their fortified camps in swamps and woods where it was difficult to be attacked. Ditches and earth embankments with wooden palisades were almost standard in Viking fortifications. From these bases they could sally up the Seine towards Paris, or the Loire into the western Frankish holdings, using their long ships. Similar bases on the Rhine and in the British Isles were also established.

At this time the Frankish kingdom, emerging from a period of instability, was divided among Charlemagne's three grandsons (the sons of Louis the Pious). The part that eventually became modern-day France was under the rule of Charles the Bald. After the Treaty of Verdun in 843 A.D. brought an agreement among the three heirs, Charles the Bald, no longer forced to fight his brothers, turned his attention on the Vikings and on his nobles, as feudalism became more deeply entrenched in his kingdom. As Charles's vassals were given the right to pass on their lands to their families they developed a greater interest in fortifying their possessions. An interesting reversal took place during this time. Whereas earlier in the Dark Ages some city walls had become, with the permission of the authorities, quarries for building materials for churches and other structures, after the onslaught of the Vikings, stones from churches and other buildings were taken back to rebuild the old city walls.

Both Charles the Bald in France and Alfred the Great on the other side of the English Channel began a policy of denying the Vikings use of the waterways.

Charles ordered the creation of fortified bridges and used them to control the Seine and then the Loire. Charles helped the Count of Paris—whose seat was not the capital of France at the time—to stop further Viking raids by erecting a fortified bridge down the river near Pitres at Pont de l'Arche, just above Rouen, in 862. This bridge was reinforced with wood and stone forts. However, the Viking raiders still managed to reach Paris. Fortified bridges were also built at Paris, but the Vikings bypassed one of them in 887 after failing to take Paris by siege and sailed further into the interior. Charles built additional fortified bridges to prevent Viking raids in the Paris Basin and elsewhere, including on the Elbe and the Loire. One of his successors, Charles the Fat, who ruled France from 884 to 888, relied upon these bridges and other fortified sites to contain the Vikings, but avoided giving battle.

The Monastery of St. Denis, the best-known and wealthiest of the Carolingian Era which helped make Paris an important city, received a defensive wall in 869. Charles the Bald assigned his poorer subjects to build and defend new forts throughout the kingdom and the walls of certain cities like Tours and Orleans

Tall towers such as this one at Cashel were built all over Ireland as refuges against invaders.

were rebuilt. Cities lacking walls, like Paris before 869, Bruges, Cambrai, and Huy, acquired them at this time. Other cities like Sens relied on old Roman walls for their defense.

When the Vikings moved up the Seine in 885 A.D. against a weakened French kingdom, the river defenses failed to stop them until they reached Paris where Odo (Eudes), the count of Paris and future king, successfully held them at bay during the siege of 885–886 A.D. Paris was a partially fortified island city at the time. It occupied the area known today as Ile de la Cite, on an island in the middle of the Seine and included a 4th-century Gallo-Roman wall and two fortified bridges that withstood the assault of an estimated 30,000 Vikings for 11 months. The smaller bridge was defended by a tower on the southern bank of the Seine. The larger bridge was also defended by a tower and each had its own moat. Assaults against the bridges failed even though the Vikings used various types of siege engines such as catapults and rams, and even launched fire ships against the larger bridge.

Eventually, early in 886, the rising river destroyed the smaller bridge, and the raiders successfully assaulted the now isolated southern tower that defended it. But all attacks against the tower defending the larger bridge failed. Relief attempts were not successful but Paris continued to resist. Finally, the raiders were bought off and they moved on to besiege Sens for half a year without success. Further north in Flanders, the Vikings encountered new fortified towns and forts by 890 and failed to make headway. The failure at Paris and further defeats in German territories disheartened the Vikings and the threat they represented to Western Europe began to wane. In 911 Charles the Simple, King of France, gave the Viking Rollo (baptized Robert) a fief centered in Rouen, and the Norse invaders were finally absorbed into the kingdom.

Meanwhile, across the English Channel, the Vikings threatened to destroy the last of the Anglo-Saxon kingdoms. By then they had already conquered a good portion of the English territory. They had established bases in England since the 790s from whence they crippled one kingdom after another. Finally, in 865 A.D., the Viking Great Army arrived in Britain after terrorizing the kingdom of the Franks from the Rhine to Bordeaux. This massed Viking force descended on Britain, and like on the continent, traded its long ships for horses to move deep inland. Only the Saxon king of Wessex, Alfred the Great, succeeded in resisting them.

As Viking forces ended their raids and proceeded to conquer England, Alfred the Great rose to meet them. He restored about 30 West Saxon burhs or forts and in the 880s assigned landowners the responsibility of maintaining them. Many of the old burhs had followed the Roman rectangular pattern with earthen ramparts and a timber palisade on top. Some, such as the one at Rochester, proved strong enough to resist the Viking onslaught. At Rochester, the Roman walls remained in use as part of the defenses during the siege of 884. This key town held out until Alfred managed to raise the siege when he arrived with a relief force. The war between Alfred and the Vikings actually involved the use of fortifications on both sides. Alfred relied on isolated island positions as sanctuaries, and, like the Romans, he built and used causeways to move his army. The old Roman fortress of Chester fell to the Vikings in 893. Alfred struck back by besieging Viking bases. By the 890s his plan for setting up the fortified towns began to bear fruit. These positions had been intended for urban development so that they would have the necessary population to defend them and surrounding territory. In addition to laying the groundwork for towns and cities in southern England, the burhs kept all points in Wessex within 50 kilometers of a fort and protected every navigable river against Viking raids. In 886 Alfred had fortified London, and in 894 a large Viking raiding force set up its base camp nearby on the Thames. Alfred resorted to Charles the Bald's methods by blocking the River Lea and building a fort on each side. The Danes abandoned their fleet which was barred from reaching the Thames and withdrew from the area. By 896 the Viking threat to the Saxon kingdom was ended.

Danelaw, the lands in England where the Danes ruled—East Anglia, Five Boroughs, and York—remained in Viking hands through the early half of the 10th century. The fortified border between the Danes and Saxons was the scene of much fighting early in the century. New frontier forts were built to secure Saxon gains, and also to threaten Danish-occupied territory with incursions against their commercial centers. Finally, in 924 A.D., the Saxons took the Five Boroughs and by the middle of the century controlled all of England. By that time much of the southern part of the country was dotted with forts. King Edward I, son of Alfred, built new burhs as he advanced. Edward's burhs, like Alfred's, were meant for the national defense. England was not yet ruled by a feudal society and the concept of the castle did not yet exist there.

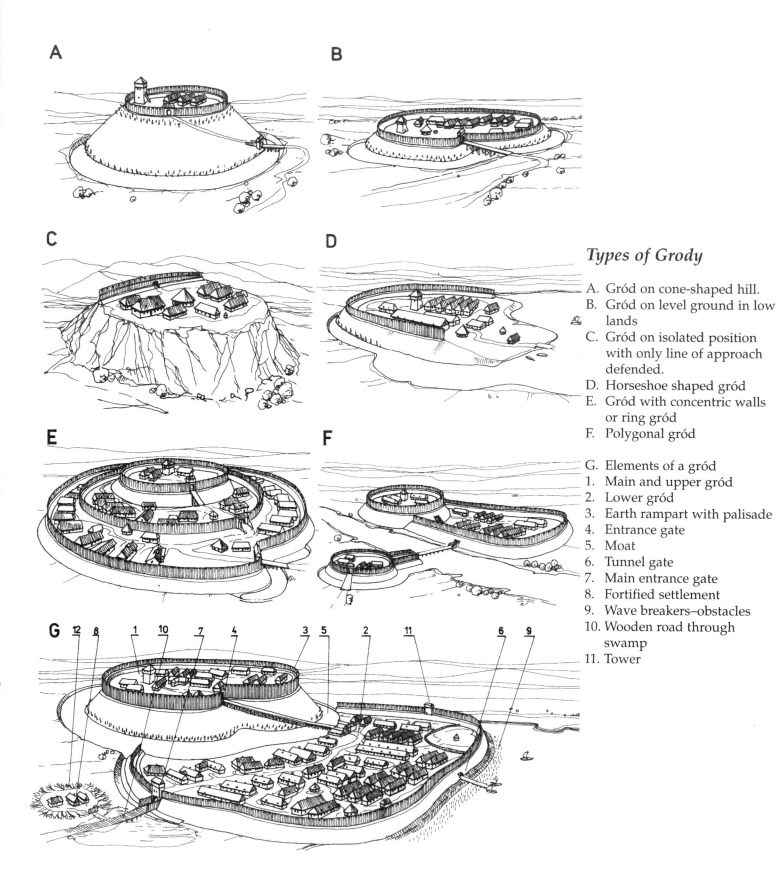

Types of Grody

A. Gród on cone-shaped hill.
B. Gród on level ground in low lands
C. Gród on isolated position with only line of approach defended.
D. Horseshoe shaped gród
E. Gród with concentric walls or ring gród
F. Polygonal gród

G. Elements of a gród
1. Main and upper gród
2. Lower gród
3. Earth rampart with palisade
4. Entrance gate
5. Moat
6. Tunnel gate
7. Main entrance gate
8. Fortified settlement
9. Wave breakers–obstacles
10. Wooden road through swamp
11. Tower

Fortifications in the Slavic Lands

The fortifications used by the Slavs in the East are not well-known in the West, despite the fact they bear great similarity to western structures. The Slavic people built fortified settlements known as *grody* (*gród* in the singular) in Polish and *grady* or *gorody* in Russian that were surrounded by a moat and usually included an earthen wall with a wooden palisade and a fortified gate. Sometimes these are referred to as ring works. The grody date back to several centuries before the birth of Christ. Just as in the West where the Latin and Germanic people had a tendency to use previous Roman fortifications and techniques, in the East, the Slavic people continued to follow the age-old style of their predecessors.

Between the 6th and the 8th centuries, after a hiatus of three centuries when no known fortification construction took place, a new building period began in the Slavic region. The simplest technique at this time was the use of a double set of basketweave wooden walls filled with earth, sand, and rubble. This technique dates back to the Bronze Age, and was used in the construction of the defenses of the island settlement of Biskupin in Western Poland. During the same period a palisade wall consisting of a double or even triple set of log walls filled with rubble was also used. However, the wooden walls were vulnerable to fire, so they were reserved for the defense of smaller settlements and individual homesteads. Larger and more important settlements were surrounded with some form of earthwork with palisades on top. The precise origin of these earthen walls is not known, but some Bronze Age Lusatian settlements in the area were already surrounded by such defenses. By the 8th or 9th century, a new construction technique was adopted. This was the "box construction," which consisted of building log boxes that were filled with soil, sand, and/or rubble. The whole was covered with earth to protect the wall from fire. Just as the west Europeans used the material excavated from the ditch to help create a wall, and in some cases a motte (hill), the Slavs covered their log boxes filled with rubble with the soil excavated from the moat surrounding the walls of the gród. The box wall sometimes consisted of two or more rows of log boxes and could reach a height of 12 meters. As the grody were usually built in areas surrounded by water courses and swamps, the weight of such large walls created problems with stability in these wet regions. To remedy this problem, layers of logs and rubble were used to stabilize the foundations. The damp climatic and soil conditions caused the

wood to rot quickly, but in some cases the earth covering protected the wood from the elements and the logs have survived to this day. The box walls, like the older earthen walls, were topped with a wooden palisade which in most cases was also reinforced. Occasionally stone was also used where it was available.

From the 9th to the 10th centuries there appeared different types of grody. Some were built to garrison military contingents, and were purely military in nature. Others were built to protect important production centers and sheltered a single type of artisan such as saddlers, blacksmiths, or weavers, who supplied the local chieftains with their goods. These settlements have kept their original names to the present day, even though they are no longer saddle production or blacksmith centers. Others were administrative centers that sheltered the chieftain's abode, his attendants, and his bodyguards. The administrative centers were not only large, but also much more complex than the other settlements. They are found mostly along the upper Vistula and in the Moravian regions, but they ranged as far north as Pomerania. Some included more advanced features such as double and triple moats. The box construction was eventually replaced with the grid construction which allowed the building of more massive and stronger defenses. These grid walls may have been in use as early as the 6th century but archaeological evidence is not conclusive on dates for the various phases of development of the grody.

The grid construction was developed as a result of efforts to correct the problems posed by the box wall. This grid type of wall consisted of layers of logs arranged in crisscross pattern alternating with layers of clay and sand which increased the stability of the wall. The wall was further stabilized by logs stuck into the ground. The grids were also attached to each other by a system of wooden hooks and joists to keep them from sliding. Often these grid walls leaned towards the interior of the gród and were shored up with an earthen embankment. The angle of the wall provided protection from siege towers because they kept the attackers away from the top of the wall. To overcome this obstacle, attackers began using ladders or portable bridges to span the distance between the siege tower and the top of the wall.

Not surprisingly, the oldest specimens of grid walls are found in the northwestern Slavic territories of Polabia and on the Polish Plain, which were dominated by swampy terrain. The grid walls never attained the popularity of the box walls, which continued to be used in the east and in the higher areas, but remains of

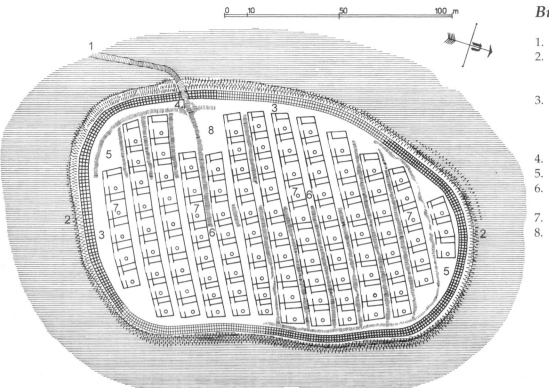

Biskupin, Poland

1. Access causeway
2. Wave breakers (sharpened logs used as an obstacle – about 40,000 of them)
3. Wall made with box type construction – covered with clay and 5-6 meters high and 3 meters wide with a wall walk.
4. Defended gate
5. Road
6. 12 parallel corduroy (made of logs) roads
7. 105 longhouses
8. Plaza

This Slavic gród at Biskupin was built in the marshes during the Bronze Age. It was typical of fortifications built in the area throughout the Dark Ages.

Close up view of the wall and obstacles (stakes) in front of the gród.

such walls were found as far east as Moscow and it appears they were used until the 13th century. The two most serious defects of grid walls were that they were not as fireproof as the box walls and that they required great amounts of wood. In addition, grid walls required frequent maintenance because the exposed wood deteriorated rapidly in the humid environment and had to be replaced regularly.

When the Swedish Vikings founded a Russian kingdom that included a large Slavic population, they built fortifications to defend it. According to one chronicle, the first Viking city was established at Staraya Ladoga on the Volkhov River, but Russians today dispute the fact that Staraya Ladoga was founded by the Vikings. Staraya Ladoga included a large settlement encircled by an earthen rampart. When Rurik of the Rus clan (the term Rus is also used to refer to both Vikings and Slavs of the new kingdom) became the Varangian leader, he built the city of Novgorod on Lake Ilmen. After Rurik, Oleg expanded the kingdom to Kiev. A stone wall was built to defend Staraya Ladoga in order to keep other Vikings out of this hybrid kingdom. Oleg, who fortified Staraya Ladoga, also founded stockaded towns to hold his conquests. Before the end of the 9th century, he was regarded as the prince of Kiev and in 907 A.D. he even marched against Constantinople.

When the Vikings arrived in the Slavic-controlled regions they referred to them as "the land of forts." These forts were circular with enclosed wooden walls above and earthen walls with a moat below them, and a form of abattis on the inner face of the water obstacle. A single entrance in the earthen wall allowed access to the fort. These forts were typical grody since the Slavic gród was a settlement located either on a prominent point which could be easily defended such as a small hill, an island in a swampy region, or at the fork of two or more water courses. The gate, or gates, were normally heavily fortified with towers. The walls were generally reinforced with earth on the inside and, where possible, covered with earth on the outside as protection against fire. Generally, there were no interior defenses within the walls.

The Slavic grody were usually built through the consensus of the local population. Construction was decided upon by the local council and was carried out by the entire population of the settlement. Archaeological and documentary evidence also indicates that each household of the gród was assigned a section of the wall to build, maintain, and defend in case of war. When the tribal chieftains acquired greater power and later became the dukes and princes of the region, the local council had to seek their approval as well before construction could be started.

These grody or grady were spread from the Elbe to the plains of Russia and the Ukraine. According to Joachim Herrmann, who described the Slavic fortifications of the North European Plain in *The Northern World* (Ed David Wilson, New York, 1980), there are over 2,000 remnants of fort or grody between the Elbe and Vistula. These forts served as focal points for groups of communities (up to 20) which emerged around them. Apparently the Baltic people used a similar fortification scheme.

In addition, to these fortifications, long earthen walls resembling the Danewirke were found in Poland and Russia. In Poland there is no solid evidence they were built as defensive structures, although it seems likely. In Russia the most famous of these walls was the Zmiewy waly located south of Kiev in modern day Ukraine. Radiocarbon dating has determined that this structure, which extended for 1,000 kilometers, was built sometime between the 2nd and 7th centuries A.D. as a defense against the Huns and other nomadic barbarians. Another line of mounds known as the Stuckinsk Line was built in the 7th century A.D. and was different in that it consisted of defenses up to 10 to 12 meters high and 20 meters wide at the base. This 200 kilometer line may have been built as protection against the Avars. The Viking fortifications bear many similarities to those of the Slavs but the Slavic ones seem to belong to a much older tradition.

Along the Baltic coast, from the Elbe River to the Vistula, the Slavic groups known as the Wends defended themselves in well-sited strongholds of the gród type with villages usually encircled by another ring work below it. The Wends, unlike the Poles and the Rus, were located on the coast. Their important towns were cleverly sited away from the coast where sea raiders could not assault them directly. Sometimes they were located at a more strategically defendable point along a river or some other outlet to the sea. Some of their strongest sites were located at Oldenburg (Stargard), Arkona, and Stettin. The port at Oldenburg was used by the Wagrians as a secure base for piracy since it could only be approached by sea after travelling through almost 30 kilometers of waterways. Arkona was situated on a headland consisting of the easily defendable coastal cliffs of the island of Rugen. Its approaches were sealed by an earthen rampart with a wooden palisade rising to almost 30 meters and an even taller fortified gate. Stettin, on the other hand, consisted of three hills surrounded by walls which were considered impregnable at that time.

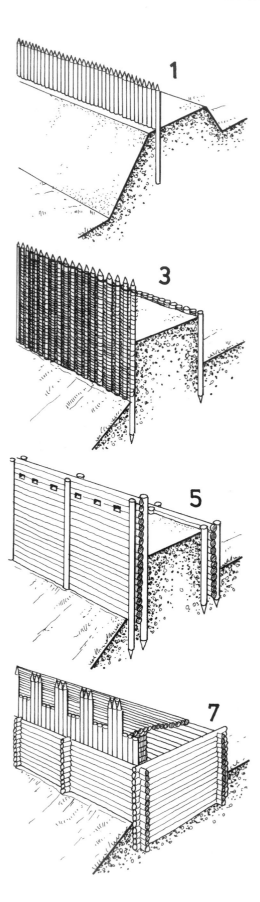

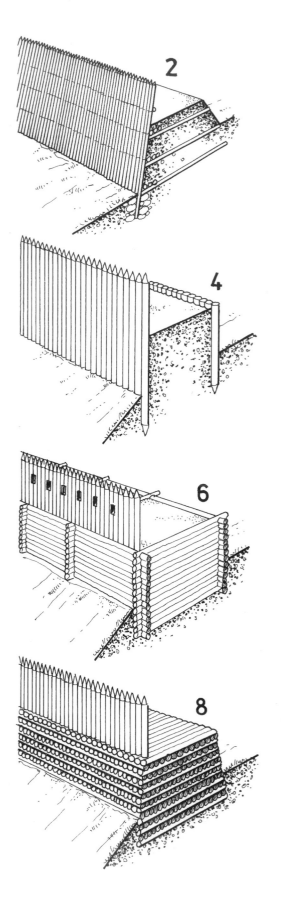

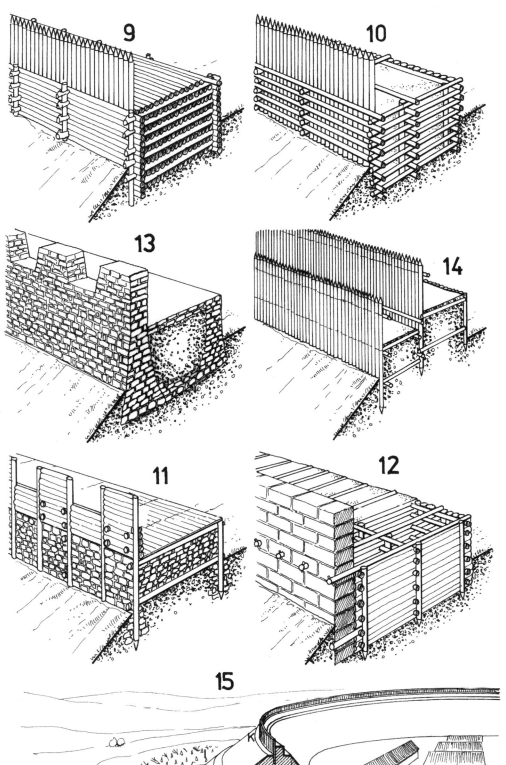

Types of Gród Wall Construction

1. Simple Wooden palisade on earthen wall
2. Palisade is built along the face of the earthen wall.
3. Basket weave construction with double palisade enclosing earthen wall
4. Similar to basket weave type but posts not woven
5. Fence wall
6. Box wall filled with earth
7. Box wall without earth
8. Stacked wall made of layers of logs
9. Hook and Stack wall. Wooden hooks to hold it in place.
10. Grid wall
11. Stone and wood wall made of mixed materials (stone foundation with wood)
12. Stone and wood wall with stone wall in front backed by earth and wood.
13. Stone wall
14. Double earth and log wall
15. Profile of a earthen enceinte of a gród.
    A. Obstacle
    B. Defensive position
    C. Settlement
    D. Area covered by fire from the walls and also including obstacles.
    E. Defensive wall and moat
    F. Defended area
    G. Counterscarp
    H. Moat
    I. Palisade
    J. Berm
    K. Earthen wall
    L. Wall

Fortifications and the Magyars

Another group of unwelcome intruders on the European scene were the Magyars. Unrelated linguistically to other European people, they invaded central Europe and launched their first assault on the Germanic Marches in the early 860s. They took control of the Danube valley in present day Hungary after pushing out the Bulgars and from there they continued to mount raids into western Europe. Henry the Fowler, King of the Germans and Duke of Saxony, solved the threat from both Magyars and Slavs by making his nobles build new fortified sites that they were obligated to garrison, and by ordering the clergy to fortify all monasteries. From the beginning of his reign in 919 until his death in 936, construction work progressed on these fortified cities. According to William Anderson in *Castles of Europe* (London, 1980), Henry organized his knights, the lower nobility, into groups of nine, one of whom was assigned the construction of a fortified town. According to another source, only free serfs were coerced into this system, which seems more likely, unless it was in combination with the nobles. The individual selected would have houses constructed for the other eight and served as part of the garrison while the others directed their attention towards agricultural activities. A portion of the food production was placed in storage in case of siege. The 10th-century Saxon historian, the monk Widukind of Corvey, claimed that Henry's success in battle was due not only to his mounted heavy cavalry, but also to his network of strongpoints.

In addition to the fortresses protecting a dozen or more settlements each, Henry set up a series of frontier forts which were to be garrisoned in shifts by the upper nobility. Some older fortified Roman sites, such as Strasbourg and Trier, were included among the empire's strongpoints. According to William Anderson, one of the most impressive of Henry's newly built castles was the one at Werla, erected in about 950. It was defended by strong towers, like those of the Slavic grody, but followed a pattern similar to the first wooden motte and baileys of western Europe. It actually had two large baileys and what appears to be a double motte position. Some German positions did bear similarities to motte and bailey and apparently a few were of that type.

The Magyars were defeated after an unsuccessful siege of Augsburg and again in open battle by Henry's successor, Otto I, at Lechfeld. They finally settled down in the Danube basin and built their own impressive fortifications. They employed a form of the box construction to form their ramparts. This technique appears to be similar to the Slav's. Jim Bradbury, who wrote *The Medieval Siege*, points out that when the log boxes were filled with clay, they were fired so that the clay turned into a type of ceramic which would become impervious to flames. This technique was probably copied from the Slavs since it was also used on the gród-type fortifications of Krakow and was likely used on other Slavic sites as well. In addition, the Magyars cleared out a zone around their fortifications to deny attackers any cover, and they employed obstacles reminiscent of the Roman era and borrowed others from their Slavic neighbors. Considering that the Magyars arrived in central Europe using only circled wagons as a form of defense for their camps, they adopted the techniques of their neighbors and even improved upon them with astounding rapidity and ingenuity. Each Magyar county had a fortified site which would eventually become a castle from which its count ruled. The king set up his residence about 35 kilometers north of modern-day Budapest on the remains of an old Roman fort at Estztergom, late in the 9th century. But Buda (modern-day Budapest—Buda was the fortified part later serving as the capital and Pest was a settlement on the other side of the Danube) did not receive its first castle until much later.

Beginning with the Romans, who set up hilltop forts after abandoning their continuous Limes and well into the Dark Ages, we see emerging the characteristics of the medieval castle and defensive warfare. Kingdoms and empires no longer attempted to defend their long frontiers, opting instead to use strongpoints to control various regions within their borders. These strongpoints, whether they were fortified towns or forts, served as refuges for the towns people who were often also employed in their defense. By the end of the Dark Ages these strongpoints appeared in many regions. Made of wood and earth or stone, depending on the available local material, they became increasingly complex and formidable. The Saxons returned to the trend of using forts to establish a defended frontier against the Vikings in the 9th century, but they also used these new forts to control and secure their conquests, like most feudal rulers that would come in their wake. Late in the Dark Ages many of these fortified positions were the property of the noble controlling a certain region given to him as a fief by his liege lord or king. These private fortifications eventually became castles in many regions and became increasingly dominant as the Dark Ages faded away.

CASTEL SANT'ANGELO, ROME.

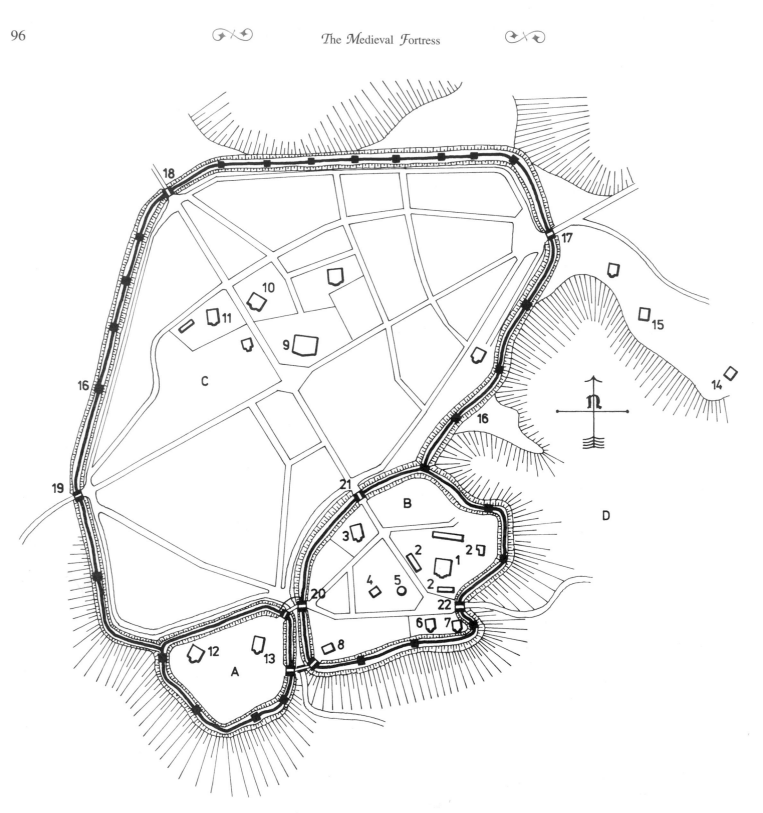

Kiev, Ukraine, 10th to 13th centuries

A. Mikhailovsaya Hill
B. Detines (Vladimir's town)
C. Yaroslav's town
D. Artisans quarter
2. Prince's Palace
3. Fedor Monastery
4. Catherine's Church
5. Rotunda

8. Vasilievskaya Church
9. Sophia Cathedral
10. Monastery of St. George
11. Monastery of St. Irene
12. Cathedral and monastery of St. Dimitri
16. Wooden palasides with towers
17. Lyadsky Gate
18. Golden Gate

19. Lvov Gate
20. Mikhailov Gate
21. Sofia Gate
22. Podol Gate

Roman Cities and New Cities of the Middle Ages

Some Roman cities would survive, expand, and retain their importance throughout the High Middle Ages:

Constantinople—New walls were added during the Dark Ages and it served as a religious center.
Rome—New walls were added during Dark Ages and it served as a religious center.
Milan (**Mediolanus**)—New wall was built around the city in the early 10th century which aided the growth of powerful merchants.
Cologne—Grew in 11th century due to trade.

BRUGES, BELGIUM. (© Corel)

Mainz—Grew in 11th century due to trade and also became cultural center.
Metz—Rebuilt in 11th century after being destroyed by the Huns a century earlier. It became a political, religious, and economic center.

Some new cities would rise to importance in the High Middle Ages:

Kiev—In 9th century was important trading center; in 10th century was capital of powerful Russian prince.
Moscow—Began with a castle in mid-12th century built to control trade.
Florence—Commercial center by 12th century.
Pisa—This merchant city was one of the wealthiest in Europe in the 10th century.
Genoa—In 10th century it became an important commercial center and its fortified harbor made it a major maritime center.
Hamburg—In 10th century it became an important commercial center and a maritime power.
Lübeck—In 12th century it became a major commercial center.
Ghent—In 10th century, after destruction of town, fortifications were built and the castle allowed the city to become a major commercial center.
Bruges—In the 9th century the town expanded around a castle and by the 10th century its harbor made it a major trading center.
London—Alfred rebuilt the towns fortifications in the 9th century after which it became the main commercial center of England.
Paris—Late in the Dark Ages it became a religious center, the capital of France, and was also fortified with walls.
Toledo—Throughout the Dark Ages it served as a capital for invaders and finally Spain. A wall and castle protected the city as it became Spain's 12th-century leading commercial center.

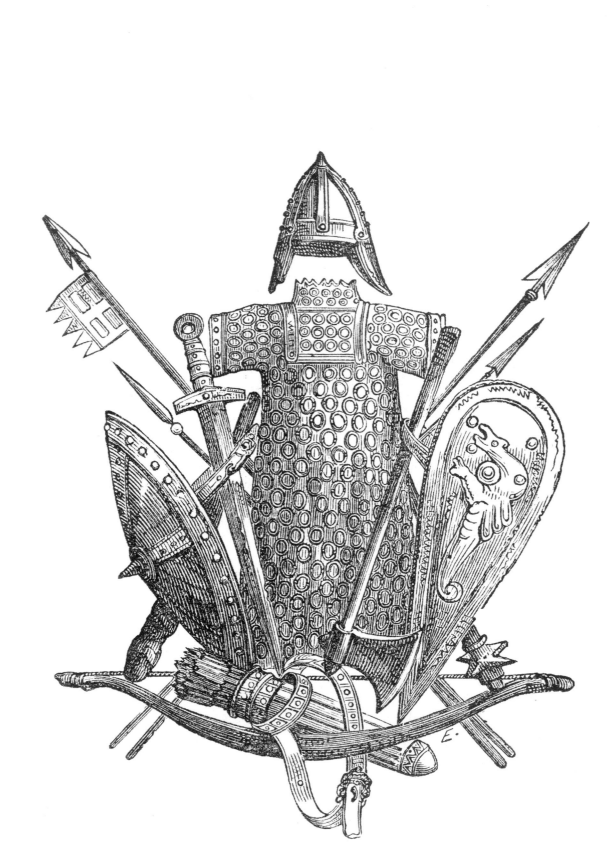

Events of the High Middle Ages

11th Century

Danish Invasion of Scotland, 1009. Danes are repelled.

HRE Henry II defeats Lombardy, 1002–1014.

HRE Henry II at war with Boleslav of Poland, 1003–1017.
—Poles take Silesia.

King Boleslav I of Poland takes Kiev in 1018 and soon after Yarolsav the Wise turns Kiev into powerful state.

King Henry I of France engages in war with powerful counts and brings them under control, 1033–1043.

King Henry I of France at war with Normans (William), 1037–1058.

Norwegian Vikings invade England, 1066; they are defeated at Stamford Bridge.

Norman Conquest, 1066.
—William the Conqueror takes England after battle of Hastings.

Norman Conquest of Sicily, 1060–1091.
—Normans take southern Italy and at war with Byzantine.

War between England and Scotland, 1077–1093.

Civil War in HRE, 1077-1106.

HRE Henry IV campaigns against Pope Gregory VII, 1081–1085.

Pope Urban II calls for Crusade, 1095.

First Crusade, 1097-1099.
—Ends with Latin Crusaders taking Jerusalem.

Civil War in Sweden, 1066-1134.

12th Century

HRE Henry V is defeated in attempt to conquer Poland in 1109.

Louis VI of France at war with Henry I of England, 1109-1112 and 1116-1120.

HRE civil war, 1125-1135. Beginning of Guelph vs. Ghibelline parties.

Second Crusade, 1146-1148.

HRE Frederick Barbarossa defeats Poland, Bohemia, and Hungary, 1156-1173; several campaigns in Italy have less success.

Henry II of England invades Ireland, 1167-1171.

War between England and Scotland and France when Henry II's sons revolt, 1173-1174; Henry II puts down rebellion.

3rd Crusade, 1190-1191.
—Richard I of England defeats Saladin at Arsuf in 1191.

War between England and France, 1194-1199 (Richard I vs Philip Augustus.)

HRE Henry VI conquers Sicily, 1191-1193.

13th Century

4th Crusade 1202-1204.
—Crusaders attack and take Constantinople in 1204.

Albigensian Crusade from 1208–1229.

Alfonso VIII of Castile inflicts major defeat over Almohads at Las Navas de Tolosa in 1212.

5th Crusade, 1217-1219—Crusaders besiege and take Damietta in Egypt in 1218

6th Crusade led by HRE Frederick II in 1229 takes Jerusalem by diplomacy.

Mongol Invasion of Europe, 1237-1241; Kiev falls in 1240; Mongol victory at Liegnitz over Prince Henry of Silesia Poles, 1241; Mongol victory at Mohi (Sajo River) over Hungarians, 1241.

Alexander Nevski of Novgorod defeats Teutonic Knights at Lake Peipus (Battle of the Ice), 1242.

7th Crusade of Louis IX of France in 1248-52 fails in Egypt.

Wars between Venice and Genoa, 1253-1299.

8th Crusade of Louis IX of France in 1270 ends with siege of Tunis.

Edward I of England conquers Wales and Scotland, 1272-1307.

14th Century

Scottish victory at Bannockburn ends English king's control over Scotland, 1314.

First major victory of Swiss Revolt (begun in 1291) at Morgarten in 1315.

War between Florence and Lucca, 1320-1323.

Hundred Years War, 1337-1457:
—Edward III of England wins naval battle of Sluys in 1340.
—Edward III wins battle at Crecy in 1346 and takes Calais in 1347.
—Black Prince defeats French at Poitiers, 1356.
—Gascon's revolt in Aquitaine in 1368 and by 1373 England has lost both Aquitaine and Brittany.

Wars between Venice and Genoa, 1353–1355 and 1378–1381.

Tamerlane at war with Toktamish, Mongol leader of the Golden Horde, 1391-1395; Tamerlane invades Russia and defeats him.

Crusade to defeat Turks on Danube ends in defeat at Nicopolis in 1396.

War between Florence and Milan, 1397-1398.

15th Century

At Tannenburg (Grunwald) Teutonic Knights decisively defeated by a Polish-Lithuanian army in 1410.

Hundred Years War continues until 1453:
—Henry V of England defeats French at Agincourt in 1415.
—Siege of Orleans begins 1428 and broken by Joan of Arc in 1429.
—English defeated at Castillon in 1453.

Hussite Wars, 1419-1436.

Turkish civil war ends in 1413 with strong Sultan; new Sultan and successors advance in Balkans and defeat Hungarian, Polish, and others in 1440s.

Turks assault and take Constantinople in 1453.

War of Roses, 1455–1485.

Reconquista ends with siege of Granada and Spanish victory, 1492.

(HRE = Holy Roman Empire or Holy Roman Emperor)

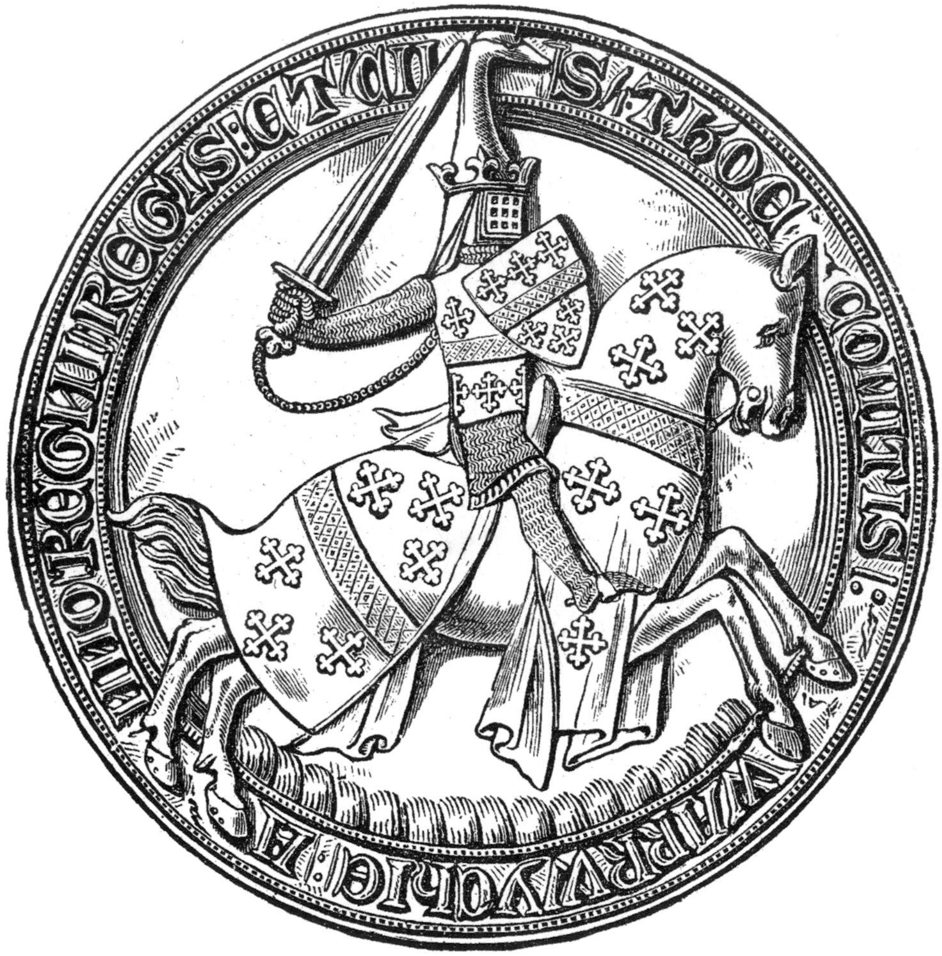

Battles of the High Middle Ages

1066 Hastings (Norman Invasion)
William the Conqueror with about 7,000 Normans vs Harold with about 7,000 Saxons.

1097-98 Antioch (1st Crusade)
Crusaders with about 1,000 cavalry and 14,000 infantry vs 75,000 Moslems.

1099 Ascalon (1st Crusade)
Godfrey of Bouillon with 1,200 knights and 11,000 foot soldiers vs Fatimid army from Egypt of about 50,000.

1187 Hattin (Fall of Kingdom of Jerusalem)
King Guy with 1,200 knights and 18,000 others vs *Saladin* with 18,000 Saracens.

1195 Alarcos
(Castilian advance south in Reconquest)
Almohads with probably 20,000 to 30,000 vs about 25,000 Castilians.

1212 Las Navas de Tolosa
(decisive battle of Reconquest against Almohads)
Almohads with up to 300,000 (Arab chronicler mentions only 160,000) vs *Christian-Crusader army* of up to 70,000 (originally may have been 62,000 French, 60,000 Castilian and 50,000 Aragonese plus troops from Portugal and Navarre with much of the force, especially French, deserting during the campaign).

1214 Bouvines
(English-German alliance threatens France)
HRE Otto IV with 6,000 cavalry, 18,000 men including English, Germans and Flemings vs France's *King Philip Augustus* with 7,000 cavalry and 15,000 foot troops.

1223 Kalka River
(Mongol invasion of Europe)
Subotai's 40,000 Mongols vs 80,000 Russians under Prince of Kiev (mostly militia with a few thousand Cumans)

1226 Yellow River
(Mongol invasion ends Chin Empire)
180,000 *Mongols* vs 300,000 Chinese.

1241 Liegnitz
(Mongol Invasion of Europe)
Kaidu's 20,000 Mongols vs Duke of Silesia with 40,000 Poles, Germans, and Teutonic Knights.

1241 Mohi (Sajo River)
King Bela IV of Hungary with 100,000 men vs *Sabutai* with 90,000 Mongols.

1314 Bannockburn
(Final battle for Scottish Independence)
King Edward II of England with 1,000 cavalry and 17,000 infantry vs *Robert the Bruce* with 500 cavalry and 9,000 infantry.

1346 Crécy (Hundred Years War)
Edward III of England with 2,500 men-at-arms and 6,500 foot soldiers (mostly archers) vs Philip IV of France with up to 12,000 knights, 6,000 Genoese crossbowmen and up to 15,000 peasant levies.

1367 Navarrette
(English expedition into Iberia to help restore
Pedro to Castilian throne)
Black Prince of England with about 20,000 men vs a 40,000-man (some estimate 70,000) Franco-Spanish army.

1380 Kulikovo
(Russian revolt - decisive battle against Mongols)
Russians with from 100,000 to 400,000 led by *Grand Duke of Moscow* revolt against Tartar army of from 150,000 to 700,000 (lower estimates for both are probably correct).

1385 Albjubarotta
(Castile attempts to invade Portugal)
Castilian army of 18,000 vs *Portuguese army* of up to 14,500 (including some English veteran troops).

1386 Sempach (Wars of Swiss Independence)
1,600 *Swiss* pikemen vs Duke Leopold of Austria with 4,000 Austrians (many cavalry).

1410 Tannenberg
(War against the Teutonic Knights)
4,000 to 6,000 Teutonic Knights vs *King Ladislas II* of Poland with 10,000 Poles and Lithuanians.

1415 Agincourt (Hundred Years War)
Henry V of England with about 750 men-at-arms and 5,000 archers vs French army of about 22,000 men-at-arms and 3,000 crossbowmen and an unknown number of peasant levies.

1453 Formigny
(one of the last battles of Hundred Years War)
French force of 8,000 vs. English force of 4,500.

1453 Constantinople (Fall of Byzantine)
The Emperors forces are estimated at about 9,000 vs the *Sultan's Turkish army* of over 50,000 and equipped with a number of small cannons and over a dozen heavy ones.

1461 Towton (War of Roses)
This was one of the larger battles of the civil war. The Lancastrian army had about 20,000 men against the *Yorkist army* of 16,000. Most battles of the war had between 6,000 to 10,000 on each side.

1476 Grandson
(War between the Swiss and Burgundians)
Charles the Bold's Burgundian army of 30,000 vs 18,000 *Swiss* pikemen.

The victor of the battle appears in italics.

Coca Castle, Spain

3

The Age of Castles

As the Dark Ages waned, the popularity of castles increased. In fact, one could say that the rise of the castle marked the transition period between the Dark Ages and the High Middle Ages, as empires and kingdoms collapsed under the onslaught of new invasions and migrations, like the Roman Empire. The Vikings shattered the feeble Celtic and Anglo-Saxon kingdoms of the British Isles, threatening the remnants of the old Frankish empire in the west. The Norsemen, mainly those from modern-day Sweden, also tangled with the Slavs of Eastern Europe, leading to the creation of the Russian kingdoms. In the south and west, the forces of Islam swept into Europe, destroying the armies of weak Christian kingdoms while Byzantium fended them off in the East from the 7th century until the 9th century of the Early Middle Ages.

Throughout the Dark Ages, the kingdoms that successfully resisted the onslaught of the "barbarians" from the North and East and the Islamic forces from the South relied heavily on fortifications for their defense. Both Viking and Moor also adopted fortified positions to strengthen their hold on the territories they occupied and to enhance their offensive operations. In the 9th century, Alfred the Great led Saxon forces against the Norse intruders, laying down the foundations of a new nation that would come to be known as England. By the time the Germanic ruler of the Latin regions of the Frankish empire in the West was succeeded by the first dynasty of Latin kings in the 10th century, the Viking problem was well in hand. Rollo's Norsemen settled in Normandy and his heirs became vassals to the Frankish king early in the 9th century. Both Hugh Capet, who founded the Latin dynasty of France, and his son who succeeded him, had to contend with their vassals more than any external enemy. The castle played an important role in their struggles to maintain their power over their dominions.

The eastern Germanic regions of the Frankish empire (East Francia) emerged from the turmoil of late Carolingian under the leadership of a Germanic leader, Henry I (the Fowler) of Saxony, who was elected king by the dukes of the other German duchies. He began the northward and eastward expansion of his own domains by fighting against the Danes and the Slavs. Henry's son, Otto I, also elected king, turned this loose union of German territories into an empire that would later be known as the Holy Roman Empire, the forerunner of modern-day Germany, after defeating the Magyar invaders threatening central Europe. Otto I also relied on strongholds to maintain control over rebellious German noblemen.

In the Iberian Peninsula, the Visigoths, who had taken refuge in the Pyrenees after their humiliating defeat of 711, began the reconquest of their former territories almost immediately. According to legend, in 718 Pelayo, a Visigothic nobleman, defeated an Arab force at Covadonga and proclaimed himself king of Asturias, the first of several Christian kingdoms that would arise in the mountains of northern Iberia. Pelayo's feats, however, were not recorded in history. The first historically recognized founder of Asturias, Alfonso I, who was crowned king in 739, launched the Reconquista which would last until the fall of Granada, the last Moorish stronghold in Spain, in 1492. As Alfonso I pushed the Moors out of the territories of Galicia and León, he consolidated his hold on his lands with fortifications and castles. In time the kingdom of Asturias-León split into several kingdoms that included León, Castile, Navarre, Aragon, and, eventually, Portugal. Aragon merged with Catalonia, the Hispanic March of the Carolingians, in 1137; Portugal seceded from León in 1139; and Castile absorbed much of the Navarrese territories in 1076 and united with León in 1230. Thus these three kingdoms became the dominant powers in the Christian part of the Iberian Peninsula and the driving force of the Reconquista. From early on, the Christian kings of Iberia maintained their gains through the use of the stone castles, many of which were taken from the Arabs they defeated. It must be noted that the formidable stone fortifications of the Moors were one of the factors that prolonged the Reconquista over a period of almost 800 years in what became "wars of position."

Throughout the Dark Ages, the last remnant of the Roman Empire, Byzantium, continued to protect Christian Eastern Europe from external threats, mainly Islamic forces, with the most impressive fortifications of the era. However, during the 10th century, the Byzantine Empire declined rapidly in the face of new invaders, the Seljuk Turks. In *Byzantine Fortifications*, Clive Foss and David Winfield reject the traditional view that the European castle evolved from the motte and bailey. According to them, the art of castle building goes back to the Roman fortified camp or walled fort which generally used a rectangular shape. The Byzantine engineers continued to renovate the Roman walls and follow the Roman model. The Arabs, who drove the Greek forces from the Middle East, adopted the same principles of fortification building. In addition, Foss and Winfield argue that in León and parts of northwestern Europe, the same Roman engineering tradition was carried on with improvements on abandoned Roman sites. According to them, new castles were not built during the Dark Ages because the art of mortar making had been lost in northwestern Europe during the Dark Ages, making it impossible to build sizable stone structures. Ross and Winfield's theory does not seem too farfetched, especially since Byzantium provided the medieval world with beautiful examples of Roman stone fortifications that could have served as models to latter day architects.

Nonetheless, the preponderance of evidence seems to point to the fact that the European castle was born in France, in the province of Anjou under the aegis of Fulk Nerra and the Count of Blois. Indeed, in that area one can observe the gradual transformation of the castle from the humble motte and bailey to the stone keep, to the elaborate complex of walls and towers of later centuries. The study of the Byzantine fortifications, may well have enhanced the European builders' skills and knowledge, but it is unlikely that it provided the necessary impetus for castle building.

PEÑAFIEL CASTLE, SPAIN   (© Corel)

Fortifications at the Beginning of the High Middle Ages

The last half of the medieval period saw the emergence of England, France, Germany (Holy Roman Empire), Russia, Portugal, and Spain (Castile and Aragon). The foundation of other European states such as Scotland, Denmark, Hungary, and Poland was also laid down. Castles were erected and cities were fortified in virtually every one of these newly emerging states at this period while Byzantium continued to improve and strengthen its old Roman fortifications.

In the west, especially in western Francia (the future France), where many city walls from the Roman era lay in ruins from disuse and were plundered for building materials, a new era or fortification building was launched. By the 11th century, the town began to return to a place of prominence as an economic center and military strongpoint in the growth and defense of a king's or a magnate's holdings in most of Western Europe. In the Slavic lands of the east and parts of central Europe and Byzantium, the town had never really lost its importance during the first half of the Middle Ages. In the Slavic lands many of the settlements and towns had been defended by earthen ramparts for centuries. In the Byzantine Empire, many old Roman walls continued in service while newer ones had been built in the Dark Ages, Constantinople being the best defended city in Europe. The population centers within the Islamic world were largely undefended unless they were on a frontier as in the case of Iberia. At the end of the 10th century, the Islamic-controlled cities in Iberia and in other regions were fortified as a precaution against internal strife and civil wars. Thus, by the beginning of the High Middle Ages almost every town or city in Europe and the Mediterranean world boasted restored or new walls. During the 11th century, many castles actually became associated with the defenses of a town or city instead of being predominately isolated strongpoints. The kingdom of Castile was even named for the castles that served as symbols of power and security. However, the fortified town also became significant in Castile's southward expansion against the Islamic kingdoms known as taifas.

SAUMUR, FRANCE. *This present-day castle sits on the site of the old fortification. Saumur was the site of conquest by Fulk Nerra in 1026.*

Castles Emerge in the West

The mental picture we form in our minds of the medieval castle today is the creation of the Romantic writers and poets of the 19th century, who invested it with an aura of heroism, mystery, and mysticism. However, the fact is that most castles fail to live up to our romantic expectations. They were usually functional structures built for war, not to house the courts of courtly love. From Europe to the Middle East and North Africa they reveal significant regional and even cultural differences. No two castle plans are alike since they were usually designed to adapt and make the most of the terrain on which they were built.

The best-known types of castles are associated with Western Europe, especially France and England. During the reign of Hugh Capet, the nobles in his realm were too busy feuding among themselves to challenge his authority successfully. Hugh's chief nemesis was his rival for the throne, Charles, Duke of Lower Lorraine (now Belgium), one of the last

Carolingians, who invaded France and took the city of Laon. Hugh was not only unable to evict Charles from the town, even after a prolonged siege, but also lost Reims to him when a gate was left open through an act of treachery. In the end, however, Hugh prevailed. His campaign, like most military actions of the High Middle Ages, involved a series of sieges of castles or fortified cities and towns. Unlike most feudal suzerains, Hugh directly ruled his counties of Orleans and Paris, which became part of his royal domain, becoming known as the Ile de France. Soon after Hugh's death, his successor, Robert the Pious, had to confront the counts of Anjou, Blois, and Troyes, who challenged his authority. In the late 10th century and the 11th century even lesser nobles defended their fiefs with the new stone castles, blocking the king's communication route between Paris and Orleans. The new stone castles not only strengthened the hold of

LANGEAIS CASTLE, FRANCE. *The remnants of the original motte and bailey castle, built by Fulk Nerra. This is the second oldest donjon in France.*

the nobles on their land grants, but also allowed them to defy and resist their king. It seems as if within the space of a generation a revolution in military architecture had taken place, putting royal power in dire peril. Yet many of the ideas incorporated in the castle had their origins in the past.

During the later part of the 10th century the Count of Anjou, founder of the Angevin Dynasty which would rule England a century later, was the teenaged Fulk Nerra. Neither Hugh Capet nor his heir Robert were able to exercise much control over this vassal or his rival, the Count of Blois. During the reign of Hugh Capet, Fulk began his campaign to consolidate and expand his holdings. A violent and aggressive man, Fulk was a keen strategist, who learned from experience that the best method to maintain the loyalty of his vassals and expand his county was to build a castle on newly occupied lands. He learned from his mistakes during his conflict with Conan of Brittany and his archenemy, Odo I (Eudes), Count of Blois. His campaigns against the latter centered on maintaining the loyalty of his own vassals south of the Loire in the valleys of the Vienne and Indre Rivers and wresting

control of Saumur and Tours from Odo. After the death of Odo, Fulk suffered a major reversal of fortunes when the forces of King Robert, then married to the Countess of Blois, moved against him to secure the holdings of Blois. However, this setback did not quell the Angevin count, who returned to his expansionist policies by slowly advancing into the holdings of his neighbors. He used his new castles to place a stranglehold on points of resistance, and by the 1020s he controlled most of the lower Loire Valley from Nantes to the outskirts of Tours. Saumur finally fell to him by 1026. Tours did not succumb until after Fulk Nerra's death, but his policy of using the stone castles to secure his lands continued. Whether the Normans and other vassals of the French king followed Fulk's example or developed one on their own is subject to debate. Whatever the case, the Normans learned quickly that the stone castle was as much a key to future success as the Norman knight, if not more.

In 992, during his campaign against Conan, Duke of Brittany, Fulk's forces were repelled in the attempt to take the fortified Breton camp at Nantes, sometimes referred to incorrectly as a castle. The position was probably little more than earth and wood, possibly consisting of a formidable timber palisade, but proved too much for Fulk's small army. Fulk did not forget this lesson. In the 990s he began the construction of more permanent stone fortifications to secure his holdings and maintain the loyalty of his own vassals. He tried to place his castles no further than a day's march from each other. The garrisons he left behind had the mission of raiding and harassing any invading force, but avoiding battle. His opponents soon learned that the only way to eliminate Fulk's garrisons would be with costly sieges rather than in open battle. They also found that laying siege to a key castle deep within Fulk's territories was a risky business, with garrisons from nearby castles only a day's march away and their line of communications also open to raids. Sieges required large forces and much time. Thus, the defender retained the advantage, since feudal armies were generally small and not ready to undertake lengthy operations. This is why the castle became so ubiquitous in medieval France.

The Roman Empire had been vanquished, in part, by warrior horsemen. The Byzantines, who adopted the use of the stirrup from the East, created the armored cavalryman, the predecessor of the Western European knight, who soon became the dominant force on the battlefield. However, although the knights played the decisive role in medieval battles, they were usually few in number because their training was lengthy and the cost of their equipment was prohibitive. Military leaders relied on peasant levees and mercenaries to fill out their battles—medieval units usually with three formations forming an army on the battlefield, right, left, and center. Morale could easily sag among the non-mounted troops, who probably felt very vulnerable, standing in an open battlefield, poorly equipped, and with little armor or protection. Thus a garrison of local levees usually felt confident behind castle walls and towers, knowing the opponents had only two options: either launch an assault under a hail of missiles or lay siege to the place, which would leave them exposed and force them to scour the countryside for food and supplies. Of course, the besiegers might also prepare special weapons to breach the walls or storm the battlements, but this required much labor and time. In either case, the besiegers' morale was much more likely to drop than the defenders' unless they could maintain their positions long enough for the garrison to run out of supplies. It is no coincidence that the campaigns of the last half of the Middle Ages usually included more sieges than pitched battles. According to Jim Bradbury, who wrote *The Medieval Siege*, medieval warfare consisted of only 1 percent battles and 99 percent sieges. Thus, there is good reason to refer to this as the Age of Castles.

Falaise Castle, Normandy

1. Great Keep - Romanesque style
2. Chapel
3. Talbot's Tower
4. Tower for secondary residence

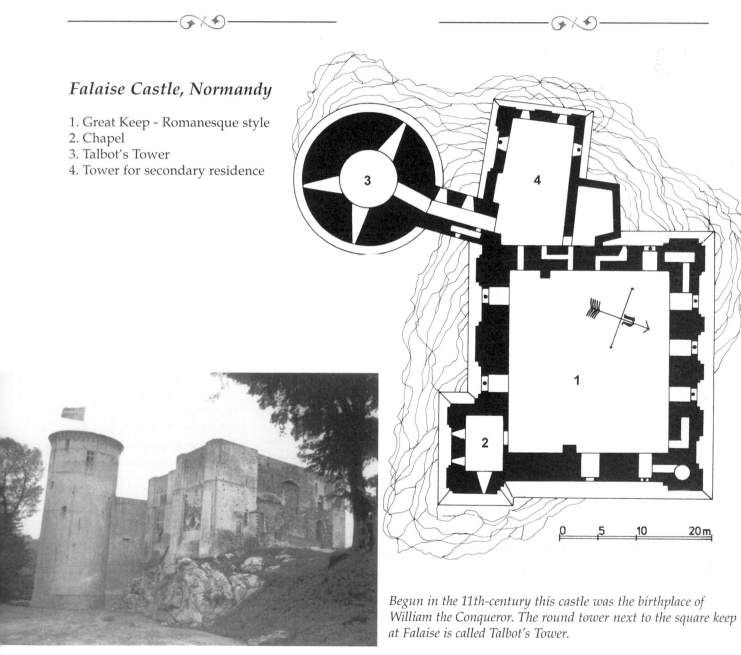

Begun in the 11th-century this castle was the birthplace of William the Conqueror. The round tower next to the square keep at Falaise is called Talbot's Tower.

Langeais Castle, France

1. Motte and bailey with remains of donjon (keep)
2. Chateau built by Louis XI

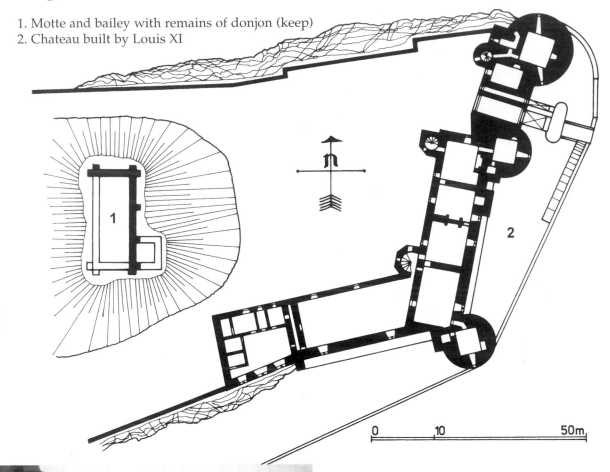

LANGEAIS, FRANCE. *The remains of the original motte and bailey fortification at Langeais built by Fulk Nerra can still be seen (see page 106) but it is dominated by the newer castle built by Louis XI to replace it in the 15th century.*

Castles of Western Europe

The earliest type castles in Western Europe belonged to the motte and bailey type. This design appears to have developed during the 10th century, although no one is certain of its exact origin. Some believe that the Vikings' timber stockades from which they raided the Frankish coastline may have been the forerunners of the motte and bailey. It is not known exactly what these defenses looked like, but it is safe to assume, based on later defenses, that they included wooden walls and possibly a ditch in front of them to protect the camp. The first motte and bailey castles, made of wood and earth, are attributed to the Vikings known as Normans, Norsemen or Northmen, who settled in Normandy. It is possible the Angevins could have developed this type of fortification before the Normans, but this cannot be proved one way or the other.

Circular fortifications using earthen mounds as ramparts and ditches at Trelleborg, Denmark, also date from the 10th century and show some similarities to the much older Slavic grody of Eastern Europe. Similar circular fortifications with earthen walls made from the excavated moat were widespread throughout the European lands north of the Alps in Western, Northern, Central, and Eastern Europe. It is possible that the Norsemen may have brought this design with them when they settled in Normandy. Although the origins of the motte and bailey may be traced to other lands, the fact remains that this type of fortification seems to have first achieved prominence in the French lands of Normandy and Anjou from whence it was taken by the Normans to England.

As discussed in an earlier chapter, the motte and bailey consisted of a wooden donjon or keep sitting atop a motte or manmade mound surrounded by a bailey or courtyard encircled, in turn, by a wooden palisade and a ditch. The motte was the last center of resistance within this fortification. The keep usually served as the residence for the noble or castellan. The larger keeps for the more powerful nobility included a great hall, living quarters, and a chapel. The encircling ditch was up to three meters deep and was backed by a rampart usually of earth and wood made from dirt excavated from the ditch. The area between the motte and the outer ditch with the ramparts formed the bailey. The wooden motte and bailey of the 10th century became or were supplanted by stone ones in the 11th century.

Until the 1970s it had been believed that the oldest known stone keep was the one at Langeais in France built by Fulk Nerra. The motte and bailey castle at Langeais was apparently begun shortly before 995 (probably in 992) at a site that controlled the route between Fulk Nerra's seat of power at Angers and his lands south of the Loire. This position also served to threaten Tours and block the route along the Loire between Tours and Saumur. The castle at Langeais was a fairly typical motte and bailey with earth and timber defenses. In *Chateaux Forts* (Paris, 1983), André Châtelain indicates that Langeais was actually one of two stone residences in Fulk's territory. Both residences consisted of a rectangular structure whose windows and doors at the ground level had been sealed. Their entrances were located on the second level (first floor in European terminology), and buttresses were added to strengthen their walls. The keeps were the dominant structures on the sites. The stone donjon was modeled after the wooden keeps of the original motte and bailey. The stone keep of the 11th century became the main fortified position instead of holding the secondary role they once had when made of wood.

Apparently though Fulk Nerra was not the first to build a stone keep in northwestern Europe. Instead, his rival, the Count of Blois may well have that honor because he had on his lands a fortified stone residence that predated Fulk's. That keep was probably erected early in the century when Fulk I the Red carved out the county of Anjou. It was located at Doué-la-Fontaine, in territory disputed between the Count of Blois and the Count of Anjou. It was probably built by one of the two men in 900, after a major fire destroyed an older wooden structure. Like the keep at Langeais, its ground floor openings were sealed and the entrance was placed above the ground level. Again, it is difficult to tell when it was transformed into a fortified keep or when it was turned into a motte and bailey. It may well have been later in the century under Fulk Nerra.

During the same period in Central Europe, the Germans built towers known as bergfrieds whose origins can be traced to the Roman watchtowers. In the Slavic lands to the east, the gród continued to dominate. During this period, the administrative grody grew to fairly large proportions, encircling major towns like Krakow, Wroclaw (Breslau), and Gniezno in Poland. The smaller ones, built by individual families, were similar to the motte and bailey-type in Western Europe. Many grody had a fortified gate, as was common elsewhere in Europe with similar constructions such as the ancient English hill forts and

Roman walls. However, the Slavic gate towers were in the main line of defense, while the keep was the main structure of the early motte and bailey serving as the last line of defense. In some cases, the grody also had an interior building that served as a last line of defense. This tower or tower-like structure served a dual purpose as residence, belfry, or granary.

There are several reasons why stone fortifications and stone keeps were not used for most of the Dark Ages. In the first place, stone had to be quarried, which required more skilled labor than tree cutting. In addition, a sizable labor force was needed to move and place the stone, and mustering the needed manpower and specialists such as masons was generally too expensive for most feudal nobles, at least the lesser nobility. It is also possible that the skills and techniques developed by the Romans for making and mixing mortar had either been forgotten or were little known in most parts of Europe during the Dark Ages for similar reasons. Finally, and most importantly, in many places wood was more plentiful and readily available than quarry stones. It was also less expensive to work with.

HOUDAN, FRANCE. *A mid-12th-century circular stone keep with projecting semicircular corner turrets.*

In *Castles of Europe* (London, 1980) William Anderson observes that Fulk Nerra probably chose to use stone for his keeps not only for defensive reasons, but also to bolster his status among his peers. His ability to finance such structures must have suitably impressed his peers, who soon began to imitate him. Fulk's early campaigns proved that a fortified position was best for maintaining control of a region, and was also difficult to capture or recapture. Since stone does not burn and it does not decay as easily as wood, Fulk's strongholds became that much more formidable. Thus the stone keep not only served to enhance Fulk's social status but also his military might.

Gradually, the donjon or keep became the focal point of the castle and more complex and elaborate defensive features were built around them. Sizes and shapes changed over time and the curtain walls surrounding the bailey became more complex. The motte and bailey remained the dominant fortification in northwestern France well into the 11th century. As the counts and dukes of the realm challenged each other, and their king took first one side then another side, stone castles proliferated. The Duke of Normandy, William I "The Conqueror," recorded numerous actions against this type of fortification as he defended his lands and later expanded his control southward toward the counties of Maine and Anjou. When William invaded England in 1066, he carried with him a portable wooden castle that would be assembled in England, which seems to indicate that wooden donjons were still in vogue even at this late date.

After the Norman Conquest, the motte and bailey castle spread throughout England, where less than a dozen fortified positions had survived from the time of Edward the Confessor. William and his successors used castles to solidify their hold on their English territories, just as they had done in their French lands. In the space of one century there were hundreds of castles built in England. Thanks to the castles the Normans were able to replace in a relatively short period of time most of the Anglo-Saxon nobility in England.

In the early part of the 12th century, so many castles went up in England that Henry I ordered those castles not built under license destroyed to maintain his control over the kingdom. The Anglo-Normans, who had moved into southern Scotland, erected motte and bailey castles when they became embroiled in a conflict with the Scots. Henry II used the same tactics when he invaded Ireland in 1168. Gradually, the motte and bailey fortifications built of timber gave way to stone

DOVER CASTLE, ENGLAND. *The Great Keep.*

structures throughout the British Isles, as they did in France. In a number of cases the wooden palisade was replaced with a wall. However, the wooden tower on the motte was replaced by a shell keep, which apparently represented an intermediate stage be-tween the wooden tower and the stone keep in some regions. The shell keep was essentially a stone enclosure atop the motte.

Sometime during the 12th century, the keep became the dominent element in fortifications in northwest Europe. Two of the largest in England were built at critical sites: the White Tower in London and the keep at Dover. Although it is possible that they both may have been originally built as part of motte and bailey complexes, it is evident that they were placed in the midst of pre-existing fortifications dating back to the Roman era. These large rectangular keeps were known in England as Great Towers. Because of their great weight, the manmade motte could not support them, and was eliminated. As the massive keeps increased in popularity throughout France and England, the motte and bailey castles were abandoned or remodeled and disappeared from the European landscape. However, the stone keeps, like their wooden predecessors of the motte and bailey type, continued to serve as the bastion of last defense.

In some cases, though, they were no longer placed in the center of the defended area or at an unassailable angle. Instead, they were linked to the curtain wall and served in the first line of defense. Because of their larger size, these keeps were transformed into residences for the more powerful noblemen who could afford to build them. They began to appear in large numbers in Western Europe after the Norman Conquest, especially in the 12th century. They were surrounded by the walls of the bailey, which, in many cases, were made of timber. A stone gate and sometimes stone towers were added to the timber walls.

Eventually, the timber palisades were replaced with stone walls. Thus in the 12th and 13th centuries, the castle consisted of walls, towers, and a keep all of stone. Early in the 13th century, the large stone keeps, many still in the motte and bailey tradition, were the dominant type of castle in Britain.

During the 13th century, the keep was gradually abandoned in favor of a larger and more powerful gatehouse. Some of the best examples of this type of castle are Harlech and Beaumaris built by Edward I during his campaigns to subjugate Wales. Edward's castles were the most modern and strongest built in Britain. The designer, Master James, incorporated in his designs many new features he had seen in other

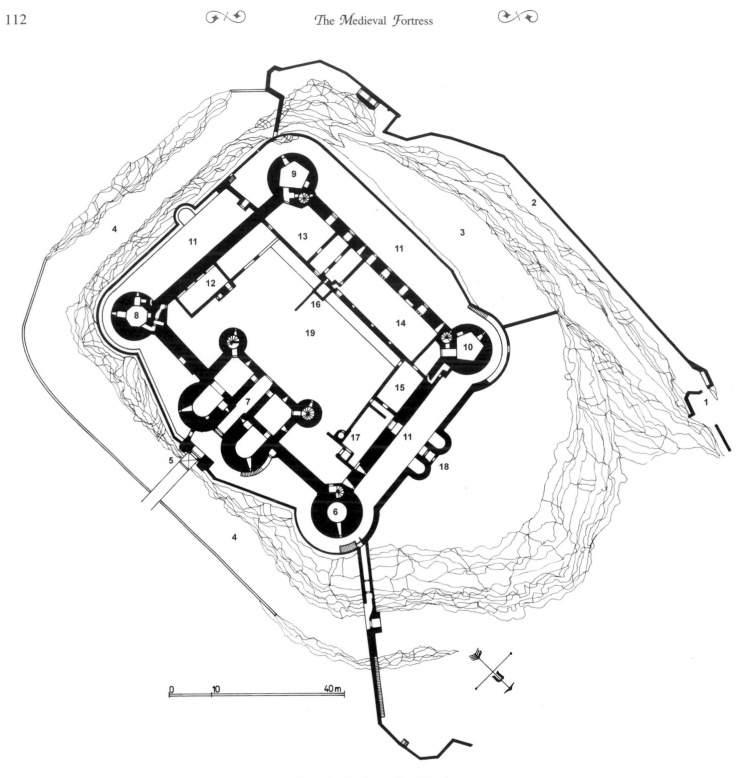

Harlech Castle, Wales

1. Water Gate
2. Outer Wall
3. Steep slope and Outer Bailey
4. Moat
5. Outer Gate
6, 8, 9, 10. Corner towers
7. Gatehouse
11. Middle Bailey

12. Granary
13. Kitchen
14. Great Hall
15. Chapel
16. Stairs
17. Well
18. Postern
19. Inner Bailey

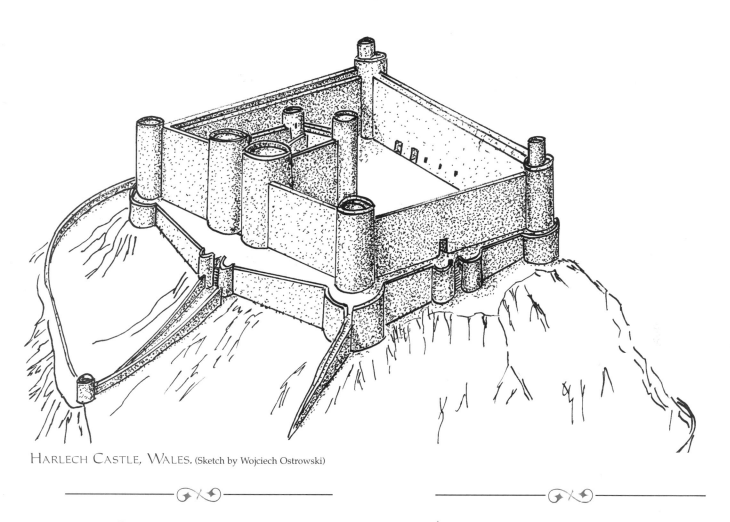

HARLECH CASTLE, WALES. (Sketch by Wojciech Ostrowski)

regions as well as some of his own, such as concentric walls with gatehouses not directly aligned with each other. Drawbridges with counterweights, plinths, and even some firing embrasures with two arrow loops came into use. Although his attention was focused on his masterpieces in Wales, King Edward did not neglect to improve his other positions such as the Tower of London.

Late in the 13th century, Edward I mastered the art of forcing his vassals to contribute heavily towards his castle building program and recruiting a massive labor force to build them. Thus he was able to assemble over 2,600 men to build Beaumaris in Wales, finishing most of it in only three years. However, Master James's entire plan for Beaumaris was never entirely completed. Many of the other great castles of Wales were built with the same remarkable speed.

New castles continued to sprout in France because of the rivalry between the Plantagenets and the Capetians and the unusual relationship between them. The Plantagenets (Angevins), who sat on the English throne also held several French territories, including Normandy, Maine, and Anjou, as vassals to the French crown. The situation became even more complicated when Henry II married Eleanor of Aquitaine in 1152. Eleanor had inherited the independent duchy of Aquitaine from her father upon his death and soon after in 1149 she had married the French king Louis VII. When the church dissolved the marriage three years later, she married the English king while Louis attempted to claim Aquitaine for himself. Thus it is that Louis VII and his son Philip Augustus launched a drawn-out campaign to retake these French territories from their English vassal. Like their predecessors, both sides' strategies consisted of taking and controlling key castles and fortified cities.

Thus in Western Europe, from Portugal to England, new castles and city fortifications went up or were rebuilt while others were captured and razed to the ground. In Iberia the expanding Christian kingdoms continued to construct castles of masonry to maintain and expand their holdings against the Moors, but unlike most of those in France and England the majority of these castles were for the king's garrisons and not private residences of the landed nobility.

Fortified Cities in the Middle Ages

The fortified city became prominent throughout Europe from the 11th century onward. In the Levant and on the Balkan and Italian peninsulas fortified cities, many fortified since Roman times or earlier, were also the chief cultural centers. Jerusalem, for instance, was fortified long before the Bronze Age and continued to remain so through this period. Its western gate had been defended for many centuries with a citadel and its oldest tower, the Tower of David, dates back to before Christ.

The citadel, which has the appearance of a castle, was a common feature in many large walled cities during the first and second millennia. The key social, economic, and political centers of the region were housed within these walls. The walls of Jerusalem were defended and strengthened by towers that had been modified and remodeled through the centuries. There are, obviously, many similarities between Rome and Jerusalem. Another such major fortified city was Constantinople, which had no citadel. Other

similar but smaller fortified cities dot the Mediterranean landscape.

In Western and Central Europe, the ancient Roman walls continued to defend many of the key fortified cities of the High Middle Ages. One such city that still remains largely intact today is Carcassonne in southwest France, which not only evolved into a heavily defended city with a citadel, but also included concentric walls. It boasts 29 towers on the inner wall, and 17 towers on the outer, which is about three kilometers in length. Its 12th century castle represents the stage of development when the keep disappeared from the castle complex. Carcassonne became one of the most formidable defended cities of the era.

In the Iberian Peninsula, the walled city of Avila remains today without a citadel but has a partially fortified cathedral which was built into the city walls. The impressive wall that encircles this city, begun at the end of the 11th century and completed early in the 12th, includes 88 towers and 9 fortified gates.

The Italian Peninsula boasts numerous examples of

Avila, Spain.

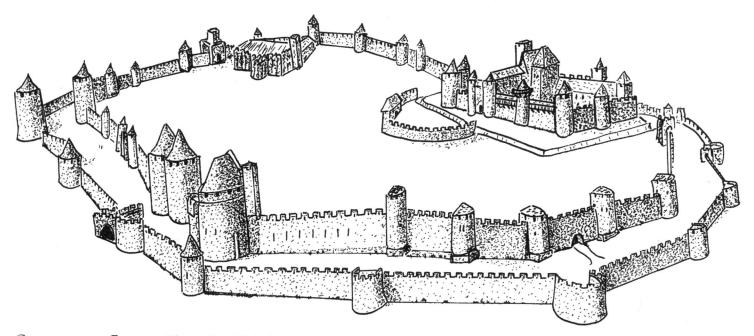

CARCASSONNE, FRANCE. *The castle with its barbican is in the upper right, the church is near the top and the Narbonne Gate on the left.* (Sketch by Wojciech Ostrowski)

fortified cities, some of which date back to the High Middle Ages. Montagnana, for instance, developed late in the 14th century instead of early in the Middle Ages. Its tall walls were made of brick, its two heavily fortified gates served as the strongholds of the town's two dominating families. Such heavily fortified gates had begun to replace the keep as the main residence of the castle since before the 14th century. The gates at Montagnana seem to have been an adaptation of this practice on the city level. The walls covered about 2 kilometers, had towers at intervals of about 75 meters, and were fronted by a wide moat. Many of the characteristics of Montagnana's defenses were found in fortifications of the next generation. Indeed, it was in the Italian Peninsula that the fortified towns and cities flourished, evolving into a new generation of fortifications. The Venetians created a trading empire and to defend it they erected a number of fortified harbors and castles along the Dalmatian coast of the Adriatic. The Genoese also fortified their overseas possessions. The works of both of these Italian republics can be found as far east as the coast of the Black Sea.

In other regions of Europe, the fortified city also took on a more important role. At the end of the Dark Ages both Paris and London, like many other cities and towns in northwest and western Europe, had received new walls. Their curtain walls were usually more expansive than those of the older cities, and, in some cases, included the remains of Roman walls. In 1190, King Philip Augustus ordered the construction of walls with 20 circular towers approximately 30 meters high on the right bank of the Seine in order to defend Paris. Twenty years later, he decided to raise a similar wall on the left bank to protect the sprawling urban population of the city. In the 14th century, the walls had to be expanded again. In the 12th and 13th centuries, other French cities that expanded beyond their older walls followed the example of Paris, building new walls to enclose their larger perimeter. In the Holy Roman Empire fortified towns continued to serve as protection from invaders from the east.

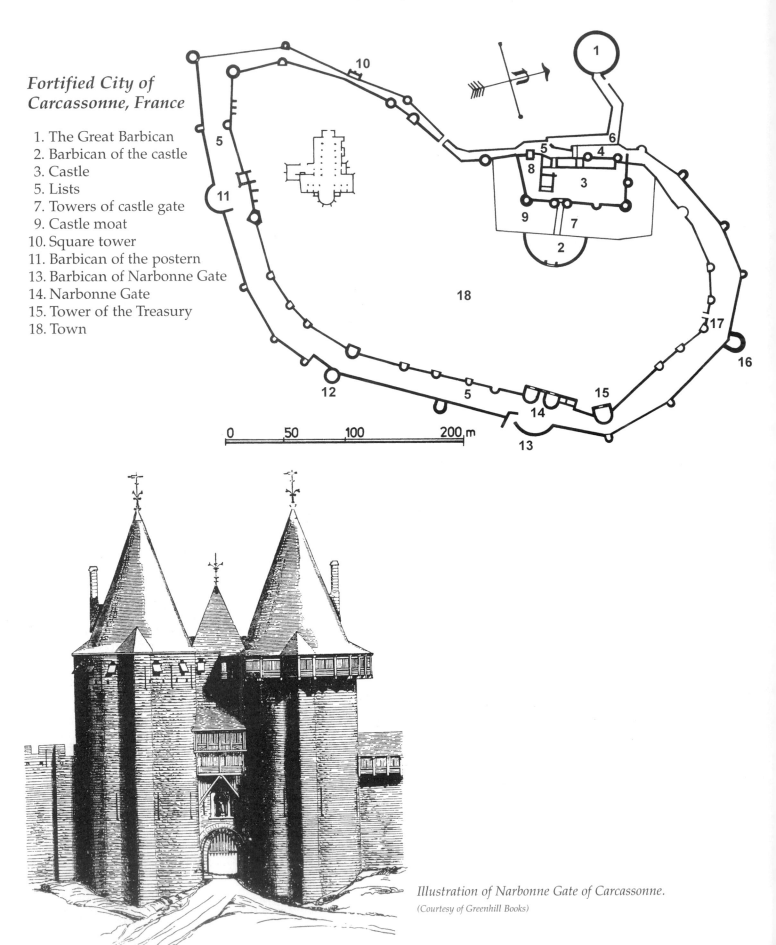

Fortified City of Carcassonne, France

1. The Great Barbican
2. Barbican of the castle
3. Castle
5. Lists
7. Towers of castle gate
9. Castle moat
10. Square tower
11. Barbican of the postern
13. Barbican of Narbonne Gate
14. Narbonne Gate
15. Tower of the Treasury
18. Town

0   50   100   200 m

Illustration of Narbonne Gate of Carcassonne.

(*Courtesy of Greenhill Books*)

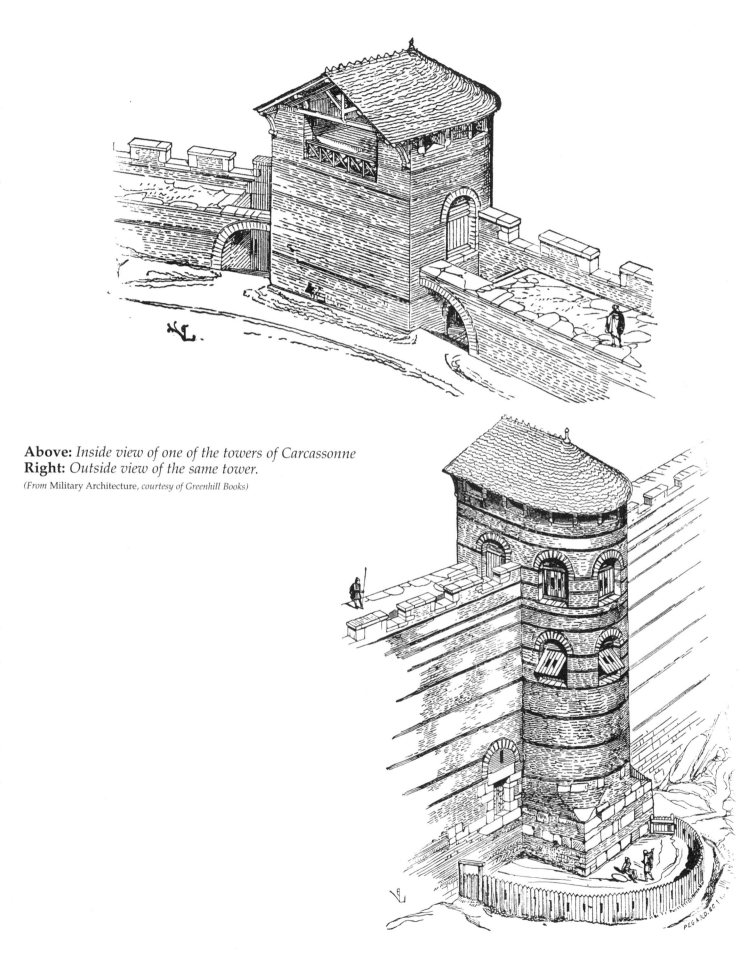

Above: *Inside view of one of the towers of Carcassonne*
Right: *Outside view of the same tower.*

(From Military Architecture, *courtesy of Greenhill Books)*

Fortified City of Jerusalem

1. Aqueduct
2. Essenes' Gate (Tekoa Tor)
3. Gate of the Spring
4. Siloe Tower
5. Golden Gate
6. Herodotus' Temple (Temple Mount)
7. Pagans' courtyard
8. Sheep's Gate
9. Antonine Fortress
10. Beautiful Gate
11. Courtyard of the women
12. Courtyard of the priests palace
13. Royal Portico
14. Double Gate
15. Triple Gate
16. Salomon's Portico
18. Calvary
19. Holy Sepulcher
20. City Gate
21. Tower of David
22. Citadel/Herodotus'
23. Royal gardens
24. Hasmonean Palace
27. Synagogue
28. Siloe Pond
29. Mount Olive

Tower of David, Jerusalem

The Grody of Eastern Europe

In the Slavic lands of the East some of the larger grody were already centuries old. Instead of stone, the Slavs continued to use mainly wood and earth. Towers, often placed on a stone foundation, were added to defend the gates during the 11th century. In some cases, especially after the early 12th century in Poland, these towers were entirely built of stone. Where possible, a wet moat protected the gates. One of the best examples of these gates was the Golden Gate of Kiev, which was built in the latter half of the 11th century.

Some of the more heavily populated towns developed a more complex set of fortifications when their population expanded beyond the original periphery of the gród. Additional walls were built to protect the newer suburbs. Many of these complex city walls appeared in Lower Silesia at the end of the 10th century.

In the kingdom of Poland, from the time of Boleslav I until the end of the 11th century, the earthen and wooden grody were the only fortifications in use. Early in the next century, under the reign of Boleslav II, many of these grody were further reinforced with wooden towers and gates with stone foundations. It was not until the 13th century that brick making was underway in Poland. In 1228, the gród of Ostrowek in Silesia was converted to masonry, like many other places. Square towers and later round ones sprouted throughout Poland by the end of the 13th century, especially in important towns like Kalisz, Lublin, and Kazimierz Dolny in Malapolska (Little Poland). In Eastern Poland it was the Belorussian dukes that were responsible for these changes. In Western Pomerania, unlike the rest of Poland, the traditional gród survived longer. The first stone or brick structures to appear in this region were large square or rectangular fortified houses more akin to the west European keep than the German bergfried, which, at this time, was also being replaced by more substantial structures in the German lands of the Holy Roman Empire. It was not until late in the 14th century that walls and additional towers were added to these keeps, which means that the old gród remained in use even longer than in other parts of Poland where the earthen and wooden walls had been replaced by masonry walls of brick.

A reconstruction of the Golden Gate of Kiev. (Photo courtesy of John Sloan.)

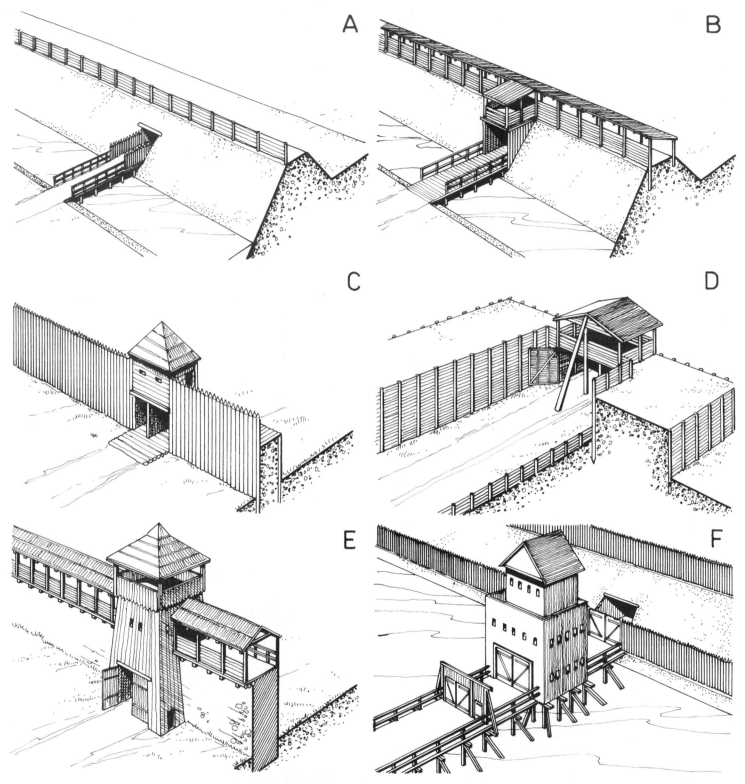

Wooden Gates used in Grody

A. Tunnel gate popular in Eastern Europe in pre-
Christian era
B. Gate projecting forward that includes an entrance
corridor

C. Gate in the face of the wall with a double entrance.
D. Wide gate supported by logs in the water
E. Gate house
F. Gate forward of the entrance on a bridge.

In northern Poland change may have also been heavily influenced by the arrival of the Teutonic Knights, who, in 1255, replaced the gród at Torun with the first masonry castle in the region and significantly enlarged it by the end of the century. They began the construction of the first monastic type castles in the East, although before this examples of fortified Polish monasteries can be found, but they were not created or designed for a fighting order of monks.

The Polish cultural center at Krakow, which had been surrounded by earthen and wooden fortifications since the 8th century, received additional work when it became the see of a bishopric in 1000. In the 11th century, the kings of the Piast Dynasty transferred their capital to Krakow whose defenses remained of wood for more than a century. The timber walls of the Wawel, the royal castle, were replaced with stone walls early in the 13th century. It was not until the next century, in 1355, that Casimir the Great began building stone defenses for the city. It is commonly said in Poland that King Casimir found a Poland built of wood and left a Poland built of brick.

Poland appears to have been typical of most Slavic lands where the older earth and wood grid walls survived until the 14th century. The preferred shapes for these large grody were square, oval, or round. As increasing deforestation gradually limited timber resources between the 12th and 13th centuries, the Slavs turned to brick and stone. However, since these materials were more expensive and harder to work with, they were at first reserved for towers and gates as in Western Europe.

The settlement of Moscow was probably founded early in the 12th century and in 1159 its ruling Russian prince built a fortification of the gród type to control the main trade route. It is reported to have had a moat, an earthen rampart, and a wooden palisade. Ivan I, still a vassal to the Mongol invaders, established the seat of his principality in the lands of the Rus. His capital would eventually become the center of the future Russian empire. In the last years of his reign from 1339 to 1340 he had new timber walls and towers made of oak added to the cities fortifications. In 1367, the Grand Duke of Moscow, Dimitri Donskoy, replaced Ivan's earth and wood fortifications with new white stone walls and a tower. He is credited with the creation of this Kremlin (citadel), but apparently the term was used as early as 1331 under Ivan's reign. The fortification was triangular with water barriers in the form of moats up to 32 meters wide or a river on each side. Late in the 15th century, from 1485 to 1495 the Kremlin was completely rebuilt. Its final tower was not completed until the end of the 17th century. The walls spanned over 2.2 kilometers and the tallest of its 18 towers was 80 meters high and the smallest, about 13 meters. The walls range from 3.5 to 6.5 meters in thickness making this citadel one of the most impressive sites of Eastern Europe.

This 1606 plan of Moscow shows the Kremlin (1), Kitai Gorad (2), the White City (3), the Earthen Moat (4), and St. Basil's (5).

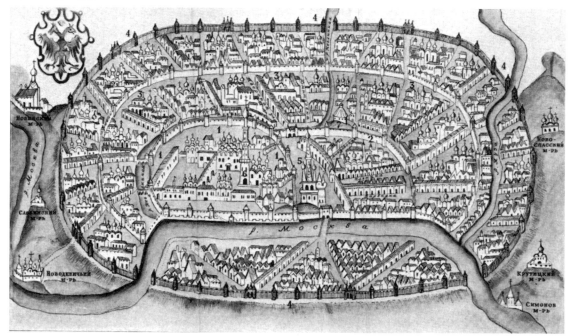

Büdingen Castle, Germany

Büdingen Castle was built in the 12th century
in Hesse. The unusual enceinte has 13 sides.
Buildings with vaulted roofs were added in
the 15th century for additional protection from
missile fire.

1. Bergfried
2. Great hall
3. Courtyard
4. Outline of buildings of the 15th century

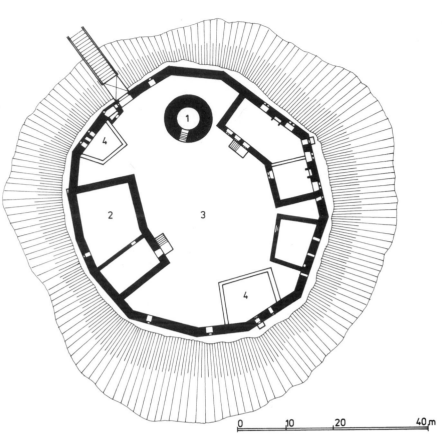

Burgschwalbach Castle, Germany

This castle was built in Hesse about 1370 and
was owned by the Counts of Katzenelnbogen.
Its bergfried towers high above the entire
position.

1. Dry moat which was also the access road
2. Lower ward with barnyard animals
3. Curtain walls
4. Chapel
5. Main gate
6. Great Hall
8. Bergfried

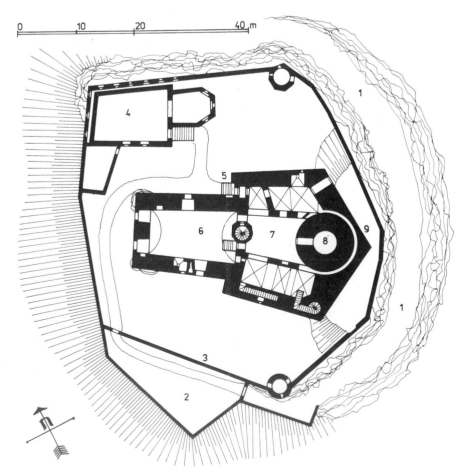

Fortifications of Central and Southern Europe

The development of fortifications in Central and Southern Europe paralleled their evolution in Western Europe. The German people occupied both plains and mountains within the Holy Roman Empire. Fortified monasteries and towns played a key role in the 10th century in warding off attacks from the Vikings and Magyars who threatened German lands. According to the Saxon historian Widukind, Henry I "The Fowler" of Germany created an effective field army and network of forts in the late 920s. Henry I's reforms and his creation of a core of armored cavalry to fight Magyars and Slavs improved the poor military reputation of his subjects, the Saxons and the Thuringians, as his army became the equal of the Frankish forces in the duchies of Lotharingia and Franconia. His son, Otto I "The Great," later defeated the Magyars at Lechfield in 955 with his famed cavalry.

The fortified towns usually grew out of a dozen or more settlements which formed a ward and were assigned to a fortress (burg). They included Merseburg, Quedlinburg, Goslar, Nordhausen, Grona, and Pöhlde. Henry I also ordered the abbeys to be walled in and saw to the repair and restoration of older walled cities. Frontier forts probably more in the tradition of a Roman fort, garrisoned by the king's bishops and counts were occupied in monthly shifts. Henry became known as "The Builder" for this work. In 933 at Merseburg, Henry's cavalry defeated an invading Magyar force that found his system of fortified towns and abbeys too heavily defended. Henry also used his system of fortifications against the Slavic peasantry in the east.

Most of the early German castles developed at about the time that the motte and bailey reached the peak of its development in the west. The main type of fortification in the German territories was the bergfried, which was similar to the French donjon or keep and was probably inspired by the older Roman watchtowers found on the German frontier. The bergfried generally served as a watchtower and strongpoint and, unlike the early French keeps, it constituted the main line of defense. Outer defenses similar to the palisade of the motte and bailey developed around it later, although the bergfried was not exploited to the greatest effect at this point. Many German castles were situated on top of hills or mountains and the area around them was fortified. Often, the Germans selected peninsula-like mountain spurs with a river looping around all but one of their sides in order to secure access to their castles.

It was not until the latter half of the 11th century, under Holy Roman Emperor Henry IV, that castle building began in earnest, becoming as important as some of the urban fortifications begun in the previous century. Before Henry IV's reign, castles had been few and far between in the Holy Roman Empire and most had been built without the monarch's permission. As Henry IV took a firm hold over his empire, he ordered many of his wooden castles to be rebuilt in stone.

During Henry's conflict with Pope Gregory VII over the investiture issue, many of his vassals tried to impede his progress to Italy from their castles. In order to reach Italy to seek absolution and have his powers restored, Henry was forced to take a long detour to the west. When he returned to power, he not only took his revenge on his vassals for this humiliation, but also on Pope Gregory VII, who was forced to take refuge in Castel Sant'Angelo in 1084. This old tomb turned into a castle was only one of many fortifications that had sprouted during the time of the Late Roman Empire. Henry IV appointed a new pope and Gregory barely escaped with the help of the Normans, who granted him refuge in the south.

After Henry IV, castle building continued to flourish in the German territories. According to William Anderson in *Castles of Europe* (London, 1980), the powerful landed German families even derived their family names from their castles' names.

After Holy Roman Emperor Otto I defeated the Magyars at Lechfield in 955, their raids into northern Italy and Germany came to an end. The Magyars finally settled on the Hungarian Plain of the Danube Basin. Not long after, King Stephen I converted his Hungarian kingdom into a Christian state, modeling many of his new state's institutions and buildings on those of his neighbors. Stephen divided his kingdom into counties with each dominated by a strong castle. He built the castles at his own expense and garrisoned them with *varkatonak* (castle soldiers) and appointed *ispans* (noblemen equivalent to counts) to run the castle-counties. Some counties were ecclesiastical, but there was an unusual overlapping arrangement with the castle-counties. The Magyar system suffered from the same type of decay as the feudal system in the West which allowed nobles to build their own castles and challenge the king's ispan and their own sovereign. Later, many towns grew up

CASTEL SANT' ANGELO, ITALY
The sketch shows the tomb of Hadrian (center) turned into a medieval fortification and post medieval additions (arrow shaped bastions). The bridge over the Tiber leading into Rome is on the left. Pope Gregory VII took refuge there from Holy Roman Emperor Henry IV in 1084. (Sketch by Wojciech Ostrowski)

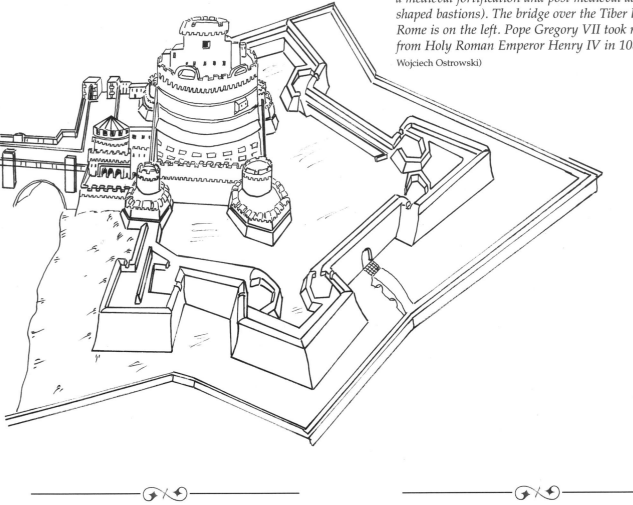

around these castles. Eventually, the earthen grody with wooden walls gave way to stone castles, which, in many cases were built on top of them.

The Mongol invasions in 1241 brought about a sudden change in Hungary. The new invaders devastated much of the kingdom and destroyed the castle at Buda. Since only the stone castles were left standing, King Bela IV commanded all castles to be built of stone henceforth. The castle of Buda was rebuilt on the hills over the eastern bank of the Danube and served as a royal residence. Other stone castles were built along the Danube, creating, in the words of King Stephen, "a river of resistance." A total of 166 royal and 132 privately owned castles sprouted during the second half of the 13th century, among them Sirok, Sümeg, Csesznek, and the castle of Boldogko.

Italy, like the rest of Medieval Europe, had its own share of castles and fortified cities. The small and growing merchant cities such as Pisa, Genoa, or Venice, found it necessary to defend themselves heavily and resorted to fortifications to protect their budding empires of the early High Middle Ages. Venice had relied mostly on its island position and its surrounding lagoon for its safety since the Dark Ages. Everywhere castles and fortified cities grew together.

The southern part of the Italian peninsula had many old fortifications that were used by a number of dukes south of Rome and by the Byzantine administrators in Apulia. Sicily had been taken by the Arabs in the 9th century. The Norsemen, who arrived late in the 10th century, established themselves in Calabria during the 11th century and proceeded to expel the Byzantine forces and the emirs of Sicily, establishing their own hold on the southern part of the Italian peninsula in the process. They brought with them the feudal system and built many castles, and, eventually, some rather impressive stone keeps.

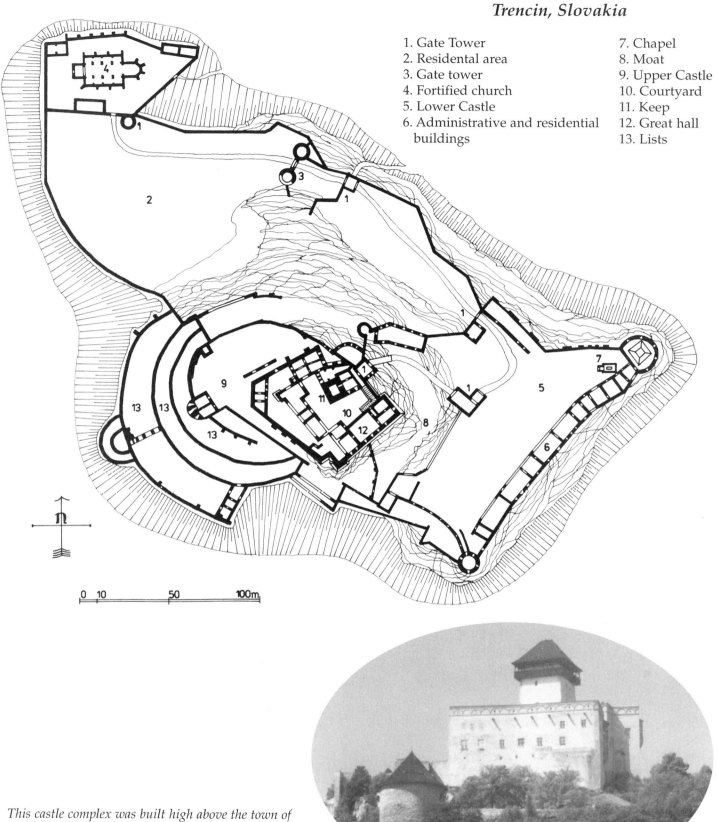

Trencin, Slovakia

1. Gate Tower
2. Residental area
3. Gate tower
4. Fortified church
5. Lower Castle
6. Administrative and residential buildings
7. Chapel
8. Moat
9. Upper Castle
10. Courtyard
11. Keep
12. Great hall
13. Lists

This castle complex was built high above the town of Trencin in the mid-13th century and was greatly reinforced and enlarged in the 15th century. Additional changes in the early 16th century included positions for artillery, making the transition from medieval castle to post-medieval fortress.

From Grody to Zamki

In Poland and Russia timber fortifications still dominated in the early part of the High Middle Ages, mainly because wood was the most readily available resource. The gród remained the most common defensive fortification between the 11th and 13th century. It was the smaller gród that eventually gave rise to the Slavic castle. Although the construction and design of the town gród and the one-family gród were similar, the latter usually included a wooden structure similar to the wooden tower of the motte and bailey castle. It is not easy to determine what these smaller grody looked like. A recent reconstruction at Grodzisko, Poland, includes a manmade hill with a wooden stockade on top enclosing a couple of wooden buildings. Access to the complex was through a gate. This arrangement is very similar to the western motte and bailey, but lacks the bailey. It is possible that more archaeological research will uncover the existence of a bailey-like area.

In *Polska technika wojskowa do 1500 roku* (Warsaw, 1994), Andrzej Nadolski points out that during this period the Slavs also experimented with stone masonry. In the Polish territories, uncut stone was first used in the foundations of the grody to stabilize the walls to prevent their settling into the marshy ground. During this period uncut stone was also added to the outer face of the walls to keep the enemy from pulling them apart and setting them afire. Other grody sported stone parapets. During the early part of the High Middle Ages, the grody were also surrounded with wider and deeper moats whose walls were lined with fascines to prevent their collapse. As in the past, the moat formed the main obstacle in front of the ramparts. The entrance of the larger grody included a single gate heavily defended by a tower. Often this gate was approached over a wooden bridge that could be as much as 300 meters long. Unfortunately, the archaeological research in the area has been limited so that the history of the gród cannot be established unequivocally.

By the 13th and 14th centuries stone fortifications replaced the gród in many areas. The Polish kings and higher nobility also built castles in the Western European style called zamki and, occasionally, single large keeps known as *wierze rycerskie* or "knights' towers." In the 14th century Casimir the Great converted most of the Polish grody and wooden castles into stone.

North of the Holy Roman Empire, the Danish kingdom developed its own form of fortifications that had a stronger affinity to the Slavic grody than to the German castles. Settlements built in the style of the gród or grad with earthen works were found in other parts of Scandinavia as well. The most dramatic change in Danish fortifications occurred when brick towers replaced the old wooden ones. They served in coastal defense, primarily against the pirate raids of the Wends. These towers appeared in the 12th century in such places as Copenhagen, Sprogo, Kalundborg, Thonburg, and Vordingborg during the reign of Valdemar I, "the Great." Brick did not spread east into the Slavic lands until the next century. In areas where stone was not an abundant resource, like in the Polish plains, brick became the most efficient replacement for wood.

Gate tower, Ziembice, Poland.

Osnus Lubus (Osno), Poland
14th century

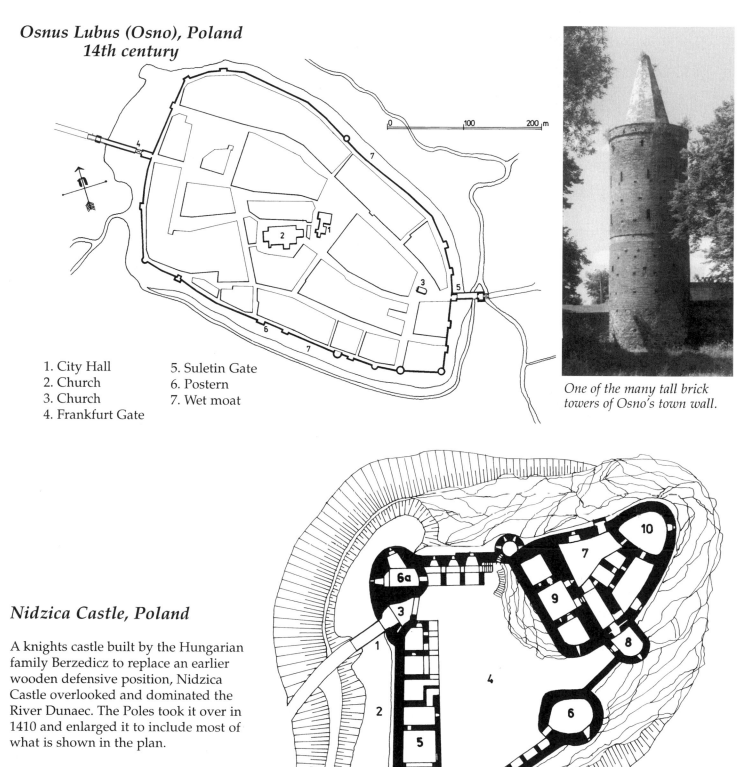

1. City Hall
2. Church
3. Church
4. Frankfurt Gate
5. Suletin Gate
6. Postern
7. Wet moat

One of the many tall brick towers of Osno's town wall.

Nidzica Castle, Poland

A knights castle built by the Hungarian family Berzedicz to replace an earlier wooden defensive position, Nidzica Castle overlooked and dominated the River Dunaec. The Poles took it over in 1410 and enlarged it to include most of what is shown in the plan.

1. Stone bridge
2. Dry moat
3. Main gate
4. Lower Castle
5. Buildings
6. Bastions
7. Courtyard of High Castle
8. Gate tower
10. Keep

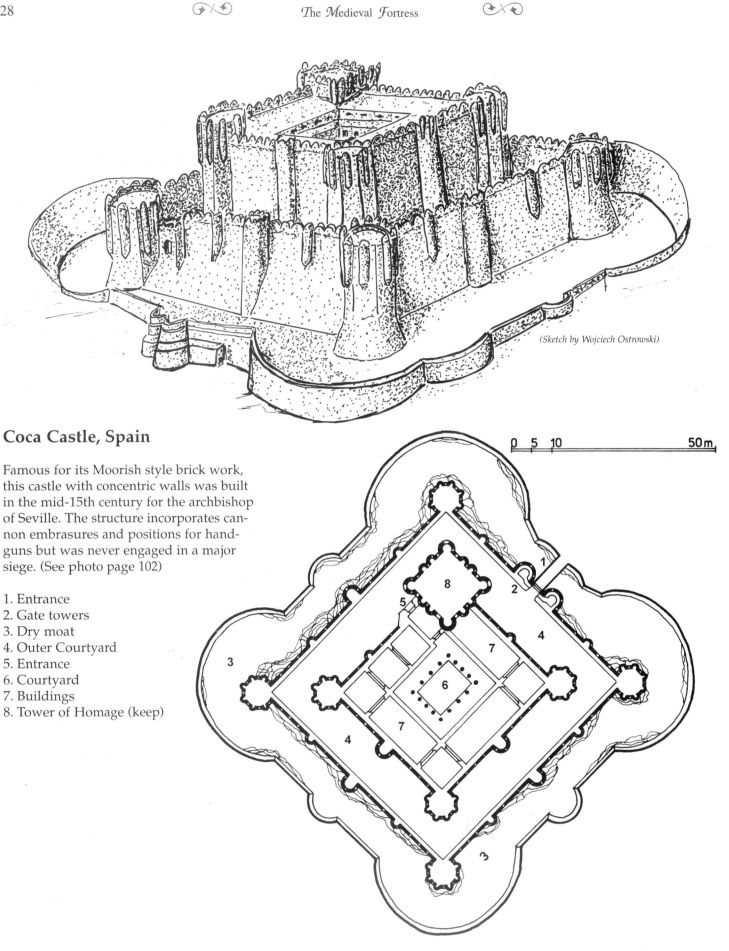

(Sketch by Wojciech Ostrowski)

Coca Castle, Spain

Famous for its Moorish style brick work, this castle with concentric walls was built in the mid-15th century for the archbishop of Seville. The structure incorporates cannon embrasures and positions for handguns but was never engaged in a major siege. (See photo page 102)

1. Entrance
2. Gate towers
3. Dry moat
4. Outer Courtyard
5. Entrance
6. Courtyard
7. Buildings
8. Tower of Homage (keep)

0 5 10   50m

ALMOUROL CASTLE, PORTUGAL.
This island castle was built on the site of a
Roman fort in 1171 by the Templars to control a
ferry crossing on the Tagus River near Tancos.

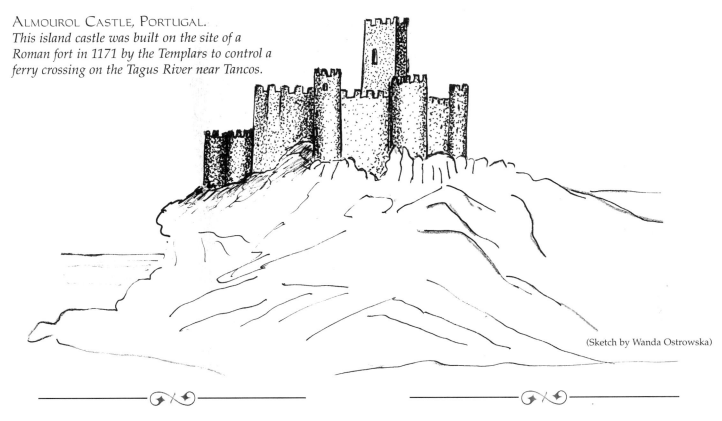

(Sketch by Wanda Ostrowska)

Fortifications of Iberia

On the Iberian Peninsula technological development in the field of fortifications was more rapid than elsewhere in Europe, probably due to the continuing confrontation between the Islamic and Christian forces. Although the Christian forces of Iberia pushed towards the Duero River in the 10th century, they became mired in internecine conflict and made little progress in the Reconquista for a time. However, as they advanced little by little, they took over Islamic fortifications, modifying and copying them as they went.

The Arabs, on the other hand, occupied, used, and even improved upon the older fortifications they had found in Iberia. At the same time their own engineering techniques reached new heights thanks to the general intellectual flowering that characterized the Islamic world of this period.

Gormaz Castle typifies the history of the Iberian castles. Between 956 and 966, Caliph El Hakim III allowed his general, Galib, to convert an old hilltop fort into a mighty castle. Since the older position had been repeatedly contested between Christian and Islamic forces, Galib's project was to consolidate the Moors hold on it. Thus he built a large castle on the upper part of the hill with a curtain wall that included 26 towers and stretched around the crest for about 1.2 kilometers. The walls consisted of large blocks and rose to a height of 10 meters. This grand castle could maintain a sizable garrison. Nonetheless, the Christians succeeded in taking it in 981, and it had to be recaptured shortly afterward.

At a time when the first stone keeps began in France, Spain was already bristling with imposing castles like Gormaz. As the Reconquista relentlessly progressed, the Christian kings captured Moorish castle after Moorish castle or built their own, long before their northern neighbors. While William the Conqueror led his feudal army against motte and bailey castles of wood and stone in northwestern France, the Castilian forces of King Fernando I were busy storming and occupying the formidable fortress of Gormaz in 1060 and in 1087, Rodrigo Díaz de Vivar, nicknamed "El Cid," was placed in charge of the fortifications of Gormaz. While other Europeans developed their own techniques in castle building, the people of Iberia adopted Islamic fortification building methods, although it may be argued that the Arabs merely copied Roman-Byzantine fortifications. Soon, however, the fortifications of the North Europeans would also come under the influence of the East as they took up the cross and sword at the urging of Pope Urban II in 1095, who called for Holy War.

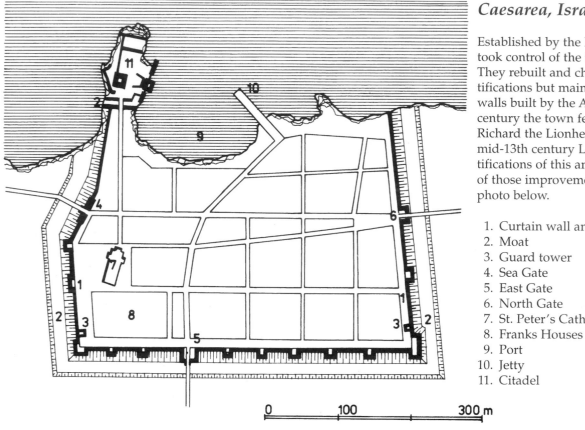

Caesarea, Israel, 12th Century

Established by the Romans, the Crusaders took control of the town of Caesarea in 1101. They rebuilt and changed the town and fortifications but maintained and improved the walls built by the Arabs. Late in the 12th century the town fell to Saladin and later Richard the Lionhearted occupied it. In the mid-13th century Louis IX improved the fortifications of this and other towns and some of those improvements are reflected in the photo below.

1. Curtain wall and towers
2. Moat
3. Guard tower
4. Sea Gate
5. East Gate
6. North Gate
7. St. Peter's Cathedral
8. Franks Houses
9. Port
10. Jetty
11. Citadel

CAESAREA, ISRAEL. *View of curtain walls and dry moat from the gate at Caesarea.*

Fortifications of the Crusades

Beginning with the First Crusade in the 11th century, generations of French, English, and other European knights and pilgrims passed through Byzantium on their way to the Holy Land and did not fail to notice the impressive fortifications along the way, especially Constantinople. As they encountered the Islamic fortified cities they admired the construction techniques both old and new. The fortifications the Crusaders encountered required more extensive sieges than they had experienced in their own lands. Few of them had experience dealing with stone fortifications since the majority of castles involved in sieges in Western Europe in the 11th century were still made of wood and earth. Only the Italians and Iberians had dealt with stone fortifications similar to those in the Levant but they formed an insignificant portion of the Crusader army. The First Crusade involved campaigns against fortified cities and ended with the fall of Jerusalem. Like in Europe the castles and fortified cities were the key to victory in the Middle East. To match their Islamic opponents, in the 12th and 13th centuries the Crusaders erected much larger fortifications in the Levant than they had ever built in their homelands. To counter the more sophisticated siege techniques of the Moslem forces, they employed more massive walls, concentric plans, and round towers. Soon the Middle Eastern landscape was dotted with impressive Crusader castles like Krak des Chevaliers and Belvoir, and fortified cities like Jerusalem, Cairo, Antioch, and Acre. The Crusaders also fortified a number of harbors like those on the islands of Rhodes and Malta. As they returned to their homelands the Crusaders took back with them both building and siege techniques. It is said that Richard the Lionhearted was influenced by the Holy Land fortifications he encountered during the Third Crusade when he built his Château Gaillard on the Seine.

The city gate of Jerusalem.

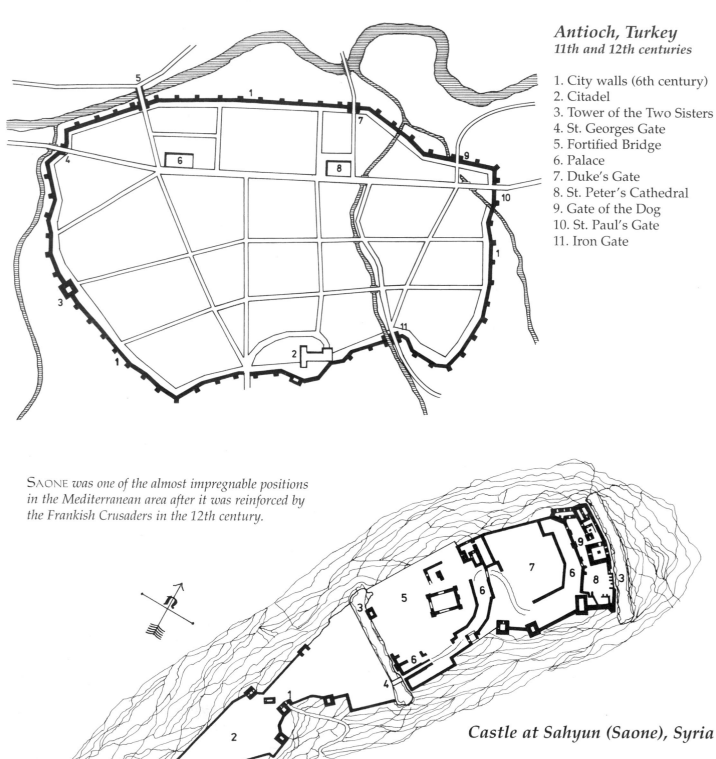

Antioch, Turkey
11th and 12th centuries

1. City walls (6th century)
2. Citadel
3. Tower of the Two Sisters
4. St. Georges Gate
5. Fortified Bridge
6. Palace
7. Duke's Gate
8. St. Peter's Cathedral
9. Gate of the Dog
10. St. Paul's Gate
11. Iron Gate

SAONE *was one of the almost impregnable positions in the Mediterranean area after it was reinforced by the Frankish Crusaders in the 12th century.*

0   50   100   150 m

Castle at Sahyun (Saone), Syria

1. Gate tower
2. Administrative and residential area
3. Moat
4. Drawbridge
5. Courtyard of Lower Castle
6. Gate
7. Courtyard of Middle Castle
8. Great Keep built by Crusaders
9. Byzantine structures and entrance

The Turning Point

The 12th century appears to be a turning point in European military history. Several European kingdoms, such as England and France, were led by strong kings who could mobilize a larger and more effective army than their predecessors. In *Western Warfare in the Age of the Crusades 1000-1300* (New York, 1999), John France points out that the castle had become one of the most dominant features in strategy and concludes, like Jim Bradbury, that more campaigns evolved around taking castles than actually engaging in major battles. Because of the vast number of castles that could hinder any invasion, entering enemy territory was akin to placing one's hand in a spider web. An aggressor had to disperse his strength to forage and to isolate the individual bastions and prevent a relief force from lifting the siege. In such circumstances, invading forces became vulnerable to raids as well as starvation. Victory for them meant bringing famine to the invaded lands by ravaging the region.

By the 12th century, the more powerful monarchs were able to muster armies equipped with sufficient siege weapons to quickly destroy all but the strongest fortifications. Many of these siege weapons were invented during the Roman period, but prior to the 12th century they had been employed on a limited scale because the cost of a siege in terms of time and money was too prohibitive. However, by the 12th century, better administrative organization and economic and agricultural improvements put enough revenue in monarchs' coffers to make it possible for them to engage in effective sieges.

There began in Europe a new armament race—ever stronger castles and fortified cities of brick or stone were built to withstand ever more effective siege weapons. Only in Eastern Europe did massive timber castles continue to be built until the end of the 13th century.

During this time many of the larger castles became more luxurious because their owners wanted to live more comfortably. Thus some of the new additions became a liability rather than a defensive asset. However, since many of these castles were so large and consisted of a series of concentric defenses, the new luxuries did not significantly weaken the overall strength of the position. But in many cases newer castles of the late Middle Ages were more palace than fortification.

During this period, the castle walls also began to encompass the adjacent town or village, especially in Flanders, where commerce was encouraged under the protection of castle walls. Even in the Levant the Crusaders found this type of arrangement very advantageous. One of the best examples of combination castle and village walls is to be found at Saone, originally a Byzantine fort located on a spur between two steep river gorges. Early in the 12th century the Frankish Crusaders built a massive keep overlooking the gatehouse. The spur was separated by a rock cut ditch about 30 meters deep. The older walls and their towers were later increased in height by the Franks. The gatehouse protected the bridge which gave the only access. Saone was considered one of the almost impregnable positions in the Mediterranean world.

Although some historians dispute the idea that the Crusaders brought back to their homelands new concepts about fortifications from the Middle East, it is difficult to prove that they did not since most of the important changes in Western Europe began to take place shortly after the First Crusade. Thus round or D-shaped towers became more widespread in Western Europe, and weapons and siege techniques, long discarded after the Roman era in Europe, were brought back into use during this period. Curtain walls became higher in response to more powerful weapons and other features were added to them.

In addition, the Holy Wars were crucial in the creation of orders of "fighting monks" in different parts of Europe and the Middle East: the Hospitalers (founded in 1070 in Jerusalem), the Templars (founded in 1119 in Jerusalem), and the Teutonic Order (founded in 1128 in Jerusalem). In Iberia orders such as the Knights of Calatrava (founded in 1158), the Order of Avis (founded in Portugal in 1162), the Order of Alcantara (founded in 1220) also came into existence. These orders' mission was to create and maintain large castles that served as bases of operations for the Crusaders in the Holy Land and Iberia. The Teutonic Order moved into Eastern Europe in the 13th century to fight the pagan Prussians. They were helped further to the northeast, in the Baltic regions, by the Sword Brothers (founded in 1200 in Riga). The German crusading orders in Eastern Europe used in their crusades against the Slavs, Prussians, and other groups similar policies as those used in the Middle East, creating in the process some of the first major stone fortifications from Poland to Russia. Torun was the first stone work of the Teutonic Knights in the East and was followed by many more.

Another significant development of the 13th and 14th centuries was the concentric castle. In this type

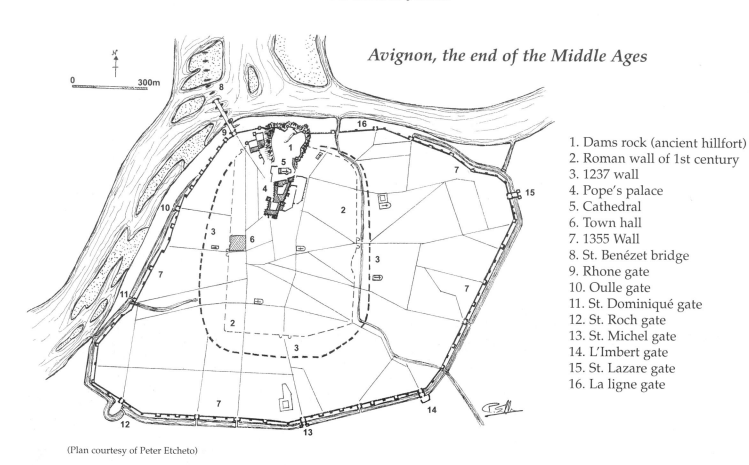

Avignon, the end of the Middle Ages

0   300m

1. Dams rock (ancient hillfort)
2. Roman wall of 1st century
3. 1237 wall
4. Pope's palace
5. Cathedral
6. Town hall
7. 1355 Wall
8. St. Benézet bridge
9. Rhone gate
10. Oulle gate
11. St. Dominiqué gate
12. St. Roch gate
13. St. Michel gate
14. L'Imbert gate
15. St. Lazare gate
16. La ligne gate

(Plan courtesy of Peter Etcheto)

PALACE OF THE POPES, AVIGNON, FRANCE.

CARCASSONNE, FRANCE. *An example of a city surrounded by concentric walls that developed in the 13th and 14th centuries.*

of fortification, the castle's curtain walls and towers were the highest, its gates were the most heavily defended positions, and the outer walls, lower and usually not as thick, were also defended by gates and towers. The towers were open in the rear where they faced the inner wall. If the outer wall fell, its positions were of no use to the attacker since the higher inner walls dominated the exposed platforms of the outer wall. The idea of concentric fortifications was not limited to castles, but also used in some cities. The oldest example of such an arrangement is Constantinople with its triple walls sealing the peninsula on which the city was located. In France, Carcassonne is a good representative of a city encircled by concentric walls.

Besides concentric fortifications, several other types flourished in medieval Europe. Fortified manor houses were not uncommon in many regions. Throughout Europe many monasteries also had some form of defense. In the Greek lands they were often built in places with difficult access, such as cliffs. In the West, abbeys acquired walls and towers like the fortified cities. Even the pope had a fortified palace at Avignon that was surrounded by a walled city.

Except for the motte and bailey, the large stone keeps, and the Slavic grody, there were no standard types of castle during the High Middle Ages. The round shape disappeared from the Western European landscape with the motte. A castle's defenses were determined by the surrounding terrain and the economical means of the castle builders. Other features, such as masonry curtain walls and towers, more elaborate gate defenses, and a central keep and bailey, each became unique and distinct. Although the Crusades may well have been a significant contributing factor to these changes, they were by no means the only one. European society and economy were undergoing profound changes at this time which must also account for the change in the character of the fortifications of the continent. Thanks to the growth of the economy and the state, an increasing number of monarchs and powerful magnates were able to muster larger armies and labor forces. In addi-

SAN GIMIGNANO, ITALY. *Four of the fourteen 13th-century towers that remain.*

tion, the rise of a highly skilled artisan class in the cities put at their disposal an army of specialists who were able to improve and refine their fortifications. As can be expected, the products of artisanry are not standardized, like the products of mass production. Thus, even though some techniques and features became quite widespread in Europe, they exhibit a great deal of variation, which can be attributed to regional tastes and conditions. The motte and bailey rose to prominence in France and England, the bergfried dominated central Europe, and families in the Italian peninsula in cities like Genoa and Florence built tall lean towers for themselves. A group of 14 out of 72 such 13th-century towers survives at San Gimignano in Italy, where new town walls were begun in 1251 to encircle the expanding city.

By the end of the 13th century, several general trends can be identified in Western Europe and the Middle East. In Europe, the tower on the motte was replaced by great keeps, which eventually disappeared, giving way to a strong gatehouse that served the same function. Masonry walls and towers grew ever higher as protection against siege weapons. The top of the towers and walls were reinforced with machicolations and their bases acquired plinth to prevent the enemy from operating there or undermining them. Moats became deeper and wider. Eventually in the 13th century, even cities were encircled with stone walls that sported many of these innovations. It must be noted that throughout Europe, design innovations usually took place in the castles and were later incorporated in urban defenses. Thus the castle remains the key in understanding the progression and importance of medieval fortifications.

In the Holy Roman Empire, the fortified cities founded during Henry I's reign seriously hindered the emperors' efforts to consolidate their power. The cities that resisted most strenuously were those on the Italian Peninsula. Meanwhile in England, the Plantagenets' armies, which were much smaller in size than those of the Holy Roman Emperors, were able to dispatch one fortified site after another both in England and in France throughout the 12th century. In the 13th century the Capetians bolstered their hold over France by reducing the number of strongpoints. Early in the 13th century Louis VII of France launched a crusade in the Langnedoc region where the heretical Cathars defended themselves in strongly fortified positions but in the end, his growing army was victorious despite the fortifications. His German neighbor, on the other hand, was losing his hold on the more numerous Italian cities. The Edwardian kings advanced into Wales and Scotland by relying on the castle and fortified town to maintain their hold. Meanwhile in Iberia, the kings of Castile continued to pursue the policy of establishing fortified towns in occupied territory, successfully foiling the Arabs' attempts to reclaim lost ground. The Christians in Iberia settled and created fortified towns and cities not only to hold on to conquered lands, but also to bolster their own forces for future offensive operations.

The most modern and advanced fortifications yet seen in Europe were developing from Wales to the Holy Land and from Iberia to Rus. Their success rested largely on the fact that the besieging armies were too small to be involved in continuous and lengthy sieges.

CASTELNAUD, FRANCE. *These are two views of the 13th-century castle at Castelnaud in southwest France. The 13th-century keep towers above it and is linked to a 13th-century curtain wall. A 15th-century barbican can be seen in front of the curtain wall's entrance. The lower walls are from a 16th-century enceinte.*

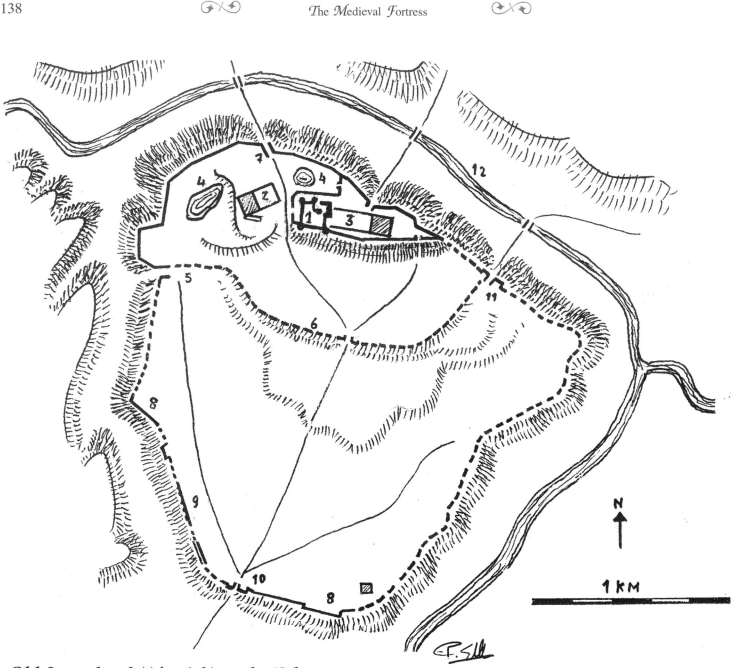

Old Samarkand (Afrasiab), early 13th century

1. Citadel
2. Great mosque
3. Royal palace
4. Cisterns
5. Namazgah Gate
6. Inner wall
7. Bukhara Gate
8. Rebuilt Greek wall
9. Buttressed wall
10. Ketch Gate
11. China gate
12. Siab River

(Plan courtesy of Pierre Etcheto)

SAMARKAND, *one of the oldest cities in Central Asia and one of the largest cities west of China, was devastated by the Mongols under Ghenghiz Khan in the early 13th century. It would later be revived when Tamerlane made it the capital of his empire in the 14th century.*

Note: The SW sector has been rebuilt in places and reveals several types of wall:
- A Hellenistic or later wall, with an inner gallery and 2 or 3 levels of frontal loopholes.
- In some places a lower advanced wall, possibly Achemenid.
- A wall with square buttresses, with frontal loopholes in the curtain and buttresses.
- There is evidence of very few, if any, towers.

The citadel has round towers. The mosque and the palace are from after the Arab conquest.

Fortifications Against the Mongols

Early in the 13th century a new wave of invaders from the East broke over Europe, swamping all resistance in their wake—the Mongol hordes led by Genghiz Khan and his successors. The bigger and stronger castles and fortified cities that already dotted the European countryside proved unequal for the job. The large European armies hastily formed in Eastern Europe were quickly smashed by even larger Mongol contingents and sometimes even smaller ones.

The reason for the Mongols' success lay far to the east. For centuries the Great Wall of China, which spanned up to 2,400 kilometers, had kept most of the barbarian tribes from the north out of the Chinese dominions. Early in the 13th century, however, many of these nomadic groups were united under the banner of Genghiz Khan, who created a large and well-organized army. The Sung Dynasty, which ruled China at the time, had adopted a purely defensive policy, believing it was possible to ward off any aggression from behind the walls of its large fortified cities. At first, the Great Khan's forces ignored the fortified cities of China, plundering the land instead. Before long, however, the Mongols realized that the cities must fall if victory was to be achieved so they worked diligently at developing their skills in siege warfare.

Not content with laying waste to China, Genghiz Khan and his hordes spilled over into the Islamic regions of Central Asia and onto the great trading cities of Samarkand and Bukhara in Transoxiana, a region that had only recently been occupied by the Khwarizmian Empire, which occupied most of ancient Persia.

The newly created Khwarizmian Empire of Alah Al Din Muhammad, which had recently broken away from the empire of the Seljuk Turks, had a large military force, at least on paper, that should have been able to effectively hold back the Mongols. Shah Muhammad's army consisted of Turks and Persians and numbered upwards of 400,000 men backed by heavily defended cities such as Samarkand and Bukhara. However, a large number of the shah's tribal allies were unreliable at best. Furthermore, the region's numerous castle-like structures were small and had little military value since they had been built by local leaders to protect themselves against common bandits, not large armies. At the beginning of Genghiz Khan's campaign, a Mongol force of 30,000 was rebuffed by an army of 50,000 led by Muhammad's son, Jalal ad-Din. However, the Mongols soon returned with an army of 200,000 men directed by Genghiz Khan and launched a two-pronged attack. In 1219, the Mongols laid siege to the heavily fortified border city of Otrar (or Utrar) east of the Aral Sea on the Syr Draya River, which reportedly held 80,000 soldiers. Otrar fell after five months but its citadel resisted another two months. Muhammad dispatched 50,000 men to meet a smaller Mongol force advancing from the south, but this time his army was destroyed. Meanwhile, Genghiz Khan, at the head of the main part of his army, swept around the empire through the desert to the north and stood before Bukhara, putting the city under siege early in 1220. Most of the 20,000-man garrison fled the city. The citadel, whose entrance was attached to the city wall, soon fell to the Mongols.

Finally, Muhammad's capital of Samarkand, encircled by a formidable brick wall, came face to face with the entire Mongol horde. The city's approximately 100,000-man garrison quickly dwindled as 50,000 were lost in a sortie against the Mongols. Of the remaining 50,000 defenders, 30,000 were Kanglis tribesmen, who abandoned the city to join the attackers. Faced with such calamity, the inhabitants of the city surrendered to the Khan, who commanded the execution of the Kanglis for their disloyalty. Still, 20,000 men held out in the citadel of the city, but they survived only a few days. Muhammad's empire virtually ceased to exist by the end of 1220 and the Shah died from illness in 1221 while trying to salvage what was left of it. These fortified cities of Central Asia were not as large as the great cities of China, which stymied the Genghiz Khan, but they were greater in size than those of Europe.

Thus the Mongols destroyed the last empire that could match their own massive armies. It must be noted that some of the fortified cities of Transoxiana were extensive enough to accommodate greater contingents than the largest European cities. Despite this, they proved incapable of stopping the Mongols. In addition, their citadels, which held huge garrisons, turned out to be very vulnerable once the city had surrendered. Besides Constantinople and possibly Rome, there were no fortifications on the scale of Samarkand and Bukhara in Europe able to hold and maintain such large garrisons. As a matter of fact, aside from the Crusader forces, it was rare to see a European army numbering in the tens of thousands before the 13th century.

Early in 1221, after his conquest of Central Asia,

(Sketch by Wanda Ostrowska)

The gate and walls of Bukhara.

Genghiz Khan sent an expeditionary force of about 40,000 into Europe under the leadership of his favorite general, Subedei. This Mongol force, moving through the Caucasus gateway, soon encountered the Christian kingdom of Georgia whose king, George IV, had been preparing a sizable army to embark on the Sixth Crusade to the Middle East. His bodyguard alone consisted of 30,000 Cuman (or Polovsty) cavalry, nomads of Turkish stock related to the Mongols who occupied mostly the steppes north of Georgia. In addition, George IV had his own army of seasoned knights and foot soldiers, who had seen action against the Persians and Byzantines during the previous century. Despite its experience, the Georgian army was smashed in battle and its king fled to his fortified capital at Tiflis. The Mongol force was not prepared to undertake a siege, so their first encounter with a European fortified position held them briefly in check. King George IV challenged them once more in the field and was soundly defeated. His medieval European knights and tactics were obviously no match for the Mongols and their well-organized hordes.

The Mongol expeditionary force continued its advance after having smashed the kingdom of Georgia, where only a few villages with defensive stone towers continued to hold out on isolated mountain plateaus. The Mongol force advanced northward onto the steppes. They defeated a Cuman army and formed a unique alliance with the merchants of Venice, who soon provided them with intelligence on the European situation. The marauding Cumans, fearing the advance of the Mongols, formed an alliance with Mstislav, Prince of Kiev and Chernigov. The 80,000 man Russian-Cuman force enjoyed a minor success, as it chased the Mongols from the Dnieper to the Kalka River in a campaign that lasted several days. Unfortunately, its success was short-lived. In 1223, a Mongol force of just over 20,000 destroyed this Russian army. Before withdrawing toward the Urals, the expedition moved to the Volga to strike at the Kama Bulgars in their strongholds. Earth and wood fortifications, and even stone ones, were useless before the Mongol onslaught.

During their first foray, the Mongols created a vacuum of power in southern Russia and they soon returned to exploit it. In 1236, led by Subedei, nominally under the command of Batu, they were back in Russia and they were unstoppable. The Kama Bulgars on the Volga were destroyed by a Tatar (Slavic term for the Mongols) army of up to 150,000 men. Next it was the turn of the Russian princes as Subedei finally crossed the Volga in 1237. The first siege took place at the city of Ryazan where three Russian princes had withdrawn after an initial defeat in the field. The Mongols isolated the city and took it by storm after a siege of less than two weeks. Soon all the cities of the principality surrendered as the Mongols began a campaign of terror. The Grand Duke of Suzdal soon lost Moscow to a direct assault. Suzdal fell next. Then his capital of Vladimir was put under siege in February 1238, and, despite its large garrison, it soon fell. By March, the Tatars moved on to Novgorod, which was only saved by the changing weather and the swamps surrounding it.

The Russian princes in the south were also beleaguered, as the great fortified city of Kiev fell in December 1240, its wooden defenses layed to waste. Only a few isolated strongholds, like those in the mountains of Georgia, were bypassed, and some, like Novgorod, remained just outside their reach. Nonetheless, every major defensive position in Russia was taken. None of the earth and timber fortified cities of the Slavs was able to withstand the Tatars. While the Mongols gave up on it, Novgorod, under the leadership of Alexander Nevsky, fought off and defeated a small invasion force of Teutonic Knights at the Battle of the Ice in 1242.

Meanwhile, in 1241, Subedei moved on to Poland and Hungary with an army of over 100,000 men. The Polish army of Boleslav V was destroyed outside Krakow and the city fell soon afterward. Prince Henry of Silesia engaged the Mongols with an army of 40,000 Poles, and about 25,000 Teutonic Knights and other Europeans (by conservative estimates), huge by medieval European standards. However, like most medieval contingents, it was poorly organized and poorly trained and was crushed at the battle of Liegnitz in April. At about the same time, King Bela of Hungary assembled 100,000 men, including Cumans fleeing from the Mongols, but was defeated at the decisive battle of the Sajo (Mohi) River.

Every European army—some of the largest created in the Middle Ages—sent against the hordes was crushed. Castles and cities defended by wooden walls fell quickly. In some cases, a few stone castles of the Hungarian kingdom resisted, although this probably was largely due to the fact the Mongols had no time to reduce them. Even the town of Pest was ravaged, but the Mongols had no time to reduce the fortress of Buda across the river.

There were no moments of glory like the battles of Marathon or Thermopilae for the Europeans. The Tatar hordes crushed every army and fortified city that stood in their path. No fortifications were able to withstand the Mongols and those that were bypassed were unable to check their advance. As quickly as they came, the hordes left, except in the lands of the Rus. They remained undefeated, only pulling back because they were recalled upon the passing of the Genghiz Khan in 1242.

For Genghiz Khan and his hordes, China was the most formidable adversary in terms of size and cultural advantages, however, the Chinese armies were not efficient and relied on massive fortified cities for the defense of the empire. In his efforts to overcome the Chinese, Genghiz Khan achieved the seemingly impossible. He wrought intertribal alliances between nomadic groups of pastoralists that led to the creation of one of the greatest armies the world has seen. A man of great genius, he also developed unparalleled siege warfare tactics. His charisma was the glue that held together the vast empire he had forged for as long as he lived. After bringing the kingdoms of Central Asia and Eastern Europe to their knees, he returned his attention to China. Only his death saved Europe from certain disaster. His successors also sent armies into the West, threatening all of Europe later in the 13th century, but by this time the Mongol empire was politically fragmented which brought an end to expansion against Europe. However, Genghiz's grandson, Kublai Khan, was able to realize his grandfather's lifelong dream by reducing the cities of China.

Polish arms and armor.

Social Organizaton and Army Size

Demographic and social organization determined not only the size of cities and their fortifications but also army sizes. In Western Europe, where feudal states predominated, armies were generally small and unstable. At this time the king of England still owned lands in France, including Normandy, and was vassal to the French monarch. The armies operating in France under Fulk Nerra in the 10th century amounted to only a few thousand men. At the battle of Hastings in 1066 the 7,000-man Norman army took on 7,000 Anglo-Saxons. In France and England after 1066 the kings relied on the nobility for their main fighting element, based on feudal obligations. These armies were generally small because of the limited pool of men to draw upon. The bulk of the English troops most likely consisted of light cavalry and various types of foot troops such as spear men and archers. Based on information provided by the Doomesday Book, it is calculated that at the end of the 11th century the king of England was able to raise an army of about 15,000 men, less than a third of whom were knights. It is estimated that more than a century later the king of England could count on a force of only 8,000 knights at most. The king of France was probably able to muster a slightly larger force. The monarchs were unable to assemble large contingents because their own vassals were as likely to defy them as fight with each other over control of the land. In 1138, after the death of Henry I of England, King David I of Scotland assembled a force of 10,000 men to invade northern England and was defeated by an English army of 8,000 men at the battle of the Standard.

In the 12th century, the populations of England and France almost doubled, but because feudalism persisted the armies did not increase substantially. Henry II, Richard I, and John never raised armies larger than 5,000 to 8,000, while the kings of France probably were able to assemble a force almost double that size. Henry II managed to raise an army of 5,000 between 1173 and 1174 to put down a rebellion. But Henry II never called up more than 2,000 knights at a time though he had many more at his disposal. He began the practice of scutage whereby his knights had the option of paying him rather than serving in person, and he hired mercenaries in their stead. Richard I opted to only call up 300 knights for his wars with France in 1197 but the number of foot soldiers serving in the field army probably varied from 2,000 to 5,000. At the battle of Bouvines in 1214, King John assembled a force of 5,000 men to join the Holy Roman Emperor with 15,000 troops against France. The French, who were able to muster an equal number of men, carried the day. During the Welsh campaigns of Edward I, the English army consisted of 15,500 men at the most in 1277, about 20,000 men in 1282-1283, 11,000 men in 1287, and 31,000 men in 1294-1295. By this time the English had managed to mobilize one of the largest armies in feudal Europe. In the 14th century, England and France finally saw the need to enlarge their armies as more and more small and medium castles and fortified cities significantly improved and had their fortifications enlarged. But although large armies were formed during the Hundred Years War of the 14th and 15th centuries, most of the combat continued to revolve around sieges.

In 732 A.D. at the battle of Tours an unusually large Frankish army of 30,000 faced off an Islamic force of 80,000. In the 10th, 11th, and 12th centuries the Holy

Roman Emperors had to contend with subduing their powerful dukes, maintaining control over an equally large Italian population, attempting to dominate the pope, and warding off attacks from the East. However, they faced the same problems as the kings of France and England in raising large forces since they had to struggle to take power away from their vassals. In 1158, Frederick Barbarossa beseiged Milan with an army of about 15,000 knights and possibly 50,000 or fewer infantryman, mostly from Italy. The city's 40,000 inhabitants surrendered after a month. The seige of Milan shows how important a large contingent was to reduce a city of this size. At the battle of Legnano in 1176, Frederick Barbarossa's 2,500 German knights and 500 Italian infantrymen met defeat at the hands of the cavalry force of over 4,000 of the Lombard League. The number of men involved in these battles clearly shows that the size of the Holy Roman Emperor's army fluctuated considerably, depending on the loyalty of his subjects and allies. Apparently a good portion of his foot soldiers were contributed by his Italian allies, and as he lost control of them his field army rapidly dwindled. Yet, late in the 12th century, Frederick Barbarossa was able to assemble and lead an army of up to 30,000 men on the Third Crusade, probably because religious solidarity outweighed regional rivalry.

In the Italian Peninsula there was a variety of arrangements for drafting armies. Some leaders, mainly in rural areas, relied on feudal ties. The cities in the more populous urban areas organized citizen militias, which were probably the most effective of the time since most of the citizens participated. These Italian forces proved extremely efficacious in defending city walls and besieging rival cities. By the 12th century, the sieges in the northern half of the Italian Peninsula were more involved than in other regions of Europe, and the armies in Italy employed more men than those in other parts of Western Europe. Increasingly cities, rather than individual castles, became the main target, which led to design innovations in that area.

Many of the Slavs east of the Holy Roman Empire had been unified to form a Polish state in 966 when Duke Mieszko I converted to Christianity. Their numerous grody, although only made of wood and earth, successfully prevented eastward Germanic expansion. At Cedynia, near the Oder River, Mieszko decisively defeated the Saxon margrave. His son, Boleslaw the Brave, was able to expand the Polish state through war using a large permanent army of

Effigy of a French prince from 1225 A.D. found in the abbey of St. Denis.

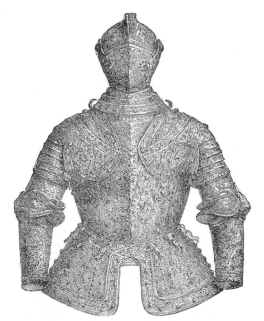

Spanish armor of the 15th century.

almost 17,000 men. To this he added local forces which also served to defend the network of grody. During his reign virtually every town was fortified. In addition, he established on his borders special military grody to hold off the enemy. The Slavic kingdoms of Poland and Rus did not suffer from the restraints of feudalism in the west. Since these two kingdoms were emerging from an earlier tribal stage, their underlying social organization still relied very much on blood ties between lineages and clans. Among the Slavs, every able-bodied man was expected to defend his lands and come to the aid of his kinsman. The Slavic rulers were able, therefore, to raise more massive armies than the feudal state societies further to the west, where membership in the warrior class was inherited. But because the leadership became increasingly centralized, the Slavic armies were more stable than the raiding parties typical of tribal societies. Along the Baltic coast, from the Elbe River to the Vistula, the Wends, a conglomeration of Western Slavic tribes, were able, like the Poles and the Rus, to call upon most of their able-bodied men for their defense. However, since they still clung to the tribal system, they had no centralized leadership. Only the Prussians and Lithuanians appear to have been able to unite and create a relatively effective force like the Poles. However by the 12th century, the Poles appear to have been better organized and technologically superior.

The kingdom of Denmark was capable of assembling an army of 7,000 to 10,000 effective soldiers as well as a sizable fleet. In conjunction with the Saxons, the Danes launched a crusade against the pagan Wends between 1147 and 1185. This was not the small-scale force usually seen in Western Europe but a sizable army. But the Danes resorted to raiding and pillaging the Wendish countryside because the Wendish strongholds were too difficult to take.

In the Iberian Peninsula, the kings of León, Castile, and the other Christian kingdoms found that they needed large armies to take on their Islamic opponents, not only in the field but in sieges of fortified cities and castles. In the 11th century, feudalism in Spain was weaker than in France, which made it possible for the kings of León, Castile, and Aragon to assemble the larger armies needed to match those of their Islamic opponents. In addition, many towns were occupied or founded with the specific purpose of serving as defensive points to hold newly won territories. Their inhabitants were required to create

Saint Louis, 1226-1270.

militias that not only defended the urban centers but also provided troops to augment the kings' army in offensive operations. Some records report that in the 13th century, at the battle of Las Navas de Tolosa in 1212, Castile, Navarre, Aragon, and Portugal managed to assemble a force of 60,000 to 100,000 foot soldiers and 10,000 cavalrymen. The Almohad army facing them consisted of 200,000 to 600,000 men, including 100,000 to 185,000 cavalry. Though these numbers may be exaggerated, it is likely that there were at least 60,000 Christian soldiers against 80,000 to 100,000 Islamic troops.

Byzantium was one of the few states able to maintain a relatively large army. But in 1071, a well-trained Byzantine army of 40,000 soldiers was smashed by a Seljuk Turks force of 70,000 cavalry at the battle of Manzikert. Large armies were rare in Europe for most of the High Middle Ages, but not in the Middle East. Soon the Byzantine strongholds of Antioch, Damascus, and Jerusalem fell one by one. As Byzantium teetered on the verge of collapse, the Seljuk Turks threatened the security of Christian Europe. After Pope Urban II called for a holy war against the Turks in 1095, it took two years for the first Crusader army to mobilize. At an estimated 50,000 men it was probably one of the largest forces ever assembled in Christian Europe of the Middle Ages. Unfortunately its leaders had little to no experience in mobilizing, maintaining, or handling such a large force. But in 1099 they attacked Jerusalem with a contingent of 15,000 men, and took the city despite the strong defense put up by 20,000 defenders and the city's inhabitants who probably numbered about 40,000.

In the 13th century Christian Europe faced one of the most critical moments of its history when the Mongols appeared on its eastern border and threatened to engulf it in a tide of flame and destruction. The Europeans with their smaller armies faced certain defeat in the face of a larger and better-organized invader and was saved only by a twist of fate that felled the Mongol khan at a crucial point.

In the 14th century, many European monarchs continued to put their faith in their fortifications and their ability to capture them, instead of making strides in the development, organization, and training of their armies. In the 15th century, Europe was threatened anew by the Ottoman Turks but despite the smaller forces the Europeans were again victorious thanks to new developments in the art of war during the Renaissance.

A suit of armor belonging to Charles the Bold.

BEDZIN CASTLE, POLAND. *The Keep.*

Medieval Poland

Until the 10th century the Slavs living in modern-day Poland and eastern Germany had tribal social organization. They were often at war with the Saxon barons of the Holy Roman Empire, who tried to dominate them, and engaged in warfare against each other. During the 10th century great administrative grody began to appear, indicating that power was becoming consolidated in the hands of chieftains who ruled the clans with increasing authority. This trend culminated in 966 with the emergence of the first Polish state under the rule of Duke Mieszko I, who converted to Christianity and founded the first Polish ruling dynasty, the Piast. This conversion was supposed to put the Polish leader on an equal footing with the Saxons who coveted his lands. His people became known as the Polanians or the people of the plains. The extensive use of their gród type fortifications, even though only of wood and earth, successfully held the Germanic barons at bay even before Mieszko's advent. In 967 he defeated the Slavs to the northwest (in modern-day Pomerania). In 972, at Cedynia near the Oder River, Mieszko fell back upon a strong gród and then decisively defeated the Saxon margrave which led to a more rapid unification with other Slavs.

Mieszko's son, Boleslaw Chrobry (the Brave), who inherited the duchy in 992, became the first king of Poland. In his struggles to include the Slavs living in lands claimed by the Holy Roman Emperor Henry, Boleslaw found himself at war with the empire. When peace was finally declared in 1018, Boleslaw controlled the lands of many of the western Slavs.

Boleslaw's next campaign was against Kievian Rus, in the land known as Ruthenia. His mission was to conquer and return these lands to his incompetent son-in-law, Swiatopelk, as Prince of Kiev. He took Kiev in 1018, but his success only served to strengthen the Russian state. However, Boleslaw managed to annex several powerful grody, including Czerwien and Przemysl, to his kingdom.

After the demise of the Khazar state in the mid-10th century, a number of Russian principalities, including Kiev, emerged in the Eastern Slavic lands. After taking Kiev, Prince Yaroslav the Wise united his people to push back the Poles and to create the strongest Slavic state east of Poland. The differences between these two Slavic nations were heightened by the fact that Boleslaw's father had adopted Roman Catholicism as the state religion, while Kievian Rus joined the Eastern Orthodox Church.

Boleslaw's Poland encompassed not only much of the territories in today's Poland but also those that were within the 1939 borders. Remarkably, he maintained a relatively large army which made it possible for him to stand up to many of his enemies. It is estimated that he maintained a standing army of almost 17,000 men, of which 3,900 were mail-clad cavalry. In the early 11th century this force most likely outnumbered the armies of the French or English (Anglo Saxon) kings. In addition, he had the ability to use the many grody in his country as a permanent line of defense, just as his father did, without having to leave his regular army to garrison them because they were largely defended by the local communities, as custom dictated. Furthermore, he was able to draw additional men from the larger grody to take part in expeditions with his army. This could increase the size of his army from several hundred to possibly several thousand depending on the location.

Poland declined after Boleslaw's death and it was not until the beginning of the 12th century that a new strong Polish king emerged. This was Boleslaw III, Krzywousty (the Wrymouth), who took over the crown in 1102. The Holy Roman Emperor, Henry V, attempted to bring Poland under his dominion by demanding that Boleslaw III become his vassal and share his kingdom with his brother. In 1109 the emperor's army invaded Poland only to be checked by the same powerful grody that had held back Germanic aggression for decades.

The German troops put the strong gród of Glogow under siege. All attacks against the fortifications failed. The defenders, consisting primarily of the citizenry, were nonetheless skilled in the defense of a gród. As the situation became desperate for the Poles, a truce was called when the defenders agreed to give hostages, which, according to tradition, included children. After receiving word that Boleslaw III was on the way, the defenders decided to continue resisting. The Germans refused to return the hostages and launched a new assault, tying the hostages to their siege towers. Despite this, the defenders repelled the attack and the arrival of Boleslaw's army forced the Germans to withdraw. The emperor's forces were decisively defeated near Wroclaw and were forced to withdraw from Polish territory.

Boleslaw III tried to maintain the integrity of the Polish state by dividing the kingdom among his sons, leaving the eldest in charge. Unfortunately, his plans failed, and soon the Brandenburgers encroached on Polish territory in Pomerania. In 1226, the Teutonic Knights were asked by Boleslaw's grandson, who ruled Mazovia in Eastern Poland, to defend his lands against the pagan Prussians. Poland would not regain its former power and prestige until the early 14th century.

Pskov, Russia. *The outer wall.*

(Photo courtesy of John Sloan)

Medieval Russia

The Russians, Belorussians, and the Ukrainians constitute a group of people known as the Eastern Slavs. Linguistically and culturally these people were closely affiliated to the Western Slavs like the Poles, the Czechs and the Slovaks, and had a similar political organization. As in the Western Slavic territories, the loosely organized tribes started coalescing into more organized principalities during the 10th century. Two of the major grady to emerge as centers of power during this period were Novgorod and Kiev. The capital of Rus was at Novgorod until 912 when it was moved to Kiev. However, the Grand Prince maintained Novgorod in his sphere of control by appointing one of his sons to rule over it. Nonetheless, Novgorod, which was governed by an oligarchy of wealthy merchants, did not tolerate the yoke of the Grand Prince for very long. In 1136 the ruling prince was kicked out, and replaced by a republican government which remained in power until the next century. Kiev, on the other hand, reached its zenith earlier under Yaroslav the Wise who made it the dominant Slavic power east of Poland.

Russia's main problem was its system for the line of succession to the throne. In theory, when the Grand Prince of Kiev died, his next eldest brother inherited his title while other brothers advanced in rank according to their order of birth. Thus Yaroslav the Wise took the throne after the death of his two brothers. When he died his eldest son inherited his title in 1036 and the cities and lands were divided among his heirs including Kiev, Chernigov, Perialslavl, Rostov, Galich, Polotsk, Smolensk, and a number of others. Unfortunately, Yaroslav's heirs were not content with this state of affairs, which gave rise to a period of civil war during which the heirs vied for the privilege of being the Grand Prince of Kiev. Finally in 1113, Vladimir II Monomakh succeeded in seizing Kiev ending the period of chaos and the others resigned themselves to ruling the lesser towns. After Vladimir's death these principalities became autonomous.

Kiev declined in importance after the 1150s when young prince Yuri Dolgoruki (Long Arms) transferred his capital to Vladimir on the Klyasma River in Suzdal. His father had created the Suzdal principality especially for Yuri in 1125. Even when he became Grand Prince of Kiev, Yuri preferred to make his home in Suzdal. Andrei Bogolubski also ruled directly from Vladimir when he became Grand Prince. Thus the center of Russian power was transferred for good from Kiev to Vladimir.

When the Fourth Crusade ended in the capture of Byzantium in 1204, Kiev's last vestiges of power evaporated. By the time of the Mongol onslaught in 1238, Vladimir was the capital and there was no local prince in Kiev. In addition, the Grand Prince at Vladimir held little control over other towns and cities of Russia. In the meantime, the merchant rulers of the republic of Novgorod selected a prince as their military commander, but denied him the right to live within the city walls. The Grand Prince had attempted to resist, but the Mongols took Vladimir and killed off his family members. He assembled an army, without the help of other princes, to meet the Mongols, but it was destroyed at the Siti River. The Mongols continued to roll on in 1240 and after sweeping through most of Russia, designated who would be the Grand Prince.

During the 12th and 13th centuries, the Russian army was able to assemble up to 20,000 men on some rare occasions. Each prince had a retinue called druzhina. In some instances the druzhina could number several thousand men, although usually it was under a 100. The druzhina consisted of heavy cavalry in the form of armored lancers and light troops serving as archers. When the time came to raise an army, the Russians were not under a feudal system of obligation. Most of the best men called to serve came from the cities. Kiev and Chernigov employed nomadic groups, including the Kypachak, to bolster their numbers. These warriors used lances, swords, and various other weapons such as knives, hammers, and maces. They also used light armor for protection.

At the battle of the Kalaka River in 1223, the Mongols were able to destroy a large Russian army of 80,000 by superior tactics and strategy. By 1240 most of Russia was under their control, while Novgorod was threatened by the Teutonic Knights. In 1241, Prince Alexander Nevsky led Russian forces against the Germanic Order and defeated them at Lake Peipus in the Battle on the Ice. Not long afterward, Nevsky became the Grand Prince of Vladimir. His grandson transferred the seat of power to Moscow after being recognized as Grand Prince by the Mongols in 1328. A Russian victory over the Golden Horde at Kulikovo in 1381 finally brought independence to the Russian state.

HAUT-KOENIGSBOURG, ALSACE.

4

Decline of the High Castle Walls

The Middle Ages slowly faded away during the 15th century, lingering in some regions for a little longer. The years 1415, 1453, and 1492, three of the dates often used by historians to mark the close of this era, are associated with decisive battles, two of which were sieges. In 1415 the battle of Agincourt marked a turning point in the Hundred Years War and the end of the dominance of the armored knight on the battlefield. In 1453 the Hundred Years War came to an end after the French drove the English from one fortified position after the other with the help of artillery. However, and more importantly, Byzantium fell to the Turks. The medieval walls of Constantinople succumbed to the Turks' modern siege tactics and weapons, including giant artillery pieces. Finally in 1492, the Islamic medieval fortress of Granada fell to the Catholic kings, Isabella of Castile and Ferdinand of Aragon, putting an end to the Reconquista and almost eight centuries of Moorish presence on the Iberian Peninsula. By this time warfare had decisively changed, along with political, economic, and other cultural activities. At the dawn of the Renaissance (which actually began well before the end of the Middle Ages) a new type of fortification made its appearance. At the same time, the castle and other medieval fortifications outlived their usefulness and went into a decline, or so conventional thought would have us believe.

In reality, castles were not abandoned at all, but continued in use long past the Middle Ages. However, new castles ceased to be built and were replaced by palatial residences with defensive features. During the Renaissance new fortifications were built to make the most of artillery weapons, while the older medieval fortification were modified to accommodate cannons. If a medieval castle was occasionally abandoned, it was because it was too obsolete to renovate and its modernization would be too costly or impractical. Most castles built in the 13th century or later were eminently suited for renovation. Some castles also lost their tactical and strategic usefulness after they were completely surrounded by the towns that had grown up around them.

Use of Cannons in the Hundred Years War

When cannons first came into use in the 14th century, they made little difference because they were too small to inflict significant damage on fortifications or even on the battlefield. In 1415, when Henry V laid siege to Harfleur, Normandy, his handful of cannons hardly facilitated his task. The port, located on the mouth of the Seine, was heavily fortified with 26 towers and large walls that included machicoulis. In addition, it was surrounded by water obstacles created by dams whose sluices could release a flood of water onto the low-lying terrain. The southwestern gate was the only one of the town's three entrances considered vulnerable by its inhabitants since it was defended by a lone water channel. Like the other gates, it was defended by a wooden barbican, however it almost reached the height of the town walls and was reinforced with fascines and tree trunks bound together with iron bands. The port facilities, located at the south end of the town, were accessed by the Lezarde River, which led to the Seine, which, in turn, was closed off with an iron chain and sharpened stakes driven into the riverbed. The river channel also cut through a water gate in the north wall that separated the western part of the town from the main part by encircling it. The part of the town unprotected by a water obstacle was the eastern section, which was covered by a great ditch running from the Montvillers

Plan of Harfleur, Normandy, 1415

1. English attacks
2. Flooded area
3. Great Ditch
4. Rouen Gate
5. Leure Gate
6. Harbor
7. Montvillers Gate

(Sketch by J. E. Kaufmann)

Gate in the north that looked over flooded lands, to the Rouen Gate in the south that faced the river. Both gates were also covered by wooden barbicans. The garrison numbering only about 400 men-at-arms confronted an army of over 10,000.

To take Harfleur, Henry V had to use his cannons and non-gunpowder artillery to breach its walls. Battering rams and belfries were not practical. Part of Henry's army, camped to the east of the town, attempted to tunnel toward the walls without success. Henry assembled his siege artillery on the west side of Harfleur to concentrate an attack on the Leure Gate whose barbican was on his side of the channel. As his men dug trenches toward the fortifications, the French blocked them with counter-trenches and countermines. Henry then tried to move forward his heavy cannon protected by large embrasured mobile screens, but his artillery men were repelled by the burghers' crossbows and guns. The French also launched sorties against the English positions.

When the artillery was finally dragged within range, according to the chronicler, it easily destroyed the masonry of the towers and splintered away the bulwarks of the wooden barbicans. The cannonballs were smeared with tar and lit before being fired at the

wooden barbican to set it afire. As the artillery bombardment continued round the clock for a week, projectiles of up to 500 pounds pounded the walls. Catapults and trébuchets of various types also took part in the action, particularly because they had a greater range than some of the cannons. The older weapons battered the fortifications quite effectively, but were eclipsed by the guns whose noise and smoke left a more lasting impression on most of the participants and demoralized the defenders. However, this severe pounding did not bring an end to the siege of Harfleur. The defenders repaired the damage inflicted by the English as the bombardment continued. French raids continued on land and sea while the garrison counter-bombarded the English with its own wall-mounted artillery. Before long disease began to spread through the English camp. Yet throughout this siege a French army sat idly by at Rouen without making a single effort to lift the siege. After little over a month, on September 16, the barbican of the southwestern gate was on the verge of collapse after being subjected to weeks of bombardment. A French raid against the protected English positions brought a brief respite. The next day, the English took the barbican and prepared to move their guns into a position from which they could fire directly upon the main walls. As their bombardment became more effective and the English forces prepared ladders for a final assault by escalade, the defenders of Harfleur, giving up any hope of relief, finally surrendered.

Although Charles Oman claims in *The Art of War in the Middle Ages* that this siege was a victory for the cannons, it must be noted that the traditional siege weapons and methods also played a significant role in the action. Henry's victory was costly since he lost almost a fifth of his invasion force. Rather than a proof of the superiority of the cannon, the battle of Harfleur is a witness to determination and grit on the part of the besieged as well as the besieger. After the reduction of Harfleur, the depleted English army went on a chevauchée that accidentally culminated in the great victory at Agincourt.

The war continued in 1417 when Henry V returned to Normandy while the French king got embroiled in a civil war with the Duke of Burgundy. Henry V took advantage of the situation to undertake the conquest in Normandy by first striking at the fortified city of Caen which was defended by thick walls and a citadel. Once again, thanks to his artillery, he was able to breach the walls of the city after two weeks. The

---

ROUEN, FRANCE. *The tower where Joan of Arc was imprisoned.* (©Bettmann/CORBIS)

castle held out for two more weeks. The pillaging of Caen exposed their king's inability to come to their aid and undermined French morale. As a result, the English were able to quickly take other fortified towns, including Alençon. The strongly fortified town of Falaise resisted until early in 1418. Henry's campaign culminated in the siege of the Norman capital and fortified port of Rouen whose walls included 60 towers and 6 gates protected by barbicans and were reinforced against bombardment from behind with a large sloping bank of earth. Desmond Seward in *The Hundred Years War* (New York, 1978) states that each of the towers mounted three cannons and the sections of curtain between towers each mounted a cannon and eight small guns. This would mean probably over 200 cannons, which might be a bit of an exaggeration, with 4,000 men at arms defending the city.

Henry V carried out his siege of Rouen by creating four fortified camps linked by trenches and blocking the Seine with iron chains. After two and a half months the French were on the verge of starvation and without hope of relief. Late in January 1419 the city surrendered, but not as a result of bombardment. Typical of most of the campaigns of the Middle Ages, this one involved few battles and many sieges, and victory resulted more from starvation than from assault. The only fortified site in Normandy Henry had failed to take was Mont St. Michel which continued to defy the English.

The campaign continued in typical medieval style with one strongpoint after another the objective, and siege the main type of tactical operation. The fortified town of Melun was placed under siege by an army of 20,000 men. The defenders only numbered 700 and the town was divided into three fortified parts by the Seine with the castle located on the island. Mining and countermining with subterranean warfare characteristic of many past sieges reached a fearsome crescendo here. Heavy English artillery smashed sections of wall, which as in other sieges, were quickly repaired or blocked. Starvation after just over four months brought the capitulation of the town. After taking Paris, Henry was involved in a few more sieges, but there were no great battles in the field and cannons alone still did not bring victory.

The Duke of Bedford and the Earl of Salisbury continued capturing fortified positions of the French king after the death of Henry V and once again defeated a French army in the field at Verneuil in 1424. In 1426 Salisbury led a force of about 4,000 men on a cam-

Caen, Normandy, 15th century

1. Castle
2. Keep
3. Moat of the castle
4. Old City
5. New City
6. Curtain walls of Old City
7. Curtain walls of New City
8. River Orne
9. Town Moat
10. Portes des Champs (Gatehouse)

CAEN, NORMANDY.
Below left: *A niche in the wall with an arrow loop that dates from the 11th century.*
Below right: *The Portes des Champs or gatehouse.*

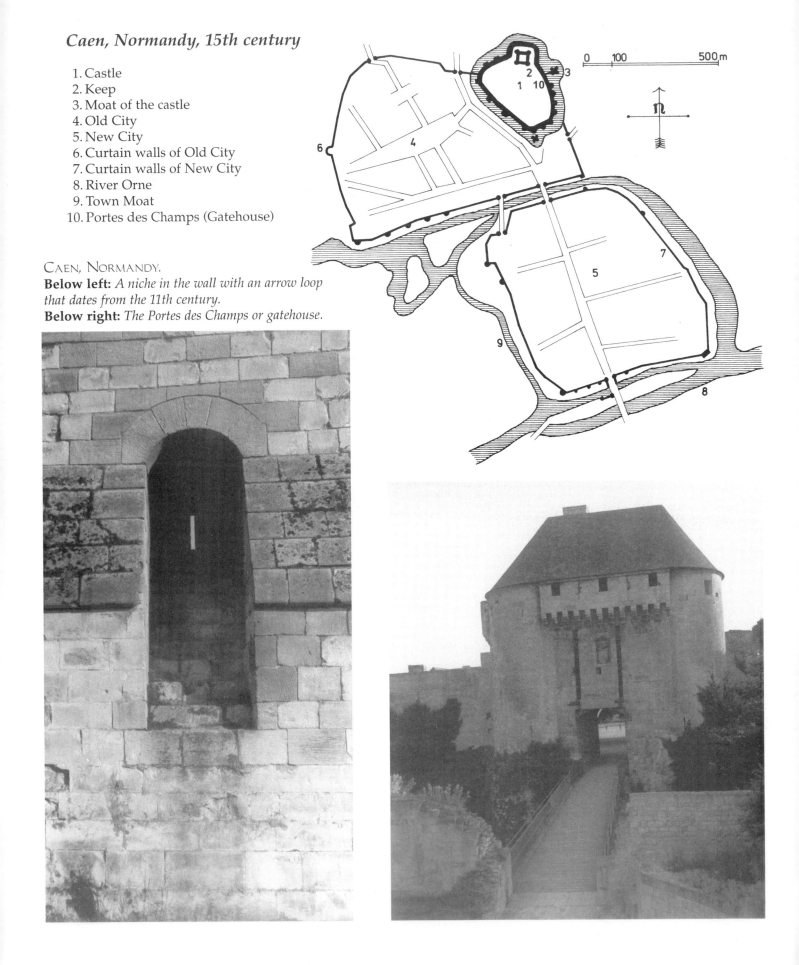

THE BASTILLE OF PARIS.

paign which took dozens of towns and fortified positions only to be stopped at Orleans in 1428. The city was one of the last great strongholds in the dauphin's territories. With over 5,000 defenders and 71 cannons mounted on the walls, the English were outnumbered. The cities walls were almost 10 meters high, and too long to be surrounded by the besieger. The English attacked the French fortified bridgehead on the south bank of the Loire which defended the bridge that crossed the river into the city. On the first arch of the bridge off of the south bank were two large towers forming a gate with a drawbridge, known as the Tourelles with a small earth and timber position (probably a barbican) in front of it on the shore. The English tried to take the Tourelles by a heavy bombardment that was followed by an unsuccessful attack. The garrison of this châtelet fled when they believed that English miners were beneath their position. The Tourelles were taken and shortly after Salisbury was killed by a round from the artillery of Orleans while inside the Tourelles. The siege continued to drag on until the late spring of the following year. The English built several bastilles, small wooden forts, to isolate the city and some of these were or included boulevards, usually a low form of earth work in front of a wall or gate which was designed to be served by cannons. In May of the following year the English siege lines were broken and Joan of Arc led the French relief force in taking several bastilles.

Then the defenders assaulted the Tourelles, held by 500 English soldiers, from the north bank along the repaired bridge and recaptured the towers, ending the siege. Again the cannons were not decisive since neither side achieved a victory because of them.

In 1435 France was reunited with Burgundy by the Treaty of Arras and England lost the valuable ally that had contributed to Henry V's successful campaigns. Despite this, it took another 18 years for the final victory. The cannon played a role, but one which has been overemphasized. Paris, which was in English hands, fell in 1436 because of starvation, desertion, refusal of the local militia to defend the city, and the locals dropping ladders over the wall to allow the besiegers access into the city. The Parisians' lack of support and downright rebellion forced the English to take refuge in the Bastille and finally to surrender. Following the capitulation of Paris, fortified towns and castles changed hands back and forth, but some strongholds like Calais, Rouen, and Bordeaux were still too well-defended to be taken back by the French.

The first significant development took place in 1441, when the French, after three unsuccessful sieges, managed to take Pontoise with the help of artillery and the guidance of Jean and Gaspard Bureau. Later, the Bureau brothers were allowed to form an artillery arm for the French army, which continued to grow in size and strength. According to Charles Oman, the artillery deployed by the Bureau brothers between 1449 to 1450

Fougères Castle, Brittany

The 11th-century border castle was destroyed and a new castle was built in the 13th century to replace it. The 13th-century castle was modified in the 15th century for cannons.

Early Castle
1. Donjon or keep destroyed in 11th century
13th to 15th Century Castle
2. The Palace
3. Boulevard and gate of Chene
4. Gate Tower of Haye-Saint-Hilaire
5. Gate Tower of Coetlogon

6. Tower of Coligny
7. 13th-century Tower of Gobelins
8. 15th-century Tower of Raoul
9. 15th-century Tower of Surienne
10. Latrine tower of 15th century–Tower of Cadran
12. Lake

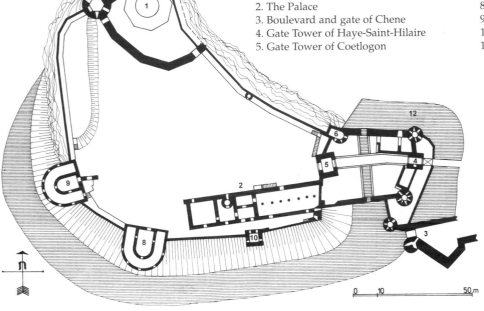

Below: *The outer gatehouse (13th-century Tower of Haye-Saint-Hilaire) with two flanking towers.*
Below Right: *The 15th-century Tower of Raoul which was adapted to mount cannons.*
Right: *The 15th-century Tower of Surienne with machicoulis and arrow loops.*

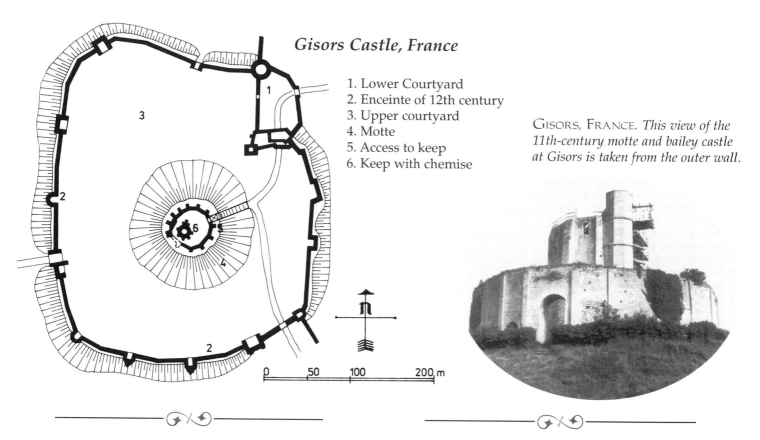

Gisors Castle, France

1. Lower Courtyard
2. Enceinte of 12th century
3. Upper courtyard
4. Motte
5. Access to keep
6. Keep with chemise

GISORS, FRANCE. *This view of the 11th-century motte and bailey castle at Gisors is taken from the outer wall.*

was responsible for 60 successful sieges. However, Oman vastly exaggerates the role of artillery in these campaigns. The fact is that it is the preponderance of numbers and local support rather than actual fighting abilities and superior weaponry that led the French to victories. It must be pointed out that Henry V had previously captured many similar positions just as quickly without much artillery and that the situation in the late 1440s had not altered greatly. In addition, during the 1440s, the English garrisons in charge of the fortified French positions were small and further suffered from desertions and lack of funds.

In 1448, for instance, the garrison of Gisors consisted of only 43 men. In 1449 a 6,000-man English expedition took the castle of Fougères by storm, but this victory would be one of the last for the English. In 1449, a French army of 30,000 men advanced into Normandy, taking one position after another with minimal, if any, resistance. Rouen gained a reprieve from siege by allowing the French forces to enter its walls without resistance. Its English garrison took refuge in the citadel, but had to surrender eventually. At Harfleur and Honfleur, the French artillery indeed opened breaches in the walls that led to the fall of these two cities. However, it must be noted that the English garrison was not as resolute in its defense as the French burghers had been years before. Although

Caen surrendered after three weeks of bombardment, the low morale of the garrison was just as responsible for the capitulation as the artillery fire. Cherbourg, the last English stronghold in Normandy, was put under heavy attack by the Bureau brothers' cannons and suffered considerable damage. However, like Henry V's forces at Harfleur many years before, the French besiegers sustained heavy losses.

After the battle of Formigny in 1450, the English, driven out of Normandy, struggled to maintain their hold on Guyenne in southwest France. Bordeaux and Bayonne surrendered to them in the summer of 1451. John Talbot, at the head of an English contingent, headed for Bordeaux and was admitted within the gates by its citizens in October 1452. However, the French returned to the region in force and put the town of Castillon under siege in 1453, entrenching themselves and their artillery. In an effort to relieve Castillon, Talbot launched an attack on the French positions where his troops were cut down by enemy guns. Soon, all English resistance ceased and the war came to an end.

Medieval fortifications were still valuable in defense, but artillery was also making enough difference to bring about significant changes and modifications to the field of military architecture.

Tarascon Castle, France

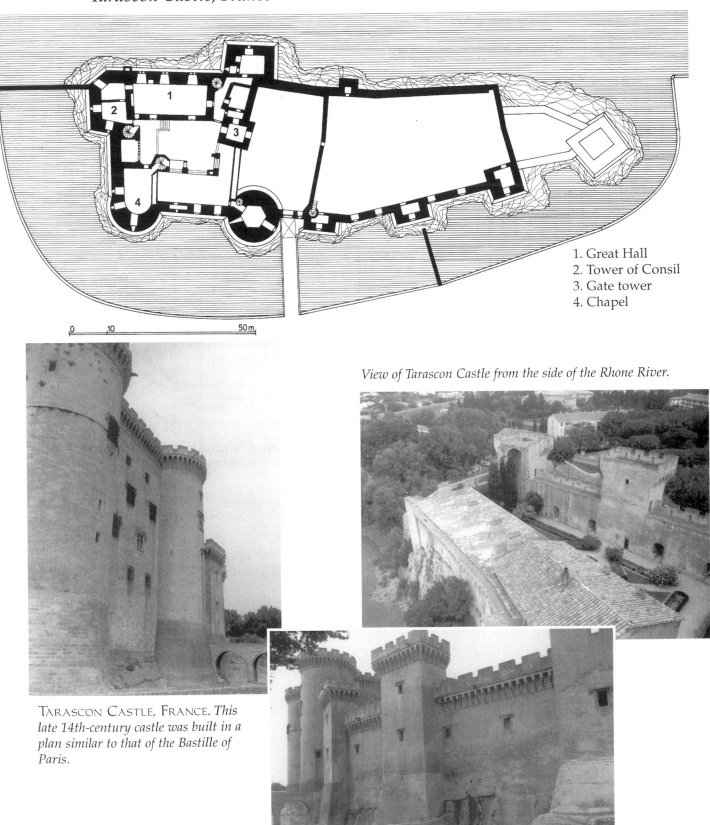

1. Great Hall
2. Tower of Consil
3. Gate tower
4. Chapel

View of Tarascon Castle from the side of the Rhone River.

Tarascon Castle, France. *This late 14th-century castle was built in a plan similar to that of the Bastille of Paris.*

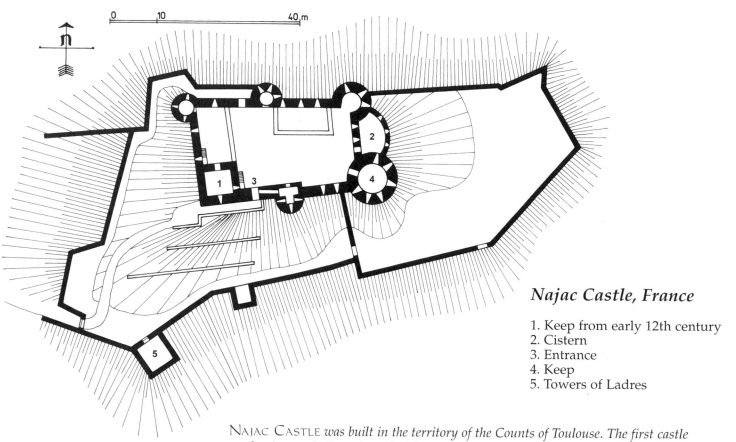

Najac Castle, France

1. Keep from early 12th century
2. Cistern
3. Entrance
4. Keep
5. Towers of Ladres

NAJAC CASTLE *was built in the territory of the Counts of Toulouse. The first castle on the site was built at the end of the 11th century and expanded during the reign of St. Louis. In the mid-13th century the large keep (#4) was added to replace the older one (#1) which then became a residential area. The castle sits on the summit of a hill from which it dominates the area and the town of Najac.*

Remains of the castle of Najac, France, from the entrance side.

PIERREFONDS, FRANCE.

PIERREFONDS CASTLE, FRANCE. *Begun by Louis d'Orleans, the brother of the Valois king, at the end of the 14th century, this large complex survived several sieges of the Reformation and was later badly damaged. Napoleon III allowed Viollet-le-Duc to restore the site in the 19th century. However, much of his work owed more to romantic fantasy than realistic reconstruction. Much of what can be seen in the photo is his reconstruction, which may be termed neo-Gothic rather than Gothic.*

Pierrefonds Castle, France

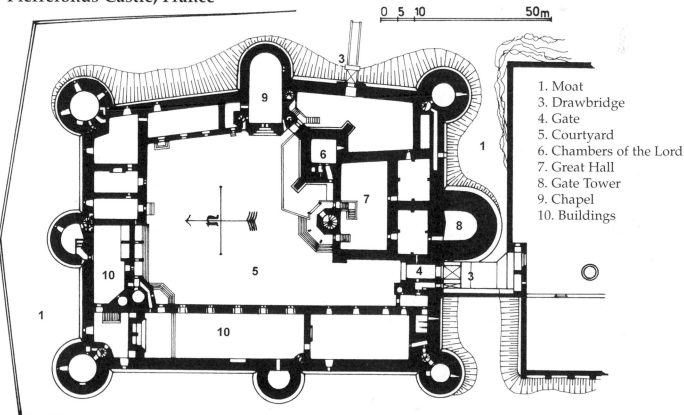

1. Moat
3. Drawbridge
4. Gate
5. Courtyard
6. Chambers of the Lord
7. Great Hall
8. Gate Tower
9. Chapel
10. Buildings

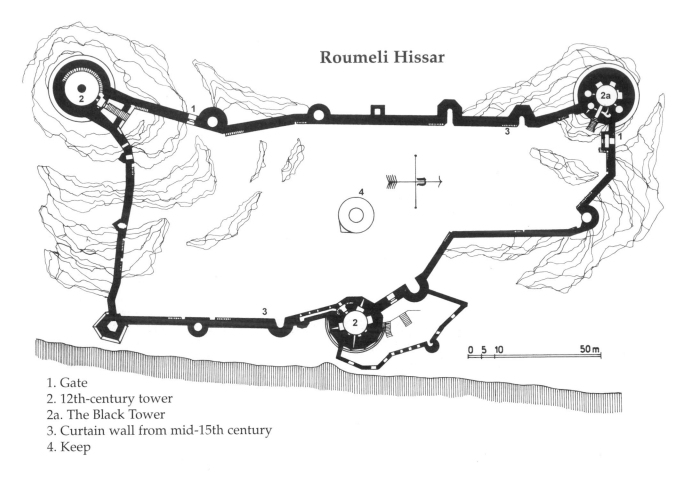

Roumeli Hissar

1. Gate
2. 12th-century tower
2a. The Black Tower
3. Curtain wall from mid-15th century
4. Keep

THE CASTLE OF ROUMELI HISSAR *sits on the European side of the Bosphorus River. Rebuilt by Sultan Mohammed II in 1452 it was armed with heavy cannons in its Black Tower.* (© *Francesco Venturi; Kea Publishing Services Ltd./CORBIS)*

The Fall of Constantinople

The year of 1453 is significant not only because it saw the end of the Hundred Years War, but also because it witnessed the fall of the great city of Constantinople and the demise of the Byzantine Empire. The fall of the city, which had held at bay for a thousand years all but the Christian warriors of the Fourth Crusade, has been partially attributed to artillery. The Turks, who had been waging war in the Balkans for years, had already been turned away from Constantinople in 1422 due to lack of time and siege equipment. They had inflicted a significant amount of damage to the city walls, which were repaired before 1453. The new sultan, Mohammed II, rebuilt, on the European side of the Bosphorus, the castle of Roumeli Hissar, known at the time as Boghaz-Kezen or "Cutter of the Throat," which stood opposite the older Turkish castle of Anadoli Hissar on the Asian side of the straits. Roumeli Hissar's Black Tower was given two additional levels. The work was completed in less than five months in August 1452. The sultan placed three heavy cannons on the tower from which he could control the straits and destroy Venetian ships.

The next year, Mohammed II advanced on Constantinople with an army estimated to number as many as 150,000 soldiers or as few as 80,000. His siege arsenal included about 100 cannons, some of which were very large. The largest, named Basilica, was built and manned by a Hungarian named Urban. Although descriptions of this monster weapon vary, most agree that it may have reached 9 meters in length and fired a projectile of either 600 or 1,200 pounds—estimates vary, based on the caliber of the weapon—at a range of up to 1.5 kilometers. According to some sources, however, its range was only 50 meters. The huge cannon took two hours to reload and could fire only about seven rounds a day. Charles Oman claims in *The Art of War in the Middle Ages* that the projectile weighed less than 800 pounds. He also points out that Urban had cast 70 other guns for the siege, 11 of which were large enough to fire 500-pound stone balls and 50 large enough to fire 200-pound stone shot. Urban had also designed the guns used by the sultan in the castles rebuilt on the Bosphorus to close the straits. Ironically, his services had been declined by the Byzantine emperor, who had considered his price too steep.

The Turkish artillery was organized into batteries, nine of which consisted of four small guns each, and five of which contained medium weapons that could maintain a more rapid fire. Most of the Turkish artillery did not arrive at Constantinople until several days after the siege had begun. However, it seems that some of the guns at least were even able to fire on Constantinople from as far as Roumeli Hissar.

The Turkish army reached the base of the peninsula facing the landward defenses of Constantinople and began the siege on April 5, 1453. The Byzantine forces numbered only 5,000 soldiers with an additional 2,000 foreign volunteers, mostly Genoese and Venetian. Their artillery was so small in number and size that it did not even match the French armament used in the defense of Harfleur at the time of Henry V's siege earlier in the century.

Before most of the artillery was even in place, the Turks directed their bombardment against the landward defenses, concentrating their efforts against the northern end of the line where a single wall encircled the Blachernae area on the Golden Horn and against a section known as the Mesoteichion where the famed triple walls occupied a section of lower terrain in the Lycus Valley and linked to the wall of the Blachernae. After two days of bombardment, the Turkish guns brought down a section of the Blachernae wall, which was rebuilt during the night. The sultan ordered mining operations and the filling of the moat while he awaited the arrival of the bulk of his artillery. In the meantime, his army attacked two small castles nearby, one of which held out for two days and the other only for a few hours.

When the artillery was finally brought into position on April 12, the bombardment resumed, lasting for over six weeks without a break. Urban's big gun was first used against the Blachernae, then on the outer wall of the Mesoteichion. Unfortunately, an explosion from the gun killed Urban during these operations. The defenders attempted to cushion the walls by suspending sheets of hides and bales of wool in front of them. This method had been used in other sieges against trebuchets, catapults, and rams, but was not an extremely effective deterrent against the Turkish cannons. Steven Runciman claims in *The Fall of Constantinople 1453* (London, 1969), that most of the outer wall was in ruin at the end of the first week, but this may be an exaggeration. Nonetheless, under cover of night the defenders blocked with earth and wood the breaches wrought by the Turkish cannons.

During these operations, the Turkish fleet attempted to break through the chain boom sealing off the Golden Horn. The plan was to attack the single wall along the Golden Horn by landing troops there and

The remains of the walls of Constantinople. (Courtesy of Stephen Wyley.)

using the warehouses as protection. This area had proven vulnerable during the Fourth Crusade of 1204, when the Crusaders had managed to take the city. However, the Turkish landing failed. The first major assault, led by the sultan's elite Janissaries, against the weakened Mesoteichion section took place on April 18. Prior to the attack, the Turks had attempted to fill the moat while the defenders sallied out at night to try and clear it. The Turkish troops carried torches to burn down the makeshift defenses and ladders to attempt an escalade. After a fierce four hour battle, the attack was repulsed and the bombardment resumed. According to Runciman, the bombardments were ceaseless and concentrated particularly on the Blachernae section. The citizens continued to repair the damaged fortifications every night and the effectiveness of the Turkish artillery is questionable because it failed, in fact, to put any section of the wall permanently out of commission, even after days of continued bombardment. On April 21, a section of the Outer Wall, including a tower was reportedly destroyed, but the defenders erected a new palisade on the rubble that evening. Meanwhile, half of the Turkish fleet was hauled overland to the Golden Horn. Morale among the defenders had been buoyed by the unsuccessful Turkish assaults by land and sea, but the lack of food was beginning to take its toll.

The bombardment of the triple walls continued through the first week of May and Urban's damaged monster gun went back into action on May 6. Finally, on May 7 the Turks launched an assault against the Mesoteichion. They charged across the filled moat and threw scaling ladders against a stockade erected on the ruins of the wall. After three hours of battle, the Turks, once again, had to retreat. An attack at the junction of the triple walls and the Blachernae the next day also failed because the walls were too strong.

The Turkish artillery began to pound on the Mesoteichion on May 16, while the Turks assembled a belfry at the height of the Outer Wall in a single night. On May 18, while the belfry was moved forward, the Turks attempted to fill in the moat under its protection to create a crossing point for it. During the night, the defenders planted powder kegs in the moat and the detonation destroyed not only the belfry but also the causeway it was supposed to cross. The next morning the Byzantines repaired their damaged stockade while the Turks built more belfries and their miners tunneled their way toward the walls, concentrating their effort against the Blachernae sector. However, Byzantine counterminers managed to intercept the miners, smoke them out, and flood the mines with water from the moat. The defenders were able to locate all the enemy tunnels because they had captured several Turks in a previous countermine operation and then tortured their captives until they revealed all the mine locations. As a result, the Turks ceased all mining operations. As Runciman summed it up, despite the heavily damaged walls ". . . the huge Turkish army with its magnificent war-engines had achieved very little."

Between May 25 and May 26, the bombardment of the land walls increased in intensity, but to no avail, since repairs were quickly made and the makeshift stockade was reinforced. During the night of May 26, the Turks moved their guns forward and brought up materials to fill the moat. On May 27, they directed their artillery against a stockade of the Mesoteichion and that night they began filling in the moat. On May 28, the bombardment stopped and the Turks rested. That evening, they began filling in the remainder of the moat and moved up their weapons and equipment. The attack began in the early hours of the morning. The Turks launched diversionary attacks all along the land walls while the main attack hit the Mesoteichion area. The first attempt at escalade was repelled in the darkness, but it was soon followed by a second assault. After sustaining heavy losses, the Turks broke through the stockade through a breach opened by the monster gun, but they were soon driven out by the defenders. Naval attacks by the Turks against the walls along the Golden Horn also failed. A third attack on the Mesoteichion was launched by the Janissaries, who struck at the exhausted defenders who were by then in their fifth hour of combat that morning.

At this time a group of Turks near the Blachernae followed a group of defenders who had launched a raid outside the walls. As they withdrew through their sally port, one of the Greeks forgot to bar the door. Fifty Turks entered the unlocked position and were soon followed by more. The defenders finally panicked. Meanwhile, the Genoese Giovanni Giustiniani, one of the key leaders in the defense, was wounded while defending the walls and had to be removed from the battle through a gate in the inner wall. At the sight of his evacuation his Genoese troops panicked and fled through the same gate. At the same time, the Janissaries, urged by the sultan, renewed their attack and by sheer numbers overwhelmed the remaining defenders. Reaching the virtually undefended inner wall, they began to fan out behind the defenders still on the outer wall, gaining the upper hand.

It seems that the turning point in the defense of Constantinople was the moment the gate was left unbarred and a key leader was wounded and removed within sight of his men. Although cannons most certainly contributed to the victory, only these two fortuitous events and force of numbers ultimately carried the day.

Thus the triple walls of Constantinople cannot have been as obsolete or useless as has often been claimed, especially since they had been modified to meet the demands of changing siege technology. One of the modifications that presaged the Renaissance was the lower wall, which formed the scarp of the moat and was a form of fausse braie, a fighting position in advance of the main walls that helped protect its base from artillery fire and other weapons. Although the Turks were able to smash down sections of this outer wall by concentrated fire, the defenders were able to build new palisades on its rubble and continue to defend the position. The main weakness in the plan for the defense of Constantinople lay mostly in the shortage of troops, which left the inner wall undefended. Once the Turks managed to break through the outer wall, there was no one to stop them at the inner wall. Had the inner walls been manned, it is doubtful the Turks would have carried the day.

———————— ❧❧ ————————

Further remains of the walls of Constantinople.
(Courtesy of Stephen Wyley)

ALHAMBRA OF GRANADA. *A keystone arch.*

The Siege of Fortifications during the Reconquista

Artillery weapons were not new to the 15th century. They had already been used in the previous century, but with no great success. Some of the earliest accounts of artillery action against fortifications date from the Reconquista. Albert McJoynt in his introduction to his edited edition of *The Art of War in Spain* (London, 1995) notes that Ismail I, the Nasrid sultan of Granada, had used cannons of unknown type in his siege of Huescar in 1324 and of Baeza a year later. No mention is made of the effectiveness of these weapons, however, it is possible that their noise and smoke alone may have had a demoralizing effect on the defenders. After all, even Urban, the Hungarian cannon maker, had cautioned the Turks not to panic when they heard the noise and saw the smoke during a demonstration of one of his cannons.

In 1407, the Muslims who held the small fortified town of Zahara located on an almost inaccessible height, surrendered after observing the damage inflicted by a few rounds fired from the besiegers' cannons. Certainly, the damage at Zahara could not have been nearly as extensive as at Constantinople which was bombarded for weeks with larger artillery nearly half a century later.

The final phase of the Reconquista was led by Isabella and Ferdinand against the Islamic kingdom of Granada during the last half of the 15th century. At the end of February 1482, Spanish forces launched a raid deep into the Caliph's territory, against the fortified town of Alhama, located between Malaga and Granada. The attack on Alhama was carried out by Captain Ortega, at the head of a contingent of 30 escaladores or scalers. The Spaniards counted on the fact that the defenders, deep in Moorish territory and atop a lofty height, would feel too secure to maintain a high state of alert. Under the cover of darkness, Ortega and his men scaled the mountain and the citadel's walls with their ladders and succeeded in eliminating the garrison. The town's citizens resisted even after Ortega's men opened the gates to the approaching Spanish army, but to no avail. The town was pillaged and sacked. A few days later, a Granadan army of 53,000 soldiers came to the rescue. However, William Prescott, in *The Art of War in Spain*, said it came with no artillery. In the meantime, the Spanish had repaired the breaches in the town's fortifications and prepared to defend their new trophy.

After losing over 2,000 men in futile assaults, the Granadans settled for a prolonged siege, cutting off the river supplying most of the town's water. A Spanish relief force broke up the siege after three weeks, but no sooner had it departed, leaving Alhama in the hands of a frontier militia, then the Granadan army returned, this time with cannons. Ferdinand sent another relief force, which broke up the siege again in mid-May. Through it all, the Moorish artillery seems to have had little effect on the outcome.

The sieges that followed were on a grander scale. An army of nearly 90,000 Spanish men proceeded to isolate Granada from the rest of its holdings. The city of Ronda was attacked in 1485. After a massive artillery barrage, which set buildings on fire and breached its walls, Ferdinand offered the city generous terms of surrender, which were accepted. The Spaniards continued the same politics in their reconquest of the remainder of the peninsula. Most towns faced with the choice between prolonged siege or graceful capitulation, chose the latter, avoiding thereby a costly battle. During the year following the fall of Ronda, the Spaniards assembled a force of over 50,000 troops to continue with the Reconquista.

At the time, points out Prescott, the kingdom of Granada was still a power to be reckoned with. Defended by mountain barriers and heavily fortified towns, it was able to field an army of up to 100,000 men. Its three main provincial garrisons of about 10,000 men each were located at Ronda, Malaga, and Guadix. The Alhambra of Granada alone could hold 40,000 soldiers within its walls. Nonetheless, the Moslems were not able to withstand the relentless advance of the Christian armies. Ronda and Malaga, to the west of Granada, fell first. After that, the Christian forces effectively sealed the remaining ports of the kingdom.

Although the Spanish forces used artillery during their sieges, it does not appear that this sufficed in bringing about their final victory. In general, the Moorish fortifications consisted of a walled town with an internal strongpoint known as the alcazaba, which was usually the most powerful and impressive part of the site. The town walls were usually neither as strong, thick, nor high as the alcazaba's. In addition, a large portion of the town walls usually covered the less accessible sections of a position on a mountain or hill and were, therefore, not likely to be very thick. According to Prescott, "The walls which encompassed their cities, although lofty, were not of

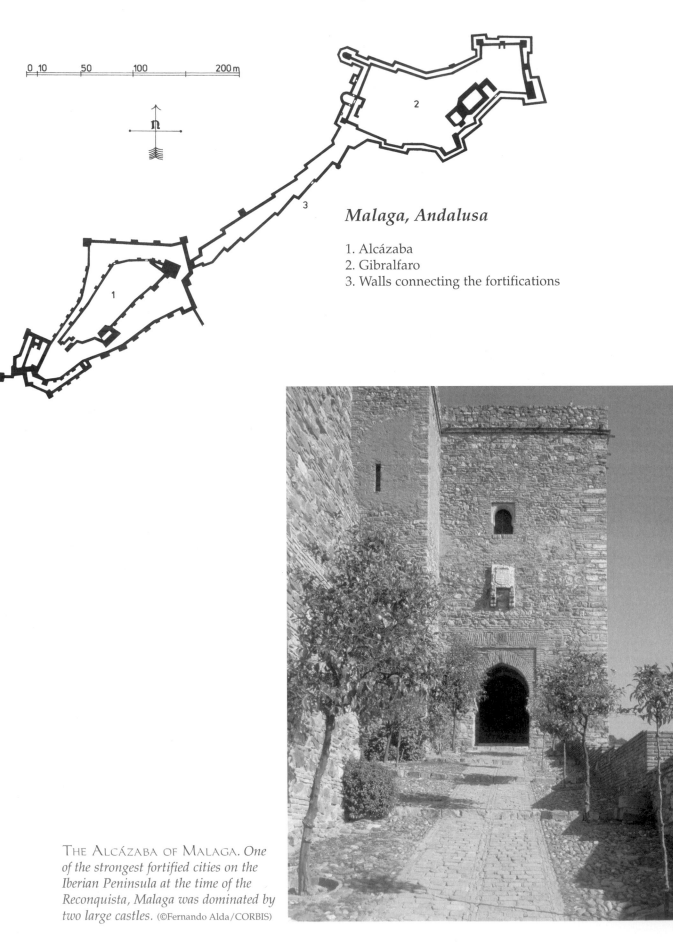

Malaga, Andalusa

1. Alcázaba
2. Gibralfaro
3. Walls connecting the fortifications

THE ALCÁZABA OF MALAGA. *One of the strongest fortified cities on the Iberian Peninsula at the time of the Reconquista, Malaga was dominated by two large castles.* (©Fernando Alda/CORBIS)

Remains of the palace at Granada, Spain.

sufficient thickness to withstand long the assaults of these formidable engines [Spanish heavy artillery]." Prescott also believes that the Moors lacked similar weapons to keep the Spanish at bay, even though they did employ some artillery in their fortifications.

Prescott also claims that Isabella and Ferdinand were convinced that artillery was absolutely necessary to reduce the last Moorish strongholds of Granada and that they imported large quantities of powder and balls from Portugal, Sicily, and Flanders. However, the weapons they acquired do not appear to have been as large, effective, or numerous as the Turks' in the siege of Constantinople. At the siege of Baeza in 1489, the Spaniards had only 20 slightly antiquated cannons. The balls they fired were sometimes iron, but usually marble. According to Prescott, the marble balls, which were made from material quarried around Baeza itself, weighed up to 175 pounds. Although these stone balls were unlikely to have inflicted much damage on the walls, they certainly could have had a demoralizing effect when they shattered behind the walls, bursting into fragments with the same effect as a small anti-personnel bomb of the 20th century.

Malaga, one of the strongest fortified cities in the kingdom, and its harbor were enclosed by a formidable set of walls. They were dominated by two castles, one of which was the alcázaba. Nestled at the base of

the mountain overlooking the city, Malaga's alcázaba was surrounded by double walls and included a palace, added in the latter half of the 11th century. It was linked by a set of walls to the Gibralfaro Castle on top of the mountain. This complex consisted of 110 large towers, 22 small ones, and 12 fortified gates. The towers were only slightly higher than the curtain walls and included positions for artillery.

The armies of Isabella and Ferdinand marched upon Malaga in May 1487 and defeated the Granadan forces that came to meet them, driving them back into their fortress. The Christians built their own defensive positions to keep the Muslims isolated in their defenses and their navy sealed off the harbor. Artillery pounded the city wall, soon opening a breach. The Spanish troops tried to storm through, but were held in check. The Moors tried to relieve the city from the east, but few of them managed to break through. Ferdinand, no longer concerned about preserving the city's buildings, set his heavy artillery into action for the first time, hammering the city until his ammunition ran out and he had to wait for new supplies. In the meantime, the Moors did not sit idly by. They responded with their own artillery fire and with constant raids against the Christian camp. Months of siege failed to bring victory. By this time the Moors were beginning to suffer from shortages of food. In August King Ferdinand asked his engineer,

Francisco Ramirez, to build belfries and tunnel toward the city walls. Some of the mines were to penetrate beyond the walls, while others were to bring them down. The Moors responded with more raids and countermines that wreaked havoc on the Spaniards.

Finally, one of Ramirez's mines managed to reach one of the city's wall towers and was filled with gunpowder and detonated. This, according to Prescott, was the first recorded instance of gunpowder use in mines. The explosion forced the Moors to retreat across a bridge that led into the city. In the meantime, the Spaniards took the tower, which housed a cannon that dominated this bridge. Shortly after this disaster, the mayor withdrew to the Gibralfaro and allowed his citizens to seek terms. The Spanish accepted the surrender of the city and the alcázaba in mid-August and the Gibralfaro's on the day they occupied the city. The Spanish artillery probably caused more damage to the city than the fortifications. In addition, the shortage of supplies and the loss of a key tower to mining no doubt demoralized the garrison to the point of surrender.

In 1489, after clearing the Moorish-held coast, the Spanish forces laid siege to the city of Baeza which was defended by 20,000 men. Its ammunition running low, Baeza surrendered in December, after half a year of siege. As a result of this siege, the well-defended cities of Almería and Guadix agreed to favorable terms and gave up with no resistance. In the spring of 1491, Ferdinand marched upon Granada itself to begin the final campaign of the war. A sally by Granadan forces early in the siege was smashed by the Christian forces. Ferdinand and Isabella proceed-

ed to build a large and comfortable camp for their army to endure the winter. Finally, realizing that his situation was hopeless, the Muslim king capitulated and the Spanish took control of the city in January 1492.

The fall of the Kingdom of Granada was more significant than the fall of Constantinople, as far as the history of fortifications and sieges is concerned. At Constantinople a massive Turkish army had faced a few thousand defenders and had resorted to almost every type of siege technique to take the city. Despite an effective concentration of artillery against weak points, many days of bombardment, and the destruction of some towers and sections of walls, final victory did not come within the Turks' grasp until two completely fortuitous events took place: an unbarred door and the fall of a key officer in front of his own men. The fall of the kingdom of Granada, on the other hand, had nothing fortuitous about it. During the final years of the Reconquista, both sides were able to muster relatively large armies and the defenders were in much greater strength in their fortified cities than the Byzantines had been in Constantinople. In addition, the Spanish Muslims were also noted for their skill with artillery and used it to great effect in their fortifications. However, as in Constantinople, artillery did not particularly favor the besiegers and was not an important factor in bringing the great Moorish cities of Malaga, Baeza, and, finally Granada, to their knees. Only at Malaga did a major Spanish assault succeed in gaining a key foothold, however its victory was due to an innovative use of gunpowder in a mine rather than artillery. As in Constantinople, breaches in the walls produced by the guns failed to bring about a victory. What was demonstrated in the Spanish campaign, was the importance of large garrisons to defend fortifications and seal off enemy breakthroughs. No longer could a few hundred soldiers successfully defend a fortified town or city, but, by the same token, neither could a small besieging army hope to take a position by achieving a breach with trebuchets, cannons, or mines.

A view of the Islamic fortress from the palace in Granada, Spain.

The Siege and Fall of Rhodes

The siege of Rhodes in 1480 is another important event in the history of fortifications. By then, the Ottoman Turks had mastered siege warfare after bringing an end to the Byzantine empire in 1453 and moving into the Balkans. However, there were still many key island bases in the Mediterranean that remained under the control of the Crusaders during the waning years of the Middle Ages. The Knights of St. John in particular had built fortifications and watchtowers on several of these islands to protect their main base at Rhodes, in the Eastern Mediterranean. In addition to the port and city, which constituted the key positions, Rhodes boasted 30 castles maintained by the Knights of St. John. Even though several of these islands were raided by the Turks after 1453, Rhodes remained steadfastly in the Knights' hands. Although the Turks were not able to bring any of their monster cannons by sea, they could bring a large force and adequate siege equipment to besiege the city.

When the Knights of St. John had taken over Rhodes in 1309, the city was defended by Byzantine fortifications consisting of high walls with square towers at regular intervals and a wide moat. Although these defenses were old, they were still formidable. Before 1450, most of the walls of the city had been rebuilt to a thickness of two to four meters and a low wall, like the one at Constantinople, was also added along the scarp. In the mid-15th century, polygonal bulwarks were further added to the square towers. The two artificial harbors were protected by towers located at the end of the moles at their entrances. The Tower of St. Nicholas was built in 1361 to guard the entrance to the harbor known as the Galley Port. The Tower of St. Angelo, erected in 1436 at the end of the eastern mole, secured the entrance to the harbor referred to as the Commercial Port. The city walls, towers, and fortified gates were crowned with machicoulis and hoardings. The Knights divided the walls into sectors and assigned their defense to men of different nationalities. Each sector was named after the country or province of its defenders and is known by that name to this very day. According to Eric Brockman, who wrote *The Two Sieges of Rhodes* (New York, 1969), the fortifications of Rhodes may have been the first to include gun ports, but this would be difficult to prove. Before the Turks began their campaign, three new towers were built and a boom consisting of a large chain was setup to protect the Commercial Port.

Old plans of the city defenses revealed to the Turks by a traitor contained a great deal of misinformation, but accurately indicated that the Auvergne section, the central tract on the western side of the city, was in a state of decay.

The campaign opened in the winter of 1479 when a Turkish reconnaissance force raided the island. In the spring of 1480, as it became increasingly clear that the Turks would return in full force, the island's population moved into the city and the defenses were prepared. The defending army consisted of a total of about 4,000 men, 600 of whom were Knights of St. John, 1,500 mercenaries, and the remainder militiamen. The Turkish fleet showed up at the end of May and landed its troops, uncontested, on the beaches. The Turkish army was led by Misac Pasha aided by Master George, a gunner who had served the Christians at Constantinople. A battery of three large guns was set up to the north of the city to bombard the Tower of St. Nicholas in the hopes of opening the harbor to the fleet.

The Tower of St. Nicholas, a circular structure over 17 meters in diameter, was surrounded by another fortification and mounted cannons on two levels. This small fort was heavily pounded with the stone balls of the Turkish guns, but, despite heavy damage, it was repaired by the garrison. In June, after 10 days of bombardment, the Turks launched an amphibious attack that failed, taking heavy casualties. Meanwhile, they also began operations against the southeastern section of the city wall known as Italy.

The Turks used all the tools within their means, including several sizes of cannons and even trebuchets, to bring down the walls. The machicolations, which were the most vulnerable parts of the defenses, and many sections of wall were heavily battered. Nine towers were brought down and the Grand Master's Palace was destroyed. The Turkish weapons wrought havoc among the structures behind the walls. By June 7, the heavy artillery was moved against the section of wall by the Jewish Quarter. Grand Master Pierre d' Aubusson ordered the evacuation of the area and prepared new positions to counter a breach. The Turks dug zigzag trenches to approach the moat and attempted to fill it in near the Italian section. The Italians excavated their own mine into the moat, removed the Turks' stones, and brought them back into the city to help build the new positions.

Rhodes, 1480 to 1522

1. Fort St. Nicholas
2. Tower of Naillac
3. Tower of St. Angelo
4. Arsenal
5. Palace of the Grand Master
G.P.–The Gallery Port
C.P.–The Commercial Port

Defense sectors by nationality:
　P.C.–Post of Castile
　P.I.–Post of Italy
　P.P.–Post of Provence
　P.E.–Post of England
　P.Ar–Post of Aragon
　P.Au–Post of Auvergne
　P.G.–Post of Germany
　P.F.–Post of France

(Sketch by J. E. Kaufmann)

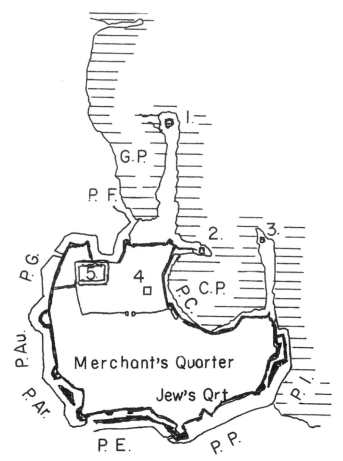

RHODES

FORT ST. NICHOLAS, RHODES.

(© Corel)

On June 13, the Turks began a heavy bombardment against the mole and Fort St. Nicholas. In the meantime, from a belfry they covered the progress of a team of engineers with missiles and handguns, while they struggled to throw a pontoon bridge across the harbor towards Fort St. Nicholas. They launched an amphibious night assault on the evening of June 18, but the bridge was destroyed by the garrison of the tower almost as soon as it was completed. By midmorning, after hours of combat, the Turks had once again been repulsed after taking heavy losses.

By June 24, the Turkish forces managed to move closer to the Italy section, placed their artillery near the moat, and proceeded to pound the wall into rubble. The Italians countered by launching a sortie from their tunnel in the moat, damaging the Turkish positions and destroying several guns. Late in July, the Italy section of the wall was almost in ruins, but the interior defenses were ready. The Turkish attack came on July 27. Like at Constantinople, the irregulars, followed by the elite Janissaries, led the way over the breach in an attempt to destroy the stockade built on the ruins of the wall. They took the Tower of Italy, advanced on the retrenchments which were part of a trap set for them by the defenders, and took heavy losses once again. The Turks lost about 9,000 men in the siege and half of the remaining 70,000-man invasion force were wounded. In August the siege was lifted and the invasion force withdrew. The medieval fortifications of Rhodes stood triumphant, despite the pounding they had received from the most modern weapons in the Turks possession.

After the siege, d'Aubusson set out to modernize the fortifications of Rhodes. Fort St. Nicholas' two towers were encircled by a thick casemate designed to mount artillery. After 1480 improvements were made to the Tower of Naillac which had been built earlier in the century to seal the other end of the Commercial Port. This tower had walls 3.7 meters thick and was 37 meters high. In places two moats formed part of the defenses, and a tenaille—fortification placed in front of the curtain wall—and other features characteristic of Renaissance fortifications were also added. Behind the old Byzantine walls several towers were enlarged and thickened. The thin walls of the fausse brai were protected by the tenaille in some sections. Early forms of bastions and caponiers appeared to provide enfilading fire. According to Athanassios Migos, in an article on these fortifications for FORT magazine, the Italian engineer Fabrizio del Carretto, who worked on these defenses, also designed curved parapet merlons on one section of the wall, a form that was later found in English coastal forts like Deal.

In July 1522, the Turks attacked Rhodes once again, bringing a large army to take on a small force of 500 Knights, 1,000 mercenaries, and 500 militiamen (according to some estimates there were actually over 6,000 defenders). The Turks began the bombardment of the modernized fortress, but their heavy batteries were unable to inflict much damage on Fort St. Nicholas, whose gunners replied with deadly counterfire. The Turkish artillery opened breaches on the city walls and sappers tunneled over 50 mines towards the walls by September, but the defenders matched them with countermines. On September 4, a mine was detonated under the English section and a ground assault gained a foothold, which was fiercely contested. Additional mine detonations were less successful. More attacks followed throughout September. The siege continued until December, when the Grand Master capitulated as his guns ran low on ammunition and he ran out of men to defend against further breaches. But the 100,000-man Turkish invasion force suffered over 50 percent casualties.

Despite more up-to-date fortifications than in 1480 and a larger garrison, Rhodes was unable to hold out against this larger Turkish army. Part of the problem may be attributed to the fact that the more modern fortifications required more defenders to effectively defend them, and these were not available—the age of the castle was coming to an end.

Alcázaba of Saxe, Spain

An Age Ends and Walls Move Downward

During most of the Middle Ages, a small number of men were enough to defend a high wall, which was able to withstand attacks from more ancient siege weapons such as catapults. The trébuchet, which became the main heavy artillery of the 13th century, was able to easily smash the battlements of a high curtain or tower, especially if it was large. Tunnels or mines beneath the same walls could also severely weaken or destroy the foundations. It was partly the combination of mining and the trebuchet that led to the creation of heavier, thicker walls in the 13th century. Although these 13th-century walls were still vulnerable to mining and bombardment by trebuchets and heavy cannons, they took a great deal of punishment before they came tumbling down.

Many of the sieges of the 11th and 12th centuries did not involve large numbers of combatants. When a breach was made, the defenders usually could match the assaulting troops trying to break through. As siege armies became larger, the besiegers needed only to effect one breach in order to prevail by sheer weight of numbers. To counter this, walls were made thicker and other architectural improvements were introduced. These advancements, in turn, triggered a proliferation of siege techniques and machines, and the creation of siege specialists such as miners, sappers, and engineers. This growth and specialization in the art of the siege prompted a corresponding progress and diversification in the art of defense. If the walls were built too high, when they fell they created a mound of rubble too high for the defenders to climb and hold securely. On the other hand, if the assaulting force managed to lodge itself on the rubble, it would be able to look down at the defenders and have them at its mercy. The solution was for the defender to build a line of interior walls and to lower the height of the curtain walls. The resultant concentric walls allowed the defender to rush troops into any breach in the outer wall. However, this remedy required larger garrisons, which was not always practical or affordable. Other solutions included various architectural designs that allowed enfilading fires along the walls and the moat. These adaptations can be observed at Rhodes, which shows a series of modifications instituted between 1480 and 1522 that illustrate the evolution of military architecture from the Middle Ages to the Renaissance.

The high walls of the medieval period were not phased out simply because they were vulnerable to artillery, but also because they were not designed to accommodate the larger and more efficient artillery of the 16th century in a very efficacious manner. Although it is commonly believed that cannons were not used effectively in defense of medieval fortifications like those of Constantinople because they weakened their walls, the fact is that cannons could be and were used in castles. The Moorish cities of Malaga, Ronda, Baeza, and Granada, for instance, had integrated artillery in their defenses.

Many of the medieval curtain walls simply did not have enough room on top to mount a cannon, whose recoil would probably have thrown it right off the battlements. In some cases, especially in towers, special platforms were prepared to accommodate artillery. In addition, larger loops were added to the walls for small cannons or guns. Medium and heavy artillery was, in fact, more effective against enemy artillery than sorties by the garrison, even when the besiegers protected their artillery with mantlets and entrenchments. Guns on a medieval wall could generally match the range of the cannons on the ground and inflict severe damage on the attackers and their makeshift defenses.

There were, however, two main reasons for lowering the walls. The first was that mining and the use of the trebuchet and cannons made it necessary for the defenders to be able to quickly rush troops in large numbers to hold breaches in the battlements. The emphasis is on the battlements rather than the wall itself, because, once the battlements were in ruins the condition of the remainder of the wall was irrelevant. The second reason for lowering the walls was to accommodate artillery. Generally, the higher the walls, no matter how thick at the base, the less room there was on the battlements for cannons. A lower wall offered more space for guns. More importantly, artillery mounted high on the walls was not very effective at short range because it covered a relatively small area nullifying the value of a low trajectory fire. Guns placed at a lower level have a grazing trajectory that covers the area between them and the target. Thus placing artillery at a lower level increased not only the chances of hitting possible targets, but also anyone or anything standing between the gun and the target. This also increased the effectiveness of the defender's guns against a mass of assaulting troops.

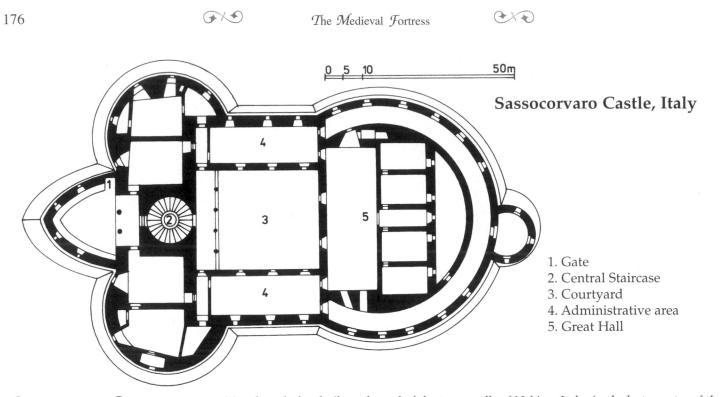

Sassocorvaro Castle, Italy

1. Gate
2. Central Staircase
3. Courtyard
4. Administrative area
5. Great Hall

SASSOCORVARO CASTLE *was a transitional castle fort built at the end of the town walls of Urbino, Italy, in the last quarter of the 15th century. It was designed to mount artillery and also to resist the new gunpowder artillery. The result was a virtual citadel with high thick rounded walls and towers.*

The changes that led from medieval to Renaissance fortifications did not happen overnight, any more than the Middle Ages ended on a certain day and the Renaissance began on the next. On the contrary, they took place gradually, over a period of a hundred years. The medieval fortifications, at least most of those built from the 13th century onward, did not become obsolete because of the appearance of any single weapon. Instead, they were simply modified, in most cases, and continued in use for many years. Such was the case of the Tower of Constance at Aigues Mortes, France, which was adapted for the use of cannons in the 16th century when its crenelated parapet was replaced with a thicker one with curved merlons, like those of Rhodes. In addition, it acquired trapezoidal embrasures that gave the artillery a wider firing angle. This type of renovation was done on similar large towers throughout France and other countries late in the 15th century and even as late as the 16th century. Many castles in England were similarly adapted for artillery, however, most of those located in Wales were allowed to fall into disrepair.

But during the 17th-century English Civil War, many of these Welsh castles were repaired and put back into service. Gun platforms for musketeers and cannons were added and, in some cases, earthworks were hastily raised for further defense. Even at this late date castles were still too strong to be taken by direct assault without a prolonged siege. The techniques used in these sieges were the same as those in vogue in the last centuries of the Middle Ages, and so were the results. However, in the 17th century, few direct assaults were undertaken during a siege. The preferred methods of bringing down a stronghold were starvation and mining. In the few instances where an assault did take place, it was launched only after a heavy cannon had created a breach in the wall. The majority of castles did not fall until after a siege of three or more months in spite of the new and more effective heavy artillery. In *A Nation Under Siege* (London, 1991), Peter Gaunt observes that many castles like those built by Edward I in northern Wales sustained little damage, even after a long and heavy bombardment. Harlech, for instance, resisted for nine months. Most of the damage to the Welsh castles was wreaked by the victors after the end of the Civil War through intentional demolitions.

Where the Welsh castles and French towers exemplify the process of adapting existing works with little or no major changes, the fortifications of Rhodes illustrate the transition from medieval to Renaissance fortifications through extensive rebuilding and renova-

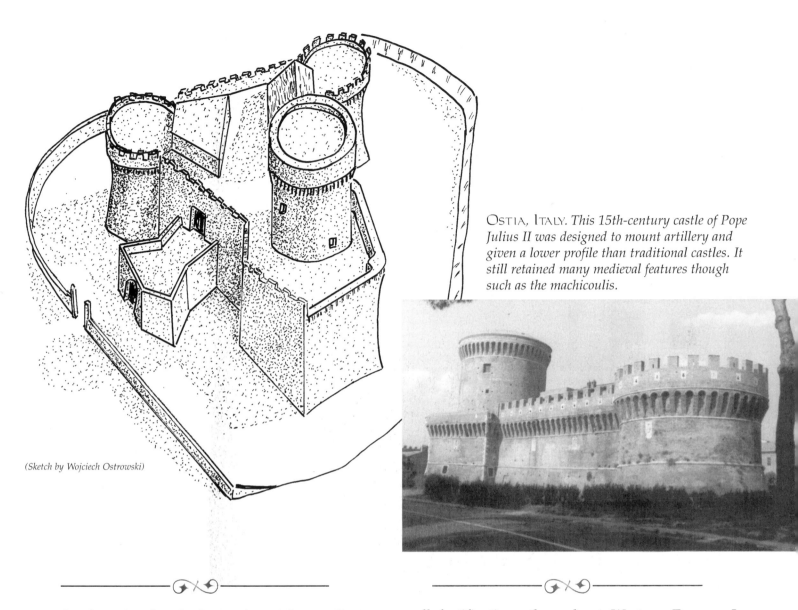

(Sketch by Wojciech Ostrowski)

OSTIA, ITALY. *This 15th-century castle of Pope Julius II was designed to mount artillery and given a lower profile than traditional castles. It still retained many medieval features though such as the machicoulis.*

tion. On the other hand, the castles of Sarzanello in Italy, Salses in France, and Deal in England, built between the 15th and the 16th century, represent the transition between the medieval castle and the modern fort. Francesco Giamberti da Sangallo, the founder of a long line of Italian architects, who designed Sarzanello in the 14th century, was not the first to lead the way in adaption. He was preceded by Francesco di Giorgio Martini, who designed Sassocorvaro not long before. Sassocorvaro included certain features like an early form of bastion whose design was improved upon and incorporated into Sarzanello. The low walls of Sarzanello gave it a Renaissance appearance, despite the presence of machicoulis. The fort was laid out in an unusual triangular shape that included three large drum towers at each corner placed in such a manner that their artillery could enfilade the curtain walls. This design was later adopted in a number of

small fortifications throughout Western Europe. In 1497, a triangular outwork was built in front of Sarzanello to protect its entrance. This was to be one of the first ravelins ever built. It had a similar function as a barbican and was linked to the fort by a bridge. Two of the drum towers of Sarzanello received new and thicker battlements for mounting artillery. The entire position was surrounded by a large dry moat and sat on a hilltop.

The castle at Ostia, built by one of Giamberti's sons for Pope Julius II, also included a large corner tower. The angular bastions added to Castel Sant'Angelo were built by Giamberti's other son. While the Giambertis innovations continued to be popular throughout the century, other improvements were also introduced until the medieval fortifications that could not be further modified were simply replaced by new ones.

SARZANELLO CASTLE, ITALY. *This triangular castle was designed in the 14th century by Francesco Giamberti da Sangallo. It is an example of the transition from medieval castle to fort for military fortifications. The tower with machicoulis can be seen (right). The triangular shaped bastion (below), one of the oldest examples of a ravelin, was built to cover the entrance, which is accessed by a bridge over the moat. (above) Another bridge crosses from the fort to the ravelin and is the only access to the ravelin.*

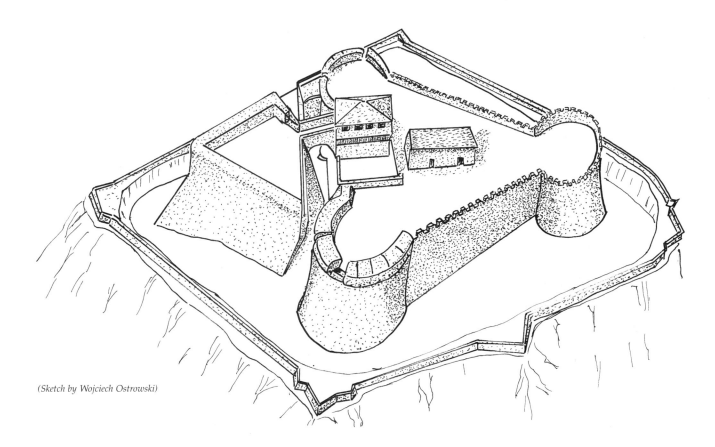

(Sketch by Wojciech Ostrowski)

Sarzanello Castle, Italy

1. Entrance
2. Guard Post
3. Dry Moat
4. Outwork–ravelin
5. Drawbridge
6. Keep
7. Quarters
8. Parapet and covered way of Renaissance fortification

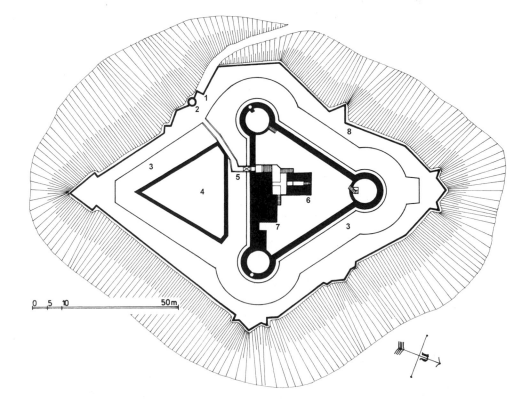

Fort at Salses, France

1. Moat
2. Chatelet with drawbridge
2a. Drawbridge
3. Demi-Lune with positions for artillery
4. Main gate
5. Courtyard
6. Well
7. Keep

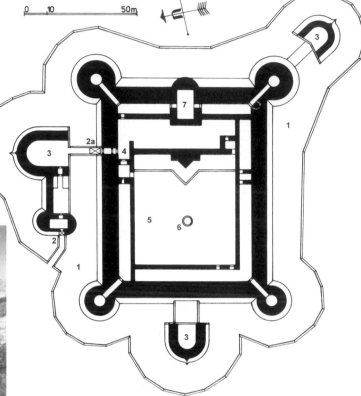

SALSES *was one of the first large castles converted for the age of artillery. It had a low profile due to a deep moat that formed parts of the walls and the shortness of its dominant tower.*

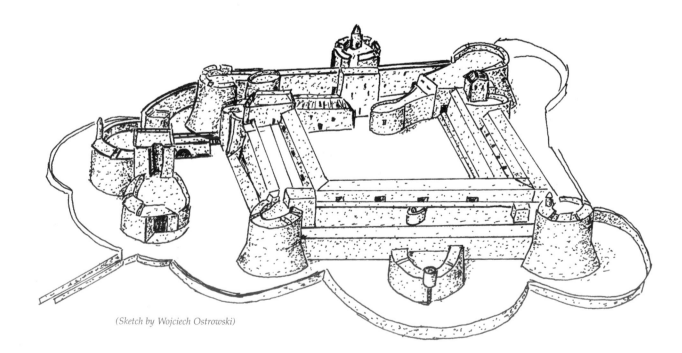

(Sketch by Wojciech Ostrowski)

CEUTA. *This Portuguese outpost built in late 15th-century on the North African coast represents a more modern generation of fortifications with bastions that were designed for artillery.*

The fort at Salses in the Roussillon, north of the Pyrenees, was designed and built by Ramiro López, a Spanish engineer, after the older castle and fortified village in the area were destroyed in a French raid. López designed this new fort for horizontal rather than vertical defense. The work was begun in 1497 and completed by 1503, when the fort was besieged by Francis I of France. After the French artillery destroyed the battlements during the siege, important modifications made to the fort and its upper works were reduced in size. López included large drum towers on the corners in his design and equipped them with artillery gun ports to enfilade the curtains. The battlements were also curved to deflect missiles and projectiles. A large five-level keep, with corners protruding into the courtyard, was built into the curtain wall. In front of it in the courtyard stood a defensive wall. The entire rectangular fort, which measured 115 x 90 meters, sat in a moat 12 meters wide and 7 meters deep, only its battlements on the curtains walls and four medieval-like drum towers were exposed to enemy fire. The moat could be flooded with water from natural springs located in the vicinity. The walls, which were originally 10 meters thick, were reinforced by the talus or batter on the lower part. The battlements above were a little less than 5 meters thick. After the siege of 1503, the thickness of the walls was increased to 14 meters. Two square curtain towers mounted cannons. Ravelins or demilunes, one of which led into an adjacent entrance

châtelet (a work built at the entrance of a passage to a fort), were added to protect the curtains. Each demilune was attached to the fort by a vaulted corridor and comprised an interior chamber and gun rooms equipped with a lift to carry ammunition to the guns placed on an artillery terrace above.

The interior of the fort of Salses was lined on three sides with arcaded buildings forming a gallery on the lower floor and a terrace on the upper floor. Below ground were stables for 100 horses and magazines and galleries for countermines. The fort, intended for a garrison of almost 1,500 men—enough to seal any breach by force of arms—held three times that number during some campaigns. It shared few characteristics with medieval castles.

In 1538, Henry VIII of England, fearing a French invasion, ordered the construction of a group of coastal forts in the region known as The Downs. The king, who was largely responsible for their design, appointed Stephan von Haschenperg, a Bohemian engineer, to oversee their construction. The so-called "castles," built between 1539 and 1540, included Deal, Walmer, and Sandown, with two more in Cornwall. They were the last fortifications to incorporate a central keep designed for fire arms and artillery. Deal, the largest of the three, was equipped with 145 embrasures for firearms and artillery positions on its bastions and towers. The battlements were rounded to deflect projectiles like at Sarzanello and Salses. The central keep and its six surrounding semicircular bas-

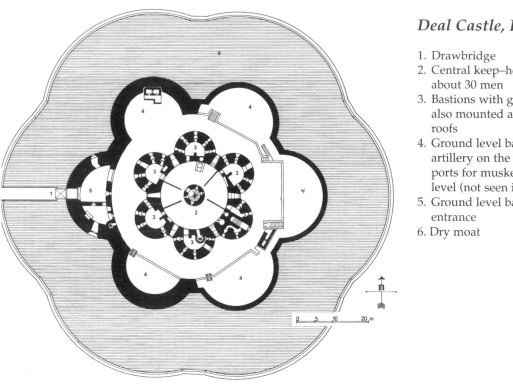

Deal Castle, England

1. Drawbridge
2. Central keep–held garrison of about 30 men
3. Bastions with gun ports and also mounted artillery on their roofs
4. Ground level bastions with artillery on the roof and gun ports for musketeers at moat level (not seen in illustration)
5. Ground level bastion with entrance
6. Dry moat

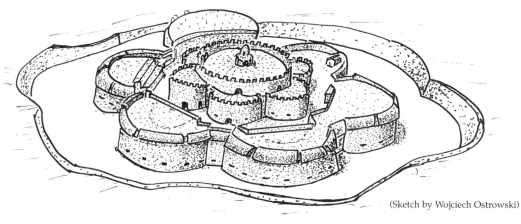

(Sketch by Wojciech Ostrowski)

DEAL CASTLE *was one of the first fortifications built for the age of artillery. Like the other coastal positions built by Henry VIII, it is actually a 16th-century fort and not a castle.*

tions, one of which housed the gatehouse were set in a dry moat. The outer works consisted of six more bastions that formed an outer curtain and were surrounded by a wide moat not far from the beach. The keep included the quarters of the garrison of only 25 men. The main artillery positions on the bastions, the tower, and in the walls faced toward the sea. The central keep bore little relation to the medieval fortifications, especially since the idea of a keep as the last and possibly strongest point of defense in the castle had been abandoned centuries earlier. Henry VIII's "castles" were the first true artillery forts, where almost all of the elements of the medieval fortifications had been modified beyond recognition and which were designed to allow the defender to take full advantage of cannons.

Although the age of castle building was coming to an end in Europe in the early 16th century, it witnessed a brief revival shortly thereafter in East Africa. In the 15th century, the Portuguese moved along the coast of Africa in their quest for a new route to the East, first establishing fortifications along the Morrocan coast. These Portuguese fortifications were more representative of the Renaissance than the Middle Ages, as can be observed at places like Ceuta, in the north, and as far east as Mombassa on the Indian Ocean.

In 1557, the first Portuguese expedition reached Abyssinia in an effort to help the supposed heir of legendary Prester John in his struggles against the Islamic armies of the Arab general Grañ. During the next century, the Portuguese helped the Christian emperors of Ethiopia to build massive high-walled castles in their capital, Gondar.

The first of these castles, built for Emperor Fasilidas, consisted of four large circular corner towers, a curtain wall, and a keep that stood against one of the walls between two towers and served as the imperial residence. Fasilidas' castle and those of his descendants were more medieval than Renaissance in design, even though most were built well into the 17th century.

In the New World, the European settlers, as they advanced inland, erected wooden stockade-type fortifications with towers somewhat similar to those of the first half of the Middle Ages, but they built more modern works on the coasts. The difference was due to the phenomenon of measured response. Simpler fortifications were sufficient to deal with Native Americans, whose armament was less sophisticated, whereas on the coast the colonists had to fight off their European rivals, who were as well-armed as they were themselves.

Thus the age of the castle waned by the end of the 15th century, giving way to the age of artillery fort. As the new age of fortifications dawned late in the 15th century, some castles continued to hold sway so that for the next few centuries both modern fortifications and castles continued to play an important role in warfare.

CASTLE OF GONDAR,
ETHIOPIA

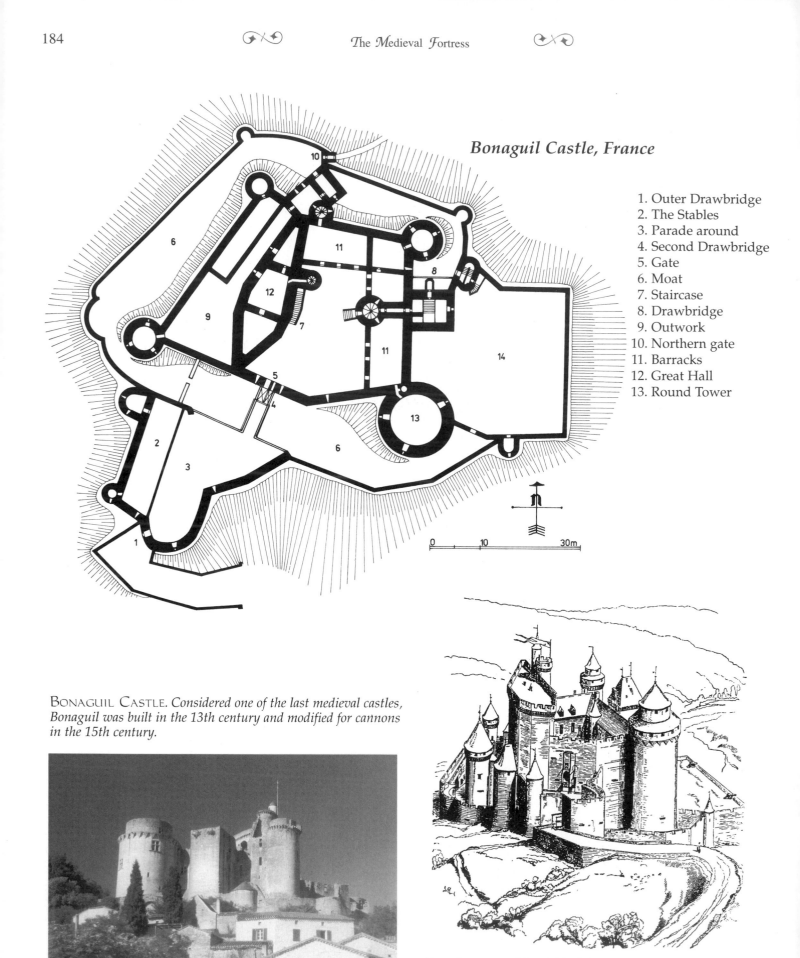

Bonaguil Castle, France

1. Outer Drawbridge
2. The Stables
3. Parade around
4. Second Drawbridge
5. Gate
6. Moat
7. Staircase
8. Drawbridge
9. Outwork
10. Northern gate
11. Barracks
12. Great Hall
13. Round Tower

BONAGUIL CASTLE. *Considered one of the last medieval castles, Bonaguil was built in the 13th century and modified for cannons in the 15th century.*

(Illustration courtesy of Greenhill Books)

Top Rankings in Medieval Siege Warfare

Most Feared and Effective Aggressors in Medieval Warfare

From catapulting the heads of prisoners into a fortification to using the children of a region as shields on siege engines to break the morale of a garrison, one group stands out above all by the use of sheer terror: the Mongols. They forced more castles and fortified cities to surrender than any other group of people. In the field of genocide and brutality, they were second to none, with the possible exception of the ancient Assyrians.

A second place mention goes to Vlad the Impaler, better known as Count Dracula, the prince of Wallachia. Vlad earned his nickname due to his habit of impaling en masse his enemies, be they Turks or Christians. His campaign of intimidation kept the enemy at bay.

Strangely enough, the Vikings, who were feared on almost every coast of Europe and even North Africa, do not rate as high as the others in the category of genocide and terror. However, their pillaging and looting left a trail of terror that burned itself much deeper in the collective memory.

Most Destructive Elements in Siege Warfare

❖ Pestilence. It could cause defeat for both the besieger and the besieged.

❖ Starvation. It usually affected the defender more than the attacker.

❖ Lack of water. It forced the quick surrender of the strongest fortified sites. A common tactic was for the besieger to poison or cut off the water supply of the besieged. Many fortified sites had wells, cisterns, or walls leading to a source of water.

❖ Time. The longer a siege lasted the more likely the besieger would abandon the siege. But if the besieged ran out of supplies, surrender came first.

Most Effective Siege Weapons

❖ The trebuchet. Used to launch a variety of projectiles, it inflicted a great deal of destruction on the battlements and behind them.

❖ The crossbow and long bow. Allowed more advantages to the defender than the attacker by allowing him to pick off the enemy from concealed positions.

❖ The belfry. It gave the besieger the ability to reach the battlements or to dominate them when it was taller than the walls. The main problem was moving it into position.

❖ Mining. It was the most effective way to bring down walls and towers, but required much time and could be defeated by counter-mining.

❖ The cannon. During the last century of the Middle Ages it had great psychological effect and could devastate weak walls.

ALCÁZAR OF SEGOVIA, SPAIN.   (© Corel)

Medieval Castles and Fortifications

*S*ince there are far too many medieval castles and medieval fortifications scattered throughout Europe to do justice to in one volume, this chapter will only focus on a selected few. We have selected some very famous fortifications as well as some more obscure, but just as interesting. Although the castles of France and England are the best known in the West, the reader should be aware that castles and urban fortifications were built throughout medieval Europe. In the Netherlands, for instance, of the original 2,000 or more fortified sites, 200 still remain standing. Belgium hosted over 3,000 castles and France as many as 30,000, over 10,000 fortifications of which still exist either reasonably well preserved or in ruins.

Each region of Europe requires its own special study. The traditional Western castle is best represented in France, England, and Wales. Many castles of the Holy Land, though also classical in design, fell in the category of medieval fortress. We have also examined the characteristics of many Eastern castles of the Slavic regions, which seem to have emerged from an altogether different tradition. Evidence seems to point, however that the Slavic fortifications may well have influenced the Western tradition by means of cultural diffusion, possibly via the Norsemen who had extensive contacts with both Eastern and Western Europe.

The Byzantine fortifications, derived from the earlier Roman period, form their own tradition and also converge with west European traditions in parts of south and southeastern Europe and the Middle East. In addition, the Islamic tradition in the field of fortifications was spread across the Middle East, North Africa, and into Iberia. It adapted itself to the works already present in those regions leaving its own distinctive mark, which can clearly be seen in Iberia, especially in many alcazabas and alcázars and later Christian castles of the region.

In some of the marginal regions of Europe are found many examples of older traditions including ringworks in the British Isles, and especially Ireland, many of which were built at the time of the Norman conquest and then adapted to include the motte and bailey. Ringworks seem to have persisted in Ireland as long as in the Slavic lands of the East. As a result, many castles of the late medieval period represent either different trajectories or delayed stages of development.

Though with so many variations and distinct regional styles, the few examples presented in this chapter can barely do justice to the art of castle building in medieval Europe, we hope the descriptions and plans will give the reader a true sense of these fortifications and will encourage further reading and study.

HARLECH CASTLE, WALES.

(© Corel)

Great Britain and Ireland

1. Arundel	9. Beaumaris	17. Caerlaverock
2. Bodiam	10. Caernarvon	18. Trim
3. Deal	11. Caerphilly	19. Limerick
4. Kenilworth	12. Conway	20. Dunguaire
5. Oxford	13. Flint	21. Cahir
6. Portchester	14. Harlech	22. Dunamase
7. Rochester	15. Rhuddlan	
8. Windsor	16. Edinburgh	

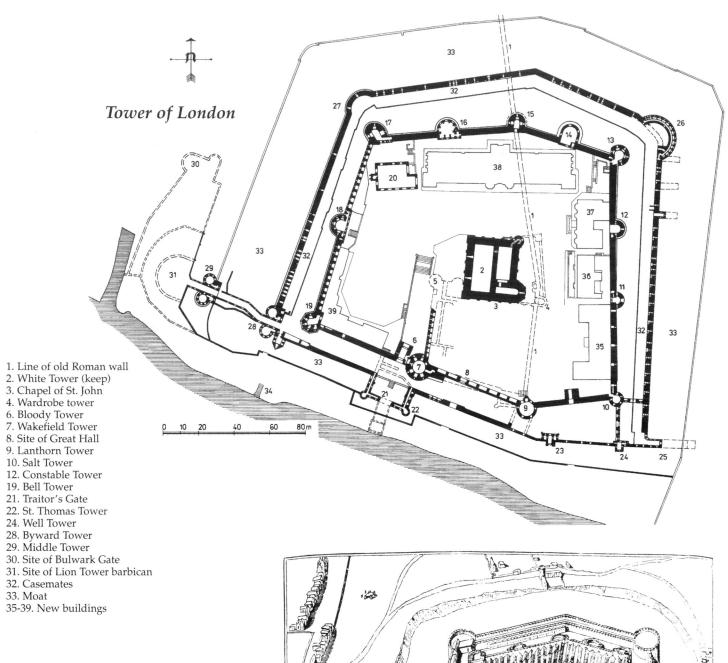

Tower of London

1. Line of old Roman wall
2. White Tower (keep)
3. Chapel of St. John
4. Wardrobe tower
6. Bloody Tower
7. Wakefield Tower
8. Site of Great Hall
9. Lanthorn Tower
10. Salt Tower
12. Constable Tower
19. Bell Tower
21. Traitor's Gate
22. St. Thomas Tower
24. Well Tower
28. Byward Tower
29. Middle Tower
30. Site of Bulwark Gate
31. Site of Lion Tower barbican
32. Casemates
33. Moat
35-39. New buildings

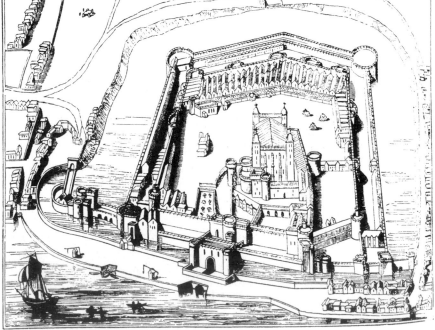

Illustration of the Tower of London.
(Courtesy of Greenhill Books)

Great Britain

After the battle of Hastings in 1066, the new Norman masters of England hurried to set up their own fortifications in the country to establish their control over it. They used timber and earth defenses first to create an enclosure and later worked on the motte and the keep. In subsequent centuries, the timber and earth were gradually replaced with masonry. Several examples of shell keeps still stand in the United Kingdom today, most notably Restormel, Cardiff, the Tower of London, Windsor, Dover, and Arundel, among others.

England

The famous **Tower of London** and especially Dover Castle, two of the largest keeps on the island, are further examples of motte and bailey castles that went through numerous stages of renovation, adaptation, and modernization through the centuries. William the Conqueror established his first defenses for London in the southeast corner of the old Roman city wall and added the White Tower or Tower of London inside this fortification at a later date. This great keep was not completed until the reign of William Rufus. It is not a perfect rectangle and only one side forms a right angle. Its sides are each a little more than 30 meters in length but none are precisely the same length. As was the case in most keeps, an outside staircase and a forebuilding led to the second level above the ground which was the entrance. The lower walls of this immense fortification are 4.5 meters thick. The keep has four levels taking it to a height of 27 meters. A dividing wall splits the keep into two unequal sections. As in most stone keeps, one or more circular stone stairways, usually located in the corners, led up to the upper levels. The floors of the keep were wooden. A chapel was situated in the east wall of the keep. In the 1241, Henry II had the structure whitewashed and added stained glass to the chapel.

The inner ward was enclosed by a wall with 13 towers built under the reign of Henry III during the 13th century. His successor, Edward I, added the outer walls, thus creating a concentric fortification. This enceinte was enclosed by a large moat, which also separated it from the Thames. Edward I built a barbican with its own drawbridge and moat on the far side of the main moat. The approaches to the causeway leading over the moat were modified numerous times over the centuries. The White Tower served as part of a royal residence for many centuries and was one of the largest of its type in Europe.

TOWER OF LONDON.   (© Corel)

Dover Castle was built at about the same time as the Tower of London, near an old Roman lighthouse and a burgh founded by King Harold before the invasion. It replaced an older castle built shortly after the Conquest of 1066. None of the work done under Williams' reign survives to this day. The great keep that stands on this location at present dates back to the 1180s and the reign of Henry II, who was also responsible for the curtain wall of the inner bailey and a large part of the outer enceinte.

Dover's great keep is considered to have been one of the strongest of the 12th century. It is almost 29 meters high, has walls varying in thickness from .8 meters to 6.5 meters, and is reinforced by a plinth. Each of its sides is over 30 meters in length. The keep includes four corner turrets. Its entrance is secured by the largest fore-building of the period in England, which includes three towers that cover the open stairs leading into the keep. Like the White Tower, the Dover keep is divided into two parts by an interior wall. It consists of three levels that are accessed by two spiral staircases located in its corner turrets. The inner wall that surrounds the keep includes 14 projecting rectangular towers that are open to the rear. The north and south barbicans defend its two gates. The outer wall consists of a number of projecting towers and the large Constable's Tower and Gate. Many of these positions were improved by Henry III in the next century. In 1216, while the barons were still in revolt against King John, Philippe Augustus' son, Louis, put Dover under siege. He assaulted the northern outer gate after taking the barbican protecting it. A mine damaged one of the gate's two towers, but the defenders managed to barricade the breach and hold the position thus preventing the fall of Dover Castle. After this campaign the Norfolk Towers replaced the damaged gateway and the sector was endowed with additional defenses. Dover Castle was modified and renovated periodically well into the 19th century, becoming a complex blend of diverse architectural styles. Matthew of Paris in the 13th century proclaimed it to be "The key of England."

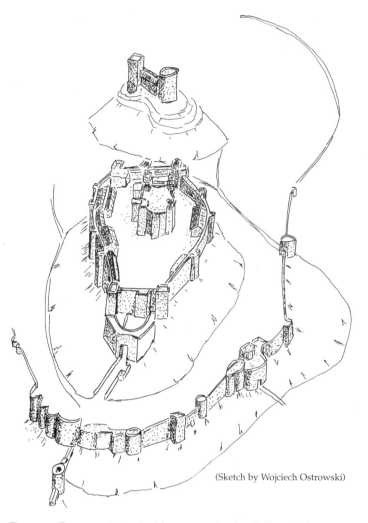

(Sketch by Wojciech Ostrowski)

DOVER CASTLE. *View looking towards the cliffs and the English Channel.*

Part of the walls enclosing the great keep at Dover.

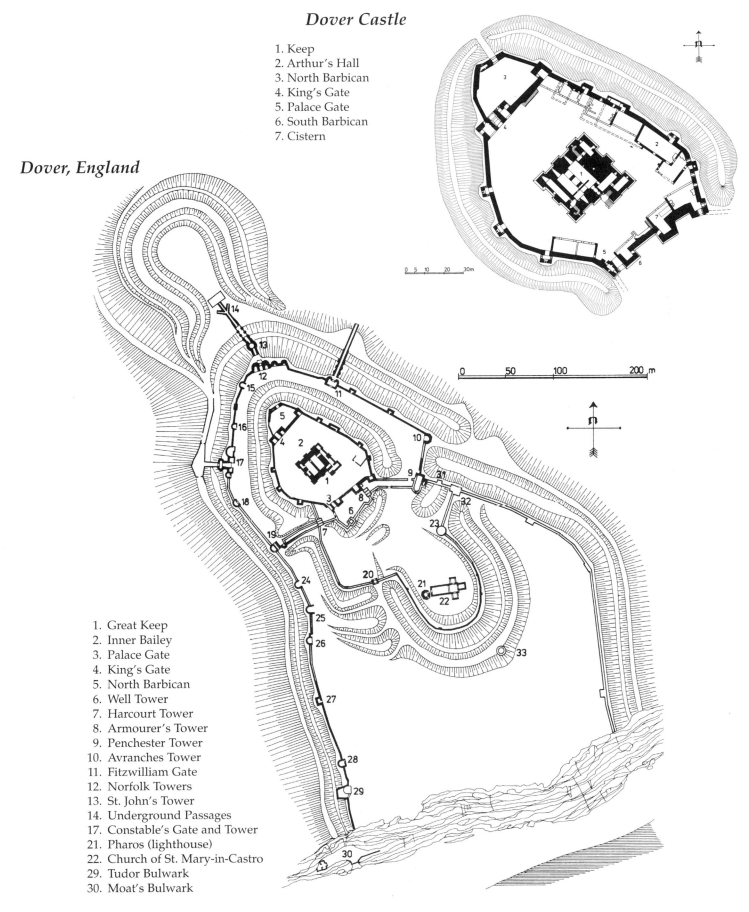

Dover Castle

1. Keep
2. Arthur's Hall
3. North Barbican
4. King's Gate
5. Palace Gate
6. South Barbican
7. Cistern

Dover, England

1. Great Keep
2. Inner Bailey
3. Palace Gate
4. King's Gate
5. North Barbican
6. Well Tower
7. Harcourt Tower
8. Armourer's Tower
9. Penchester Tower
10. Avranches Tower
11. Fitzwilliam Gate
12. Norfolk Towers
13. St. John's Tower
14. Underground Passages
17. Constable's Gate and Tower
21. Pharos (lighthouse)
22. Church of St. Mary-in-Castro
29. Tudor Bulwark
30. Moat's Bulwark

Rochester Castle, England

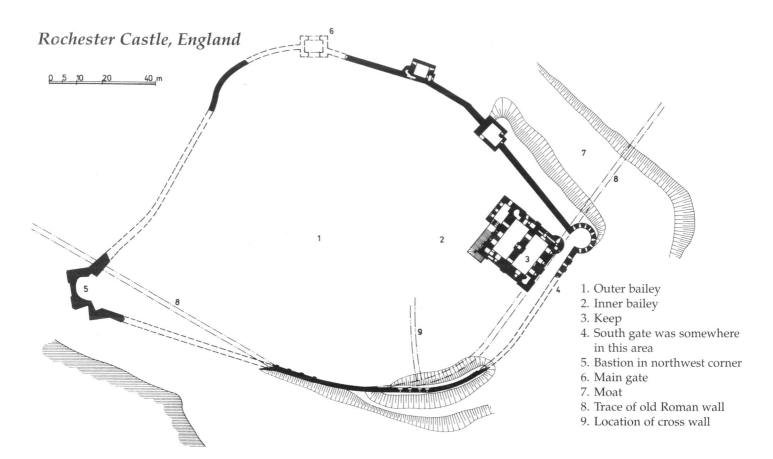

0 5 10   20   40 m

1. Outer bailey
2. Inner bailey
3. Keep
4. South gate was somewhere in this area
5. Bastion in northwest corner
6. Main gate
7. Moat
8. Trace of old Roman wall
9. Location of cross wall

ROCHESTER CASTLE. *The keep.*

Rochester Castle also goes back to the reign of William the Conqueror. A motte and bailey castle was first built on Boley Hill shortly after the Norman Conquest. In the 12th century, Archbishop William de Corbeil erected the great tower about 100 meters north of the old site on Boley Hill. It was built in the southern corner of the bailey. The almost square shaped keep measures about 27 meters on each side, rises to almost 35 meters in height, and has walls about 3.6 meters thick at the base. Buttresses placed in the middle and corners of the keep supported its enormous weight and plinths protected the base of its walls from mining.

The keep consisted of four levels and was divided in half by a cross wall. The battlements included supports for wooden hoardings and the four corner turrets added to the defenses. The fore-building consisted of three levels and was connected to the entrance by a small drawbridge. The entrance itself was located in a small tower standing before the fore-building and was accessed by a shallow staircase. A portcullis secured the gate.

A stairway descended from the ground floor to the basement that housed an underground cesspool where the keep's garderobes drained. This cesspool was probably emptied twice a year. The well was in the center of the cross wall and accessible on all levels. The upper three levels had two fireplaces each and were connected by two circular stairways. The second floor (third level) included a minstrel gallery with pillared arches forming an arcade in the cross wall. All levels had windows to provide light. The chapel was located on the second floor of the fore-building. The third floor housed mainly apartments for the ruling family. The roof above the third floor was probably made of lead.

A wall cut across the castle's enclosure, creating an inner bailey about one-fourth the size of the outer bailey. The enceinte was surrounded by a moat, probably water filled, with the Medway River on the northwest side. The size and location of the outer wall changed between the 12th and 14th centuries when parts of the old Roman wall were incorporated in the defenses. The new curtain included a gatehouse with a draw-bridge on the eastern side as well as a couple of towers. Further changes were made under the reign of Edward I and later.

The castle at Rochester, like the one at Dover, endured a major siege during the reign of King John, who had suffered a series of reversals. Following the loss of Normandy in 1206 after the fall of Château Gaillard, King John engaged in a dispute with Pope Innocent III, who placed England under an order of interdiction. Philip Augustus was about to invade England in support of Innocent III, when John prudently decided to give in. Later, while campaigning again on the Continent, John suffered a major defeat at Bouvines in 1214. Next he lost control of his own barons, who forced him to sign the Magna Carta in 1215. Subsequently, the mercenary army he hired to deal with the barons turned against him, seizing Rochester Castle. John advanced on the castle, which was held, according to the chroniclers, by no more than 140 knights and archers. The town was quickly taken in a surprise attack and John's men proceeded to lay siege to the castle. The chroniclers are not clear on whether it was King John's siege machines or his miners that breached the outer walls but the garrison had to retreat into the great tower. The miners next worked their way under the southeast corner of the keep, successfully bringing down a large section of it. The defenders continued to resist using the keep's cross wall, but they eventually had to surrender, vanquished by exhaustion and starvation.

The damaged section of the keep was rebuilt about two years later by the new king, Henry III. The outer wall was extended and a drum tower was put in the southeast corner near the damaged part of the keep. In 1264, the castle was besieged again during another revolt of the barons. Once more, the bailey fell and the defenders took refuge in the keep, which was bombarded by catapults for about a week while mines inched toward its walls. Only the timely arrival of the king's army caused the besiegers to retreat. It was not until the next century that the damage suffered during this siege was repaired and improvements were made at the direction of Edward III.

Caerlaverock Castle, Scotland

1. Earthen wall, probably with a palisade
2. Drawbridge
3. Wet moat
4. Gate towers
5. Courtyard
6. Great Hall
7. Quarters

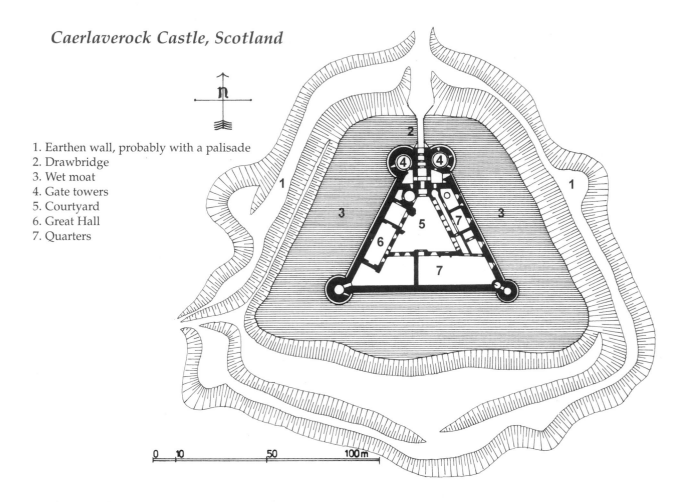

CAERLAVEROCK CASTLE, SCOTLAND. *One of the first concentric castles ever built.*

(© Corel)

Scotland

Scotland too, is famous for its castles, one of the finest of which is at **Edinburgh**. This castle was built in the 11th century and served the Scottish kings for many centuries with many renovations. It was besieged in 1296, destroyed in 1314, and attacked several more times after the Middle Ages.

Another notable castle in Scotland is **Caerlaverock**, built between 1290 and 1300. Although it is not certain whether it was first erected by the Scots or the English, it is a fact that it stands on Scottish soil. Caerlaverock has the distinction of being one of the first concentric castles ever built. Purportedly built in the French style, this triangular castle stands on a rock formation. At the apex of the triangle stands a huge gatehouse composed of two drum towers that served as the keep. These gatehouse towers were crowned with machicoulis. In addition to these two towers, there was a round tower at each of the other corners.

The water-filled moat was surrounded by an earthen embankment that served as an additional line of defense. Caerlaverock was dismantled and rebuilt several times over the centuries.

Wales

Wales is home to some of the most impressive and most famous castles in Europe: Caerphilly, Flint, Rhuddlan, Conway, Caernarvon, Harlech, and Beaumaris. Most of them were built in northern Wales in the 13th century by Edward I in order to maintain control of the Welsh lands. Except for Caerphilly, their design is attributed to a master mason or architect by the name of Master James. These castles gradually evolved from the heavily fortified castle with a keep to the truly concentric castle where the functions of the keep were taken over by a great gatehouse. These Edwardian castles in Wales, with their complex gatehouses, were considered the most formidable and expensive in Europe and were copied elsewhere, especially Harlech and Beaumaris.

EDINBURGH CASTLE, SCOTLAND.

(© Corel)

Caerphilly Castle, Wales

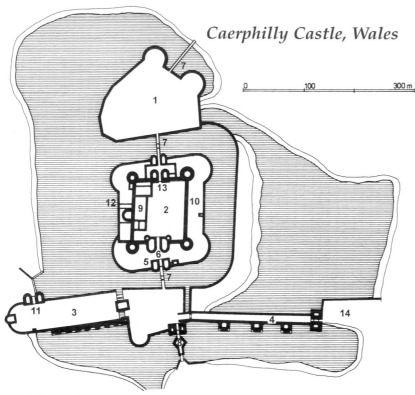

1. Hornwork
2. Inner Ward
3. Southern Platform
4. Northern Platform
5. East gatehouse to middle ward
6. East gatehouse to inner ward
7. Drawbridges
8. Barbican and two drawbridges
9. Great Hall
10. Middle Ward
11. Gatehouse
12.. Water Gate
13. West Gate
14. Gate

Top: *The barbican's gatehouse which at one time held the drawbridge. Inside the gatehouse were a portcullis with murder holes in the ceiling and strong wooden doors behind it.*
Middle: *View from the south of the inner walls and massive east gatehouse to the inner walls and smaller east gatehouse to the middle ward.*
Left: *East gate of inner wall. The tower to the left of the gate was partially destroyed during the English Civil War.*

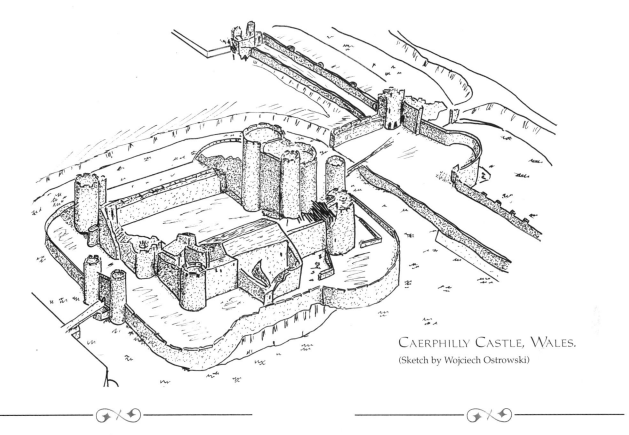

CAERPHILLY CASTLE, WALES.
(Sketch by Wojciech Ostrowski)

The strength of castles in North Wales was only rivaled by the baronial castle of **Caerphilly** in South Wales erected by Gilbert de Clare. Founded in 1271, six years before the famous Edwardian castles of North Wales, Caerphilly was probably the strongest of the fortified sites in South Wales. It stood near the location of an earlier castle built by Gilbert in 1268 that had been burned down by Prince Llywelyn ap Gruffydd in 1270. It was also the probable emplacement of a much older Roman fort. No sooner had the construction on Caerphilly started, than Llywelyn put it under siege. Fortunately he was diverted before the castle's occupants could be forced to surrender, and Gilbert was able to complete it by 1295.

Like most of the Edwardian castles that followed, Caerphilly has impressive concentric defenses and gatehouses rather than a keep, and some of the most impressive water defenses in Europe. The outer curtain on the east side was used to dam the marsh and nearby stream and formed two lakes that surrounded the stronghold. These lakes created a barrier over 400 meters wide on the north and south side. The inner ward was surrounded by a curtain wall with four corner drum towers and two well-defended gates between two large towers. The great hall and other structures rested against the southern wall of the inner ward, which also included a water gate. The

middle ward, which encircled the inner ward, included two gateways consisting of two half-round towers each. The largest of the two entrances, the Eastern Gatehouse, consisted of three levels and housed the constable's residence on the top one. The entire position was surrounded by the inner moat and the Southern Lake. A drawbridge led from the heavily defended gate to the Eastern Front or Great Curtain that stretched for almost 400 meters. The Eastern Front consisted of the Southern and the Northern Platform, which included sluices and were separated by a defensive screen wall near the large gatehouse in the center. Posterns were located at the extremity of each platform. The gatehouse included guard rooms, machinery for the drawbridge, heavy double doors, and a portcullis. The outer moat lay in front of the Eastern Front. The Western Gatehouse of the middle ward consisted of only two levels and led to an island that served as a hornwork.

In 1316 Llywelyn Bren, a local Welsh prince, attacked Caerphilly Castle with an army of 10,000 men, but the small castle guard beat off his surprise attack. The water barriers prevented mining and also kept the walls out of range of the besiegers' catapults. In 1326, Edward II set up his headquarters at Caerphilly as his queen, Isabella, moved against him with her army. In November of 1326, the queen laid

Conway Castle, Wales

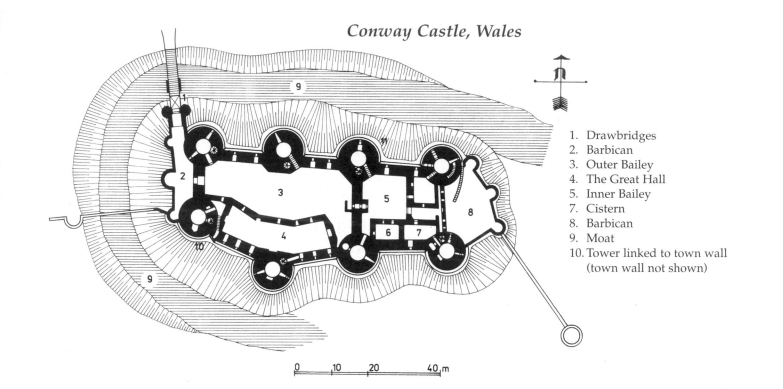

1. Drawbridges
2. Barbican
3. Outer Bailey
4. The Great Hall
5. Inner Bailey
7. Cistern
8. Barbican
9. Moat
10. Tower linked to town wall
   (town wall not shown)

Above: *Looking towards the inner ward with the great hall on the right.*
Right: *Towers of the outer ward and west barbican.*
(Both photos are courtesy of Bernard Lowry)

siege to the castle that lasted through January and February 1327. The castle finally surrendered when the garrison accepted favorable terms in February. The defenders were still well provisioned when they gave up. In the meantime, Edward II was captured and abdicated in January 1327 in favor of his son.

In 1403 the castle once again played a key role when it was taken and occupied by the Welsh leader, Owen Glyndwr. In the 17th century, during the English Civil War, the Parliamentarians did their best to destroy and dismantle Caerphilly.

The most modern Welsh castles of the 13th century were the Edwardian castles of Conway, built between 1283 and 1287, Caernarvon, built between 1285 and 1322, Harlech, built between 1285 and 1290, and Beaumaris built between 1295 and 1320, but never completed. **Flint**, the first of these Welsh castles, was the only one that still had a keep. The others were integrated into the fortifications of the nearby town. Both Conway and Caernarvon are elongated and follow the contours of the rock formation upon which they stand.

Conway Castle includes drum towers and two gateways located between two of the towers, at each of its east and west ends, the narrowest sides of the castle. Both gates are defended by barbicans. At one time the battlements of the towers accommodated wooden hoardings, which were later replaced with machicoulis. Some sections of the gateways are also protected by machicolations. In addition, several of the towers are equipped with high turrets for observation. A great hall and garrison area were located in the outer bailey, which covered the western two thirds of the castle. The royal apartments and offices stood on the east side of the inner bailey. A postern accessed by a rope ladder was situated in the south wall of the outer ward. The wall walk linked all parts of the castle. The town wall connected with the drum tower separating the two baileys on the north side. The River Conway flows on the eastern end of the castle and Gyffin Stream runs below its southern face. The remainder of the castle was surrounded by a wide moat. The town walls extended for over one kilometer, were about 1.7 meters thick, rose to a height of 9 meters, and included 21 towers and several gates, adding significantly to the castle's defenses. In 1284, the garrison numbered only 30 men, but in 1401 it was increased to 75. Conway Castle was besieged twice in its history: the first time in 1401, when it surrendered to the Welsh, and the second time in 1646, during the Civil War.

FLINT CASTLE, WALES.   (© Corel)

1. Eagle Tower
2. King's Gate
3. Queen's Gate
4. Moat
5. City wall
6. River

Caernarvon Castle, Wales

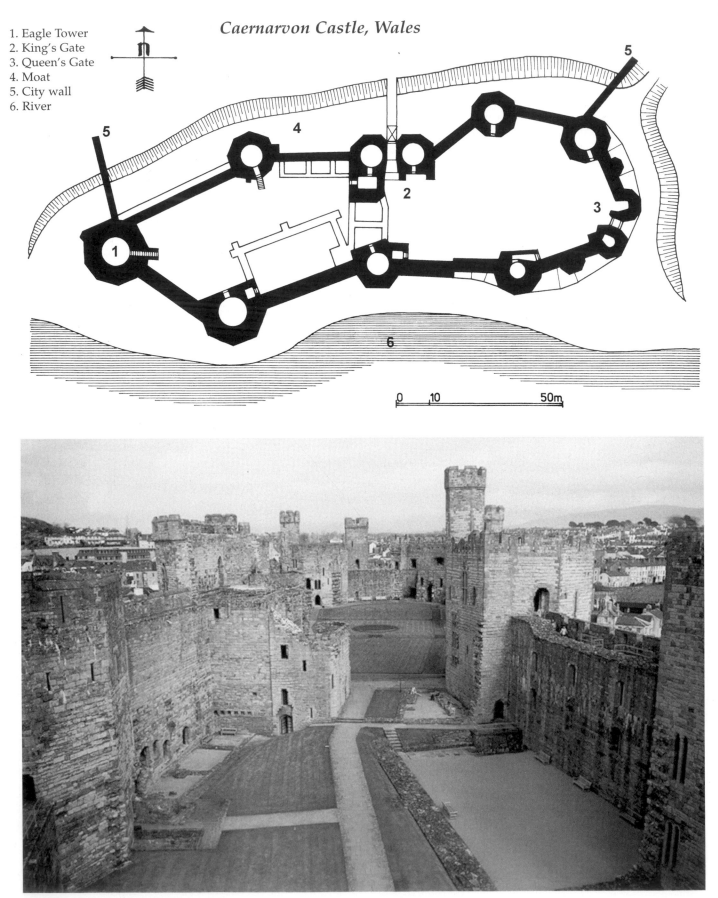

0   10   50m

(© Corel)

Caernarvon Castle is not perched as high as Conway, but it stands between the river and the town. It was built on the site of an old Roman fort and a Norman motte and bailey. Like most of the more modern Edwardian castles, its strongpoint is the gatehouse rather than a keep. A water moat that covers its north side links up with the river which forms an obstacle on the south side of the castle. A large gatehouse known as the King's Gate allows access to the north of the castle and towers over the town. Master James had planned to include six portcullises, five doors, and interior arrow loopholes and murder holes to this gatehouse, but the work was not completed.

The town wall links up at the west end of Caernarvon Castle with the polygonal Eagle Tower, which is similar to a keep and rises to a height of 36 meters. A tower on the northeast side connects the castle to the other end of the town wall, which runs for almost a kilometer and has two well-defended gateways. The Menai Strait protects the north side of the town and castle and the River Cadnant the south side. A second gatehouse is on the east side known as the Queen's Gate with two portcullis and murder holes and behind it is the old motte. The allure passed through the polygonal towers as in Carcassonne, which allowed the defenders to block any section of the curtain that might be captured. The towers were decorated with a banded pattern copied from the fortifications of Constantinople because the English believed that bones found on the site belonged to Emperor Constantine's father. The king thought it also a good idea to tie the new castle to those of Imperial Rome, going even as far as ordering carvings of eagles for the Eagle Tower. There were high turrets for observation on several of the towers, including the Eagle Tower which had three. In 1284, Caernarvon Castle housed a royal garrison of 40 men and there were 200 in 1401. The castle was put under siege several times by the Welsh, including in 1403, but it was never taken.

Harlech and Beaumaris are similar to Caernarvon because they are laid out along a more regular, rectangular shape and include concentric defenses with powerful gatehouses. **Harlech Castle** (see page 112) overlooks the town of the same name from a high hill and is defended by a large moat. Unlike the other Edwardian castles, it was not built as part of the town defenses. Four large projecting drum towers, two with turrets, sit at each corner of the inner wall. The gatehouse on the east wall is formed by two large D-shaped towers that frame the entrance and two smaller towers on its inner corners. It too served as a keep. The eastern section of the wall is 2.6 to 3.5 meters thick. The inner curtain, up to 24 meters high, towered over the cliffs behind the castle, which dropped off for 60 meters. The middle bailey is bounded by a surrounding lower outer wall and an outer gate leading into the gatehouse. An outer bailey is encompassed by a wall that surrounds the northern and western sides of the castle that are not covered by the moat and extends about 50 meters down the steepest side of the hill. The wall of the outer bailey encircles it down to the base of the hill, giving the impression of a giant ball with a strap around it. The castle was designed in such a fashion that even if the walls of the outer bailey fell, the besieger gained little advantage. Construction of Harlech Castle began in 1283 and was completed by 1290. In 1401, the castle was occupied by a garrison of 40 men. In 1294, it was attacked by the Welsh, who were having little success when they were driven away by an English relief force. Owen Glyndwr put the castle under siege again in 1401 with the help of the French, keeping it isolated from the sea. Eventually he forced the small garrison to submit. He held the castle from 1403 until 1409 when the English recaptured it with a force of a thousand men. Harlech Castle was subsequently involved in a longer siege during the War of Roses, when the Lancasterian garrison of 28 men surrendered in 1468 on favorable terms after two years of resistance.

Beaumaris Castle lays near the coast and is much larger than the other Edwardian castles. Although it has concentric walls, the gates of the outer wall are set out of line with those of the inner wall so that if they should fall, the aggressor would not have direct access to the inner gate. Two powerful gatehouses in the north and south walls give access to the castle, which is surrounded by a wet moat and includes a dock linked to the sea. In addition to the four projecting drum towers in the corners, like those of Harlech, Beaumaris has one tower in the center of the two walls without gatehouses. The lower outer wall, which was not added until 1316, includes numerous small projecting towers. Beaumaris was never completed because trouble in Scotland diverted King Edward's attention and funds and it did not face a siege until the English Civil War.

Beaumaris Castle, Wales

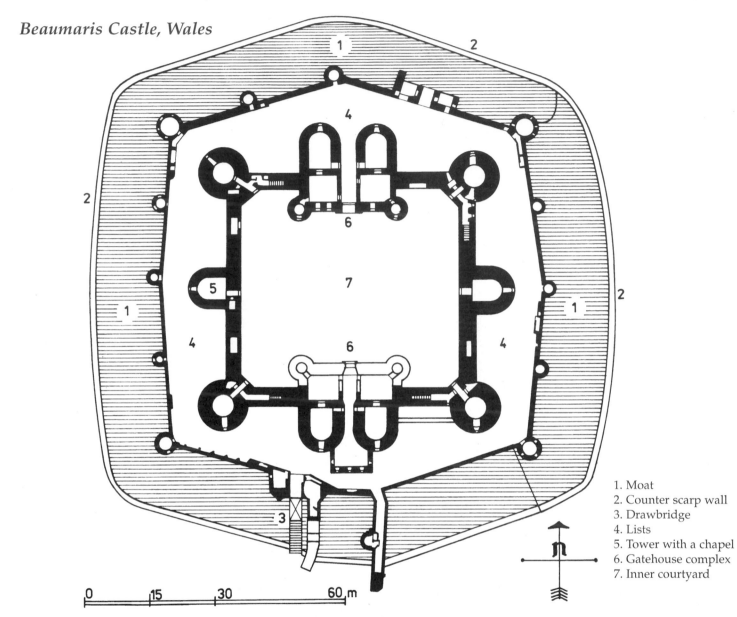

1. Moat
2. Counter scarp wall
3. Drawbridge
4. Lists
5. Tower with a chapel
6. Gatehouse complex
7. Inner courtyard

0   15   30   60 m

BEAUMARIS CASTLE. *An aerial view of the ruins.*

(© Corel)

Cardiff Castle in Wales, still has its motte and bailey to which other features were gradually added over the centuries to bring it up-to-date both as a defensive structure and as a residence. In 1090, after invading Wales, Robert Fitzhamon quickly erected a motte in the northwest corner of the remains of an older Roman fort. Fitzhamon's timber keep that crowned the motte was transformed into a polygonal stone shell keep late in the next century. Fitzhamon rebuilt the Roman walls and added towers and living quarters. The enceinte was later converted to stone and received a large gatehouse on its south side, transforming Cardiff Castle into a large fortified structure that serves as a good example of a 12th- to 14th-century castle.

CARDIFF CASTLE, WALES. *A view of the original motte and bailey castle from inside the newer walls.*

BEAUMARIS CASTLE, WALES. *The gatehouse.*

(© Corel)

DOOLIN TOWER, *also know as Doonagore Castle, Ireland. This post-medieval work overlooking the Atlantic on the Irish west coast was built in the 1580s by the O'Connors as a residence in the medieval style.* (© Corel)

Ireland

The tradition of building fortifications in Ireland is very old, going back to the raths, or stone circular stone wall fortifications that many chieftains maintained. The Celtic tribes that occupied the island also built spectacular earth works like Tara. Later, in the Dark Ages the countryside was dotted with ringworks—earthworks with a moat that are much larger than the enclosed area—whose remains can still be seen today. The most notable examples of ringworks can be found at Castlerahanin in County Cavan, Kilpipe in County Wicklow, Loughcrew in County Meath, and Dungar in County Offaly.

Around the 12th century, Henry II's Anglo-Normans arrived at a time of political strife and they soon replaced the ringworks with motte-and-bailey castles. In many cases the motte was built in the middle of existing ringwork forts, and the keep was erected on top. The outer earthworks of the ringworks were preserved to protect the bailey. What distinguishes the Irish motte-and-bailey castles from those found in the rest of Europe is their unusually good state of preservation. Some of the most notable examples of Irish motte-and-bailey castles are Rathturtle Moat at Deerpark in County Wicklow, the mottes of Milltown in County Meath and Cloncurry in County Kildare, and Clonmacnoise Castle in County Offaly. Motte-and-bailey castles were built in Ireland well into the 13th century.

In some places, the motte-and-bailey castles were replaced with stone structures almost as soon they were built. One of the most important Anglo-Norman castles in Ireland is **Trim Castle** in County Meath. It was founded by Hugh de Lacy, who was appointed by Henry II to administer the conquered lands and to keep in line rivals like Richard "Strongbow," Earl of Pembroke. De Lacy built Trim Castle in 1173 on the emplacement of an older ringwork fort on the southern bank of the River Boyne. Between 1200 and 1224, Hugh de Lacy's modest motte-and-bailey, which had been burned down a few years earlier, was replaced with a massive stonework structure. The massive keep of Trim Castle occupies almost the entire area formerly enclosed by the earthworks of the old ringwork. The keep was surrounded by a moat, long since filled, and was defended on the northeast by a forebuilding and a mantlet wall. A causeway spanning the moat ensures access to the keep from the lower ward. The roughly triangular-shaped lower ward was entirely surrounded by walls at one time by Geoffrey de Geneville, Hugh de Lacy's grandson. The southern section of the wall, running from the River Boyne to the southeast corner is still protected by four semi-circular towers, two of which are corner towers. The eastern section of the curtain wall, overlooking the River Boyne, was guarded by two rectangular towers. This section of the wall is now gone. The northwestern wall had no towers, except the northeast corner tower, which was the largest of the whole complex and abutted the great hall. Three gates gave access to the castle. The southern gate, or Dublin gate, was protected by a barbican; the northwest gate was protected by a square gatehouse. The third gate was a water gate, which gave access to the castle from the river and was probably defended by hoardings on the battlements above it.

TRIM CASTLE, COUNTY MEATH, IRELAND.

(Sketch by Lizbeth Nauta)

Cahir or Caher Castle in County Tipperary, stands on a rocky outcrop that forms an island in the middle of the River Suir. It was built by the Butlers, descendants of Philip of Worcester, who was granted lands in the area in 1192. The most ancient part of this castle, dating back to the 13th century, consists of a squarish inner ward protected by curtain walls, three square corner towers, and a round corner tower in the southeast. The entrance to the castle was guarded by a massive gatehouse. The solar, or main residence of the lord's family, was located in the large square tower in the northwest corner of the inner ward. The entrance to the solar was located on the ground floor, in the one-storied great hall. In the 15th century, the access gate to the inner ward was walled off, and the gatehouse became a keep, the main residence of the family. A new gate was opened in the southeastern curtain wall, between the keep and the round corner tower. The 13th-century portcullis and its mechanism were moved to this new gate. Also in the 15th century, a rectangular outer ward was added to the castle. A barbican was built to guard access to this ward on the east side. The curtain walls of the outer ward were protected by two round corner towers. A causeway leading to the barbican on the east side of the island was also protected by a defensive wall. In the 16th century an inner wall to the south of the keep divided the outer ward into two sections: the middle ward and the outer ward. After a major siege in 1580 involving artillery, a round bastion projecting beyond the wall was added near the northeast tower in the 17th century.

❧❧❧

Dunamase Castle in County Laois was built on an imposing site overlooking and dominating the entire area. Like many Irish castles, it was built on the site of a pre-existing fortification, which was occupied by Strongbow at the end of the 12th century. In the 13th century, Meiler FitzHenry built the impressive defenses, which were later expanded by William Marshal, who used the place as his seat of power. A large keep, which served as the great hall, occupied a central point on the highest elevation of the position between the upper and lower bailey. The whole complex was surrounded by curtain walls pierced by two gates. The southern gate probably served as the postern. The eastern gate, which was the main entrance, included a gatehouse whose ruins remain standing to this very day. An outside wall with a barbican extended along most of the length of the eastern curtain wall. The outer defenses included a wide moat and probably other obstacles. Although in ruins, the remaining structures of this massive castle retain their original majesty.

CAHIR CASTLE, IRELAND.   (© Corel)

Tower houses are another important feature in Ireland. They seem to have proliferated mainly in the 15th century with the encouragement of the English king. One of the more interesting of these towers is Clara Upper in Kilkenny County. It is a rectangular structure consisting of five levels and a small bailey protecting the entrance. A bretèche at the top level still projects directly above the ground-level entrance. Often these tower houses were surrounded on two or more sides by a low defensive wall reinforced, more often than not, by small corner towers. This type of walled enclosure was called a bawn. The tower house of Aughnanure in County Galway is surrounded by a complex system of defenses. Originally it was surrounded by two sets of walls, the inner wall separated the outer ward from the inner ward. The River Drimneen served as a moat on the northern side of the inner ward, which was accessed by a drawbridge on the eastern side. The outer ward enclosed a much larger area and included a square tower in the middle of the southern and western walls, one round tower at the southwestern corner, and a square corner tower at the northwestern corner. The outer ward housed a banqueting hall, now razed to the ground. The majority of these tower houses were square or rectangular.

However, there are a few, like the tower house of Balief in County Kilkenny, and of the post-medieval Doolin in County Clare that are circular.

Dunguaire Castle is located on a site that has been fortified since the beginning of the Middle Ages. The 7th-century Irish king of Connaught was the first recorded occupant of this rocky outcrop overlooking Galway Bay near Kinvara in Shannon. No detail is known of the structure built there before 1520 when a member of the O'Heynes family built the present-day castle. This structure appears to have the characteristics of both the Irish tower house and the older keep-type stronghold. The main tower or keep rises just over 20 meters and includes a bawn like many tower houses. The entrance and windows on each side of the tower are protected by a bretéche on the battlements. The enclosing walls of the bawn and the roof of the tower include battlements and an allure. A small corner tower flanks the gate of the bawn. For a post-medieval structure, this castle retains mostly medieval characteristics which was common in many outlying areas of Europe.

DUNGUAIRE CASTLE, SHANNON, IRELAND.

COCHEM CASTLE, GERMANY. *This castle was built in the 12th century and enlarged in the 14th century. The tall conical shaped roofs of its towers are typical of those in northern Europe as they made them more resistant to heavy snowfall.*

Western Europe

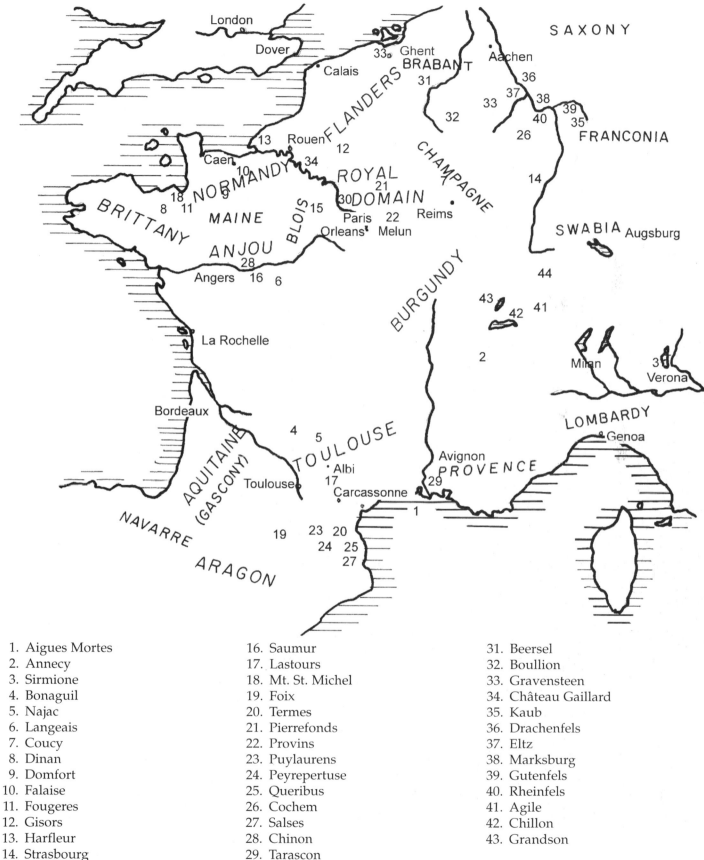

1. Aigues Mortes
2. Annecy
3. Sirmione
4. Bonaguil
5. Najac
6. Langeais
7. Coucy
8. Dinan
9. Domfort
10. Falaise
11. Fougeres
12. Gisors
13. Harfleur
14. Strasbourg
15. Etampes
16. Saumur
17. Lastours
18. Mt. St. Michel
19. Foix
20. Termes
21. Pierrefonds
22. Provins
23. Puylaurens
24. Peyrepertuse
25. Queribus
26. Cochem
27. Salses
28. Chinon
29. Tarascon
30. Vincennes
31. Beersel
32. Boullion
33. Gravensteen
34. Château Gaillard
35. Kaub
36. Drachenfels
37. Eltz
38. Marksburg
39. Gutenfels
40. Rheinfels
41. Agile
42. Chillon
43. Grandson

VINCENNES CASTLE, FRANCE.

France

In France, a number of motte and bailey castles, most in ruins, still survive. One of the two oldest masonry castles of this type in Europe is to be found at **Langeais** (see page 106 and 108). Only a large section of the original wall stands on the site today, not far from the new castle, which was built to replace it.

At **Gisors** (see page 157) one can visit one of the best preserved and restored shell keeps on a motte and bailey, originally built in the late 11th century by the Normans. The stone walls of the polygonal keep, called chemise in this type of construction, were rebuilt in 1160 and enclosed a chapel, a well, and a kitchen. The entire position sat on a 20-meter-high motte with steep sides situated in the center of an almost square bailey with rounded corners. The original motte was built by William Rufus in 1096, who also added the first keep. A stream forming a moat covers three sides of the castle. The fourth side, which slopes down toward the town, includes the gate which is covered by a large barbican. In 1123 Henry I of England built the surrounding walls and the flanking towers that projected beyond the walls. These were the first flanking towers to be built in France during the Middle Ages. They were open in the rear so they could not be used against the defenders in case they were taken. After taking the castle from Richard the Lionhearted in 1193, Philip Augustus of France built the large circular Tour du Prisonnier, or Tower of the Prisoner, in the southeast corner at a point where the town wall met with the barbican and the castle's bailey wall.

With a bailey large enough to hold 1,000 troops, Gisors remained a strategic position throughout the Hundred Years War. In 1438, it was garrisoned with only 90 Englishmen and in 1448, with 43. As a result, it quickly fell to the French in the last years of the war, like so many other under-garrisoned English castles in Normandy.

Besides Gisors, King Henry I of England was responsible for the construction of over 25 stone castles in Normandy, which helped him secure his French territories against the French monarch.

After Richard I of England conceded Gisors to Philip Augustus of France in 1195, he built **Château Gaillard** to secure his Norman frontier. This new castle, Richard's masterpiece, was built in a loop of the Seine River, on a spur almost 90 meters above the towns of Grand and Petit Andelys, from which it dominated the entire area. The castle, completed in three years, incorporated many new defensive features and consisted of three baileys.

The inner ward of Château Gaillard, which was laid out at the end of the spur near the cliffs, housed the living quarters and the great keep, which was rounded and had a beak that jutted toward the only possible direction of attack. The walls of the keep were almost 2.5 meters thick and included oblique surfaces to deflect projectiles and an impressive plinth against mining. The keep had absolutely no facilities, not even a fireplace, and was probably intended only for a last stand. The lower story was used for storage and the upper housed the guard room. Today, the battlements above the guard room are gone. Château Gaillard's machicoulis, known as *machicoulis en arche*, rested on a system of arches and were similar to those of the Palace of the Popes at Avignon. The keep was built into one of the walls of the bailey, which were also 2.5 meters thick and were reinforced with buttresses.

The middle ward included two large towers that protected the entrance, a large chapel, latrines and other mural towers. Contemporary illustrations of the castle show wooden hoardings on the walls rather than the machicoulis found on the keep. The triangular outer ward was at the only side of the castle that was easy to access and it served almost as a barbican. It was separated from the middle ward by a dry moat that was 9 meters wide and 6 meters deep and was crossed by a fixed bridge.

Château Gaillard was supposedly the first castle in France to be built with stone machicoulis. Its towers protruded beyond the walls, like those of Gisors, to give flanking fire. The tower walls were slightly less than 3.5 meters thick. The curtain walls were reinforced with a plinth and rose to 9 meters in height. The walls facing the direction of attack were 3.5 meters thick and the others about 2.5 meters. In addition to the castle, Richard I fortified an island on the Seine so he could close the river in the event of an attack. The island was linked to the walled town of Petit Andelys, which occupied a small peninsula. A stockade closed the river just above the town and was linked to a wall running down the cliff from Château Gaillard.

Château Gaillard, Normandy

1. Outer bailey or barbican
2. Middle bailey or lower court
3. Inner bailey or upper court
6. Well
7. Chapel
8. The keep
9. Postern gate or sally port
10. Drawbridge
11. Moat

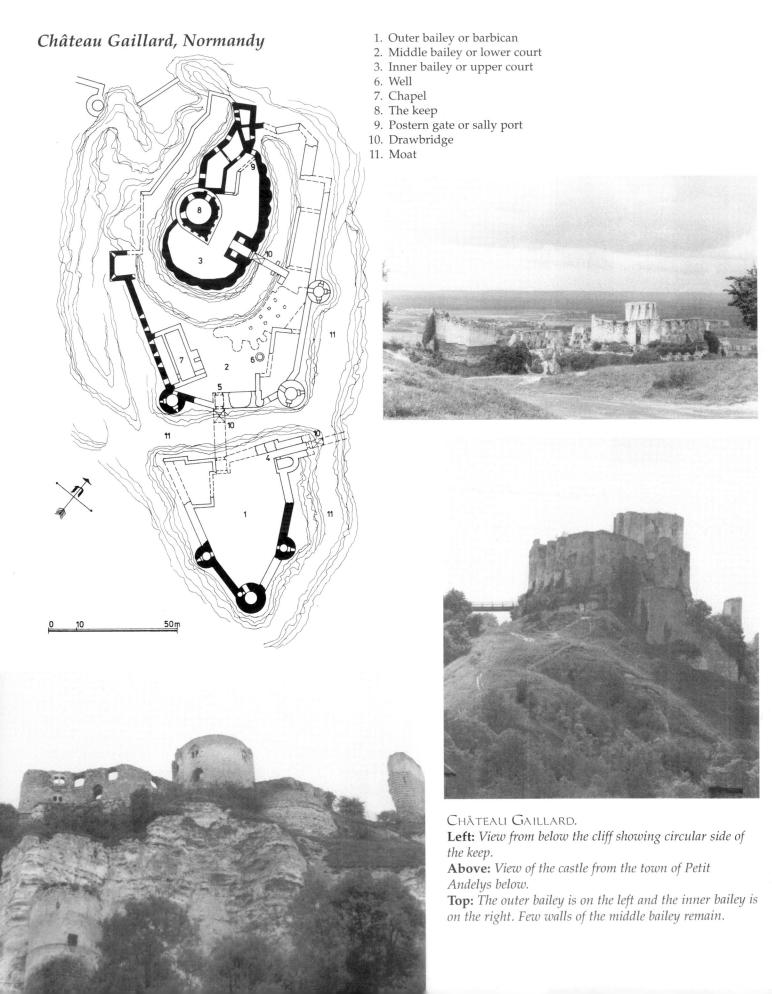

CHÂTEAU GAILLARD.
Left: *View from below the cliff showing circular side of the keep.*
Above: *View of the castle from the town of Petit Andelys below.*
Top: *The outer bailey is on the left and the inner bailey is on the right. Few walls of the middle bailey remain.*

Keep at Château Gaillard.
(Illustration from Military Architecture courtesy of Greenhill Books)

Philip Augustus of France began the siege of Château Gaillard in 1203. The defended island and stockade closing the river were the first positions to fall. Roger de Lacy, who commanded the castle's garrison, had to force out the elderly, the women, and the children to save his food stores. The French refused to allow a second group of refugees to leave, forcing them to live in the ditches during the winter until Philip finally relented. The removal of "useless mouths" was a common practice in the Middle Ages. So was the refusal of the besiegers to allow refugees safe passage. The French assault on Château Gaillard began in the spring of 1204. As a belfry and catapults hurled projectiles at the defenders, the sappers began filling in the ditch inch by inch and undermined the base of the large tower under the protection of mantlets. According to one source, the tower collapsed, according to another, it was a section of the curtain wall that came down. Be that as it may, when the breach occurred the outer ward was quickly taken and the defenders retreated to the middle ward. The French discovered an unguarded garderobe shaft on the cliff side through which they crawled into the castle and through an unblocked window of the chapel. As they took the chapel, the garrison withdrew into the inner ward. A large trébuchet, which had done little damage on walls of the outer bailey, went to work against the thinner walls of the inner bailey. The sappers mined beneath the walls only to be intercepted by a countermine. Both mines weakened the substructure of the castle and the trebuchet finally brought down a section of wall, forcing the garrison to surrender the supposedly impregnable castle. The surviving 140 defenders were taken prisoners. Like so many other castles, Château Gaillard was repaired until 1603 when the first Bourbon king ordered the dismantling of its defensive elements.

Mont St. Michel, Brittany

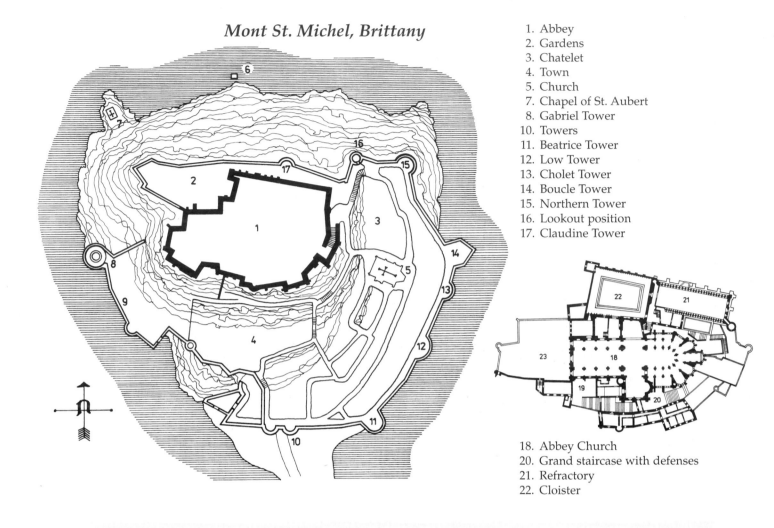

1. Abbey
2. Gardens
3. Chatelet
4. Town
5. Church
7. Chapel of St. Aubert
8. Gabriel Tower
10. Towers
11. Beatrice Tower
12. Low Tower
13. Cholet Tower
14. Boucle Tower
15. Northern Tower
16. Lookout position
17. Claudine Tower

18. Abbey Church
20. Grand staircase with defenses
21. Refractory
22. Cloister

MONT ST. MICHEL, BRITTANY. *The monastery sits atop the island and the town walls lie below. The island is surrounded by water only at high tide.*

MONT ST. MICHEL. *Fortified approaches to the monastery and church looking west from #3 on the plan opposite.*

On the border between Brittany and Normandy was a Benedictine monastery built atop a rocky island in the 10th century known as **Mont St. Michel**. A Romanesque monastery replaced the older one in the 11th and 12th centuries under the jurisdiction of the English king. During the next century, under the kings of France, Gothic additions were made. The monastery was fortified with crenelations and the town at the base of the island was enclosed with an enceinte and several towers that were linked to the abbey above. The town walls included an almost continuous line of machicoulis. Three fortified gates covered the approaches to the monastery. At the top of the winding path to the monastery stands a structure called a *châtelet* in French. It is a small work at the end of an approach protecting an entrance. In 1434 only 119 French knights were able to repel an English assault at this point. The island of Mont Saint Michel was easily accessed at low tide across the sand flats, but it became totally inundated at high tide.

MONT ST. MICHEL, BRITTANY. *A closeup view, taken from #10 on the plan opposite.*

Coucy-Le-Château, France

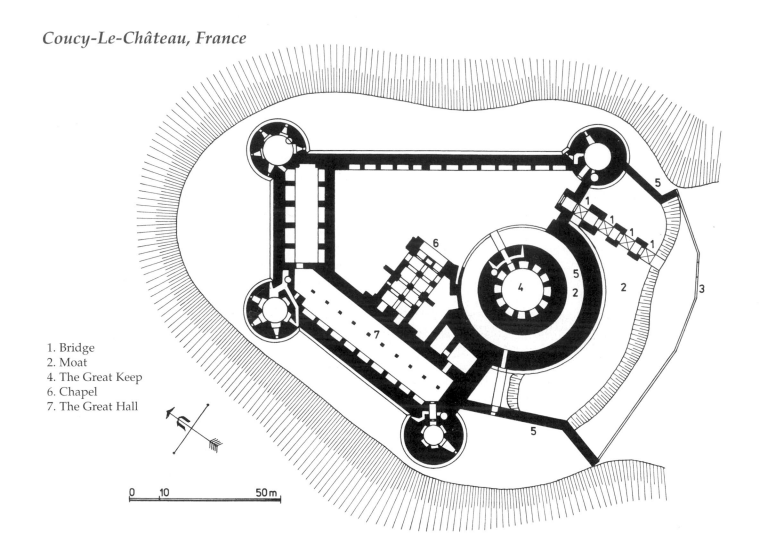

1. Bridge
2. Moat
4. The Great Keep
6. Chapel
7. The Great Hall

0 10   50 m

The remains of Coucy-Le-Château's with what is left of the great keep on the left that was destroyed by the Germans in World War I.

Another of France's impressive fortified sites is **Coucy-Le-Château**, which had one of the largest keeps ever built. The town and castle of Coucy were sited on top of a hill with steep sides. The fortified town was enclosed by turreted walls which connected to the castle. Enguerrand III of Coucy began construction of the great donjon in about 1220. Between 1225 and 1240 the town and castle fortified complex was completed and included 32 towers, most of which flanked the walls, and four of which were the large corner towers of the castle. From this site, which overlooked the valley of the Ailette and the Oise, Enguerrand and his descendants dominated the entire surrounding region as well the approach to Paris from the north for many years.

A vast lower bailey lay between the castle and the town, from which it was separated by a gated wall. The courtyard housed the stables, two barracks, the church for the garrison, administrative buildings, and other facilities. In later centuries it became the parade grounds or Place d'Armes. The lower bailey was protected by an enceinte with 13 towers and had several sally ports.

The castle of Coucy was quadrangular and had four massive corner towers. It had only one entrance that was accessed by a drawbridge and long causeway spanning a large outer moat. The massive keep, or *tour maîtresse*, was built into the wall facing the lower bailey. It was separated from the lower ward by a moat and a semicircular defensive wall called a chemise, which was about 20 meters high. It was also set apart from the upper bailey by an interior moat. The keep rose to a height of 54 meters, had a diameter of 31 meters, and walls about 7.5 meters thick at the lower level. It was equipped with its own drawbridge, a portcullis, two doors, an iron grille, a staircase, and access to the garderobe. It also had a well about 64 meters deep that supplied the occupants with fresh water on the lower level. On the second level, a postern was equipped with another drawbridge that allowed contact with the allure of the chemise. The third level included a great hall with a surrounding gallery and wooden balconies about 3 meters above the floor, which is said to have accommodated the entire garrison of up to 1,500 men. Finally, the fourth level allowed access to the battlements and a large two-story wooden hoarding. The interior of this keep was decorated with many fine carvings and had impressive Gothic vaulting. The keep of Coucy was no doubt one of the finest seigneorial dwellings in medieval France. The castle was entered through a single gate located next to the keep. Its interior walls were lined with a residential building on the northwestern side, which held the great hall and the seigneorial apartments, which were renovated by Enguerrand VII. A chapel projecting into the interior courtyard led to one of the great halls. The castle also included subterranean works.

The first major siege of Coucy took place in 1411 during the civil war between the Armagnacs and the supporters of the Burgundians during the Hundred Years War. The next siege did not occur until the 17th century, when members of the Fronde tried to use it as their base, after which the castle's defenses were dismantled in 1652. The castle managed to survive in reasonable repair until 1917, when the Germans decided to install their Paris Gun nearby and blew up the great keep before they withdrew.

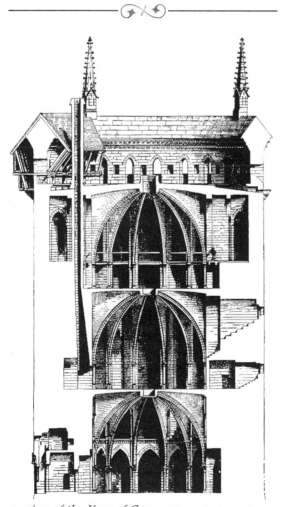

Cutaway view of the Keep of Coucy (Illustration from Military Architecture *courtesy of Greenhill Books)*

Vincennes Castle, France

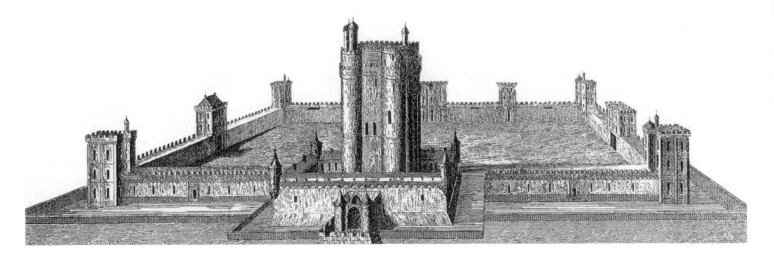

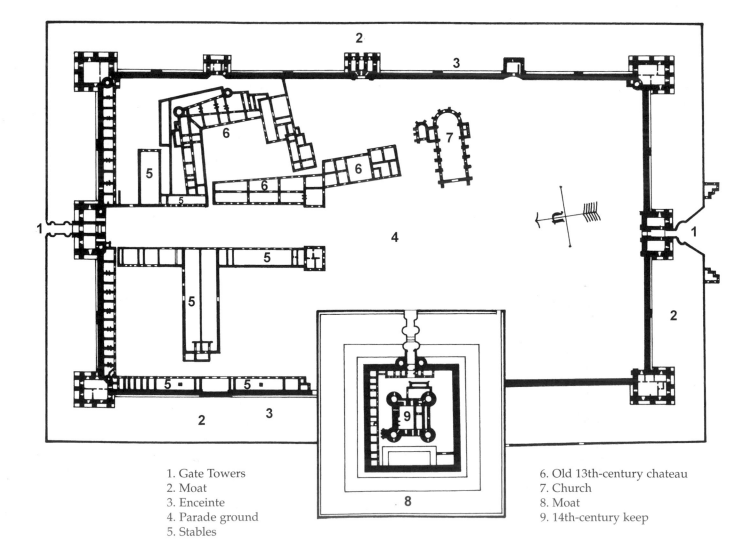

1. Gate Towers
2. Moat
3. Enceinte
4. Parade ground
5. Stables

6. Old 13th-century chateau
7. Church
8. Moat
9. 14th-century keep

Another brilliant example of medieval military architecture is the royal castle of **Vincennes**, which became one of the most important in France. Originally, in the 12th century, it had been a small hunting lodge of the kings of France in the Paris forest. Louis IX added a keep in the 13th century and Philip the Fair added the courtyard. Philip VI built the present great keep about 50 meters west of the old one over a period of about 30 years beginning in 1337. The 66-meter-high keep consisted of five stories and included four circular corner towers and a well protected entrance. Charles V enclosed this keep and a huge area around it with an enceinte that included nine rectangular towers, four of which were corner towers, and three entrances. The large keep and its original enclosure sat on one side of this new curtain wall. A huge wet moat, which was drained in the Renaissance, surrounded the enceinte.

Vincennes became one of the largest royal residences of the 14th century and rivaled in size the Palace of the Pope at Avignon. Only the keep at Coucy was larger. The chemise enclosing the keep had a plinth and continuous machicoulis, with bartizans or watchtowers on each corner. A barbican surrounded by its own moat protected the two large towers of the entrance to the royal compound.

Vincennes was the scene of many important events during the Hundred Years War. King Henry V of England died there in 1422 after agreeing to a truce with the French king. It was reoccupied by the English in 1430 and became the residence of Henry VI of England until it was recaptured by the French in 1432. The castle eventually was converted into a prison and remained as such for a number of years until it was restored and put back into use by the kings of France.

❧✦☙

Southwestern France is particularly rich in medieval fortifications, which include not only the city of **Carcassonne** (see pages 115-117) but also a series of castles that were occupied in the 13th century by a heretical sect known as the Cathars. These castles played an important role in the Albigensian Crusade launched by Pope Innocent III in 1208. The king of France sent Simon de Montfort at the head of a French Crusader expedition from the north to invade the region. Count Raymond VI of Toulouse, who tolerated this sect in Languedoc, attempted to defend his territory from the invaders, but was defeated by Simon in 1213.

After the count's defeat, the French crusaders continued their massacre of the Cathars. In 1218, Simon de Montfort was killed by a stone launched from a trebuchet during his siege of Toulouse. Louis VIII then personally led a new crusade in the 1120s. The last resistance ended with the fall of the castles at Montségur in 1244 and Quéribus in 1255.

The fortified city of Carcassonne, ruled by the Viscount Raymond-Roger Trencavel, was an early objective of this crusade. At the time it included only its original set of Roman walls. When the siege began in 1209, the city held 4,000 people, including about 2,000 combatants, while the besiegers numbered 20,000 men. In August 1209, after only 15 days, its water supply started running low, so Viscount Raymond-Roger rode out under a flag of truce and was taken prisoner. As a result, the town surrendered, and Simon de Montfort appointed himself Viscount and ruler of Carcassonne and was later succeeded by his son. Louis VIII turned the city into a royal fortress. The last of the Trencavel, in an effort to regain his family's holdings, attacked Carcassonne in 1240. However, he was forced to lift his siege when Louis IX's army came to the rescue, putting an end to his ambitions. The king moved the city's population across the Aude River where he founded a new town. He then proceeded to strengthen the old city by ordering the construction of an outer wall not as high as the inner one. The new wall included 15 towers, mostly open in the rear, and 2 barbicans. However, instead of having the older defenses razed, the king ordered them rebuilt. The work was completed by 1285 and the city became known as "The Maid of Languedoc."

The Black Prince of England avoided attacking Carcassonne during the Hundred Years War. However, the city lost its strategic importance when the Spanish frontier was pushed further south during the 17th century.

❧✦☙

The Cathar Castles high in the surrounding mountains included Minerve, Termes, Lastours, Peyrepertuse, Montségur, Puylaurens, and Quéribus. Located north of Carcassonne, **Lastours** consisted of four castles built along a rocky mountain crest. The oldest of the four, Cabaret, dated from 1063. Fleur-Espine, which included a keep and a walled enclosure, was built in 1153. Quertinheux, which was built on a rock, was built slightly later. Finally, the Régine or Royal Tower, built near Quertinheux, was added by the

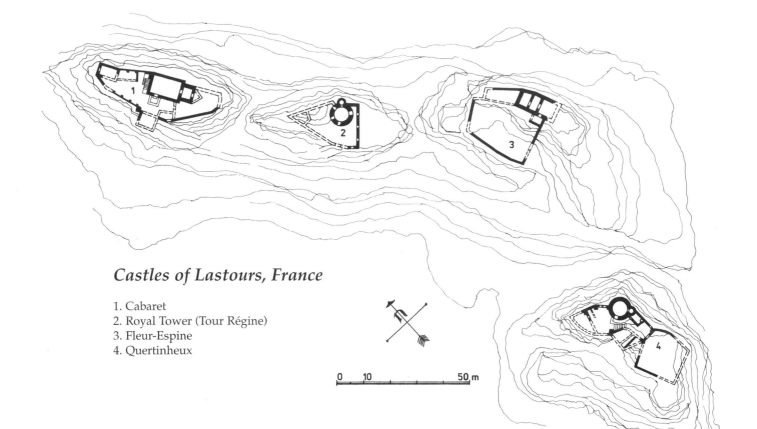

Castles of Lastours, France

1. Cabaret
2. Royal Tower (Tour Régine)
3. Fleur-Espine
4. Quertinheux

0   10   50 m

QUERTINHEUX, *one of the four castles of Lastours. The king had it, the Royal Tower, and Fleur-Espine built as counter-castles to watch over and block access to Cabaret Castle.*

CABARET CASTLE, LASTOURS, *with badly damaged keep.*

king's forces after they took the site from the Cathars. According to legend, the people of Carcassonne escaped by underground passage to Lastours when the city fell in 1209. Simon de Montfort put Cabaret under siege in 1209, but was not able to take it. The Cathars abandoned the castle in 1211.

The fortified village of **Minerve**, to the northeast of Carcassonne and northwest of Narbonne, stood on a spur surrounded by two ravines. It served as a refuge for the Cathars under the protection of Viscount Guillaume of Minerve. Its enceinte covered most of the village, except on the side of the cliffs. In July 1210, Simon de Montfort put the city under siege and bombarded it with four catapults, one of which was named *Malevoisine* or "Bad Neighbor," and was probably a trebuchet. Its heavy projectiles created so much havoc in the castle that a small sortie was launched to destroy it, but the defenders failed in their mission. Almost seven weeks after the beginning of the siege, as the death toll mounted and with nowhere to bury the dead on the rocky spur, the situation inside the castle became intolerable. Viscount Guillaume surrendered and the Cathars taken prisoner were massacred when they refused to renounce their faith.

Peyrepertuse Castle rests at the top of a mountain over 730 meters in altitude with difficult approaches.

The site was fortified since Roman times. The castle, first mentioned in 1020, included a large square keep and a church. After it fell to St. Louis (Louis IX) in 1240, additions made in 1245 included a large new circular tower next to the keep and extensions to the 12th century walls which stretched for almost 100 meters, creating a large courtyard that enclosed this section of the mountain. The walls were highest along the northeast face, which is the only part of the approach that affords enough, though limited, space to assemble troops for an assault on the walls. Another castle was built above Peyrepertuse, on the mountain crest overlooking it. This was the castle of Saint Jordy, which included a keep, a large chapel and a wall running from the keep to the northern edge of the cliffs. This castle was built between 1245 and 1280.

Puylaurens Castle stands at the summit of a rocky mountain crag and dates back to the 10th century. A series of walls forming a chicane that protects the steep uphill approach to the castle's entrance was not added until the 17th century. The castle's circular towers at each corner were added by the king of France after he took Puylaurens from the Cathars in 1244. The square keep near the entrance that is overlooked by one of the circular towers is the only part of the original Cathar structure.

PEYREPERTUSE. *The keep of the lower castle.*

Peyrepertuse Castle, France

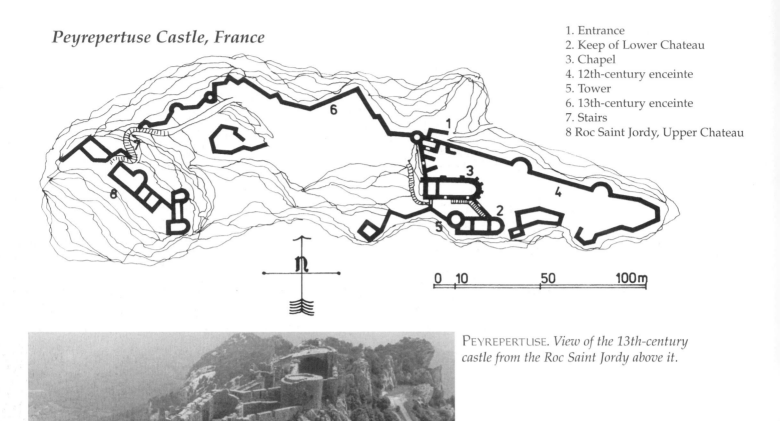

1. Entrance
2. Keep of Lower Chateau
3. Chapel
4. 12th-century enceinte
5. Tower
6. 13th-century enceinte
7. Stairs
8 Roc Saint Jordy, Upper Chateau

PEYREPERTUSE. *View of the 13th-century castle from the Roc Saint Jordy above it.*

PUYLAURENS CASTLE.

Puylaurens Castle, France

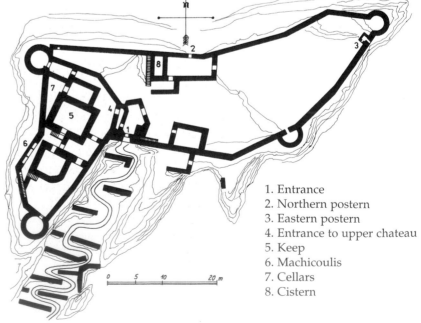

1. Entrance
2. Northern postern
3. Eastern postern
4. Entrance to upper chateau
5. Keep
6. Machicoulis
7. Cellars
8. Cistern

Montségur Castle was also built on the summit of a mountain at an altitude of 1,200 meters and had limited access like the other Cathar castles. It included a large keep at one end and an enceinte with three sides covering over 40 meters on the longest side. This enceinte was apparently only a low weak wall during the Cathar occupation and was raised and strengthened by the king after the defeat of the Cathars. Montségur was built early in 1204 and evidence suggests that it had served as a religious center for the Cathars. Louis IX sent an army against it in 1243. The approach up a winding path was a difficult one. The crusaders stealthily carried the parts of a catapult up the mountain and set it up on the opposite side of the castle so they could effectively bombard it. However, their siege machines were smashed by the machines of the defenders. It took nine months for the Cathars to surrender. When they finally did, they were promptly massacred and their remains were burned, as custom dictated in the case of witches and heretics.

Quéribus rested upon another lofty peak. It had a large keep that included access through a subterranean chamber to a small position overlooking a steep approach that offered, nonetheless, enough room for a besieger to install artillery. The entrance to the castle was located at a distance of about 40 meters from the keep, at a lower level. A series of walls covered the approaches. Quéribus resisted the Crusaders until 1255 and served as the last stronghold of the Cathars. The king's men managed to bring a trebuchet to the back of the castle at the location covered by the small underground position. Although they smashed some sections of the walls and its hoardings, they did not inflict enough damage to allow their miners to work against the walls. A number of projectiles from this assault can still be found embedded in the defenses.

As a rule, the Cathar castles had no circular nor projecting towers. Whenever these types of towers are found in Cathar fortification, they can usually be attributed to King Louis IX, who reinforced some of the castles of the Roussillon and used them as border outposts against Aragon. Puylaurens, Peyrepertuse, Aguilar, Termes, and Quéribus were the few selected for continued service out of about 50 castles in the region. Montségur and Puivert were also reinforced to maintain control over the region since the population's loyalty was questionable after the crusade.

The ruins of Montségur.

Montségur Castle, France

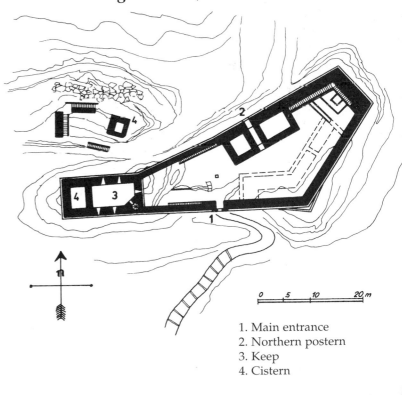

1. Main entrance
2. Northern postern
3. Keep
4. Cistern

Quéribus Castle, France

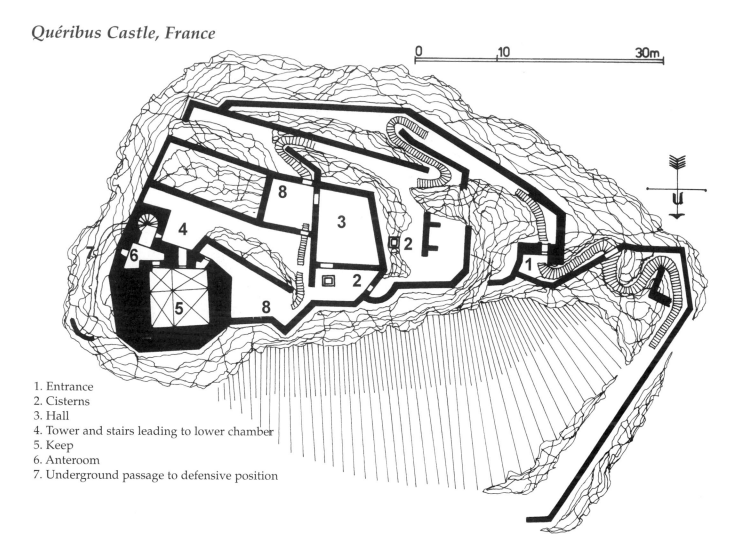

0   10   30m

1. Entrance
2. Cisterns
3. Hall
4. Tower and stairs leading to lower chamber
5. Keep
6. Anteroom
7. Underground passage to defensive position

QUÉRIBUS. *The remains of the castle. The approach to the castle is on the right but during an assault the design allowed the defenders to take up positions on the left.*

Louis IX also built the large fortified port of **Aigues Mortes** in the marshes of the Rhone delta between 1240 and 1250 in preparation for his crusade against Islam. Saint Louis first built the great round keep, or Tower of Constance, which had walls almost six meters thick and was surrounded by a moat. The tower stood outside the town walls and was linked to them by an arched bridge which gave access to the second level (European first floor). Except at the upper level, the Tower of Constance had no loopholes. Its battlements were modified for artillery at the end of the Middle Ages. The town walls, when they were finally completed by Philip III the Bold and Philip IV the Fair in 1295, formed a rectangular enceinte of about 1.7 kilometers surrounded by a moat. Five gates, each consisting of a châtelet with two large semicircular towers, and several posterns gave access to the town. An advanced work called the Tower of Carbonnière, which controlled the road leading to the town through the marshes, was built about three kilometers from the town. It too was later modified for artillery. This fortified harbor was considered Louis IX's most impressive achievement, even though its military value was not lasting.

———————— ✍ ————————

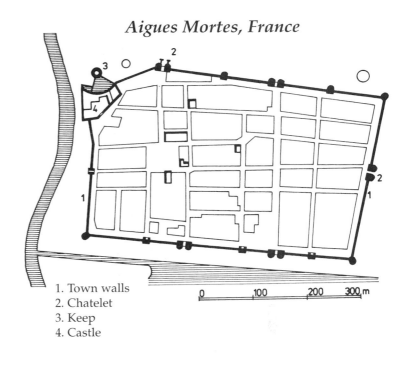

Aigues Mortes, France

1. Town walls
2. Chatelet
3. Keep
4. Castle

0   100   200   300 m

AIGUES MORTES. *One of the gates of the town wall. Note the garderobes on either side.*

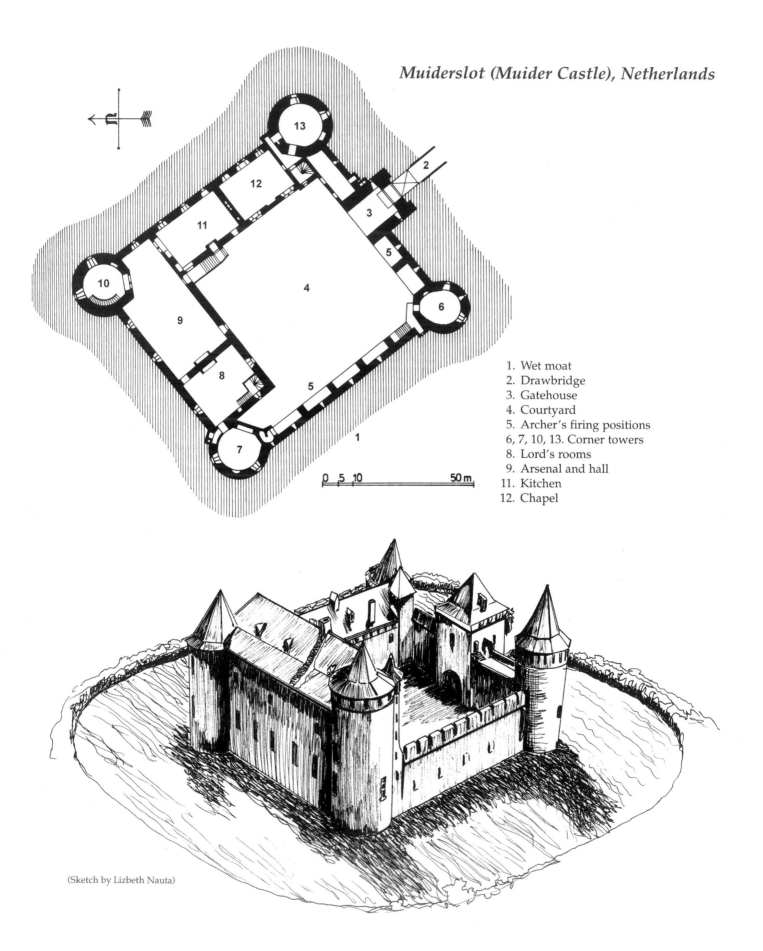

Muiderslot (Muider Castle), Netherlands

1. Wet moat
2. Drawbridge
3. Gatehouse
4. Courtyard
5. Archer's firing positions
6, 7, 10, 13. Corner towers
8. Lord's rooms
9. Arsenal and hall
11. Kitchen
12. Chapel

0 5 10   50 m

(Sketch by Lizbeth Nauta)

The Low Countries

Although Belgium, The Netherlands, and Luxembourg were part of the Holy Roman Empire, their fortifications were heavily influenced by west European designs. In The Netherlands, most castles were built with water defenses, since the land elevations were generally low.

One of the finest examples of Dutch castles is **Muiderslot** or **Muider Castle** (slot means castle), which clearly shows the influence of the Edwardian castles of Wales. It was built about 1280 when Count Floris V ordered its construction in the middle of the Vecht River. Like most Dutch castles, this castle is built of brick in a rectangular pattern with four large drum towers projecting beyond its curtains. Its square gatehouse includes bretèches and a drawbridge. A great hall occupies the back wall of the castle. Much of this castle was rebuilt at the end of the 14th century since it was largely dismantled after the assassination of Count Floris in 1296. The new castle was built on the ruins in 1370 by the Count of Holland, a Bavarian duke. The great hall was one of the last additions and the castle saw no action until the 15th and 16th centuries.

One of the most important castles in Belgium is the **Château des Comtes**, also known as **Gravensteen**, which served the counts of Flanders. It was founded in 1180, when Count Philip of Alsace built a large keep at Ghent on the site of an older one dating from the previous century. He based his design on fortifications he had observed in the Levant during the Crusades.

A barbican standing about 20 meters in front of the outer curtain is linked by a double wall to the gatehouse, whose entrance is covered by a bretèche. The keep, a large rectangular structure with walls 1.7 meters thick built in 1180, stands in the center of the bailey. Its loopholes, located 1.8 meters above the floor, were reached by means of a scaffolding. The present keep shows that it consisted of three floors with firing loops in two of them. The first two floors of the older castle were incorporated into it, forming its basement. Other structures of the castle were placed along the front and side of the keep and included the residence of the castellan and the kitchens. The palace of the counts was built behind the keep, along the curtain wall.

The bailey wall consists of 24 semicircular turrets supported by wall buttresses. Each tower has two levels, a lower level with arrow loops and an upper level crowned with merlons, embrasures secured with wooden shutters, and machicolations. One of these towers was larger than the rest, had embrasures in the walls, and was covered by a small roof. The wall walk passed through its lower level. The curtain walls of the castle were surrounded by a water-filled moat.

The burghers of Ghent took Gravensteen by siege in 1301 and 1338. The second time, the curtain was breached. In the centuries that followed the gatehouse and keep were used as prisons and the counts used the palace as a court of justice until 1708.

Not far from the modern-day capital of Brussels, in the Brabant region, stands the water castle of **Beersel**. The first fortification on this site was built under Henry I, Duke of the Brabant, in the 13th century. It was one of three similar castles in the region and sited in terrain where water could be easily incorporated into its defenses. Beersel was originally built as a simple stone-walled enclosure but additional work transformed it into a castle over time. Its moat is formed by a small lake. Its D-shaped towers are designed to resist gunpowder weapons. The upper level of one of its towers served as permanent quarters for the garrison, but in wartime the other towers could be similarly used. Because mercenaries were heavily used in the late Middle Ages, provisions were made to quarter the local garrison in a separate tower from the others, in case the mercenaries became unreliable. Machicoulis topped the curtain walls and the towers. The gate tower included a portcullis and murder holes in addition to the drawbridge and its mechanisms. Weapons were maintained in the castle and a garrison of 50 men was considered sufficient to hold it. Its most distinctive feature are the Flemish style stepped gables added to its towers in the 17th century. Beersel was taken twice by siege and was rebuilt in 1491, when its present three towers were erected.

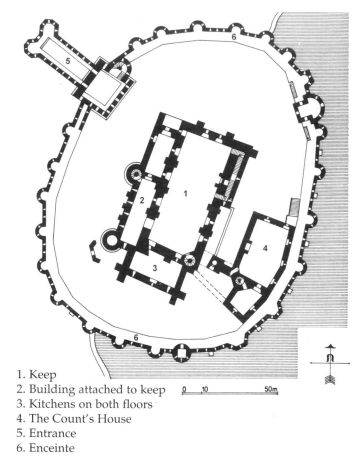

1. Keep
2. Building attached to keep
3. Kitchens on both floors
4. The Count's House
5. Entrance
6. Enceinte

View along the restored eastern wall with the upper level of the Count's House visible behind the outer wall.

Gravensteen, Ghent, Belgium

View from the northeast of the semicircular bartizan and behind it the restored keep.

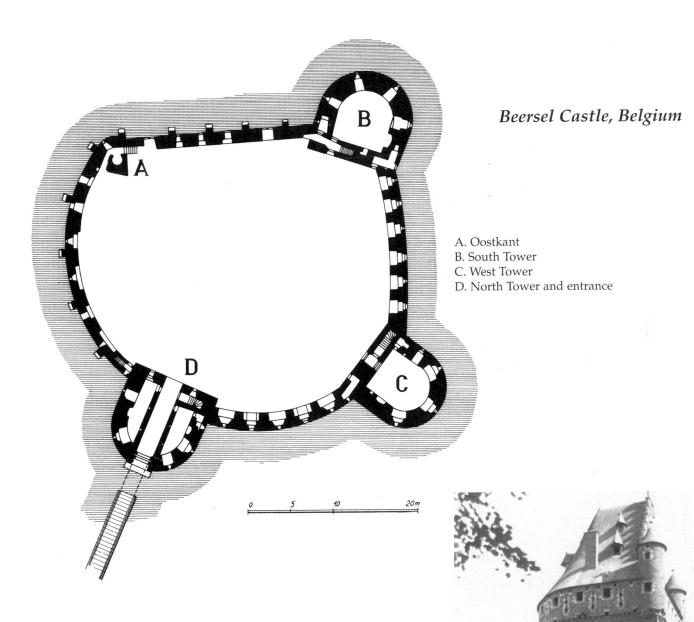

Beersel Castle, Belgium

A. Oostkant
B. South Tower
C. West Tower
D. North Tower and entrance

0 5 10 20m

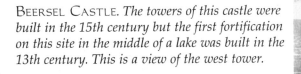

BEERSEL CASTLE. *The towers of this castle were built in the 15th century but the first fortification on this site in the middle of a lake was built in the 13th century. This is a view of the west tower.*

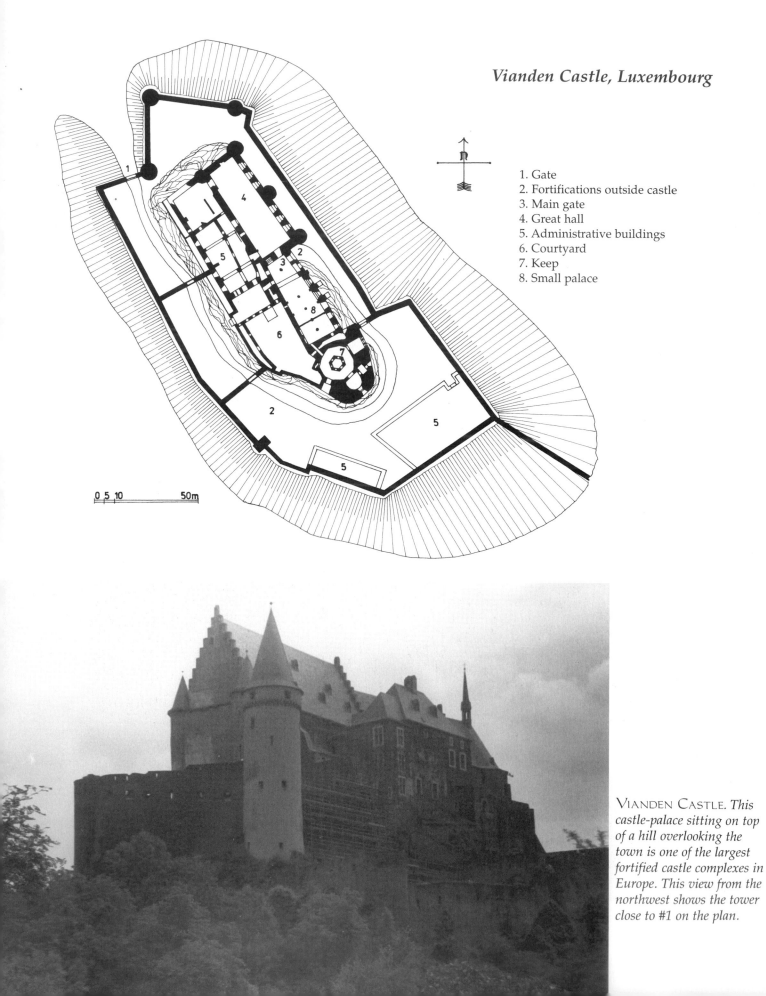

Vianden Castle, Luxembourg

1. Gate
2. Fortifications outside castle
3. Main gate
4. Great hall
5. Administrative buildings
6. Courtyard
7. Keep
8. Small palace

0 5 10   50m

VIANDEN CASTLE. *This castle-palace sitting on top of a hill overlooking the town is one of the largest fortified castle complexes in Europe. This view from the northwest shows the tower close to #1 on the plan.*

In the Ardennes region of Belgium the castles are sited on higher elevations, as is the case of **Boullion**, the seat of Godfrey, the leader of the First Crusade. This 11th-century castle stretched along a rocky ridge at the neck of a peninsula formed by a bend in the Semois River. While dominating both sides of the bend in the river from its lofty position, it still included a deep dry moat at its entrance. Boullion was heavily modified and extended in the 17th century by Vauban, who adapted it for artillery, and admirably illustrates the evolution of fortification from castle to modern fort.

⟡

Vianden Castle in Luxembourg is a combination castle-palace. Its origins go back to the 11th century, when it was built on the ruins of an old Roman fort and a 9th-century Carolingian palace. It is located on top of a hill overlooking the town and the river. The counts of Vianden apparently used the castle to force tolls on those traveling by land and river. The 11th-century castle included a square keep, a circular chapel on the other side of the enceinte, and a large palace in between. In the 12th century a second palace and a larger keep were added. The remains of a 13th-century octagonal tower near the center of the courtyard indicate that its function was toll collection. The early masonry of the castle is Romanesque with the typical herringbone pattern of the period. The 13th-century construction on the complex clearly belongs to the Gothic period and includes a new grand palace with a huge great hall capable of holding 500 men. The approach to the castle is covered by three successive gates that guard the path that passes beneath the castle walls along the new enceinte. Between the 13th and 15th centuries additional work resulted in the castle's high curtain walls protected by projecting circular towers. The town around the base of the hill extends to the river and bridge and is also protected by walls. Vianden became one of the largest fortified castle complexes in Europe.

BOULLION CASTLE. *The castle of Boullion, Belgium, was built by King Godfrey, the leader of the First Crusade. It sits atop a ridge in a loop of the Samois River.*

Chillon Castle, Switzerland

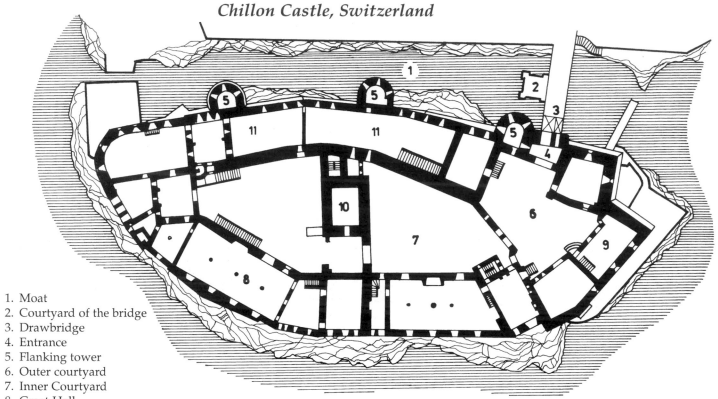

1. Moat
2. Courtyard of the bridge
3. Drawbridge
4. Entrance
5. Flanking tower
6. Outer courtyard
7. Inner Courtyard
8. Great Hall
9. Administrative building
10. Keep
11. Open space between walls

CHILLON CASTLE *on Lake Geneva. The keep is the tallest structure in the photo.*

Switzerland

Switzerland was and still is at the confluence of the German, Italian, and French traditions and its castles reflect the influence of all three. The 13th century residence of the Hapsburgs, **Hapsburg Castle**, in northern Switzerland can be numbered among its German-style castles. Its surviving bergfried dates to the 11th century and other additions were made over centuries. In western Switzerland, **Grandson Castle** towers over Lake Neuchâtel. Its tall curtain walls, three large, round corner towers, and two smaller semicircular towers date from the 13th century. The rest of the castle was heavily rebuilt in the 15th century when it came under the control of the counts of Chalon. A fausse braie also dates from this period.

The most famous of the Swiss castles is, without a doubt, **Chillon Castle** on an island on Lake Leman (also known as Lake Geneva) built, at least in part, by the bishops of Sion. The oldest of Chillon's towers may go as far back as the 10th century. This large rectangular tower at the center of Chillon is probably the old bergfried. However, most of the present structure, erected in the 13th century, can be attributed to Peter II of Savoy. It consists of the outer wall, towers, and buildings. The four large towers and the curtain facing landward are reinforced with machicoulis. During the 14th and 15th centuries, the walls and towers were given added height and the gate was rebuilt. Chillon remained in the possession of the Savoy family until it was taken over by the Bernese, who used it as an arsenal for their flotilla on the lake in 1536. Later still, it was used as a prison for a short time.

Grandson Castle, Switzerland

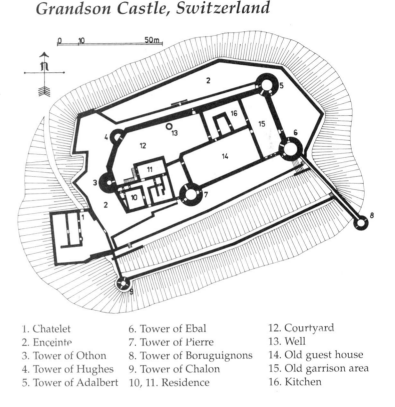

1. Chatelet
2. Enceinte
3. Tower of Othon
4. Tower of Hughes
5. Tower of Adalbert
6. Tower of Ebal
7. Tower of Pierre
8. Tower of Boruguignons
9. Tower of Chalon
10, 11. Residence
12. Courtyard
13. Well
14. Old guest house
15. Old garrison area
16. Kitchen

GRANDSON CASTLE. *The major battle of the same name was fought next to this castle in 1476. Grandson was built in the 13th century and later rebuilt in the 15th century. Two of the tall circular towers are pictured here—notice that the curtain walls almost reach the height of the towers.*

THE PFALZ *in Germany was known as the "Ship of Stone."*

GUTENFELS CASTLE *overlooking the Rhine with one of its circular towers in the foreground.*

MAUS CASTLE. *Built on a square plan, this was one of the best designed 14th-century castles on the Rhine.*

Holy Roman Empire

The greatest concentration of castles in any river valley in the Holy Roman Empire was to be found on the Rhine, between Mainz and Bonn. The German barons built castles on this stretch of the great river to control the trade route. Between Mainz and Cologne alone there were 30 structures set up to collect tolls. These castles, which fell under the control of the Electors of Mainz, the Palatinate, Trier, and Cologne included Eltville, Klopp, Ehrenfels, the Mouse Tower, Rheinstein, Sooneck, Heimburg, Furstenberg, Stahleck, Gutenfels, Pfalz, Schonburg, Marksburg, Maus, Boppard, Stolzenfels, Ehrenbreitsteing, Lahneck, Martinsburg, Hammerstein, Arenfels, Reineck, Drachenfels, and Godesburg.

Many of these Rhine castles stood on outcrops above the valley, from where they could dominate the river. Most consisted of one or more tall towers that dominated their surroundings; a few actually were built along the river; and one, known as the **Pfalz**, was situated in the river. The Pfalz, which was built in 1327 by King Ludwig of Bavaria as a toll station, became known as the "Ship of Stone" and was modified over the centuries. It was dominated by a pentagonal keep that stood at the center of a large courtyard and was first built to serve as a toll station. A decade later the central tower was surrounded by a hexagonal structure. It is overlooked by **Gutenfels Castle**, which stands above it, on the east bank of the Rhine. Gutenfels, with its 35-meter-high bergfried, a three-story-high great hall, and strong curtain walls, is more typical of the medieval German castle.

Many of the Rhine castles were controlled by the infamous "Robber Barons" and were so much out of control during the 13th century that the League of Rhenish Cities was created in 1254 to challenge their domination of trade along the river. In 1272, Emperor Rudolf finally crushed their power, destroying the castles of Rheinstein, Reichsenstein, Sooneck, and Rheineck. However, he was unable to take Rheinfels. Many of these castles served in the Thirty Years War and later.

One of the best preserved of the Rhine castles is **Marksburg**, which is perched on a high crag overlooking the river. Built early in the 13th century by Count Eberhard II von Eppstein, it includes an unusual triangular-shaped courtyard. Its largest structure is the palace on its least accessible side. A structure known as the Rheinbau occupies the eastern side of the courtyard and another, the Nordbau, the north side. Between the palace and Rheinbau rises the large Kaiser Tower. Another smaller, round tower stands at the other end of the Rheinbau. The four-level bergfried in the center of the courtyard rises to a height of 40 meters. Its turret towers over the castle and gives a commanding view of the region. An outer curtain wall, added below during the 15th century, encircles the high castle and was eventually adapted for artillery. Marksburg was the only one of the Rhine castles that did not fall in the Thirty Years War of the 17th century.

RHEINSTEIN CASTLE.

Marksburg Castle, Germany

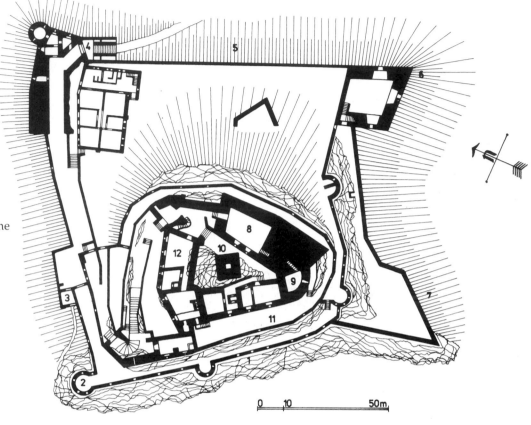

1. Lower wall facing the Rhine
2. Tower of the Constable
3. Entrance
4. Bridge Tower
5. Wall
6. Pulvereck
7. Sharp angle
8. Palace
9. Kaiser Heinrich Tower
10. Bergfried
11. Rheinbau

MARKSBURG CASTLE *sits high above the Rhine River with a 40-meter bergfried that gives a commanding view of the region.*

Otzberg is a classic example of a German hilltop castle derived from a bergfried, which overlooks the town from the top of a hill. This circular tower was built purely for observation and defense and afforded no space for accommodation. It stands in the center of the inner ward of the castle and is surrounded by high walls against which lean the other structures of the castle. The outer ward encircles the inner ward which in turn is surrounded by a large moat. No detailed information is available about the site, but it appears to have been built in the 13th century.

❧❧❧

In the Odenwald, **Breuberg Castle** was begun during the 12th century and was the property of the imperial abbey of Fulda. It was built on top of a large hill overlooking the town of Neustadt. Its enceinte, between 10 and 14 meters high, was laid out in an almost rectangular shape and enclosed a ward about 55 by 38 meters. A tall, square bergfried that dates back to 1160 occupies the center of the courtyard. Several of the buildings of this inner ward, the Romanesque entrance gate, and the chapel on the northeast wall were added in 1350. Most of the other buildings, including the palace, were erected between 1475 and 1510. The outer castle with two additional gates were constructed in the 15th century. A large moat surrounded the entire castle complex. Four circular towers designed for artillery were built between 1482 and 1507. Breuberg is a fine example of a castle adapted to the era of gunpowder by the 16th century.

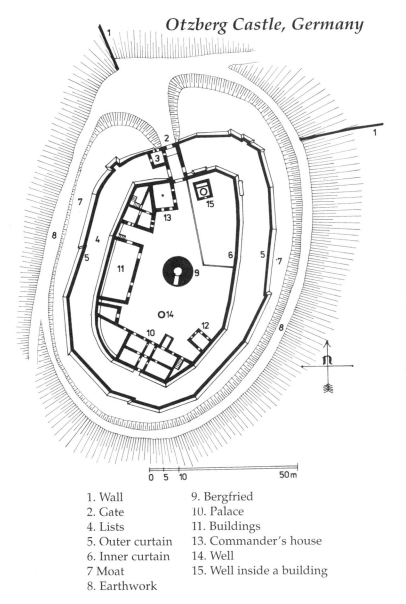

Otzberg Castle, Germany

1. Wall	9. Bergfried
2. Gate	10. Palace
4. Lists	11. Buildings
5. Outer curtain	13. Commander's house
6. Inner curtain	14. Well
7 Moat	15. Well inside a building
8. Earthwork	

OTZBERG CASTLE, GERMANY. *Part of the remains of the enceinte with the battlements gone.*

Breuberg Castle, Germany

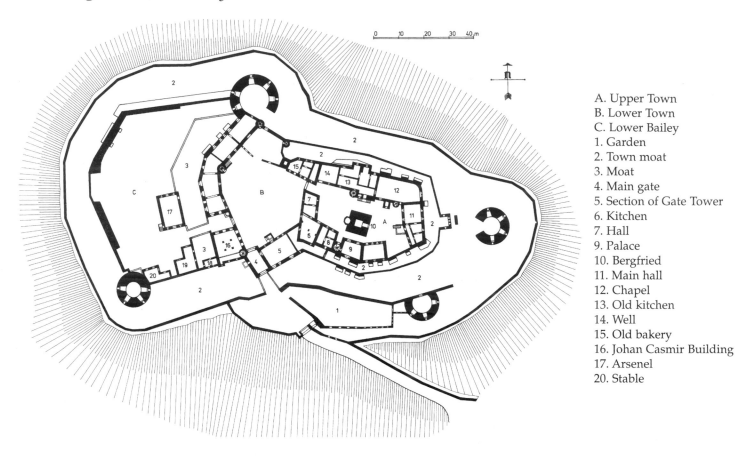

A. Upper Town
B. Lower Town
C. Lower Bailey
1. Garden
2. Town moat
3. Moat
4. Main gate
5. Section of Gate Tower
6. Kitchen
7. Hall
9. Palace
10. Bergfried
11. Main hall
12. Chapel
13. Old kitchen
14. Well
15. Old bakery
16. Johan Casmir Building
17. Arsenel
20. Stable

BREUBERG CASTLE *overlooks the town of Neustadt, Germany. The photo on the left is a view looking east toward #2 on the plan with the main gate (#4) in the middle background.*

German castle building extended beyond the empire into the lands of Prussia, where the Teutonic Knights had established their headquarters. Their most important and largest castle was **Marienburg** (now located in Poland and known as Malbork Castle), which was the seat of the Grand Master and can be categorized as a convent-castle. In 1280, the Teutonic Knights had moved their convent from Zamtyr, near the confluence of the Vistula and Nogat rivers, to a new location higher up the Nogat River. The new site stood on a finger of land jutting out into the Zulawy Marsh, which straddled the river at this point. The work on this site had actually begun two years earlier. The moats, linked to Lake Dabrowka by a canal that extended for 10 kilometers, were dug first. Among the first structures to go up on the south side of the site was the large square structure known as the High Castle, which included the chapel and corner turrets for defense. The so-called Gdanisko Tower to the southeast of this structure was added soon after. Next came the Middle Castle, which included the palace of the Grand Master. Both the High and Middle Castles were surrounded by a moat. Concentric walls finally completed the defenses. The fortified complex was accessed through a high gate tower in the Middle Castle on its north side. The area in front of the Middle Castle, called Fore-Castle,

included facilities such as the stables, workshops, and armories that served the occupants of the castle. This area was enclosed within the fortifications and became the Lower Castle. After the castle was built, a town grew alongside it. The castle's defenses absorbed the town walls in 1365. The towers and walls include machicolations and the galleries and towers are built in the Gothic style. The area covered by the defenses was 800 meters long and up to 250 meters in width at one time.

In 1280, Marienburg was placed under the supervision of Henrich von Wilnowe, Commander of the Order. In 1309, Grand Master Siegfried von Feuchtwangen transferred his headquarters here. Between 1320 and 1350 a new construction phase resulted in the creation of the three sections of the castle. In 1410, the castle was put under siege for two months by the Poles, who failed to take it. After that, the Teutonic Knights adapted the castle for gunpowder weapons and later in the century successfully resisted further Polish attacks. Finally, in 1454, King Casimir of Poland managed to capture Marienburg. The castle underwent further modifications in the 17th century under the Swedes and later it fell into disuse and was not restored until after World War II. Today, it is considered to be one of the largest brick fortresses in the world.

MARIENBURG (MALBORK), POLAND. *View of the Bridge Gate (#5) on town plan on page 242.*

Marienburg Castle (Malbork), Poland

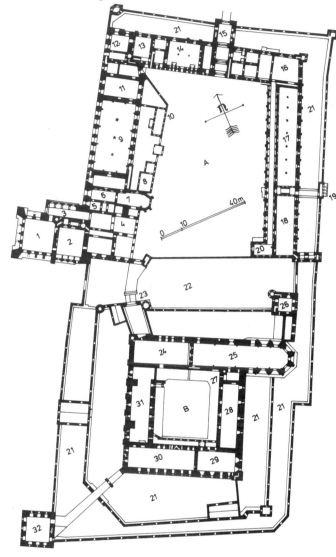

A. Middle Castle
B. High Castle
1-18. Palace of the Grand Masters
15. Entrance gate and drawbridge
21. Lists
22. Moat
23. Drawbridge
25. Church of St. Mary
28. Knight's Hall
29. Room of the Convent
30. Convent Refectory
31. Great hall
32. Gdanisko Tower

Town of Marienburg, Poland

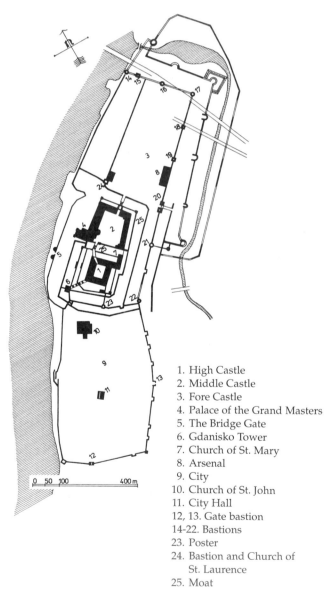

1. High Castle
2. Middle Castle
3. Fore Castle
4. Palace of the Grand Masters
5. The Bridge Gate
6. Gdanisko Tower
7. Church of St. Mary
8. Arsenal
9. City
10. Church of St. John
11. City Hall
12, 13. Gate bastion
14-22. Bastions
23. Poster
24. Bastion and Church of St. Laurence
25. Moat

MARIENBURG *is one of the largest brick fortresses in the world.*

The Baltic Region

SWEDEN

Olavinlinna · Viborg

Hame

· Abo

Stockholm

NOVGOROD

Koporye

Narva

Reval

Novgorod

ESTONIANS

Fellin

Pskov

PSKOV

Wolmar

LIVS

Wenden

Rigo

LETTS

Kalmar

BALTIC SEA

CURONIANS

LITHUANIANS

POLOTSKA

RUSSIAN PRINCIPALITIES

DENMARK Copenhagen

Memel

Arkona

Rostock

RUGIANS

Konigsberg

PRUSSIANS

Danzig

Elbing

POMERANIANS

LIUTIZIANS

Marienburg

Christburg

Rheden

Stettin

Torun

VOLHYNIA

KIEV

H.R.E.

POLAND

· Dobrzyn

KALMAR CASTLE, SWEDEN.

(Sketch by Lizbeth Nauta)

Kalmar Castle, Sweden

Late 12th century castle rebuilt in the 13th century and heavily changed in the 16th century.

1. Artillery wall (16th century)
2. Artillery bastions (16th century)
3. Gate
4. Magazines under walls
5. Gate tower
6. 13th century ward
7. Palace
8. Residence
9. Well

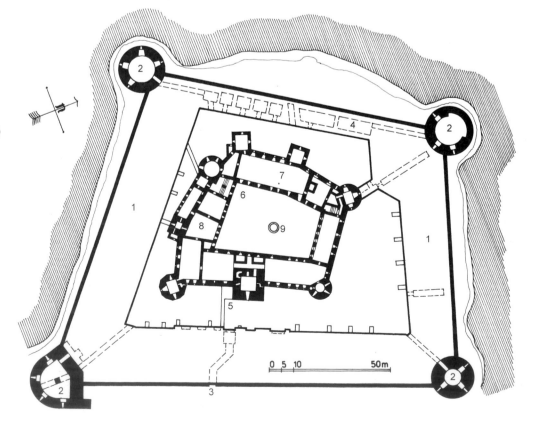

Scandinavia and Finland

The history of fortifications in this region is tangled and confused. The Danes dominated during the early part of the High Middle Ages. The Swedes, on the other hand, did not establish a strong kingdom until the 14th century. In 1397 the Union of Kalmar united the kingdoms of Norway, Sweden, and Denmark under the leadership of the Danish monarch Queen Margarita. Meanwhile, the Duke of Mecklenburg's son held Stockholm and claimed the Swedish throne. During this time the number of castles increased, many of them privately built. In southwestern Sweden, along the coast, were the ruins of a 12th-century fortification that served as a Danish toll station on the narrow straits. In 1370, Danish King Valdemar IV rebuilt the position in brick, giving it extremely thick walls. However, castle building in Sweden did not begin in earnest until after 1250.

One of the oldest castles in Sweden is the 13th century fortification of **Kalmar**, located on the southeast coast. It may have been constructed as early as the 1250s. Its oldest structure is a round tower, which was built at the same time as several other buildings that do not remain standing today.

This castle initially served to check the activities of Slavonic pirates. By the end of the century an enceinte with round projecting flanking towers was completed and a gatehouse was added on the west wall. The castle was surrounded by its own moat and occupied most of the island on which it stood. Its design may have been influenced by the Edwardian castles. Kalmar, like many other Swedish castles, stood near a walled town whose fortifications were built at the beginning of the 14th century. Turrets, open on the sides that faced the castle, flanked the town's curtain wall.

Across the straits, on the island of Öland, stood **Borgholm Castle** built in a similar style as Kalmar. However, here a large, round tower rose inside the curtain wall and a large corner tower projected out of its almost square enceinte. Known as the "Key to Sweden," Borgholm has endured many sieges and undergone many modifications that include towers for artillery. Interestingly, a similar fortification, with a round tower dating to the mid-13th century and the same type of enceinte, was also built at Stockholm, but it was made of brick. Like Borgholm Castle, **Stockholm Castle**, also stood on an island and acquired its castle and town walls in the 1250s.

Viborg Castle (Viipuri), Karelian Isthmus, Finland

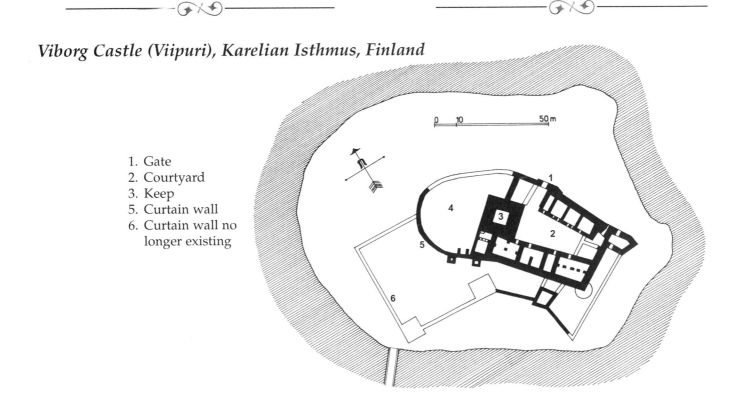

1. Gate
2. Courtyard
3. Keep
5. Curtain wall
6. Curtain wall no longer existing

Raseborg Castle, Finland

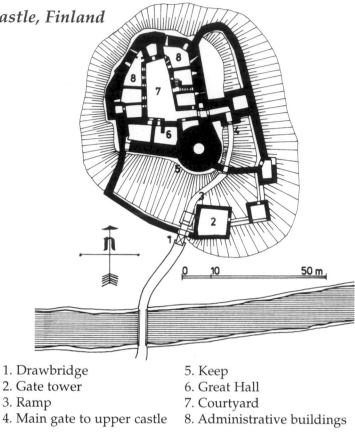

RASEBORG CASTLE, FINLAND. *Large square granite castle built in 1374 and used by the Swedish king's bailiff to administer southern Finland.* (Photo courtesy of Jaroslaw Chorzepa)

1. Drawbridge
2. Gate tower
3. Ramp
4. Main gate to upper castle
5. Keep
6. Great Hall
7. Courtyard
8. Administrative buildings

However, of the three Swedish castles mentioned only Kalmar retains its original defenses today.

❦❧

As the Swedes conquered Finland, they consolidated their power with fortifications. At the key trading post of **Viborg** (Finnish Viipuri), on the Karelian Isthmus, the Swedes built a strong castle on a small island in 1293. The first curtain wall enclosed a rectangular bailey. A large, four-level square tower about 20 meters high was built later. The tower walls were about 3 meters thick and about 15 meters in length. In the 14th century, increased trade led to the creation of the town of Viborg, whose walls were not erected until the latter half of the next century.

❦❧

Raseborg was a coastal castle built in the latter half of the 14th century. Located to the west of Helsinki, it is situated on a small rocky knoll that was then surrounded by water. From its position the Swedes could

challenge the dominace of the Hanseatic seaport of Reval. The Swedes, Danes, and pirates all attempted to hold this key position until the beginning of the 16th century.

❦❧

Häme Castle was another Swedish castle built in Finland by an earl early during the 13th-century crusade against the Finns. In 1260, when it was first established, it was a fortified camp consisting of 7-meter-high walls about 33 meters long on each side and three towers. Between 1270 and 1300 the Greystone fort, a complex of rooms inside the enceinte, was added. Between 1300 to 1350 the gate tower, which served as a keep, was erected. The tower was built of brick, except for the upper floor which was wooden. Between 1330 and about 1500, the castle was entirely converted to brick and built in the Gothic style. It was expanded and adapted for gunpowder weapons.

❦❧

Olavinlinna or **Olof's Castle** was built in Finland in 1475 by Erik Axelsson Tott, a Danish knight and governor of Viipuri Castle, to defend Sweden's eastern border in an area that was disputed with the Grand Duchy of Moscow. Erik began building a stone wall around the city of Viipuri, which extended for about 2 kilometers and included towers. Next, he erected the Castle of Olof on the small rocky islet of Kyrönsalmi. The builders worked under the protection of wooden defenses erected to deter hostile Russian incursions. Olof's Castle is an example of the transition period between medieval and gunpowder warfare with round towers adapted for cannons. When Erik died in 1481, his brother replaced him and work continued on the castle until the structure was largely completed in the 1490s. The castle incorporated three great bastions along the seaward side as well as three 20-meter-high medieval wall towers which rose above the level of battlements along the other side. Bastions and towers alike mounted cannons many years later. The medieval walls rose to over 10 meters and linked the towers to each other. The island location precluded mining and kept the walls out of reach of medieval war machines. The only weapon that could effectively engage the castle was the cannon.

After the Swedes refused to give up St. Olof in 1495, war broke out and Viipuri was put under siege by the Russians. At Olof's Castle, Bishop Pietari Kylliäinen had under his command a garrison of about 150 men, including peasant troops. He used his men to attack the Russians besieging Viipuri in a long-range sortie and finally forced them to abandon the siege after a major Russian assault on the walls failed. The Russians returned early in 1496 and wiped out a relief force sent to the castle before withdrawing. In the summer, the Russians returned and made another serious effort to take the castle but failed. In the next century, Olof's Castle underwent more modifications and continued to play an important role as a border position.

OLOF'S CASTLE, FINLAND.

(Sketch by Wojciech Ostrowski)

Karlstejn Castle, Bohemia

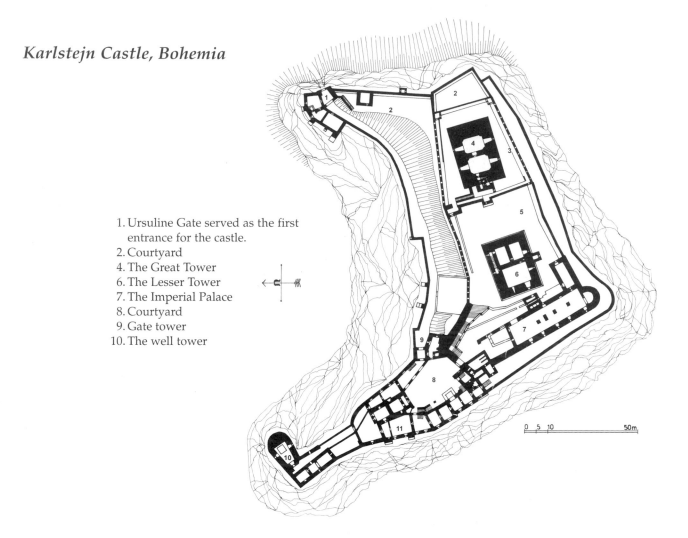

1. Ursuline Gate served as the first entrance for the castle.
2. Courtyard
4. The Great Tower
6. The Lesser Tower
7. The Imperial Palace
8. Courtyard
9. Gate tower
10. The well tower

KARLSTEJN, BOHEMIA. **Below:** *A hilltop castle begun in the mid-14th century by the Hungarian king. This view shows the Imperial Palace with round tower on the the left and the Lesser Tower with the Church of Our Lady on the right.*

Right: *View from the courtyard looking at the inner gate with the Lesser Tower behind it on the right and the Grand Tower behind it on the left.*

Central Europe

Although there were many castles in the territories of present-day Czech Republic and Slovakia, few examples that have not been either heavily modified or fallen in ruin remain today.

The Bohemian **Karlstejn Castle** stands out as one of the largest in the Czech Republic. This castle was built between 1348 and 1357 by Charles I of Hungary, who was also Holy Roman Emperor Charles IV. It was intended to guard the main road and to protect the emperor's treasures and religious relics. Situated on top of a mountain, it includes a massive four-level Great Tower that rises to a height of 37 meters and a Lesser Tower, which is massive nonetheless. The Imperial Palace stands along the south wall of the castle. The round well tower at the southwest corner of the castle was connected, according to legend, to underground passages that led to the river. A fourth circular tower rises at the corner of the palace, and a fifth near the commander's residence along the south wall. Karlstejn's defenses, which included wooden hoardings at one time, are considered typical of most castles in central Germany. Karlstejn was besieged during the Hussite Wars but successfully held out.

One of the most interesting medieval castles in Slovakia is **Spissky Hrad**, located on an elevated site overlooking the trade route between Hungary and the Baltic Sea. The first defensive position on the site was built by the Hungarians and consisted of a large stone tower standing at the highest point, 634 meters above sea level. The tower was surrounded by a wooden palisade. These fortifications were brought down by an earthquake in the 12th century and a large stone castle and Romanesque palace were erected on the site in the 13th century. When the Mongols swept through the Polish and Hungarian kingdoms in 1242, Spissky Hrad remained unscathed but the king brought in Italian master artisans to improve the castle's defenses. In the 14th century, a second castle was built near the first, and is now referred to as the Lower Castle. It enclosed a large area with a curtain that included two square towers and a gatehouse. At the end of the 15th

KARLSTEJN CASTLE.

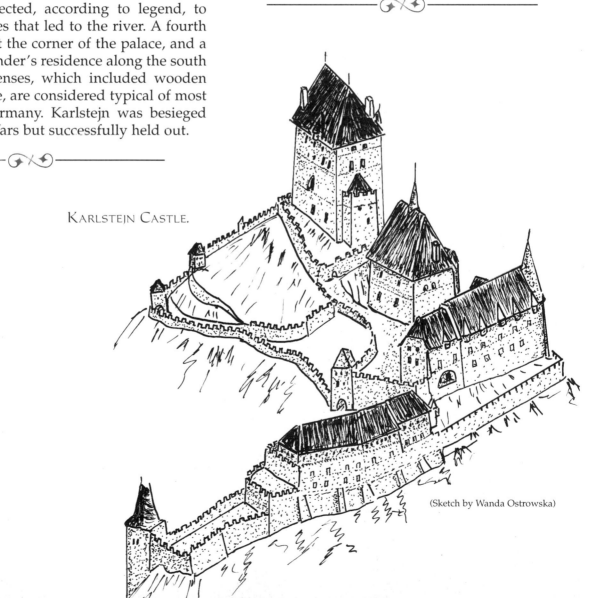

(Sketch by Wanda Ostrowska)

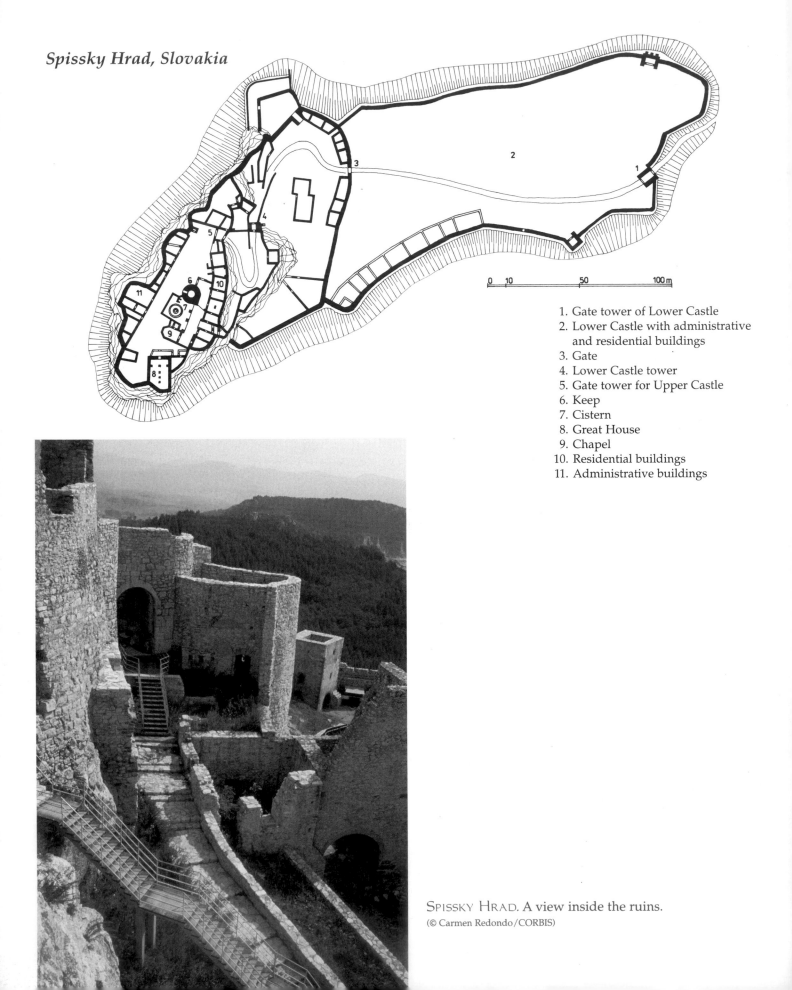

Spissky Hrad, Slovakia

1. Gate tower of Lower Castle
2. Lower Castle with administrative and residential buildings
3. Gate
4. Lower Castle tower
5. Gate tower for Upper Castle
6. Keep
7. Cistern
8. Great House
9. Chapel
10. Residential buildings
11. Administrative buildings

SPISSKY HRAD. A view inside the ruins.
(© Carmen Redondo/CORBIS)

century, the Upper Castle was rebuilt and served as a center of Hussite power. During the next century, further improvements were made to the entire castle complex, which was adapted to artillery, and the palace was turned into an arsenal.

Hungary is also rich in castles, many of which resisted the Turkish onslaught at the end of the Middle Ages. **Esztergom Castle** on the Danube north of Budapest was built in the 10th century on the site of an old Roman fort, becoming an impressive complex in the 12th century under King Bela III. From its inception it served as the residence of the Hungarian kings and was the site of the coronation of St. Stephen in 1000. Situated on top of Castle Hill, it included a large polygonal keep overlooking the river, a walled enclosure, and several large buildings and towers. Numerous post-medieval additions transformed it into a veritable palace complex by the mid-15th century.

Buda Castle, located on Castle Hill across the Danube from the old town of Pest, was built by King Bela IV after the Mongol invasion. A Gothic palace was added to it in the 14th and 15th centuries only to be destroyed by the Turks in the 17th century and rebuilt. Some of its medieval walls have been restored.

Other notable Hungarian castles include the 11th century **Visegrád Castle**, which served as a royal residence in the 14th century and was expanded during the 15th. It sits on top of a high hill overlooking the Danube and the city below where the impressive Solomon's Tower was built.

Further south, in Slovenia, overlooking Lake Bled, stands the 11th-century **Bled Castle**. This early 11th-century castle, the oldest in Slovenia, rises from a cliff. It was first mentioned in 1011, when the Holy Roman Emperor, Henry II, gave it to the Bishops of Brixen. The castle includes a lower and upper bailey and a curtain wall. The lower bailey walls, which include a round tower of Gothic design standing near the cliff

and a gate tower, are Romanesque. The upper bailey includes a Gothic style chapel and the residence.

In addition to Bled, there are other castles in Slovenia such as **Ljubljana Castle**, a massive, though heavily reconstructed, stronghold. **Celje Castle**, also built on top a rocky cliff, is one of the largest castles in the region but was abandoned in 1400. It includes a large rectangular keep, encircled by curtain walls running along the top of the ridge, and several other towers. At one end a square stone tower stands on a motte located in a separate, elongated bailey.

BUDA CASTLE. *This southwest corner tower was reconstructed after World War II.* (Courtesy of Chris Szabo)

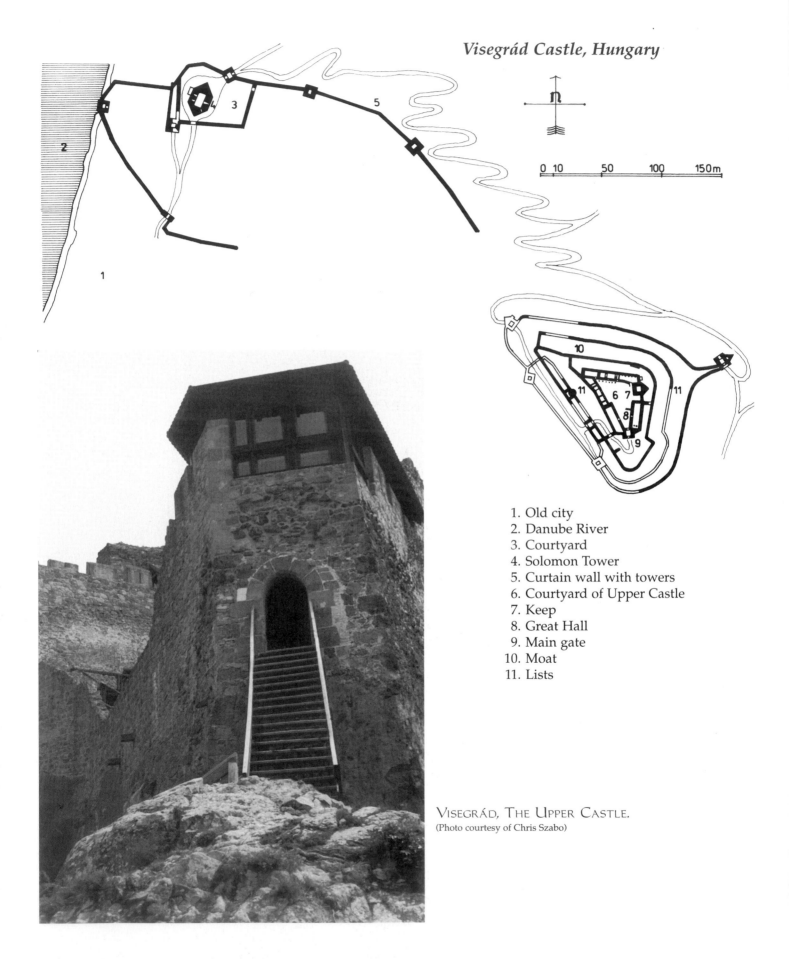

Visegrád Castle, Hungary

0 10   50   100   150m

1. Old city
2. Danube River
3. Courtyard
4. Solomon Tower
5. Curtain wall with towers
6. Courtyard of Upper Castle
7. Keep
8. Great Hall
9. Main gate
10. Moat
11. Lists

VISEGRÁD, THE UPPER CASTLE.
(Photo courtesy of Chris Szabo)

Bled Castle, Slovenia

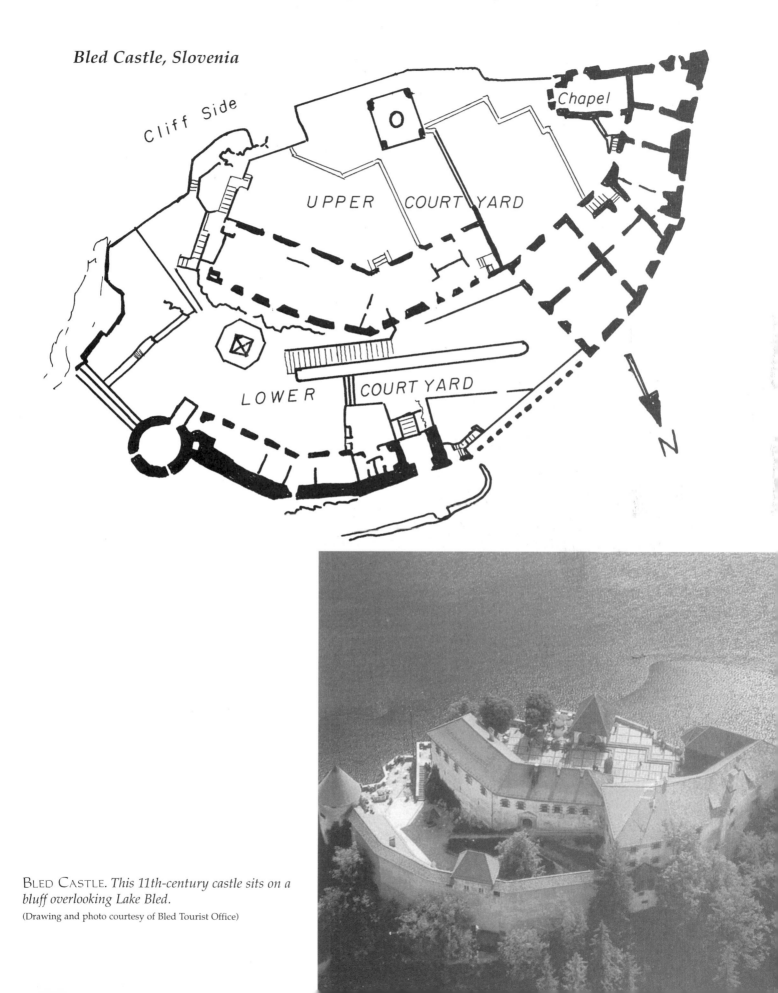

Cliff Side

Chapel

UPPER COURTYARD

LOWER COURTYARD

N

BLED CASTLE. *This 11th-century castle sits on a bluff overlooking Lake Bled.*

(Drawing and photo courtesy of Bled Tourist Office)

BEDZIN CASTLE, POLAND.

Poland

In Poland there are many castles in various states of preservation. Since the country's borders and political situation changed so much through the centuries many of these castles have been significant in the development of the nation.

The most impressive medieval site in Poland is the **Wawel of Krakow** which is located on a rocky hill overlooking the Vistula. From the 1050s until the 1500s it served as the royal residence. When the kings of the Piast Dynasty ruled from there in the 10th century, they built their residence in stone, but surrounded it with earth and timber fortifications. The position was divided into the Upper and Lower Castle separated by a moat. The residence and cathedral were located in the Upper Castle. Although some stone and brick positions were added over the centuries, the greatest change did not take place until after 1320, when the entire castle, including its outer defenses, was rebuilt in masonry in the Gothic style. Casimir the Great expanded the site in the mid-14th century, adding new churches and the two tallest defensive towers. After the Middle Ages the Wawel became more palace than castle, in the style of many of the French royal châteaux.

Radzyn Chelminski was a timber and earth castle built by the Teutonic Knights in the early 13th century. In the 14th century it was built in brick and became the seat of the military commander of the order. It was heavily damaged in the 17th century wars with the Swedes.

Ogrodzieniec was a knight's castle on a small hill among limestone rocks between Krakow and Czestochowska built by Wlodek Sulimczyk. His descendants resided there until 1470, when they sold it to a family from Krakow. It was rebuilt in the next century and converted into a Renaissance structure but was twice destroyed by invading Swedes in the 17th century and early 18th century. It is a large complex sitting upon a hill that includes a gatehouse for the approach, which is from the rear, and several round towers.

Radzyn Chelminski, Poland

1. Keep
2. Room of the commandant
3. Church
4. Refectory
5. Sanitary tower
6. Galleries
7. Courtyard
8. Gateway
9. Drawbridge
10. Courtyard
11. Curtain wall
12. Moat
13. Counterscarp
14. Lower Castle

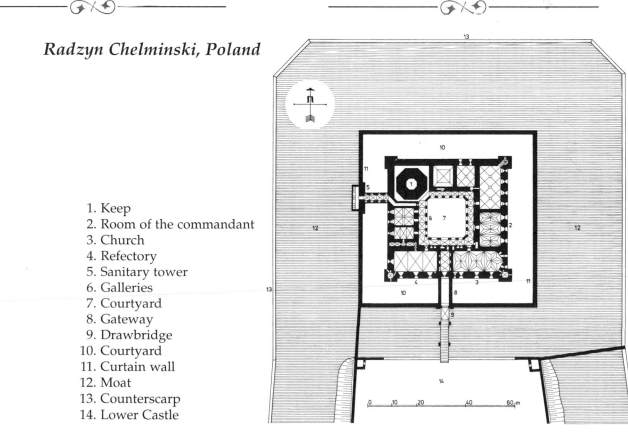

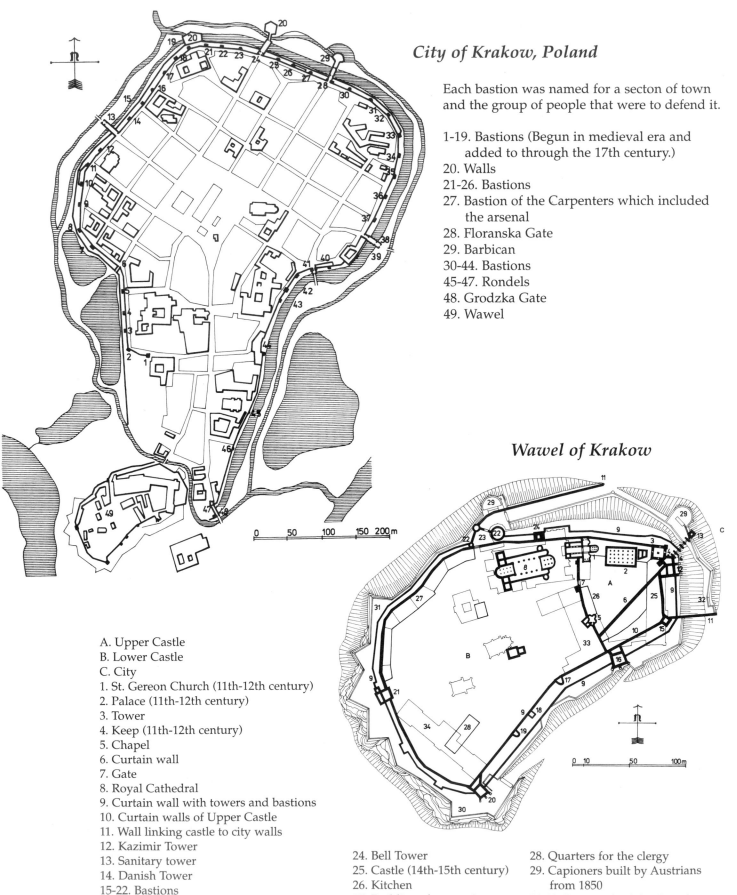

City of Krakow, Poland

Each bastion was named for a secton of town and the group of people that were to defend it.

1-19. Bastions (Begun in medieval era and added to through the 17th century.)
20. Walls
21-26. Bastions
27. Bastion of the Carpenters which included the arsenal
28. Floranska Gate
29. Barbican
30-44. Bastions
45-47. Rondels
48. Grodzka Gate
49. Wawel

Wawel of Krakow

A. Upper Castle
B. Lower Castle
C. City
1. St. Gereon Church (11th-12th century)
2. Palace (11th-12th century)
3. Tower
4. Keep (11th-12th century)
5. Chapel
6. Curtain wall
7. Gate
8. Royal Cathedral
9. Curtain wall with towers and bastions
10. Curtain walls of Upper Castle
11. Wall linking castle to city walls
12. Kazimir Tower
13. Sanitary tower
14. Danish Tower
15-22. Bastions
23. Lower Gate

24. Bell Tower
25. Castle (14th-15th century)
26. Kitchen
27. Buildings for courtiers

28. Quarters for the clergy
29. Capioners built by Austrians from 1850
30-32. Bastions built by Austrians

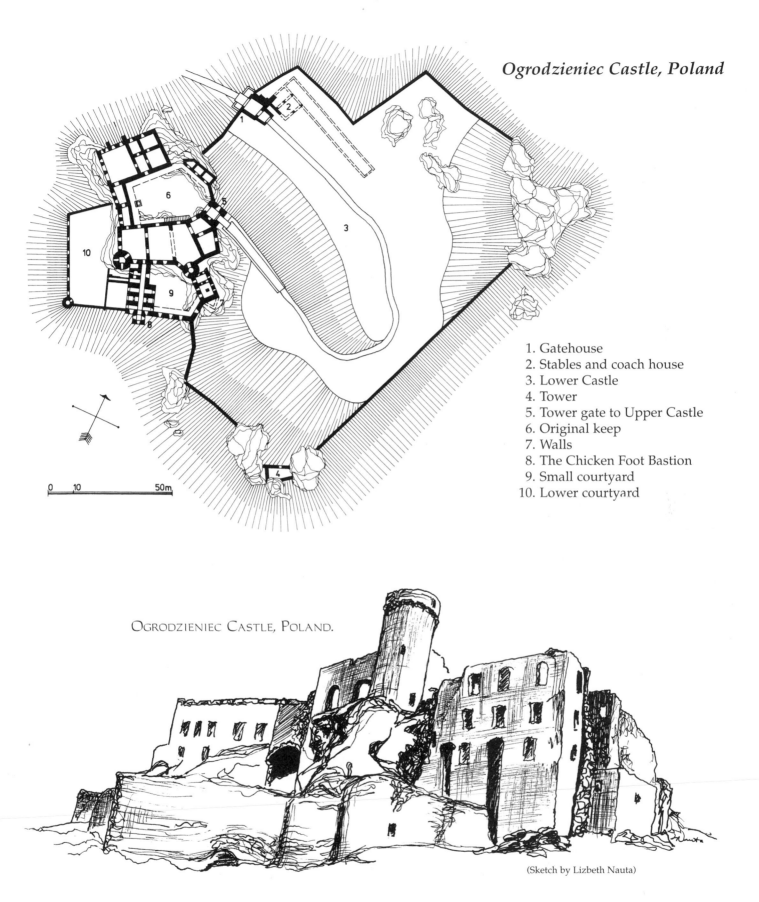

Ogrodzieniec Castle, Poland

1. Gatehouse
2. Stables and coach house
3. Lower Castle
4. Tower
5. Tower gate to Upper Castle
6. Original keep
7. Walls
8. The Chicken Foot Bastion
9. Small courtyard
10. Lower courtyard

0   10   50m

OGRODZIENIEC CASTLE, POLAND.

(Sketch by Lizbeth Nauta)

Olsztyn Castle, Poland

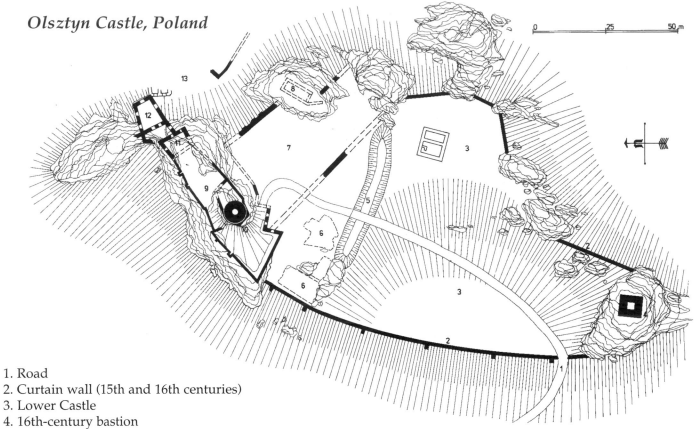

1. Road
2. Curtain wall (15th and 16th centuries)
3. Lower Castle
4. 16th-century bastion
5. Dry moat
6. Cellars
7. 14th-century courtyard of Lower Castle
8. 14th-century residence
9. Courtyard of the Upper Castle
10. Keep
11. Great House
12. Three-level residence tower of 16th and 17th centuries
13. Ruins of the Lower Castle

OLSZTYN CASTLE, POLAND.
This view of the ruins shows tower #12 in the foreground with the Great House (#11) behind it and the keep (#10) behind that.

In **Szydlow** a knight's castle or keep was built on an island in the marshes during the mid-15th century by Stanislaw Szydlowiecki. Szydlow is a walled town with a small castle in one corner. The town walls enclose a synagogue, a church, and the entire town. One of its remaining gatehouses is still quite impressive with interior defensive features and two observation turrets.

Olsztyn was a royal castle built on a rocky limestone formation by Casimir the Great on the site of a 12th- or 13th-century gród. It is located west of Krakow and served as a border castle. It consisted of two castles, sometimes considered three, and is rather complex. The Upper Castle, which sits on top of a hill and includes a circular tower and a large masonry structure, is the oldest section and dates from the 14th century. It was built on a rectangular plan from the local limestone. On the southwest corner a round tower that was about 20 meters high protects the nearby entrance. The tower's entrance is eight meters above the ground and its battlements provide a breathtaking view of most of the surrounding area. This tower was raised another six meters with an octagonal shaped addition during the 15th century. Behind the tower lays a small courtyard surrounded by masonry buildings, which included a square residence that was replaced with two larger three-level buildings and later by residential towers. The Lower Castle, four times as large as the upper one and irregular in shape, was surrounded by a curtain wall. It was built between the 15th and 16th century, consisted of two baileys, and probably included an entrance on the south side. Two outworks, each surrounded by walls and a moat, were added to serve as barbicans. Between 1393 and 1396, the Poles and Hungarians fought for control of Olsztyn as a result of a border dispute. In the 15th century, the dukes of Silesia attacked the castle several times as the site continued to grow larger. In 1488 a town was founded at the bottom of the hill. The castle was expanded and rebuilt in the 1550s and besieged in 1587 by Maximilian of Hapsburg, who inflicted heavy damage to it. In the 17th century, the Swedes attempted to destroy the site as they did many other fortified sites in Poland.

Szydlow, Poland

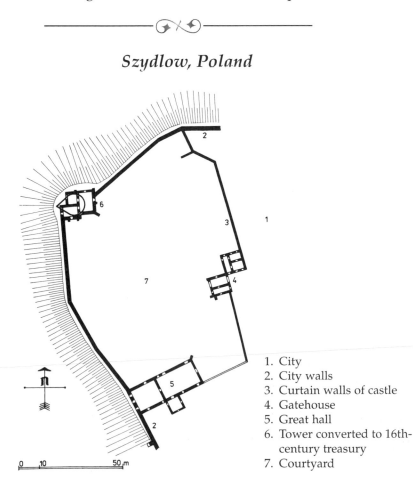

1. City
2. City walls
3. Curtain walls of castle
4. Gatehouse
5. Great hall
6. Tower converted to 16th-century treasury
7. Courtyard

SZYDLOW, POLAND. *Elaborate city gate rebuilt after destruction by Swedes in the 17th century.*

Another notable castle in Poland is the royal castle of **Bedzin**, built by Casimir the Great in the mid-14th century on the site of a 10th-century gród, which had been destroyed in the 12th century. It is located between Krakow and Katowice and dominates the main crossroads leading to Silesia. In 1228 a wooden castle with stone foundations and a stone tower occupied the site but it was burned by the Mongols in 1241. King Casimir replaced the timber castle with a masonry structure in 1358 to strengthen his defenses of Poland against attacks from Silesia. Inside the enceinte the oldest structure on the site, a large round tower with four-meter thick walls rose to twice the height it reaches today. A large, square keep housed the residence of the castle. Another tower, also four-meters thick, was attached to the keep. These two towers were connected by a drawbridge and formed the upper bailey surrounded by a 8- to 12-meter-high curtain. A second curtain wall about 5 meters high formed the lower bailey. There is also a deep moat and, on the river side, a third wall connects the city wall to the castle's curtain walls. The city walls of Bedzin were not built until 1364. Two gates led into the castle from the side of the river and were defended by the battlements of the curtains.

———— ❧❧ ————

BEDZIN CASTLE, POLAND.

Bedzin Castle, Poland

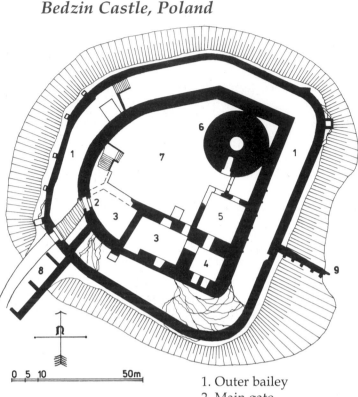

1. Outer bailey
2. Main gate
3. Great Hall
4. Square tower
5. Administrative building
6. Keep
7. Inner Bailey
8. Foregate
9. Curtain wall

Czersk Castle was built on the cliffs overlooking the Vistula, south of Warsaw. The present castle stands on a manmade hill that resulted from the leveling of the walls of an older gród that consisted of an upper and lower bailey linked by a bridge. Czersk is located on the site of a marketplace at the crossroads of two trade routes, one on the Vistula and the other overland. At the end of the 11th century, Boleslav the Bold added a gród to protect the marketplace and the village that arose intermittently on the site from the 6th century. The oval-shaped gród was protected on three sides by the terrain and by earthworks on the side leading to the town, and overlooked the river, which has shifted since then.

In the late 14th century, Czersk Castle was entirely rebuilt and became the first brick fortification in the region. The earth and timber walls of the gród were leveled and served as a foundation to the new masonry structure, which has retained the rough outline of the older fortifications. The longest section of wall is about 50 meters on the west and 40 meters on the east, forming a trapezoid. The walls are 1.8 meters thick on the northeast side and are set on a stone foundation, which, in turn, sits on the old gród. A projecting four-level square gatehouse rose to a height of 22 meters at one time, and has walls over three meters thick. It includes a postern and a regular entrance with a drawbridge, but no portcullis. The upper levels housed the living quarters of the captain of the guard. The battlements accommodated permanent wooden hoardings and a high triangular roof. However, it is debatable whether these hoardings actually served a military propose or were added as decorations in the 16th century, when the top floor may have also been added. The curtains were probably about 10 meters high and the two round projecting towers on the southern and western corners were probably of the same height. The allure was accessed by stairs and from the towers. The southern tower has few openings and may not have been a defensive position. The two round towers consisted of several levels and their height may have been increased after the 14th century. Both were provided with supports for wooden hoardings. Czersk Castle was destroyed by a Swedish army in the 17th century.

CZERSK CASTLE, POLAND. *View from entrance gate which is accessed by a bridge over the moat.*

Checiny Castle, Poland

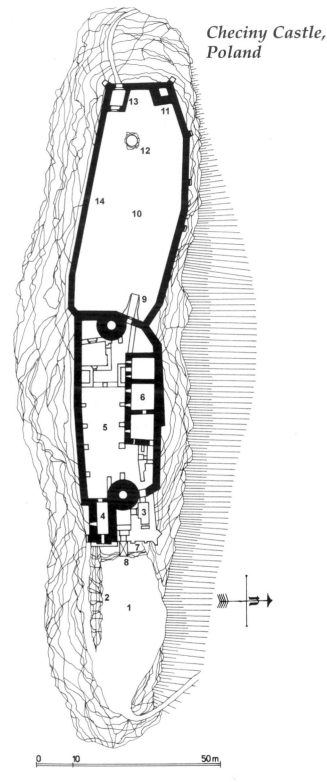

Checiny is an elongated hilltop castle from the 14th century built along the crest of a ridge overlooking the town of the same name. The oldest part of the castle was built by the bishop of Krakow by order of King Vaclav II of Poland and Bohemia in 1300. It became one of the strongest castles in Poland and in 1318 became the royal treasury of the Polish king. During the 14th century important prisoners from the wars with the Teutonic Knights were held there. The upper ward in the eastern section was the oldest part of the castle and was accessed by two entrances at each end that guarded a large round tower each. In the 15th century, the lower ward and a square tower were added near the west end of the extended enceinte. A tunnel near the well led from the lower ward to the church of Checin below the hill. The main entrance to the lower ward opened on the east side of the castle and was protected by a drawbridge. A building housing the chapel on its lower level and the treasury on its upper level was built against the south wall, near the round tower at the east end of the upper ward. This tower was also the final point of defense and could only be entered from a window on the second level. It also contained food stores for the defenders. Checiny Castle burned in 1607, but was never taken by siege. The upper levels of the two tall round towers appear to have been rebuilt after being damaged in World War I.

CHECINY CASTLE. *View from the eastern tower of the Lower Castle. The tower in the background is #11 on the plan.*

1. Bailey
2. Stone wall
3. Gate tower and chapel
4. Treasury
5. Courtyard of Upper Castle
6. Great Hall
7. Moat
8. Drawbridge
9. Gate and ramp
10. Courtyard of Lower Castle
11. Round tower with square foundation used as prison in later years
12. Cistern
13. Entrance gate to Lower Castle
14. Curtain wall

Lithuania

Troky Castle, initially made of wood and rebuilt in the 14th, 15th, and 16th centuries, was located on an island of Lake Galve. The present structure was started in the late 14th century by a Prince Giedymin of Lithuania and was finished in the next century. In 1383 the castle was taken by the Teutonic Knights and then retaken by Prince Jagiello in 1392. Two buildings of two levels formed part of its inner enceinte. The castle also had a set of rectangular, concentric walls and a five-level square gatehouse that also served as a residence. An outer bailey, added at a later date, occupied the remainder of the island. The residential structures consisted of three floors, and a great hall stood in the oldest part of the castle. A moat separated this section of the castle from the outer bailey. The castle was made from rough stone, which can be seen on the lower level, and red brick. The curtain wall of the outer bailey included three corner towers that were square at the base and circular above and were designed to accommodate cannons.

Troky Castle, Lithuania

1. Gate tower for Lower Castle
2. Courtyard
3. Quarters for the garrison
4. Stables
5. Moat
6. Drawbridge
7. Gate Tower
8. Lists
9. Upper Castle

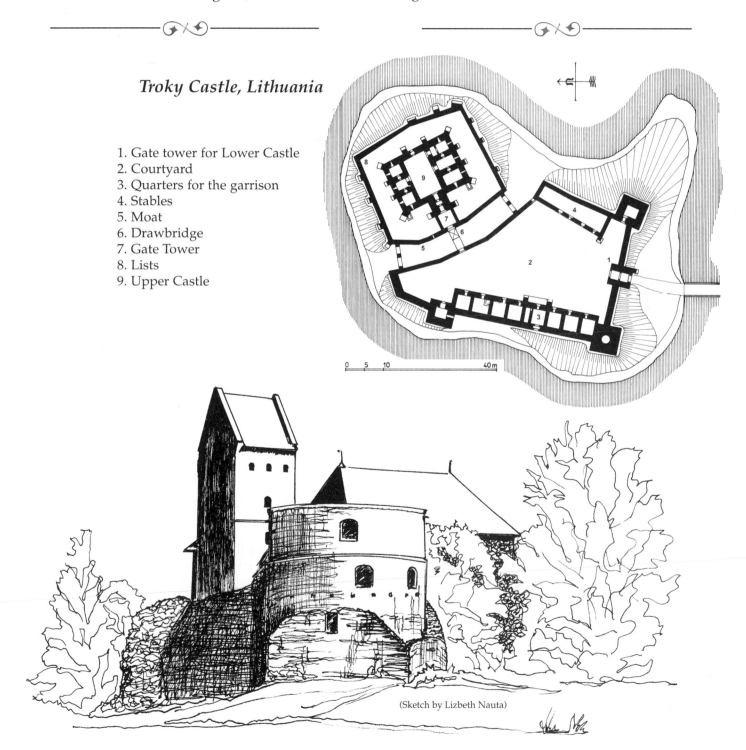

(Sketch by Lizbeth Nauta)

Ukraine

Chocim Castle, Ukraine

One of the most imposing fortifications in the Ukraine is the Polish castle of **Chocim**, which includes a tower that dates back to the last half of the 13th century. Most of the work, however, was done between 1457 and 1480 by Stephen III of Moldavia, who struggled to break away from the Turks. Chocim is situated on the Dniestr River and is surrounded by high walls along its irregular perimeter. The curtains are reinforced with six towers which include large corner towers, two circular wall towers, and a gatehouse. The battlements of the curtain walls reach the same height as those of the towers. The three-level keep stands in a corner and projects beyond the curtains. The castle's courtyards were raised about eight meters. Chocim was surrounded by a large moat and the river. In the mid-16th century, the Poles occupied the castle and rebuilt one of the towers, the gatehouse, and the walls to the south and added a moat and two drawbridges. The castle continued to act as a border castle through the 17th century and exchanged hands many times.

———————❧❦———————

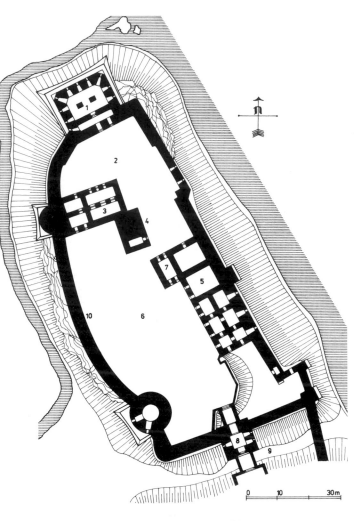

CHOCIM CASTLE, UKRAINE.

1. Keep
2. Courtyard
3. Great Hall or Palace
4. Tower
5. Garrison building
6. Courtyard
7. Chapel
8. Gate tower
9. Moat
10. Curtain wall

(Photo courtesy of John Sloan)

Russia

Before the Mongols overran much of Russia, with the exception of Novgorod the land of the Rus consisted mostly of independent principalities like that of Kiev. One of the oldest medieval fortifications in the area is **Kopor'ye** or **The Rock**, built sometime before 1240. The castle stands on a rock that drops off for 30 meters on one side and is protected by a deep moat from the higher ground on the other side. In 1240, it consisted of timber walls and was originally built by German knights, who controlled the traffic on the Luga and Plyussa rivers. This first fortification was destroyed by Alexander Nevsky, who attacked the site in 1241 in retaliation for the Teutonic Knights' seizure of Pskov. After the battle of the Ice in 1242, the knights returned to fortify new positions.

In 1280, the Novgorodians decided to rebuild the fortress in stone to protect the city of Kopor'ye and secure their borders. The nobleman in command of the castle tried to set up his own kingdom, but was removed in 1282 and the castle was dismantled. In 1297, the encroachment of the Swedes forced the Novgorodians to rebuild their fortifications once again, but this time their defenses turned out to be larger and more complex.

In 1338, the German knights returned only to be defeated in their attempt to storm the castle. Subsequent invasions by Germans and Swedes met with failure. A new fortress built at Yam in the 15th century near the Livonian border eventually reduced the importance of Kopor'ye. When Yam was attacked three times in the 1440s, the Novgorodians decided to strengthen Kopor'ye, but it was not until the next century that it was reconstructed to better meet the demands of gunpowder warfare. The five-level circular towers of Kopor'ye that rise to a height of 20 meters and the walls that vary from 4 to 4.5 meters in thickness were probably late additions. The gateway includes two large, projecting towers that give flanking fire along the walls. Kopor'ye continued in service through the 17th century.

Long after the invasion of the Mongols, a Russian state slowly emerged at Moscow when Dimitri Donskoi successfully broke away from the control of the Golden Horde in 1381. Moscow was defended by an earth and timber fortress that was replaced by stone in 1367. After 1462, probably in 1485, Ivan III, Grand Prince of Moscow, ordered the construction of a brick fortress to rival Rome and Constantinople. The triangular-shaped **Kremlin** was accessed through four gates and a postern on the side along the Moscow River. Its walls run for 2.5 kilometers and are 20 meters high and 3.4 meters thick. Three round corner towers, more than a dozen square towers, and the gatehouses along the enceinte include positions for cannons. The Kremlin was updated over the centuries as it continued to serve as the official imperial residence for the rulers of Russia.

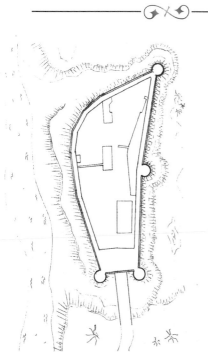

(Sketch by Wojciech Ostrowski)

KOPOR'YE, RUSSIA. *Large drum towers covering the gate.*
(Photo courtesy of John Sloan)

Kremlin, Moscow

1. Walls
2, 4, 5. Synod
3. Belfry
6. Palace
7. Postern
8. Water tower
9. Forest Gate
10. Trinity Gate
11. Barbican
12. Bastion Sobakina
13. Nicolas Gate
14. Spassky Gate
15, 16. Bastions

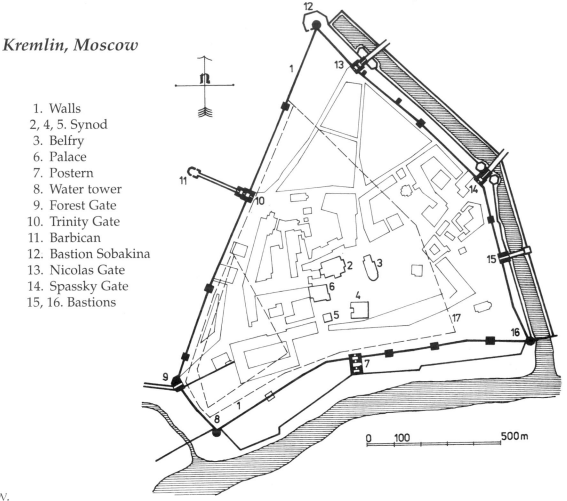

0 100   500 m

THE KREMLIN, MOSCOW.

Eastern Mediterranean

The Eastern Mediterranean area along the Adriatic coast to Constantinople, from the Balkans to the Levant, is strewn with Byzantine fortifications that include old fortified and refortified sites from Roman times. Added to these are the castles built by the Crusaders and the Arabs, each with their own distinctive style of architecture. The walled city of Jerusalem, in continuous use since Biblical times, was repeatedly updated throughout the Middle Ages. The Crusaders refortified many other cities and built numerous castles adopting methods used by Byzantine and Islamic architects alike, combining them with their own.

Of the many castles built in the area, **Belvoir** was one that stood out for its innovative style and imposing presence. It was erected by the Hospitalers on the western heights, 480 meters above the valley of the Jordan River, not too far south of the Sea of Galilee (Lake Tiberias). Built in 1168, it is the first known concentric castle. It is thought to have been built in the style of a Roman castrum, with a square bailey of a type popular only in the 12th century. This huge work reportedly bankrupted the Hospitalers.

Set within the huge moat, Belvoir's defenses span about 100 meters on each side forming a square, and consist of an inner and outer defense line. The surrounding moat was about 20 meters wide. Along the east side, overlooking the valley, rose a large tower whose upper level was even with the bottom of the moat. The outer wall included seven square towers and a gatehouse that stood on the side that overlooked the steep slope of the Jordan Valley. The curtain wall comprised three mural towers reinforced with plinths that projected into the moat. A couple of these towers gave access into the moat. At the southeast corner was the Eastern Gate which covered to the path leading into the castle. This path made a "U" turn on reaching the wall connected to the large east-

ern tower and led back toward the southeastern corner tower where it made a 90-degree right turn before it reached the inner gate. The entire approach was controlled by arrow loops in the corridors. The south wall included the stables and storage areas. The outer bailey included a large vaulted cistern and a steam bath that were part of the barracks for mercenaries. The square inner bailey, which housed the convent, was designed mainly for religious functions, according to Jonathan Riley-Smith in *The Atlas of the Crusades* (New York, 1990). It served as a cloister and included its own gatehouse, the dormitory for the brother knights, a refectory, and a chapel. The inner walls comprised a square with projecting towers on each corner and arrow loops in the walls that covered the outer bailey. Although Belvoir has been practically razed down to its foundations, it still exhudes an aura of power and strength.

After the Christian defeat at Hattin in 1187, Saladin launched his attack on the Christian Kingdom of Jerusalem. The population of Jerusalem surrendered after a siege of two weeks. As most of the other Christian strongholds fell one by one, Belvoir continued to resist for over a year, delaying Saladin's attack on Tyre thus saving that city. Belvoir was returned to the Crusaders in 1241 by the sultan of Egypt, when it was restored and served until 1247.

Belvoir Castle, Israel

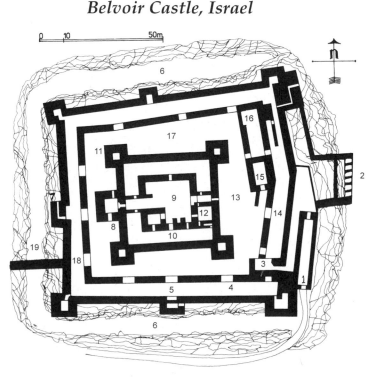

1. Outer Eastern Gate	11. Inner corner tower
2. Outer Eastern Tower	12. Kitchen
3. Inner Eastern Gate	13. Eastern courtyard
4. Storage and stables	14. Storage and stables
5. Postern	15. Water cistern
6. Moat	16. Bath
7. Postern	17. Northern courtyard
8. Inner Western Gate	18. Outer Western Gate
9. Inner courtyard	19. Bridge
10. Refectory	

In Syria today stands one of the most impressive castles built during the Crusades—**Krak des Chevaliers**. A Hospitaller castle, like Belvoir, it occupies a site about 650 meters above the west bank of the Orontes River near Homs. It was originally an Islamic-Byzantine castle used by the Count of Tripoli to defend his borders until he turned it over to the Hospitallers in 1144, who subsequently improved it and turned it into a Romanesque castle.

Krak des Chevaliers was positioned on a site that could only be approached from one side. Its inner curtain included three massive, interconnected towers overlooking a combination moat and reservoir located between them and the outer curtain. The outer wall, which surrounded the inner enceinte, was not added until the 13th century when modifications were made to the inner works.

Krak des Chevaliers underwent at least two periods of major renovations in 1142 and at the end of the century. In addition, it was damaged by earthquakes in 1157, 1170, and 1201, so that it had to undergo major repairs before and after these periods of remodeling. During the second phase of renovation, the castle acquired an outer wall with semicircular towers. Either during this period or at a somewhat later date, the Hospitallers built a vaulted passage that allowed an armored knight to ride on his horse all the way from the main gate to the inner bailey without dismounting. This passageway made three 90-degree turns before it reached the inner ward and included arrow loops and a portcullis that could turn it into a trap if necessary. The inner enceinte and the central tower of the castle also were improved during the second remodeling phase. Machicoulis crowned the towers and numerous bretèches covered the base of the curtains. It is claimed that even the latrines could be turned into bretèches if the need arose.

Krak des Chevaliers was besieged in 1188 by Saladin, who was not able to take it. Early in the 13th century, the garrison of the castle consisted of about

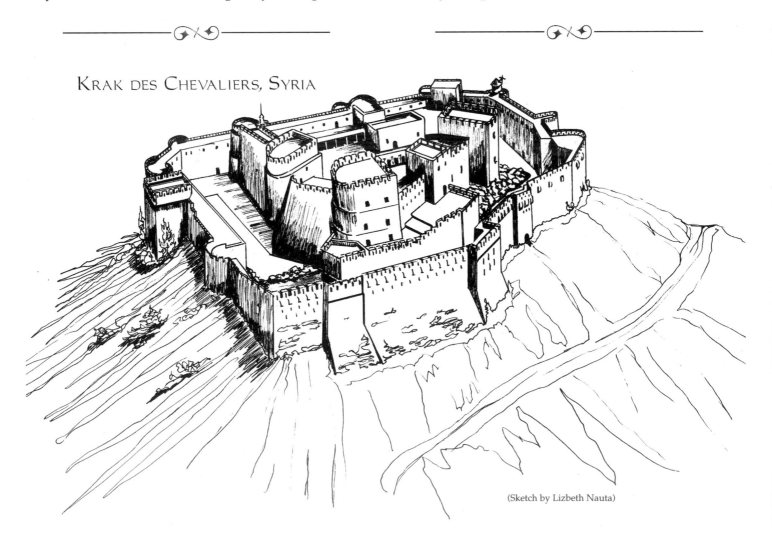

KRAK DES CHEVALIERS, SYRIA

(Sketch by Lizbeth Nauta)

2,000 men. The castle was besieged repeatedly in 1207, 1218, 1229, 1252, and 1267, and managed to survive. In 1270, the Mamlukes launched a raid not only against the castle but also on the surrounding region, which had adverse effects on the morale of the garrison. As a result it fell to the Mamlukes led by Sultan Baibars in 1271 after a siege that began early in March and lasted only about six weeks. The garrison numbered little more than 200 knights at the time. Baibars' siege engines inflicted a great deal of damage on part of the outer wall and towers. The gate tower was taken after a short bombardment, which forced the inadequate garrison to withdraw to the inner curtain. Once the outer ward fell, mining brought down one of the towers of the inner curtain, forcing the Hospitallers into their last stronghold. Finally, Baibars

METHONI, GREECE. *Turkish tower built on the adjacent island in 1572, seen from the sea gate.* (Courtesy of Peter Etcheto)

avoided another costly assault by convincing the knights to surrender on favorable terms, allowing them to return to Tripoli. The Arabs repaired and maintained the castle for several more centuries.

On the Greek islands and the coastal region under the domination of Byzantium there were numerous fortified sites, including Constantinople, the strongest and largest of them all. One of these sites is at **Methoni** on the southwest coast of the Peloponnesus, near Pylos, which has been a fortified position since the Classical Age. The Methonians engaged in piracy early in the High Middle Ages, incurring the wrath of the Venetians, who attacked their town and destroyed their old citadel in 1124. The Byzantine Empire regained control over Methoni the following year. During the Fourth Crusade, Geoffrey of Villehardouin took over the ruins of the old citadel and ceded them to Venice in 1205. The Venetians temporarily lost the site to the Genoese, but took it back and refortified it during the 13th century, changing its name to Modon. The new city wall built by the Venetians included small square towers open at the rear and low walls around the peninsula. The castle sealed the north end of the peninsula. Within the new enceinte stood a cathedral and the town and port, which prospered due to its location on the trade route to the Levant. The Genoese retook Methoni in 1354, but lost it again to the Venetians in 1403 after a naval battle that took place within sight of the town. During the 15th century, walls were erected along all sides of the rocky promontory, a moat was dug across the landward side, and a fausse braie was added in front of the walls on that side.

Despite these strong defenses, the Turkish sultan's forces conquered Methoni in 1500 and proceeded to make their own additions. Soon after the defeat of Lepanto, the Turks began strengthening Methoni and other positions. They built a sea gate in the medieval style that gave access to a rocky islet where they erected the Bourzi Tower. This octagonal structure, also in the medieval style, included positions for artillery to cover the port area.

Attempts by the Knights of St. John in 1531 and by Don Juan of Austria after the battle of Lepanto to recapture Methoni failed. In the next three centuries the position changed hands many times between the Christians and the Turks, who continued to remodel and renovate it.

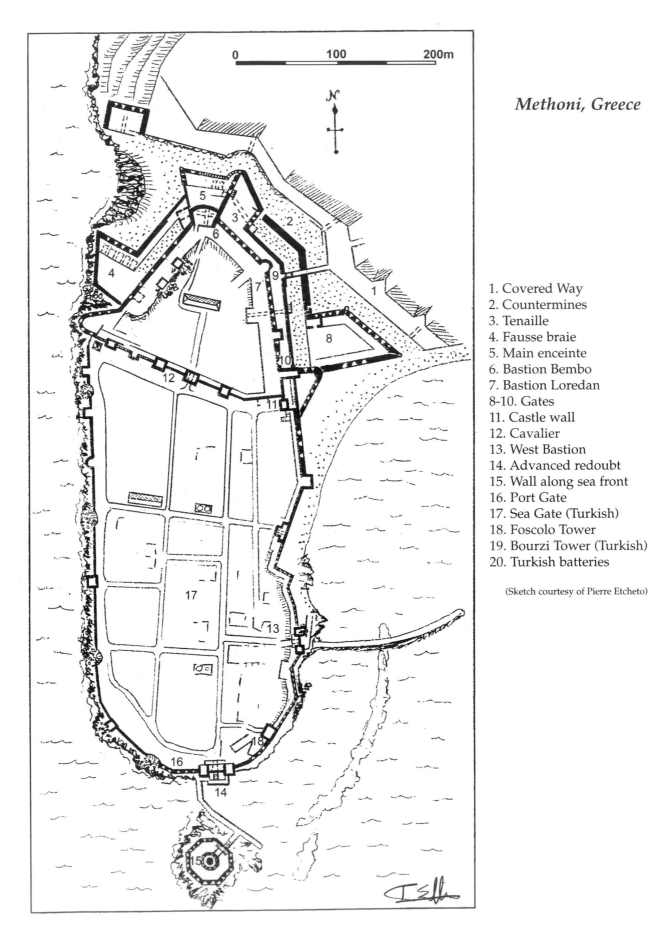

Methoni, Greece

1. Covered Way
2. Countermines
3. Tenaille
4. Fausse braie
5. Main enceinte
6. Bastion Bembo
7. Bastion Loredan
8-10. Gates
11. Castle wall
12. Cavalier
13. West Bastion
14. Advanced redoubt
15. Wall along sea front
16. Port Gate
17. Sea Gate (Turkish)
18. Foscolo Tower
19. Bourzi Tower (Turkish)
20. Turkish batteries

(Sketch courtesy of Pierre Etcheto)

METHONI, GREECE.
Above: *South front of the castle showing Venetian wall of the 13th century.*
Below: *The Sea Gate. (Both photos are courtesy of Pierre Etcheto)*

FERRARA CASTLE, ITALY. *Type of castle built in the late 14th century in northern Italy. It included square towers, machicoulis, and a surrounding moat.*

Italian Peninsula

The Italian Peninsula served as a link between all corners of the Mediterranean world and, as the cradle of the Renaissance, was the point of origin of many innovations in military architecture. The innumerable castles and fortified cities throughout the peninsula often present unique features. Most Italian city walls and castles reflect, more than any other fortifications in the West, the technological changes that took place through the millennia.

Emperor Frederick II founded many castles in Italy and is credited with construction of the palace at **Lucera**, near Foggia. However, the data seems to indicate that he was only responsible for a great square tower with an octagonal-shaped upper level and a lower level in the Norman style. The tower stood on a huge base that measured 50 meters on each side and included a gallery containing firing slits for archers on all sides. It was destroyed late in the 18th century. Charles of Anjou, the king of Naples between 1270 and 1283, asked his architect, Pierre d'Agincourt, to rebuild three sides of the original enceinte around the polygonal site. The new curtain had 24 towers that included pentagonal shaped interval towers, unusual for the period. The entire position sat on a spur, surrounded by steep wooded slopes on all sides and a deep manmade moat separating the castle from the town. Pierre added two large, round corner towers to the wall along the moat side. The castle of Lucera was known as the "Key to Puglia."

Frederick II is also credited with incorporating some Islamic features into his buildings. According to some sources, he is said to have imported Islamic builders for Lucera, but according to others, these men were actually rebellious Moslems who had been moved from Sicily to Puglia. Frederick appears to have been enchanted with the octagonal shape, which he used more than once, and which is a feature that appears to be more common in Byzantine and Islamic works. At **Castel Del Monte** at Apulia in southern Italy, the octagonal plan appears again, not only in the outline of the castle, but also in the layout of the eight towers at each corner. This castle served more as a hunting lodge than a defensive position and was later used as a prison by Charles of Anjou.

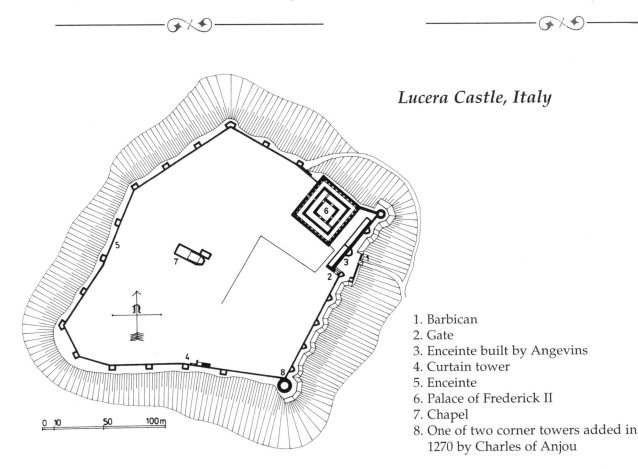

Lucera Castle, Italy

1. Barbican
2. Gate
3. Enceinte built by Angevins
4. Curtain tower
5. Enceinte
6. Palace of Frederick II
7. Chapel
8. One of two corner towers added in 1270 by Charles of Anjou

CASTEL NUOVO, NAPLES.

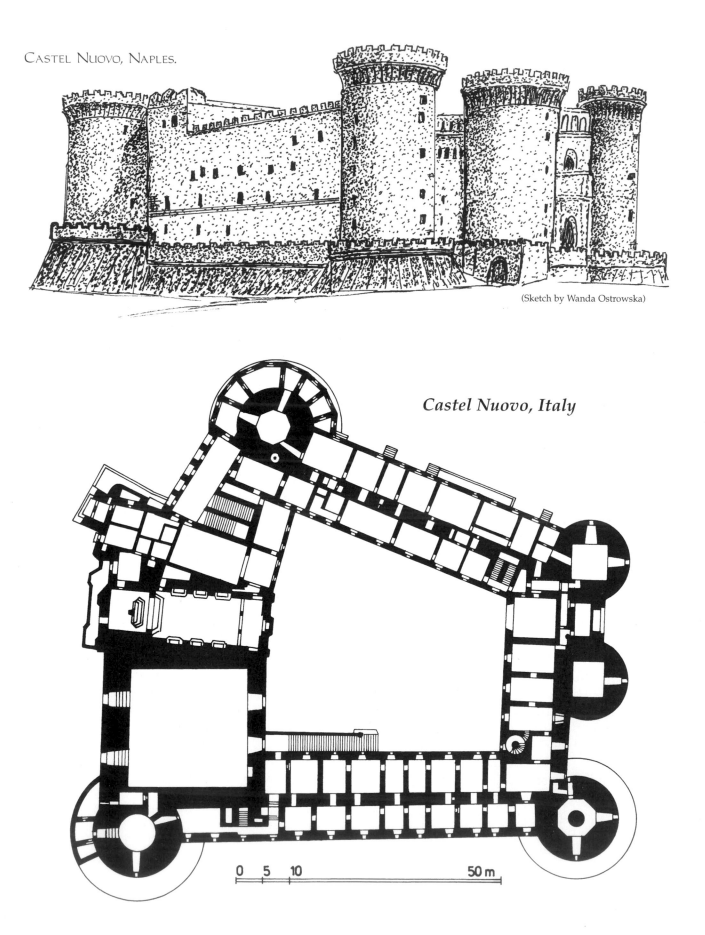

(Sketch by Wanda Ostrowska)

Castel Nuovo, Italy

0 5 10   50 m

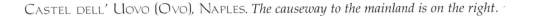

CASTEL DELL' UOVO (OVO), NAPLES. *The causeway to the mainland is on the right.*

(Sketch by Wojciech Ostrowski)

Castel Nuovo in Naples was originally designed by Pierre d'Agincourt for Charles of Anjou. The king ordered this new castle to be built at the same time as he was renovating **Castel dell' Uovo** (or **Ovo**), a high-walled citadel built in the gulf on a rock islet about 200 to 300 meters from the shoreline. The bridge on the causeway leading to it was easily removed. The original castle was built in 1220 by Frederick II and destroyed by the Spanish in 1503. In conjunction with several other castles, including Castel Nuovo, Castel dell'Uovo formed a protective ring around Naples. The present structure dates from the 17th century.

At Castel Nuovo five huge, machicolated drum towers dominate the entrance and walls. One stands at each corner of the castle and the fifth is in the center of the wall, between the entrance and a corner tower. The high inner curtains were surrounded by a much lower outer wall forming a concentric ring at the edge of the moat. The entrance is defended by the central mural tower and a corner tower. Some work was done to adapt the castle for artillery and the outer wall is probably a fausse braie that resulted from that effort. Most of these additions, which remain to this very day, were ordered by Alfonso I of Aragon in the 1440s and 1450s and carried out by Italian and Iberian architects.

One of the castles owned by the Scaligeri family was **Sirmione**, located on a peninsula on the south end of Lake Garda, which was designed to maintain strategic dominion of the area. Control of this lake gave the family the same power as the robber barons of the Rhine. Construction on the brick castle began at the end of the 13th century and was completed early in the next century. What sets it apart is the harbor within its walls. A square tower crowned with machicoulis located in the southeast corner overlooks the harbor and the castle. Three square corner towers and two gatehouses dominate the walls. The castle sits on a narrow part of the peninsula and is separated from the mainland by a wide moat filled with lake water. Only a drawbridge leading into the gatehouse of the castle and a second gate next to the castle leading into the city provide access across the moat, which isolates the fortified end of the promontory. The moat also branches off to surround the other two sides of the castle. The second gatehouse is on the west side. The position is very impressive and never underwent siege.

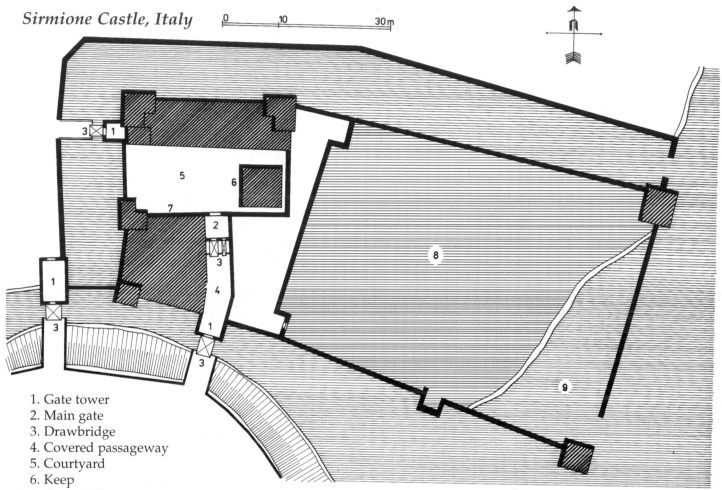

Sirmione Castle, Italy

0   10   30 m

1. Gate tower
2. Main gate
3. Drawbridge
4. Covered passageway
5. Courtyard
6. Keep
7. Great Hall
8, 9. Harbor

SIRMIONE CASTLE *on Lake Garda.*

THE CESTA, *one of the three castles of San Marino, a small country surrounded by Italy, viewed from the oldest of the three, the Rocca. The castles span the high crest of a ridge and are linked by a wall which runs along the ridge.*

ALMANSA CASTLE, SPAIN.

Iberian Peninsula

1. Alhambra of Granada
2. Baeza
3. Baños de la Encina
4. Coca
5. Montealegre
6. Gormaz
7. Guimarâes

8. Medina del Campo
9. Fuensaldaña
10. Peñafiel
11. Saxe
12. Almonvol
13. Torrelobatón
14. Zahara

Ávila, Spain

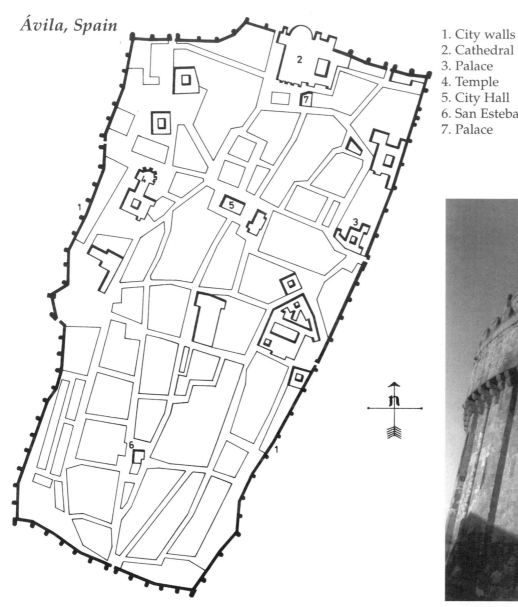

1. City walls
2. Cathedral
3. Palace
4. Temple
5. City Hall
6. San Esteban
7. Palace

ÁVILA, SPAIN.
Above: *Fortified walls of the church which was built into the city walls.*
Left: *San Vincente Gate of Avila.*

Iberian Peninsula

The Iberian Peninsula is dotted with medieval fortifications built between the 8th and the 15th century, during the entire period of the Reconquista. Its fortified cities played a key role in the liberation of Iberia. In addition to fortified cities which held the frontiers, almost continuous lines of castles and watchtowers mushroomed over the landscape as the Christian-Islamic frontiers shifted across the peninsula.

One of the oldest fortified cities is **Lugo** located in Galicia, the northwest corner of the peninsula. The quasi-circular Roman wall from 270 A.D. surrounds the city, covering 2.14 kilometers. It is 12 meters high and varies in width between 4.5 and 7.0 meters. In the true Roman style, the wall is made mostly of cement with stone facings of slate and granite blocks. It is believed that it was entirely covered with cement during the Roman occupation, which lent it a white color. The slate was probably a medieval addition. The city is entered through five Roman and five medieval gates. The walls included 85 projecting square and semicircular towers, 72 of which still stand. Most of the towers probably consisted of two levels to accommodate archers. Because of their northern location in Iberia, these fortifications exhibit no Islamic characteristics.

One of the best known fortified cites in Spain is the city of **Ávila** at the edge of a plateau overlooking the right bank of a tributary of the Duero River. The town is still surrounded by a 2.5-kilometer-long medieval enceinte and over 80 towers that are thought to have replaced an earlier Roman wall. Ávila's walls are up to 3 meters thick and 12 meters high. The town includes nine gates, the most impressive of which is the San Vincente Gate with its two large towers protruding from the walls and its arched entrance. The San Vincente Gate, in its present state, probably dates from the 15th century. A nearby tower has an unusual set of double battlements. In 1090, King Alfonso VI of Léon asked his brother-in-law, Raymond of Burgundy, to rebuild the walls of the city. French masons were brought in to work with 3,000 Spaniards, Moslems, and Jews on the project. It is

though that the construction took until the end of the decade. It must be noted, however, that the records are not precise on the subject, so that there is no certainty about the dates of construction. The merlons on the walls are capped in the pyramidal style so typical of Moorish architecture. The semicircular towers are unusual for the time period. The city had no citadel, but a cathedral, built between the 12th and 14th centuries, is incorporated into the urban walls. The cathedral is a fine example of transition between the Spanish Romanesque and Gothic style.

ÁVILA, SPAIN. *One of the most heavily defended towers of the city walls.*

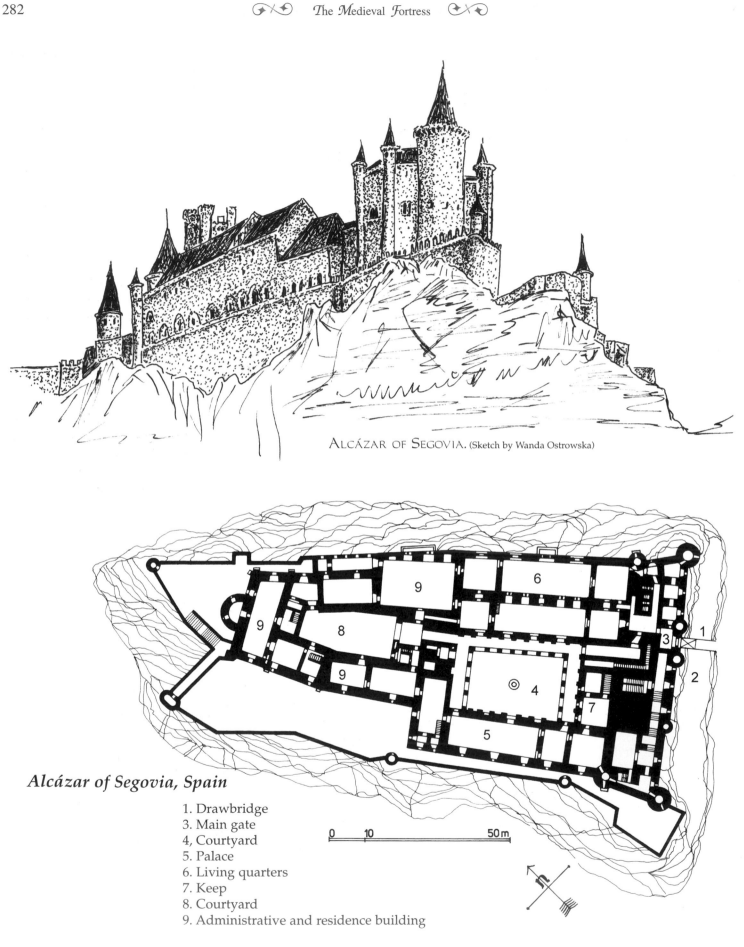

ALCÁZAR OF SEGOVIA. (Sketch by Wanda Ostrowska)

Alcázar of Segovia, Spain

1. Drawbridge
3. Main gate
4, Courtyard
5. Palace
6. Living quarters
7. Keep
8. Courtyard
9. Administrative and residence building

0   10   50 m

One of the earliest Moorish citadels or alcazabas in Spain is located at **Baños de la Encina**, in the southern province of Jaén. Built during the reign of Caliph Al-Hakam II of Cordoba in the 10th century, it stands on a hill dominating a pass between Castile and Andalusia. This well-preserved castle shares many traits with the Byzantine fortifications, to which it apparently owes much. Its oval enceinte, only about 100 meters long, includes 14 protruding square towers and a gateway with the double horseshoe arch typical of Islamic architecture. A keep was added in the 13th century, when Christians occupied the castle after the battle of Las Navas de Tolosa in 1212.

Another type of castle in Moorish Spain was what the Moslems called the alcázar, a fortified royal palace usually more spacious and more luxuriously appointed than the alcázaba. The most famous alcázar in Spain is the **Alhambra of Granada**, which derives its name from the red stone from which it was built. The third largest of its kind, this jewel of Spanish-Islamic architecture is nestled among the snowy peaks of the Sierra Nevadas and is in an excellent state of preservation. The Alhambra is dominated by a small alcázaba that stands on the site of an older fortification from the 9th century. The present alcázaba and the Alhambra are attributed to the Nasrid dynasty, which

was also responsible for the construction of the city walls with 24 towers. Their construction took place between the 13th and 15th centuries. The city of Granada was the last stronghold of Islam in Iberia.

The term alcázar was eventually adopted by the Christians to refer to fortified royal or aristocratic residences. The most famous of these residences is, no doubt, the **Alcázar of Segovia**, whose most famous occupants were the Catholic kings. It was founded in the 11th century by Alfonso VI of Léon on the site of a Moorish castle. Its construction and renovation continued through the 16th century as it became a primary residence of the kings. The castle was located on a rocky spur overlooking the confluence of two small rivers that form a moat along its steepest sides. An arched bridge crosses a deep moat on the landward site. One of its ends, shaped like a ship's prow, includes several turrets attached to a large rectangular tower and another round tower. The rectangular tower was actually the old keep. Another large structure near the front of the castle dating from the 15th century is known as the Torre de Juan II. It includes turrets, two at each corner, and machicoulis decorated in the Mudéjar style, which combines Islamic and Gothic elements.

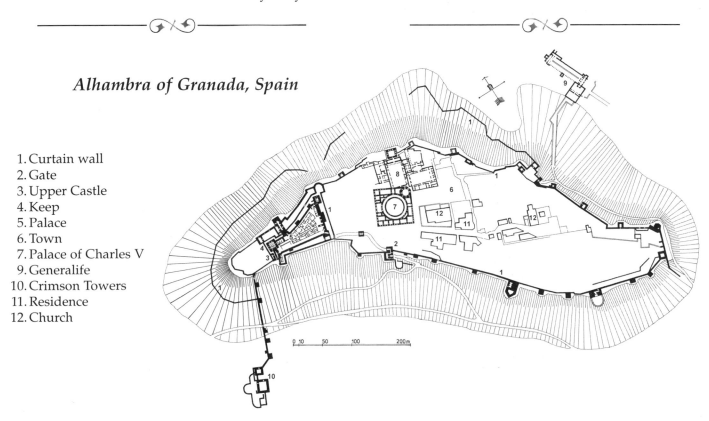

Alhambra of Granada, Spain

1. Curtain wall
2. Gate
3. Upper Castle
4. Keep
5. Palace
6. Town
7. Palace of Charles V
9. Generalife
10. Crimson Towers
11. Residence
12. Church

The School of Valladolid

by Ismael Barba García

Different styles or schools of castle construction developed in many regions of Europe during the Middle Ages. The "School of Valladolid," is a particularly distinctive style that developed in the Duero Valley in Spain during the second half of the 15th century. The style followed the specific instructions issued by King Enrique IV for the construction of the royal castles of Medina del Campo, Portillo, and "Torre Nueva" of Segovia. The construction of the castles followed the same pattern as the royal castles, which consisted of a square plan and a great Homage Tower or keep. The height of the walls was equal to half the length of one side of this square. The great Homage Tower rose to a height equal to the length of one side or twice the height of the surrounding walls. Generally, minor noblemen, who had fewer economic resources, had to be satisfied with smaller castles, but maintained the same proportions. Thus, their castles were actually reduced scale copies of the castles of the great lords. Typically the castle of a great lord measured 40 meters in height while that of a lesser gentleman was only 25 meters in height.

The great noble families of the region soon followed the example of their king by building their own castles on the same model. Such is the case of castles such as Torrelobatón, Fuentes de Valdepero, Peñafiel, and Fuensaldaña. Interestingly, most of the castles belonging to the school of Valladolid were built for newly ennobled middle-class families, many of Jewish origin, that were fighting for acceptance among the old aristocracy.

Most of these castles were built following a similar process that usually took two generations to complete. Influential men from the cities of the Duero Valley achieved high positions in administration thereby coming into close contact with the Royal Court. These men next strove to obtain small lordships by purchasing a nearby town like Fuensaldaña or Villafuerte, a process that could take up to 20 years. Once their title of nobility was secured and they received the right to keep their royal land grants within their family, they proceeded to build a castle, as a symbol of their social status.

These castles with a great Homage Tower became obsolete in a few years because of the appearance of artillery, and were reduced to the status of simple symbols of ostentation on the part of their builders.

FUENSALDAÑA CASTLE, SPAIN

The region of **Valladolid** is particularly famous for its numerous castles, such as Montealegre, Fuensaldaña, Torrelobatón, and Medina del Campo.

Montealegre is one of the most impressive and strongest castles of the region with its high curtains and unusual pentagonal tower, known as the Torre del Homemaje or Tower of Homage, the Spanish term for keep. The uppermost part of the three-levels of this keep has been destroyed. One of Montealegre's corners overlooks the plain below. Its walls are 4 meters thick and about 20 meters high. The present structure dates from the early part of the 14th century and includes square corner towers and round towers in between. The entrance included a drawbridge over a moat, which has now been filled.

Torrelobatón Castle was built in the 14th century and owes its design to the same school of architecture as most of the castles in the vicinity of Valladolid. Torrelobatón's three-level keep—some of whose floors were probably further subdivided—was built in the early part of the 14th century and stands in a corner of the enceinte. The castle also comprises three round corner towers crowned with machicoulis. It was heavily modified in subsequent periods.

Fuensaldaña Castle was begun in the 1430s and was designed by a Muslim master mason named Mohamed. Except for the keep, it is very similar to Torrelobatón. Its four-level vaulted keep, whose large upper floor was subdivided into two more floors, was started in 1453. The longest side of this large rectangular structure of about 20 by 15 meters is incorporated into one of the four sides of the castle. Four round towers rise at corners of the curtains, and bar-

MONTEALEGRE CASTLE, SPAIN.

TORRELOBATÓN CASTLE, SPAIN.

tizans stand on the center of the longer walls and on the towers.

The castle of **La Mota at Medina del Campo** dates back to the 12th century, but the only parts of that early castle that survive to this day are the lower portions of its walls. La Mota was remodeled repeatedly between the time of Alfonso VIII in the 13th century until the 15th century. The present brick structure dates from the 1460s and its battlements were restored in the 20th century. The castle consists of a large square keep that stands in one of the corners and rises to a height of about 30 meters. The keep consists of three levels, the lowest of which is further subdivided into three floors and gives access to the castle's subterranean galleries. The keep stands out because of the unusual double turrets or double bartizans on each of its corner, similar to those of the Alcázar of Segovia. Machicoulis were built between the bartizans. The inner wall includes five rectangular towers and is surrounded by a deep, wide moat with defensive positions within it. The outer wall surrounding the entire castle was added in the 15th century and includes four circular corner towers, two circular ones at the drawbridge entrance, and smaller semicircular ones between the round ones. The walls were reinforced by plinths and were adapted for firearms.

La Mota, Medina del Campo, Spain

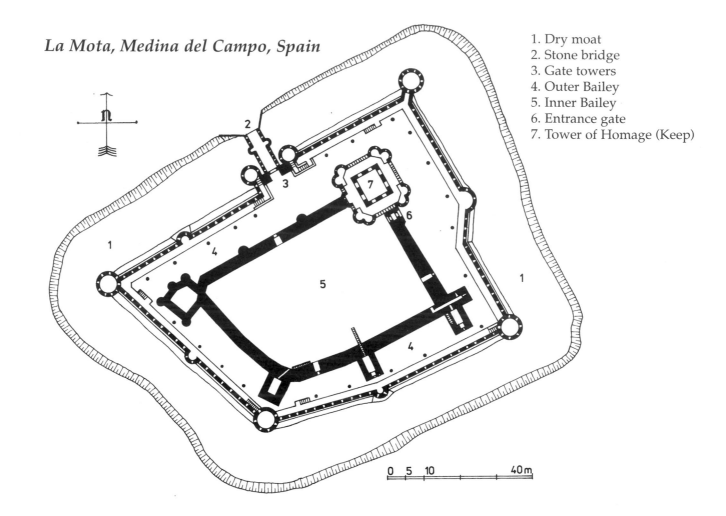

1. Dry moat
2. Stone bridge
3. Gate towers
4. Outer Bailey
5. Inner Bailey
6. Entrance gate
7. Tower of Homage (Keep)

LA MOTA, MEDINA DEL CAMPO, SPAIN.
Left: *The walls and towers. The adaptation for cannons can be seen on the outer towers.*

PEÑAFIEL CASTLE.

(Sketch by Wanda Ostrowska)

Peñafiel Castle, to the east of Valladolid, "Castile's Faithful Rock," has the appearance of a ship rising above the surrounding plain of the Duero. The castle stretches for over 150 meters along the crest of a hill. The space between its upper walls that forms the courtyard is no greater than about 10 meters in width. Its large keep stands in the center, dividing the castle into a northern and southern ward. The rectangular keep has three levels which may have been divided into additional floors and rises to a height of over 20 meters. The outer enceinte, which dates back to the 11th century, consists of the oldest walls and is about 210 meters long and about 20 meters wide.

Peñafiel was formerly a Moorish fortification which was taken from Almanzor by Count Sancho García, who renovated it in the 11th century. It was controlled for a time by one of El Cid's lieutenants. The upper or inner walls, added during the 14th century, included 8 towers and 21 turrets mounted on corbels typical of many Spanish castles of the period. Only the two corner towers are not solid and have an interior. The upper walls, the keep, and towers are lined with machicoulis. The gate in the outer wall opened at an angle onto the inner wall so that the approach route could be guarded from the keep and the inner walls. Don Pedro Girón, Master of the Order of Calatrava, was responsible for the final modifications made to the castle in the 15th century. One of the most famous of the Peñafiel's occupants was Don Juan Manuel, nephew of King Alfonso X, the Wise, who penned his famous treatises and *Conde Lucanor* within its walls between the 13th and 14th century.

Peñafiel Castle, Spain
The tower of homage (keep) is in the center.

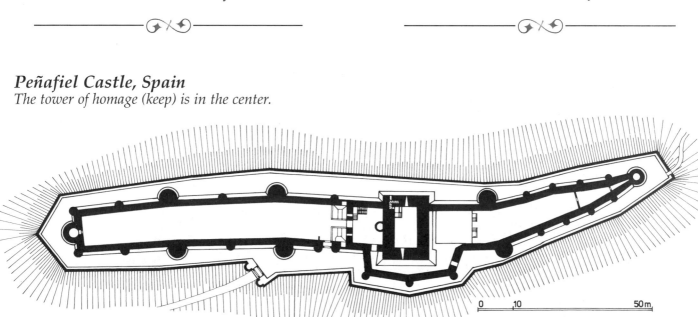

0   10   50m

ALMANSA CASTLE
View showing the Tower of Homage (keep) which tow-
ers over the three-level castle perched over the town.

(Sketch by Wojciech Ostrowski)

Almansa Castle, similar to Peñafiel but much larger, lies to the east (to the southwest of Valencia). It was erected on the site of a small Arab fortification of the 9th century that had been expanded by the Moors in the 10th century. By the 12th century, it had been taken over by the Christians, who added new walls. In 1255, the king of Aragon renovated Almansa and gave it to the Templars, who garrisoned it. This impressive castle rests on a rocky formation dominating the plain. Its large keep, which stands at its highest point, was not added until the 15th century. It rises on the north side, overlooking the cliff, and is approached by a long stairway on the south side. It is protected by walls and towers that follow the rock formation at various levels and drop down to the town that huddles at the foot of the cliff.

Not far from Almansa is the Moorish Alcázaba of **Saxe**, which stands on the crest of a ridge overlooking the town. It includes a large square keep and what appears to be a Moorish corner tower on the east end linked to each other by walls. The keep and the ruins of two round towers on the west end were probably Christian. The only approach is from the side facing away from the town on the north side. In many ways, Saxe is typical of the numerous Moorish and Christian strongholds that dot the Spanish countryside.

(Sketch by Wojciech Ostrowski)

ALCÁZABA OF SAXE.

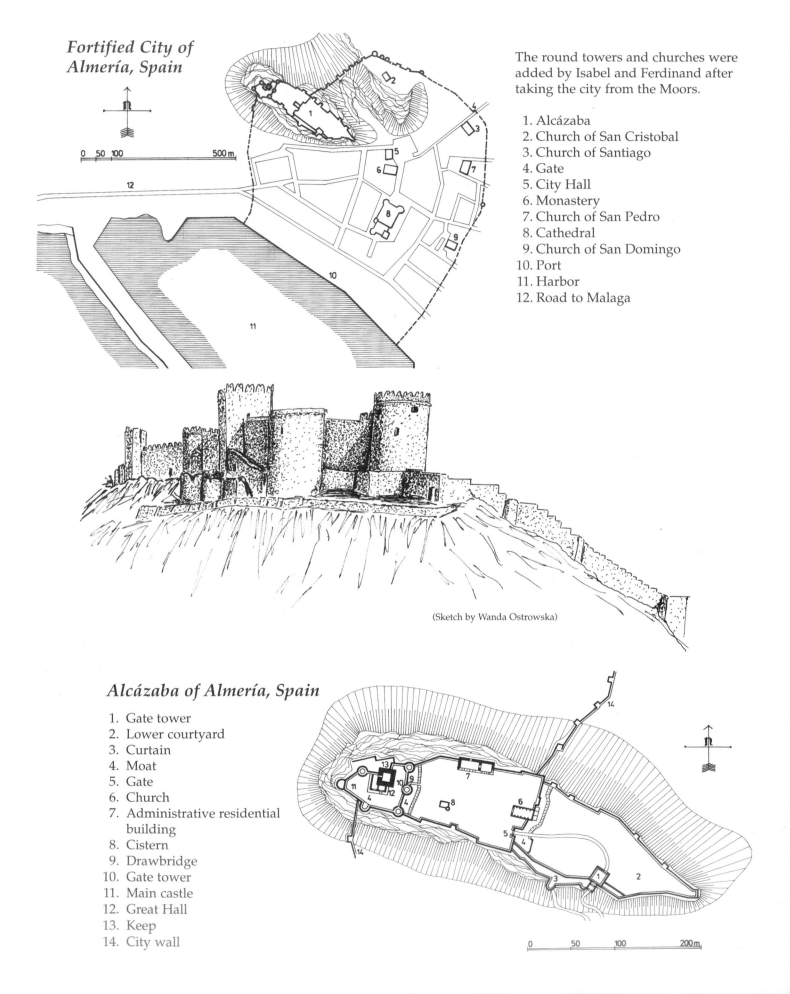

Fortified City of Almería, Spain

0   50 100   500 m

The round towers and churches were added by Isabel and Ferdinand after taking the city from the Moors.

1. Alcázaba
2. Church of San Cristobal
3. Church of Santiago
4. Gate
5. City Hall
6. Monastery
7. Church of San Pedro
8. Cathedral
9. Church of San Domingo
10. Port
11. Harbor
12. Road to Malaga

(Sketch by Wanda Ostrowska)

Alcázaba of Almería, Spain

1. Gate tower
2. Lower courtyard
3. Curtain
4. Moat
5. Gate
6. Church
7. Administrative residential building
8. Cistern
9. Drawbridge
10. Gate tower
11. Main castle
12. Great Hall
13. Keep
14. City wall

0   50   100   200m

One of the most spectacular Moorish fortified cities of Spain is **Almería**, nicknamed Mirror of the Sea. Its alcázaba stands on a ridge 65 meters high that overlooks the town and is only accessible from the south. Almería's alcázaba, as first built by the Moors in the 8th century, rests on the ruins of a Phoenician citadel. The castle comprises three wards with flanking towers on the curtains. The water reservoirs were located on the north side of the lower ward. The middle ward included a mosque, baths, and underground prison cells. The upper ward, separated from the rest by a moat, still houses a keep with Gothic ogival openings added after Isabella and Ferdinand captured Almería in the 15th century. The upper ward also included underground galleries and three additional large towers, one of which was connected to the scarp by a tunnel, and another of which served as the quarters for the harem. The last of the three towers overlooked the wall and gate that led up to the castle's entrance. A wall linked to both sides of the castle encircled the town.

Alfonso VII of Castile took Almería in 1147 with the help of the Genoese, but lost it again to the Moors 10 years later. Abu Sidi improved the city's fortifications, turning Almería into one of the "Keys to Granada." Jaime II recaptured the castle and ransomed it back to the king of Granada. Almería finally fell to Isabella and Ferdinand in 1489.

Almería, Spain.
Above: *View from the castle of the walls encircling the town.*
Right: *The walls encirling the city with the castle in the background.*

The kingdom of Portugal was not devoid of castles and fortifications. **Lisbon** was occupied and fortified by the Moors until it fell to the Crusaders in 1147, so many of the Portuguese fortifications exhibit strong Islamic characteristics. One of the exceptions is **Guimarâes Castle** in the north, which is more European than Arabic in character. Originally built in the 10th century as a tower in Christian style, it acquired an enceinte late in the 11th century when it was occupied by the king of Castile. The present-day structure, which owes its layout to 15th-century renovations, is trapezoidal and includes square corner towers and a large keep that stands inside the enceinte instead of being incorporated into the curtain walls.

Castelo dos Mouros, located at Sintra, includes walls and towers that run along the rocky ground, winding over the terrain and along cliffs. In 1147, Castelo dos Mouros surrendered without resistance to Portugal's first king after the crusaders took Lisbon. This victory was the first for a Portuguese king. The architecture of Castelo dos Mouros is characteristic of the Mudéjar style, also known as the Andalusian style, which originated in Al Andalus in the 8th century. The Mudéjar style was characterized by the use of concrete made with earth, gravel, lime, and straw developed in the 10th century. It also included features such as towers linked by bridges to the main wall and huge underground water cisterns like the ones found at Almería. The Mudéjar style persisted in Islamic Iberia and Morocco in the Magreb, with a few modifications from the 10th through the 13th century.

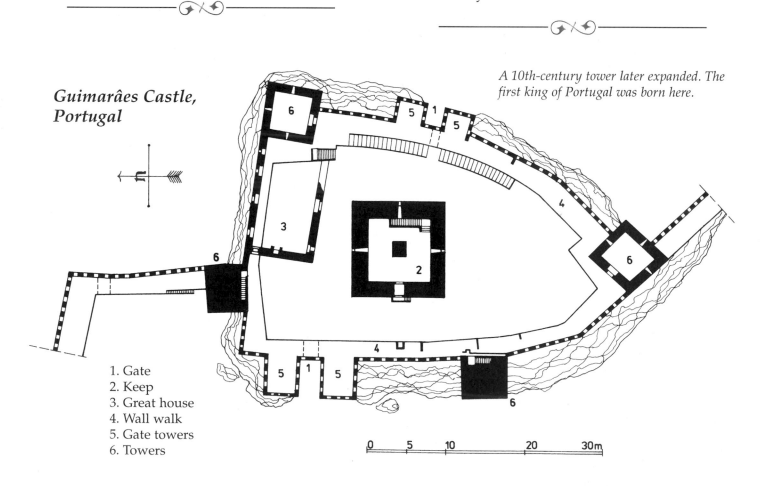

A 10th-century tower later expanded. The first king of Portugal was born here.

Guimarâes Castle, Portugal

1. Gate
2. Keep
3. Great house
4. Wall walk
5. Gate towers
6. Towers

0   5   10   20   30m

North Africa

In **Morocco** city walls, alcázabas (casbahs), and alcázars have survived unchanged through the ages. The walls of **Marrakech**, some of the oldest in Morocco, may date back to the 11th century when the Almoravids took the town. At the other end of North Africa, the town of **Al Qahira** near Cairo, founded by the Fatimids in 969, is a magnificent example of a royal acropolis in the Islamic style. In 1087, the vizier surrounded it with a stone wall, square towers, and fortified gates. **Cairo** boasts Saladin's great citadel built between 1176 and 1183 just to the southeast of Al Quahira. Saladin's walls, which spanned 1,200 meters, included small semicircular towers every 100 meters and several impressive fortified gates. In 1207, Al Kamil reinforced the towers and gates and added five huge square keeps. The Mamlukes erected two more walls on the southwest to protect the palaces, barracks, and storage areas. In the 16th century, the Turks built two large circular towers to control the citadel. Thus the fortifications of Cairo span the entire period of the High Middle Ages.

CAIRO. *Part of the walls of the citadel.* (Photo courtesy of Pierre Etcheto)

Left: RABAT, MOROCCO. *Gate through 14th-century walls.*
Below: ALEXANDRIA. *Qait Bey Castle built on the site of an old lighthouse that was one of the seven wonders of the world.*

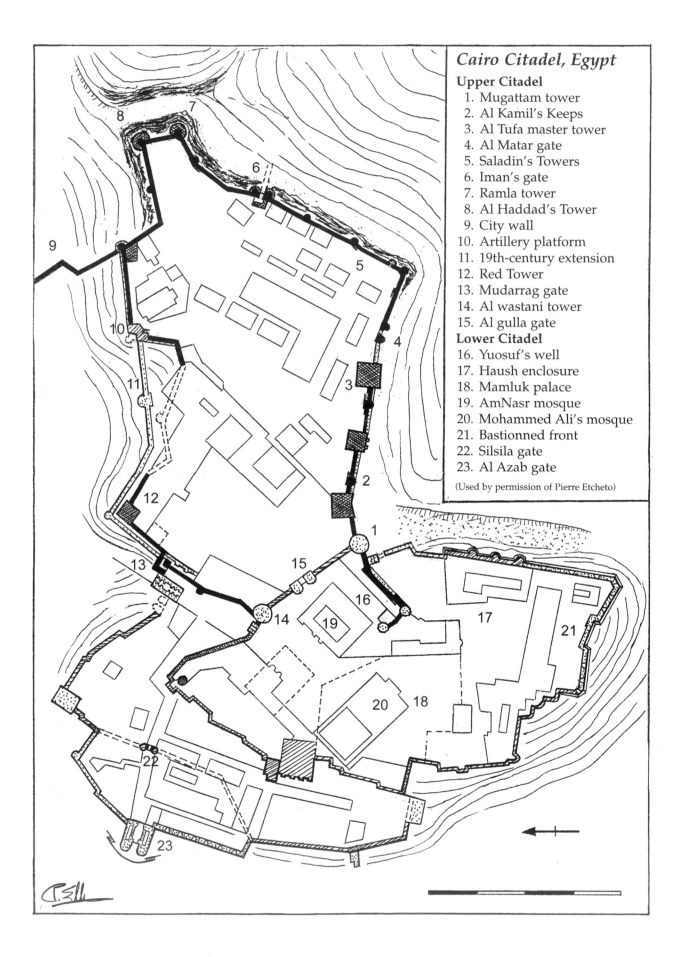

Cairo Citadel, Egypt

Upper Citadel
1. Mugattam tower
2. Al Kamil's Keeps
3. Al Tufa master tower
4. Al Matar gate
5. Saladin's Towers
6. Iman's gate
7. Ramla tower
8. Al Haddad's Tower
9. City wall
10. Artillery platform
11. 19th-century extension
12. Red Tower
13. Mudarrag gate
14. Al wastani tower
15. Al gulla gate

Lower Citadel
16. Yuosuf's well
17. Haush enclosure
18. Mamluk palace
19. AmNasr mosque
20. Mohammed Ali's mosque
21. Bastionned front
22. Silsila gate
23. Al Azab gate

(Used by permission of Pierre Etcheto)

Builders and Architects of Medieval Fortresses

The names of the men responsible for the design and construction of the castles and other fortifications of the Middle Ages are mostly lost to history. Historians of the era tended to focus on those who commissioned the works rather than those who carried out the actual plan and construction. Usually those in charge of the projects were master masons and carpenters who had reached their high office through years of experience, those whose work was recognized and highly praised by their peers. Many of them had worked on other large projects other than fortifications, such as churches and stone bridges. Titles given to these men varied from country to country and throughout historical records they are usually referred to by their title with their name going into obscurity. But a few of the names did survive and below we list some of the more prominent ones.

Langred: France, late 10th century; designed Ivry.

Gundulf of Bec: Normandy and England, 11th century; adviser to William the Conqueror.

Benno II, Bishop of Osnabruck: Holy Roman Empire, 11th century; adviser to Henry IV; designed Harzburg.

Robert de Belleme: Normandy and England, late 11th and early 12th centuries; built castles at Arundel and Gisors.

Prince Jury Dolgoruky: Russia, 12th century; helped design and ordered the construction of the first citadel (Kremlin) in Moscow in 1156.

Richard I, King of England: 12th century; designed Château Gaillard in France.

Hugh de Noyers, Bishop of Auxerre: France, late 12th century; improved the episcopal castles at Varzy and Noyers.

Frederick II, Holy Roman Emperor: Italy, 13th century; designed Castel del Monte and other structures.

Edward I, King of England: 13th century; involved in design of castles especially in Wales.

Edward II, King of England: 13th century; involved in design of castles especially in Wales.

Master James of St. George: Savoy, 13th century; over 30 years designed and supervised the construction of 10 of the most modern castles of the time for Edward I in Wales including Harlech and also did work for Edward in Scotland.

Eudes de Montreuil: France, 13th century; designed and supervised work on Aigues Mortes and other fortifications for Louis IX and Philip III.

Philippe Chinard: France, 13th century; a master mason who worked on Castel del Monte for Frederick II.

Pierre d'Agincourt: France, 13th century; built walls of Lucera in Italy.

Raimond du Temple: France, 14th century; worked on Vincennes.

Guillaume d'Arondel: France, 14th century; worked on Vincennes.

Jean Lenoir: France, 14th century; designed Pierrefonds.

Dmitry Donskoy, Prince: Russia, 14th century; helped design and ordered construction of the white brick Kremlin of Moscow in 1367.

John Lewyn: England, 14th century; a master mason who worked on Bolton Castle in Yorkshire, England.

Mikolaus Fellenstein: 14th century; best known designer of the castles of the Teutonic Knights.

Juan Guas: Castile, 15th century; worked on the castles of Mombeltran, Belmonte, and Manzanares and the cathedral of Toledo.

Ali Caro (Christian name: Alonso Fonseca): Castile, 15th century; worked on the Castle of Coca.

Juan Carrera: Castile, 15th century; worked on the castles of Coria and San Felices de los Gallegos.

Fernan Gomez de Maranon: Castile, 15th century; worked on the castles of Almeria, Fuenterrabia and Peñafiel, and the tower of the castle of Fuentes de Valdeparro.

Lorenzo Vazquez: Castile, 15th century; worked on the castles of Calahorra and Cihuela.

Luis Fajardo (a converted Muslim): Castile, 15th century; worked on the castles of Velez Blanco, Mula, Alcázar de Murcia.

Aristiotel Fioraventy (Italian ancestry): Russia, late 15th century; ordered by Prince Ivan I Kalita to build the red brick walls of Moscow's Kremlin.

Giuliano da Sangallo and Antonio da Sangallo: Italian city-states; these brothers from Florence

worked on several important transitional fortifications including the moderization of Castel Sant' Angelo in Rome (1493) and Civitacastellana (1494-1499). Their nephew, Antonio the Younger, became the Pope's architect and worked on a number of 16th century fortifications.

Lorenzo de Donce: Castile, early 16th century; worked on the Castle of Grajal de Campos (1519) and the restoration of Simancas (1521).

Feodor Savelievich Kon: Russia, late 16th century; worked on the walls of White town of Moscow, the walls of Smolensk (1595-1602), and the walls of other Russian cities.

Titles of Builders and Architects

FRANCE:

Master Carpenter	*Maître charpentier*
Construction Master	*Maître de chantier*
Master Mason	*Maître maçon*
Stone Cutter	*Tailleur de pierre*
Quarry Stone Cutter	*Carrier*
Architect	*Architecte*
Engineer (17 century)	*Ingénieur*

❦

PORTUGAL:

Master Carpenter	*Mestre Carpinteiro*
Construction Master	*Mestre das Obras*
Architect	*Arquitecto*
Engineer (17th century)	*Engenheiro*

❦

SPAIN:
For castles made of stone:

Master Engineer	*Maestro Mayor**
(in charge of all others; also served as architect)	
Master Stone Cutter	*Maestro Cantero**
(also served as architect)	
Construction Master	*Maestro de Obras**
Stone Cutter	*Cantero*
(cut and polished the stone)	
Cutter	*Pedrero*
(less skilled than the cantero, usually worked with rough stone or in the quarry)	

*The *maestro mayor, maestro cantero,* and *maestro de obras* could be the one and same person. They were mostly Jews or Muslims and served their Christian or Moorish customers with equal competence.

For castles made of brick or adobe:

Master Builder	*Maestro Alarife**
Brick Layer	*Albañil*

*The term alarife is derived from the Arabic. The maestro alarife was usually a Moor or a descendant of a Moor.

Late 15th-century terms for builders of fortifications:

Military Engineer (Architect)	*Capitán*
Construction Engineer	*Maestro*

THE NETHERLANDS:

Master Mason	*Bouwmeester*
(There is little information on the identity or exact titles of these men.)	

❦

SWEDEN:

Master Mason	*Byggmästare*
(There is little information on the identity or exact titles of these men.)	

Mid-16th century

Master Mason or Master	*Byggmästare* or *Mästare.*
(There is little information on the identity or exact titles of these men.)	

❦

RUSSIA:

Artist-Architect	*Zodchij*
(builder of fortifications and churches)	

Appendix II

Chronology of Sieges

Even though the number of medieval sieges both large and small probably can never be accurately estimated, the number of fortifications can give us a clue. The number of medieval fortifications in Europe and the Mediterranean World probably was well over 50,000 and if only one-tenth of those were ever engaged in warfare, the number would still be extremely high. Since many medieval sieges only involved a small number of men this is not impossible, so here we have selected a number of sieges with some significance.

673-678 Siege of Constantinople. Five year siege by Arabs ended after they took heavy losses.

717-718 Attack on Constantinople. The Arabs lost another 40,000 men in this siege. Both this and the 7th-century siege secured the Balkans from the Islamic threat for centuries.

885-886 Siege of Paris. Despite an all out attempt on the part of the Vikings, Paris did not surrender. This great siege left a major impression on Franks and Vikings alike.

955 Siege of Augsburg (August 8-9). Otto I arrived at the head of a Saxon army to break the siege and the next day the battle of Lechfied was fought, ending the Magyar threat.

1016 Siege of London. After Edmund Ironside was made king of England in April, the Viking Canute the Great put London under siege although he could not maintain the encirclement and Edmund managed to break out. But Edmund died a year later, giving Canute an opportunity to take the throne of England.

1049 and 1054 Sieges of Domfront. William the Conqueror began the expansion of his Norman territories. The long siege of the stone castle of Domfort, an extremely strong castle in Angevin territory, failed in 1049, but succeeded in 1054, after the garrison heard of how William treated the defenders of Alençon without mercy after taking that town while Domfort was under siege. William continued to expand his power through more sieges.

1071 Siege of Manzikert. The siege of this Armenian town in Asia Minor caused the Byzantine emperor to send a relief army, which was crushed in open battle. Subsequently Byzantium's power rapidly declined in the Middle East.

1081 Siege of Dyrrachium (near Durres in Albania). The Norman Robert Guiscard laid siege in July. In October, a Byzantine relief force was smashed by the much smaller Norman force. The Normans successfully assaulted the town in February. Byzantium, already driven from southern Italy by the Normans, was thus threatened on a new front in Europe.

1083-1084 Siege of Rome. Pope Gregory VII was placed under siege in Castel Sant' Angelo by Holy Roman Emperor Henry IV. In May 1084 the siege was broken by a Norman/Lombard force attacking from the south.

1093-1094 Fall of Valencia. Starvation forced the city to surrender to El Cid after a nine-month siege.

1097 Siege of Nicaea in Asia Minor (May to June). The Crusaders built and employed all types of siege engines. After defeating a Turkish relief force, they catapulted the heads of the dead into the city. The Byzantine emperor ordered ships hauled up to help the Crusaders attack from the lake side. Mining brought down a tower of the outer wall and catapults smashed part of the outer wall before the Turks surrendered. This was the first major siege and victory of the First Crusade.

1097-1098 Siege of Antioch (October to June). This is considered one of the great sieges of history. In October Crusaders besieged the city. Starvation affected both sides heavily. The Crusaders built three towers to blockade three of the city gates. On December 29, a sortie by the garrison failed. On December 31, a Turkish relief force was defeated. On February 9, a larger relief force was also defeated. In March, the garrison launched another unsuccessful sortie. The Crusaders again catapulted the heads of Turks into the city. Kerboga led a new relief force, but before he arrived in June, the Crusaders had taken the city when a traitor opened a gate. The Turks held the citadel until Kerboga's arrival. Kerboga attacked the town from the citadel, but was repelled. He besieged the Christians in the city. The finding of a supposed holy relic fired the Crusaders to march out of the city and smash Turkish army in open battle under the leadership of Bohemond of Taranto. The path to Jerusalem was open.

1099 Siege of Jerusalem. A Crusader army of less than 10,000 arrived in June to put 20,000 defenders plus the city's population under siege. With the fall of Antioch there was no chance of relief. The Crusaders built three large belfry's mid-July and began filling the moat so the towers could be advanced against three different points on the wall. Turkish catapults on the walls responded and padding was dropped over the walls to protect them. Raymond IV's attack in the south was temporarily held. Godfrey of Boullion's attack in the north succeeded after his men opened the gate. Anyone in the path of the Crusaders was slaughtered and the remaining defenders withdrew to the Tower of David and surrendered. The First Crusade ended in success for the Crusaders.

1109 Siege of Glogów. The Holy Roman Emperor Henry V attempted to take this Polish gród using hostages as human shields. However, his siege failed when King Boleslav of Poland arrived with a relief force. This battle was decisive in defeating Germanic attempts to take over the Polish state.

1111-1112 Siege of Tyre. Baldwin I of Jerusalem had attempted for several years to take several coastal cities, but had limited success. In November he attacked Tyre, one of the strongest coastal cities controlled by the Fatimids. The defenders destroyed the huge belfries (some equipped with rams) with fire and also used grappling irons and ropes to defeat them. In April, a Muslim army came to relieve the city and besieged Baldwin's camp, which was made of earthworks. Baldwin broke off the siege and withdrew.

1124 Siege of Tyre. In February Baldwin renewed his siege of the island city with the help of the Venetian navy. He cut off the city's only fresh water source which was supplied by an aqueduct. The only approach was along the manmade isthmus created by Alexander the Great centuries before. The garrison finally surrendered in July, after months of exchanging artillery fire, and despite the defender's use of Greek Fire and the failed assaults by Baldwin's forces.

1144 Siege of Edessa. The Turkish sultan Zengi attacked the fortified town in November. On Christmas Eve, his engineers breached the walls by using caves to tunnel to the walls and took the city. In another two days the citadel surrendered, which led to the Second Crusade.

1147-1148 Siege of Lisbon. A 30,000-man force of Portuguese, Anglo-Norman, Flemish, and German Crusaders moved against the Moors who held the city with 5,000 men. The Anglo-Normans brought up a 28-meter-high belfry, which was destroyed by the Moors with fire arrows and projectiles from catapults. Another belfry was built and suffered a similar fate. In September, a mine was intercepted by a countermine of the Moors. However, the Moors were defeated in a skirmish below the ground and the mine brought down a large section of wall in October. The Crusaders were stopped in their attempt to storm the breach. Along another section of the front a new 24-meter-high belfry was built and moved up to the wall, causing the Moors to surrender. The new Portuguese king now had a capital.

1153-1154 Siege of Ascalon. In January King Baldwin of Jerusalem laid siege to the city with his entire army and blockaded the port by sea. After several months, the Fatimids sent a naval force from Egypt to resupply the defenders. One of the tall siege towers allowed Baldwin's forces to fire over the walls, directly into the streets. The tower was set afire in a sortie, but the fire caused a breach in the wall which allowed the Templars to storm through. The defenders eliminated the attacking force and repaired the wall. In August, heavy bombardment convinced the garrison to surrender. This was the last important conquest of the kings of Jerusalem.

1158 Siege of Milan. Frederick Barbarossa, who had tried to restore imperial control over Northern Italy since 1154, laid siege to Milan in 1158. The Milanese surrendered in September, after a month-long siege.

1159-1160 Siege of Crema. The siege began in July as a result of continued defiance on the part of Milan. In frustration, Frederick Barbarossa had hostages tied to a belfry before he advanced it toward the walls of the city. Undaunted, the citizens of Crema continued to resist for another six months, until starvation forced them to surrender. The emperor ordered the walls and city razed to the ground.

1161-1162 Siege of Milan. The conflict between Frederick Barbarossa and Milan continued. He placed the city under siege again in May. After almost a year, in March 1162, the city surrendered. Its citizenry was removed and the emperor had the place leveled.

1174-1175 Siege of Alessandria. The North Italian states of the Lombardy League defied the Holy Roman Emperor in 1167. One of the cities of this league, Alessandria, consisted in 1168 of two towns on the Tanaro River, each with earth and timber defenses, and was named after Pope Alexander III. The siege began in September after the citizens refused to destroy their city and return to their former towns. Despite the use of a secret tunnel and deep mining, all attempts by Frederick Barbarossa to take the city failed. In April the siege was lifted.

1187 Siege of Jerusalem. After his victory at Hattin, Saladin advanced on Jerusalem and put it under siege in September. In a desperate effort to mount a defense, Balian of Ibelin, the commander, knighted every available male, including boys. In nine days Saladin's miners breached the walls, but were held back by the defenders. Short on men, Balian finally surrendered.

1188 Siege of Saone. Saladin and his son al-Malik al Zahir besieged Saone. Saladin attacked the east wall across the deep moat with four catapults and damaged the northeast corner. Al Zahir's forces used two siege engines to establish themselves on the north wall. Al Zahir's troops made a breach

and quickly rushed through, overrunning the town. The heavily outnumbered defenders fled to the great tower and negotiated a surrender.

1189-1191 Siege of Acre. After the fall of the Kingdom of Jerusalem, Conrad of Montferrat arrived in time to save Tyre. In August 1189, he and King Guy attacked the garrison of Acre, a city located on a strong position on a peninsula. For a time Saladin besieged the besiegers. Over the period of a year, both sides took heavy losses from disease and starvation. Assaults with belfries in May failed. After the fall of the castle of Beaufort in July 1190, Saladin sent troops to Asia Minor to meet Frederick Barbarossa's Crusaders. Richard the Lionhearted and Philip Augustus joined in the siege as part of the Third Crusade in 1191. Phillips' attempt to take the town with new siege towers failed in April 1191. Countermining stopped his underground efforts. Richard built a huge four-level siege tower which was not destroyed until it almost reached the walls. The defenders finally surrendered in July. Despite the hard-won victory, the Third Crusade began to fall apart.

1203-1204 Siege of Château Gaillard. In September 1203, Philip Augustus put the castle under siege. King John's commander, Roger de Lacy, surrendered the castle in March after a successful French assault. This victory opened the Seine River to the French and made it possible for them to eventually drive the English from Normandy.

1204 Attack on Constantinople. Forces of the Fourth Crusade were carried by Venetians to the city and helped return a deposed emperor to power. When the emperor ordered them to leave, they assaulted the city, which fell for the first time to an invading force. After this siege, Byzantium's might was seriously crippled and its lands temporarily under Latin control.

1209 Siege of Carcassonne. The siege took place as part of the Albigensian Crusade. After two weeks of fighting in the suburbs, Viscount Raymond-Roger attempted to negotiate with the Crusaders. During the parley he was taken prisoner, which led the city to surrender soon afterward. After the siege, the city became a royal stronghold in the king's crusade against the whole of Languedoc.

1211 Siege of Toulouse. Simon de Montfort, leader of the Crusade against the Albigensians, was unable to surround the city whose walls extended over six kilometers. While supplies reached the city, it was Simon's Crusaders who ran out of food. An assault with siege engines failed.

1215 Attack on Rochester Castle. The rebelling barons attempted to hold the stronghold against King John. The curtain wall and the corner of the keep were successfully mined and the castle was taken.

1216 Siege of Odiham. King John's small and insignificant castle at Odiham was garrisoned by three knights and ten sergeants but held out for two weeks against 140 soldiers of French Prince Louis during the Baron's Revolt in England. This clearly demonstrates the strength of strongholds against the typical armies of the first part of the High Middle Ages, a period of transition, when armies were only beginning to organize more efficiently for siege warfare.

1216 Siege of Dover. Prince Louis of France landed in England in 1216 and joined the rebels fighting King John. The king's garrison refused to surrender even though all the Cinque Ports had fallen. In 1217 the commander of Dover intercepted the French fleet arriving with reinforcements and defeated it at sea. After an English victory at Lincoln, the siege was lifted.

1217 Attack on Toulouse. Raymond of Toulouse defended the city against Simon de Montfort in September. Although the city was virtually unfortified, Simon's forces were engaged in heavy street fighting. Simon was killed by a stone from a catapult and the siege was abandoned. The king himself had to lead the next crusade against the Cathars and attack Toulouse in 1219.

1218-1219 Siege of Damietta. The 5th Crusade landed in the Nile Delta and began a siege that lasted 16 months. The Crusaders finally launched a successful assault in November 1219. Discovering a wall that the garrison, weakened by disease, had not manned, the Crusaders quickly swept over it and scaled the inner wall, taking the city.

1220 Fall of Bukhara and Samarkand. These two major fortified, and heavily defended, Central Asian cities quickly fell to the Mongols. The size of the Mongol forces and the defending forces by far exceeded any armies the European nations could muster.

1220-1221 Fall of Herat. This city quickly surrendered to the Mongols, but later revolted. In the ensuing six-month siege the city was forced to surrender and the population was executed as a lesson to any who would oppose the horsemen from the east.

1224 Siege of Bedford Castle. This castle, held by rebellious mercenaries, was attacked by the royal forces. The besiegers built towers for mounting catapults to keep the walls under constant bombardment. Henry III of England, in a common tactic of the day, warned the men of the garrison that he would execute them all if they did not yield. When his miners succeeded in badly damaging the inner wall and the keep, the defenders surrendered and were hung.

1226 Attack on Avignon. During the Crusade against Cathars, Louis VIII of France attacked Avignon, which was controlled by Raymond of Toulouse. Although the defenders mounted a vigorous defense, using trébuchets, Avignon fell and the king destroyed it fortifications. Later the walls were rebuilt and the Palace of the Popes was added.

1236 Attack on Cordoba. After the troops of King Ferdinand III of Castile stormed the city, more victories over the Moors followed in the south, drastically reducing the foothold of the Moors in Iberia to the kingdom of Granada.

1238 Siege of Brescia (July to September). A year after defeating the Lombardy League, the Holy Roman Emperor, Frederick II, laid siege to Brescia. It took him one year to assemble a large enough force for the siege. The imperial force included many non-Germanic elements such as Englishmen, Spaniards, Saracens, Cremonans, and Greeks. His mixed army could not prevent sallies by the garrison. He built huge belfries for the assault in September, but bad weather caused him to break off the siege. In 1241 Frederick put the small city of Faenza under siege. Faenza held out for half a year, preventing him from taking Bologna. Both sieges demonstrated that the imperial forces of the time were not capable of undertaking the sieges of cities, whose defenses were more complex than those of castles.

1240 Assault on Kiev. On December 5, the Mongols stormed the weakly held city after heavily bombarding it with their catapults. Despite suffering heavy casualties, the Mongols seized the city. The next day, Vladimir Gród (the citadel) was assaulted along with the Sophia Gate where the last defenders were holding out. The population was massacred and the city burned to the ground. Russia remained under Mongol domination for more than a century.

1241 Fall of Krakow. After the Polish army was defeated in battle outside the city, the Mongols quickly took the Polish capital.

1244 Siege of Montségur. The fall of this Cathar castle was a decisive event in bringing a close to the Crusades. What is of interest about this siege are the methods used by the attackers. The king's men were able to carry a catapult up the mountain and reassemble it on the opposite side of the castle in order to bombard it with greater efficiency.

1258 Attack on Baghdad. The Mongols advanced on Baghdad and laid siege to it in January. In February, heavy bombardment brought down parts of the eastern wall. Later in the same month, the Caliph surrendered. He was executed and his city was razed.

1266 Siege of Kenilworth Castle (July to December). Henry III undertook a major siege since the rebels defending the castle numbered over 1,000 men. In addition, almost the entire castle was protected by large water barriers that included an artificial lake and ponds. The site may have ranked with Dover in strength. The defenders answered the massive catapult bombardment by the royal forces with their own counter-bombardment, succeeding in destroying two great belfries and even some artillery. The attackers placed catapults on vessels to bombard the outer wall from the lake. The defenders made raids on the besiegers but finally, starvation convinced the defenders to negotiate a surrender.

1268 Siege of Antioch. Baibars, sultan of Egypt, advanced on Antioch after taking Caesarea and Arsouf in 1265 and Jaffa in 1268. In May he launched an assault on Antioch and defeated the outnumbered defenders. He than had the fortifications destroyed. Baibars' success signaled the collapse of the Crusaders' foothold in the Holy Land.

1271 Siege of Krak des Chevaliers. Baibars launched a full-scale assault against a depleted garrison, using trébuchets and mining. He also built towers, one of which dominated the south wall. All these efforts resulted in victory.

1291 Siege of Acre. Sultan al-Ashraf assembled a large number of siege engines from his domain and had ordered a hundred new ones built, two of which were probably huge trébuchets. The siege, which involved over 220,000 men, began in April. The population of Acre did not even reach 40,000 souls, including 15,000 knights and soldiers. Two thousand reinforcements arrived in May. The sultan used projectiles with explosives and assigned 1,000 miners to tunneling toward each tower of the double walls that sealed the peninsula. In May, the miners brought down the towers and sections of the outer wall. The defenders pulled back to the inner wall in the face of the assaulting Mamelukes. Soon, the inner wall was breached as well and the Christians attempted to flee by sea. The castle near the inner walls held out longer and was brought down by mining. Thus the last major Crusader stronghold in the Holy Land was gone.

1300 Siege of Caerlaverock Castle. King Edward I, at war with the Scots, put this castle under siege. After heavy bombardment the 60-man garrison accepted terms.

1304 Siege of Stirling. The city surrendered before Edward I could use his huge trébuchet he had planned on bringing into action. Most of the Scottish fortifications proved to be no match for Edward's huge siege engines during this campaign.

1305 Siege of Swiecie Castle. This castle was actually a gród that dominated a strategic site near the Vistula River and withstood a 10-week siege. A traitor damaged the catapults and crossbows forcing the garrison to accept terms from their besiegers, the Teutonic Knights. For the next 150 years Poland had no access to the Baltic.

1308 Fall of Gdansk (Danzig). Teutonic Knights took the city at the invitation of the citizens to protect them against the Brandenburg Knights. After taking the castle, the Teutonic Knights massacred the citizens thus beginning the first war of the century between the Poles and Teutonic Knights.

1344 Siege of Algeciras. Alfonso XI put this seaport under siege and destroyed the city after its surrender. Only the Islamic kingdom of Granada remained in Iberia after the fall of Algeciras.

1346-1347 Calais. After the victory at Crécy in the Hundred Years War, Edward III put Calais under siege. Supposedly bombards were employed during the siege. When a relief army failed to reach the city, its garrison surrendered. Calais became a key base for operations in France for the English for the next century.

1372 Fall of La Rochelle. The illiterate English commander of the garrison of La Rochelle was tricked by the French mayor into believing that a letter from the king called for him to parade the castle garrison in the town. He was led to believe that they would finally be paid (a Castillian fleet had already stopped the ships carrying the payroll from arriving). He brought out the entire garrison and walked into a French trap resulting in his surrender. The Mayor gave the city and its defenses to Bertrand du Guesclin.

1390 Siege of Vilno Castle. Teutonic Knights accompanied by the future king of England, Henry IV, failed to take the castle. Polish troops lifted the siege and relieved the Lithuanian garrison.

1396 Siege of Nicopolis. Sigismund of Luxemburg, King of Hungary, led an international force of as many as 60,000 Crusaders against the Turks. A string of several quick victories over Turkish garrisons in Bulgaria preceded the siege of Nicopolis, on the Danube. When several direct assaults failed, the crusaders began mining and preparing for an attack by escalade since they lacked siege machines. The sultan, at the head of a relief army, arrived about two weeks after the siege began, drew the Crusaders into battle, and defeated them.

1415 Siege of Harfleur. After landing in Normandy to renew the Hundred Years War, Henry V put Harfleur, the main port in the region, under siege. He used artillery with some success. This siege led to the campaign that resulted in the decisive battle of Agincourt.

1417 Siege of Caen. In September, Henry V returned to Normandy and proceeded to attack the city of Caen, the key to Normandy west of the Seine. After reducing Caen by assault, other French cities fell one by one in the course of the next year. The campaign culminated with the surrender of Falaise and Cherbourg.

1418 Siege of Rouen. Henry V turned on Rouen, the key to the remainder of Normandy and the road to Paris. The city surrendered in January 1419. Additional sieges followed until 1422, leading to the defeat of the French king.

1428 Siege of Orleans. The English had not completed the siege of Orleans when Joan of Arc, having managed to inspire the French forces, broke up the siege. The defeat of the English at Orleans was the turning point in the Hundred Years War.

1449-50 The 60 Sieges of the Bureau Brothers. The Bureaux brothers, employed by Charles VII, were instrumental in developing the efficient use of cannons in siege warfare during the Hundred Years War. This type of campaign heralds the phasing out of medieval-type fortifications.

1450 Siege of Kruja (Albanian fortress). After five months of futile attacks and incurring 20,000 casualties, the Turkish sultan lifted the siege. George Kastrioti Skanderg became the national hero of the Albanians and continued for many years to hold off the Turks.

1453 Siege of Castillon. The French siege of this town near Bordeaux caused the English under the leadership of John Talbot to march to its relief. The English were defeated in this last battle of the Hundred Years War.

1453 Fall of Constantinople. The Turkish sultan prevailed against the Byzantine defenders thanks to the use of all types of siege weapons, including cannons. The fall of Constantinople, which dealt a death blow to the Byzantine Empire, is sometimes used to mark the end of the Middle Ages. Subsequently, the Turks advanced through the Balkans almost unchecked.

1454 Siege of Malbork (Marienburg). The main seat of the Teutonic Knights had been improved as late as 1450 with a new enceinte. In March the site was put under siege by a Polish army. Both the defenders and besiegers employed artillery. The Poles lifted their siege in September and withdrew.

1456 Siege of Belgrade. Hungarian Janos Hundayi successfully defended the city for three months against Muhammed II's army, temporarily halting the Turkish advance.

1472 Siege of Beauvais. Charles the Bold of Burgundy marched against Beauvais, Picardy, because King Louis XI of France did not honor an agreement to turn over certain cities to him. Beauvais had a garrison of about 80 men, some auxiliaries, and a few pieces of artillery. Its defending force rose to about 15,000 in July. The besieging army numbered possibly over 40,000 men in late June. Despite almost two weeks of constant and heavy bombardment which managed to breakdown some of the defenses, the Burgundians failed to take the city and Charles was defeated.

1480 Siege of Rhodes. The Turks failed to take the city despite their use of artillery. This is one of the few checks the Turks encountered in their relentless advance through the Eastern Mediterranean.

1492 Siege of Granada. In many ways the siege of Granada was almost an anticlimax as the finale of a major campaign. However, it brought an end to the last Moorish state in Iberia, completed the Reconquista, and led to the expulsion of Moors and Jews and the beginning of the Spanish Inquisition.

1495 Assault on Viipuri. During their invasion of Finland in September 1495, the Russians laid siege to the Finnish city of Viipuri. The Finns awaited Swedish aid that never arrived, but they held out until November 11 when the siege culminated in the Viipurin pamaus or "The Great Bang of Viipuri." According to popular history, the Russians had already captured the powder tower of the castle and were on their way down, when the castle commander, Knut Posse, blew up the tower with the Russians in it. The superstitious Russians considered it an ill omen and left the castle alone. They also failed to take the Olavinlinna Castle, although they continued to raid southern Finland up to the vicinity of Turku and Häme. However they were unable to take and hold these strategic fortified centers.

1520 Siege of Rhodes. In this second siege of Rhodes, the Turks heavily bombarded the newly modernized fortifications and took them by storm. The last Crusader foothold in the East fell.

1521 Siege of Belgrade. With less dynamic leadership than in 1456, the Hungarians succumbed after Turkish mines destroyed sections of the walls and a massive assault brought victory.

1529 Siege of Vienna. A force of 100,000 Turks was unable to breach the city walls held by 20,000 men. After three weeks, the Turks withdrew. The siege of Vienna finally broke the tide of the Turkish advance into Europe.

History of Medieval Artillery

Before the advent of the cannon, besiegers had a wide variety of weapons at their disposal. The catapult and the ram were probably the most ancient, going back to antiquity. The ram was simply a log that was used to hit gates and walls until they crumbled. Catapults came in various sizes and were used to launch stone projectiles or incendiaries over city and castle walls. When they landed on the walls themselves the projectiles usually inflicted little damage except in the case of weak masonry, wooden palisades, or timber hoardings. Since they had a high angle of fire and their accuracy was limited, chances of scoring direct hits were not great. In addition, most catapults had a firing range of about 200 meters, which made them vulnerable to the defenders' catapults which had a longer range if they were placed on the towers or walls. However, catapults were often used with deadly effect in psychological warfare. For instance, they were used to hurl dead animal carcasses and cadavers over the walls to spread pestilence among the enemy and terrorize the population.

Sometime in the 12th century, a more deadly and accurate siege weapon made its appearance the trébuchet. It replaced the torsion weapons such as the catapult and associated projectile throwing machines as the main heavy artillery weapon. Instead of torsion, it relied on counterweights to provide the momentum for launching heavy projectiles. Although several types of trébuchets are mentioned by the chroniclers, there are no accurate descriptions of this weapon in any medieval source. It is known that a very large one was used at Acre in 1291 and that it took 100 carts to transport after it was dismantled. The trébuchet used at the siege of Orleans in 1428 filled 26 carts. According to a medieval chronicler, one particular trébuchet required 50 tons of sand to fill its counterweight bucket. We are also told by the chroniclers that some of these weapons reached ranges of 500 meters and lobbed projectiles weighing as much as 200 to 300 pounds.

Tests with reconstructed weapons done in 1999 by Professor Wayne Neel of the Virginia Military Institute with a group of specialists and Renaud Beffeyete, a French restorer of castles, for the Public Broadcasting System program series NOVA near Urquhart Castle overlooking Lochness, confirmed that the trébuchet was capable of hurling projectiles of 250 pounds with surprising accuracy, but not the long ranges reported by the chroniclers.

It has been theorized the height of walls increased in order to intercept projectiles and protect the area within the enceinte. However, this seems unlikely because the higher the wall, the weaker it would be. In addition, a high wall would present a larger target. The high trajectory of the descending trébuchet projectiles would allow them to gather enough momentum to inflict serious damage.

The first gunpowder weapons appeared in the 14th century, and by the 15th century several types of artillery came into use. Handguns and light artillery will not be mentioned here since they did not seriously affect the medieval fortifications other than the creation of a different type of firing loop for their use by the defenders. Medium and heavy guns were important in that they could lay down a continuous barrage against the defenses. It appears that it was more practical and effective to deliver several batteries of guns to a siege than to create several batteries of trébuchets. Before the effects of the shock of their noise and the initial damage had worn off, these 15th-century guns appear to have been effective enough to cause most defenders to surrender immediately.

When they first came into use on a large scale during the Hundred Years War their shock effect caused many premature capitulations.

The 15th-century cannons changed greatly from the less effective ones of the 14th century which were mostly crude wrought iron tubes with iron hoops reinforcing them— generally referred to as bombards. Many of these early bombards were as dangerous to the crew as to those being targeted, especially the breechloaders. During the first centuries of use they were built by and manned by civilians and this did not change until about the 17th century. Transport was not easy since most weapons were not mounted on a mobile carriage and had to be broken down. There were no standardized sizes, which also meant the stone, lead or iron projectiles might not fit all of the cannons being used during a siege or battle. Many different types of artillery came into use. The smallest fired a projectile which only had an anti-personnel capability. Some of them could do damage to earthen and wood ramparts. A medium-sized weapon found in France between 1360 and the end of the next century, called a "courtaud," weighed over 1,000 pounds. These fired balls of up to 18 pounds. The heavier and more familiar muzzleloaded bombards which used direct fire, as opposed to the larger caliber bombards that were similar to a mortar, were the most effective against various types of fortifications. There are a number of surviving examples. Many of these fired stone balls weighing over 100 pounds and some could fire a round weighing up to 280 pounds.

Cannon rounds had a greater velocity than tré-buchets but sometimes did less damage since they would be hitting the walls straight on and with so much force that they might embed themselves in the walls without bringing them down. The advantage of the cannon was that it could usually stand off a greater range and became less vulnerable to counter-fire. Although enemy gunpowder-type artillery could eliminate that advantage. Also, the further away the cannon was placed, the less effective a long-range

round would be against the walls. If that were not the case, the siege engineers of later centuries would not have dug parallels and zigzag trenches to help move their guns forward. Transporting and firing these guns required a large train. The mortar type of bombard was used for lobbing heavy rounds over and against the enemy walls. One built in Laon during the 15th century weighed over 1,000 pounds and fired a stone ball weighing about 60 pounds.

France was the first country to attempt to standardize sizes of the bombards under the direction of the Bureau brothers. They created seven types ranging from 2 pounds to 64 pounds during the 15th century.

Most weapons from the 15th to 16th centuries would be classified with the following names. The sizes of projectiles are from several sources:

Falcon, Cerbottana–fired 1- to 2.5-pound projectile.
Serpentine–fired 6-pound projectile.
Saker–fired 5-pound projectile.
Demi-culverin, Mignon–fired 8-pound projectile.
Basilisk–fired 20-pound projectile.
Culverin–fired 20- to 24-pound projectile.
Courtaud–fired 60- to 100-pound projectile
Cannons or bombards–fired normally 50- to 300-pound projectile.
Mortar - fired 300-pound projectile.

The giant weapons were less common and only appeared in a few major sieges.

Some of the monster weapons, like Urban's big gun used against Constantinople, included one built at Ghent which weighed 30,000 pounds and fired a ball weighing almost 800 pounds at a range of 1,000 meters. The Burgundian Mons Meg weighed 12,000 pounds and fired a ball weighing almost 550 pounds and used 100 pounds of gunpowder. It fired a round every six minutes which was considered fast. The largest cannon built was the Russian "King of Cannons" built in 1502 which fired a 2,000-pound stone ball.

Glossary

Adulterine castle A castle that was unlicensed.

Alcazaba Spanish term derived from the Arabic referring to a castle or citadel occupying the high point of a city or town. It is supposed to come from the Arabic term casbah which referred to a fortified place of a lord or chieftain in North Africa.

Alcázar Spanish term derived from the Arabic referring to a fortified palace which in many cases is not much different than a castle serving as a residence.

Allure The wall walk along the top of the curtain. *Chemin de Ronde* in French.

Ashlar Stone cut into blocks and given a smooth surface with squared edges as opposed to rough cut stone.

Bailey Courtyard.

Barbican Fortification placed in front of the gatehouse to protect it. Also known as an outwork.

Bartizan Small turret, usually a lookout post built on a corner of a tower or wall in the latter part of the High Middle Ages. Characteristically it was supported by corbels. They were quite common in Renaissance fortifications. In medieval fortifications the corbels are generally not as close to the top of the wall. They were used along the middle part of the wall as well as the corners.

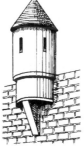

Bartizan

Bastide Originally a town developed in France as a fortified settlement.

Bastilles Initially small timber forts that were garrisoned and used by a besieging army to protect their own positions. The French also referred to these as *châtelets*. The French later used the term bastille and châtelet to refer to masonry fortifications consisting of one or more towers that were used to block a passage.

Bastion Salient that projects beyond the walls to provide flanking cover.

Batter A talus-like slope in front of the wall that gives it added thickness and strength. Same as plinth and also known in French as talus.

Battles Medieval formation referring to a group of soldiers under one leader. Many armies were divided into three battles and during movements one usually followed the other. In combat many times they lined up with a right, left, and center battle.

Belfry Mobile siege tower made of wood.

Bergfried German term referring to a tall tower which in many respects is similar to a keep. Its origin is different in that it is not related to the motte and bailey and that it also did not always include space for any type of a residence. It appears, however, that some larger bergfrieds are really no different than some of the smaller keeps in the west. The bergfried generally occupies much less space than a western keep.

Bossed masonry or *Bossage* French term used to describe the outer surface of a wall of cut stone with the face uncut or the face actually carved with bump-like features probably for both decoration and defensive purposes.

Boulevard French term referring to a low earthwork placed in front of a gate or section of a wall to mount cannons. Also, can refer to a terreplein or flat area behind a rampart usually for placing artillery on a post-medieval masonry fortification.

Bretèche French term referring to a type of stone machicolation which opens over a window or doorway.

Buttress Projection that supports a wall. In French they are called *contreforts*.

Castle Term derived from the Latin *castellum*. Common terms in other languages for a castle are: French–*château-fort*; German–*burg, schloss*; Italian–*castello*; Polish–*zamek*; Spanish–*alcázar, castillo*; Russian–*zamok*.

Bretèche

Châtelet French term referring to a type of gatehouse position that normally had two towers and the typical array of defenses. It was linked to the city walls but could operate independently of them. The English appear to have no term for this other than gatehouse. Sometimes a châtelet may be confused with a barbican and the French also have a secondary meaning (see Bastilles) which sometimes leaves some confusion.

Chemin de Ronde French term for the allure or wall walk.

Chemise Wall surrounding a donjon or keep on top of a motte used in the 12th century. A keep may be attached to it, but this wall usually created a shell keep. Later in artillery forts of the 16th century it evolved into a slightly different feature.

Classical Era Term referring to the latter part of ancient history, which began with the Greeks and ended with the Romans. Many important developments in fortifications made during the Roman period profoundly influenced medieval military architecture.

Corbel Stone or wooden support used on parapets for hoardings and machicolations.

Counter-castle Term synonymous with counter-fort and siege-castle referring to a strong fortification, often similar to a motte and bailey. It was built by the besieger to block an escape route or possible relief route which the besieged may attempt to use. This type of fortification was usually of a temporary nature and did not survive to this day in most cases.

Counter-fort Fortified position, sometimes of masonry, built by a besieging force to protect their siege lines.

Crenel Opening between merlons.

Curtain Walls between towers.

Donjon French term for the English keep.

Drum tower Round tower.

Enceinte The walls encircling a castle.

Fausse braie Low wall usually in front of the counterscarp that helped protect the fosse and main walls, especially after cannons were developed. This type of wall was usually designed as a low enceinte to protect the base of the main walls of the enceinte.

Garderobe Latrine.

Gatehouse Defensive position usually consisting of a tower or towers through which the entrance through an enceinte or any set of walls is made.

Gothic Era Phase of architecture that began in the 12th century and dominated through the 15th century. Many of its characteristic features often were found in churches, included flying buttresses, high walls, pinacles and Gothic vaults. Some of these features can also be found in the fortifications of the period.

Greek fire Incendiary type weapon based on a secret formula developed in the Byzantine Empire. It probably consisted of a mixture of sulphur, quicklime, pitch, and other ingredients.

Gród, Grad, Gorod, Grody, Grady, or Gorody Slavic terms for a fortified site varying from a small position to a fortified town that was defended by earth and timber walls.

Herse French term for portcullis.

Hill-top fort Iron Age fortification associated with Celtic settlements. Usually a hill-top position fortified and defended. Many hill-top forts were found in northwest Europe, especially the British Isles where they remained in use during the Dark Ages.

Hoarding Wooden structures which extended over the stone walls and had openings so the defender could cover the face of the wall in addition to crenels for covering the area to the front of the wall.

Hrad Czech word for a gród or castle.

Keep The most fortified position in a castle, usually square until late in the 12th century. The keep served as the residence of the owner of the castle. Initially it was called by the French term "donjon." The word "keep" was not used until after the Middle Ages.

Loops Narrow slits in the walls which could be used for allowing in light, or if designed with sufficient space they were for the use of weapons like bows and crossbows.

Machicolation Works added to the battlements which extend beyond the wall and allow the defender to use openings in the floor to control the face of the wall.

Machicoulis French term referring to machicolations that extend across the battlements of a wall or tower as opposed to a bretèche which is only above a gate, door, or window.

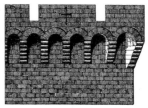

Machicoulis

Machicoulis sur arche French term referring to machicoulis that is inside an arch which can be found on walls and over entrances.

Mantlet Large wooden shield protecting assault troops and sappers.

Merlon Section of the battlements between two crenels.

Machicoulis sur arche

Meurtrière French for "murder hole." Usually found in the ceiling in an elaborate gateway so that anyone forcing entry was subject to fire from above.

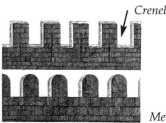

Crenel

Merlon

Mural Tower Tower connected to the mural walls.

Mural Refers to the walls.

Murder hole See Meurtrière.

Motte French term referring to the artificial hill used in motte and bailey type castle.

Oillet Small round opening in the wall or part of an arrow loop for observation.

Parapet Sometimes referred to as the protective wall with merlons and embrasures adjacent the allure.

Plinth See Batter.

Portcullis Grid-like gate that is usually of wood and shod in iron which drops vertically. Known as a *herse* in French.

Postern Sally port in the form of a small door or gate.

Rath Circular enclosure that was sometimes referred to as a ring fort which may have an earthen rampart and a ditch or be formed on a hill top which might be leveled. In Ireland it generally refers to a type of ring fort used only for single families.

Ringwork Circular defense usually formed with earth and timber works in use since ancient times. There is not much difference between a ringwork and a ring fort, except for the fact that the former usually has earthworks and a fosse that are larger than the enclosed area. Many ringworks were in use during the Middle Ages. They were similar to the East European gród, although the gród might be considered more of a ring fort. They maintained their popularity well into the 11th century in England and even later in Ireland.

Romanesque Era Architectural period dominant in the 11th and 12th centuries, although it began a few centuries earlier. Usually best exemplified in churches with thick walls and heavy buttresses among other features. Some Romanesque features were found in fortifications of the period.

Sally port Small gate used as an exit from a fortified position or for launching a raid upon besiegers.

Shell keep Keep that is actually circular with an open courtyard in the center.

Shell keep

Siege-fort See Counter-Castle

Solar Private chamber in a castle, but usually refers to a well-lit room.

Tenaille Fortified position placed in front of the curtain wall and usually between bastions of post-medieval fortifications. This provided additional protection for the enceinte.

Ward Courtyard, bailey.

Zamek Polish term for a castle made of masonry.

Bibliography

Abel Vilela, Adolfo de. *Guía de la muralla romana de Lugo*. Lugo, Spain: Grafic-Lugo.

Aigle: Suisse depuis 500 ans. Imprimerie A. Boinnard, 1976.

Alcock, Leslie. *Was This Camelot? Excavations at Cadbury Castle 1966-70*. New York: Stein and Day, 1972.

Amelchenko, V.V. *Druzjiny drevney Rusy*. Moskow: Military Edition, 1992.

Andrews, Francis B. *The Mediaeval Builder and His Methods*. New York: Dorset Press, 1992.

Arxznski, Marian. *Budownictwo warowne zakonu krzyzackiego w Prusach (1230-1454)*. Torun, Poland: University Mikolaja Kopernika, 1995.

Balard, Jean. "Des châteaux forts en Palestine." *L'Histoire* 47: 94 -101.

Banaszak, Dariusz, Tomasz Biber. *An Illustrated History of Poland*. Richard Brzezinski (trans.). Poznan, Poland: Podsiedlik-Raniowski & Co. Ltd., 1998.

Banks, Arthur. *A World Atlas of Military History*. New York: Hippocrene Books, Inc., 1973.

Belohlávek, Miroslav. *Hrady, zámky a tvrze v Cechách, na Morave a ve Slezsku, Západni Cechy*. Prague, 1985.

Bennett, Matthew. *Agincourt 1415*. London: Osprey, 1996.

Billings, Malcolm. *The Crusades: Five Centuries of Holy Wars*. New York: Sterling Publishing Co., Inc., 1996.

Bishko, Charles J. "The Spanish and Portugese Reconques 1095-1492." *A History of the Crusades*, Vol 3. Ed. Harry W. Hazard. Madison, WI: University of Wisconson Press, 1975. 396-456.

Blackburn, Donald S. "Collision of Faiths." *Military History* June (1994).

Bogdanowski, Janusz. *Sztuka obronna*. Cracow: Zarzad Zespolu Jurajskich Praków Krajobrazowych, 1993.

—. *Architektura obronna w krajobrazie Polski*. Warsaw: Wydawnictwo Naukowe PWN, 1996.

Borowiejska-Birkenmajerowa, Maria. *Barbakan Krakowski*. Cracow: Wydawnictwo Literackie, 1979.

Bottomely, Frank. *The Castle Explorer's Guide*. New York: Avenel Books, 1979.

Boyle, Charles, ed. *The Domestic World*. Alexandria, VA: Time-Life Books, 1991.

—, ed. *The Domestic World*. Alexandria, Virginia: Time-Life Books, 1991.

Bradbury, Jim. *The Medieval Siege*. Rochester, NY: The Boydell Press, 1992.

Brereton, Goefrey ed & trans. *Froissart Chronicles*. Bungay, England: Penguin Books, 1978.

Brockman, Eric. *The Two Sieges of Rhodes: The Knights of St. John at War 1480-1522*. New York: Barnes and Noble Books, 1969.

Brown, R. Allen, Michael Prestwich and Charles Coulson. *Castles: A History and Guide*. Poole, UK: Blandford Press, 1980.

Brunet, Roger. *Le Languedoc et le Roussillon*. Paris: Libraairie Larousse, 1977.

Budzinski, Tadeusz. *Zamki i palace Polski poludniowo-wschodniej*. Rzeszow, Poland: Libri Resssovienses, 1998.

Bugay, A.S. *Zmiewy waly-letopis' zemli Rusko*.

Bujak, Adam. *Zamki i zamczyska*. Warsaw: Editions Spotkania.

Bujlo, Violetta and Wojciech Kapalczynski. *Zabytki i muzea województwa Jeleniogórskiego*. Jelenia Góra, Poland: COIT, 1992.

Burne, Alfred H. *The Crecy War*. Novato, CA: Presidio Press, 1990.

Cardberg, C.J., and Knut Drake. *Turku Castle*. Christopher Grapes (trans.). Turku, Finland: Turku Provincial Museum, 1998.

Catherine, Cécile. *Aimer les châteaux de la Loire*. France: Editions Quest, 1986.

Cauvin, André. *Découvrir la France cathare*. Limbourg, Belgium: Nouvelles Editions Marabout, 1978.

Chambers, James. *The Devil's Horsemen*. London: Caswell, 1979.

Chanas, Ryszard and Janusz Czerwinski. *Dolny Slask -przewodnik*. Warsaw: Wydawnioctwo Sport i turystyka, 1977.

Chatelain, A. *Architecture militaire medievale*. Paris: L'Union R.E.M.P.ART., 1972.

Chatelain, André. *Châteaux forts: images de pierre des guerres médiévales*. Cahors, France: L'Imprimerie Tardy Quercy, 1983.

Chodynski, Antoni Romuald. *Malbork*. Warsaw: Arkady, 1982.

—. *Zamek malborski w obrazach i kartografi*. Warsaw: Panstwowe Wydawnictwo Naukowe, 1988.

Christiansen, Eric. *The Northern Crusades: The Baltic and the Catholic Frontier 1100-1525*. Minneapolis: University of Minnesota Press, 1980.

Cipolla, Carlo M. *Before the Industrial Revolution: European Society and Economy 1000-1700*. Norton, 1994.

Contamine, Philippe. *War in the Middle Ages*. Michael Jones (trans.). New York: Basil Blackwell Inc., 1984.

Corfis, Ivy A. and Michael Wolfe, ed. *The Medieval City Under Siege*. Woodbridge, England: Boydell Press, 1995.

Cosman, Madeleine P. *Fabulous Feasts*. Trans. Anthea Bell. New York: George Braziller, 1996.

Curry, Anne and Michael Hughes, ed. *Arms, Armies and Fortifications in the Hundred Years War*. Rochester, NY: Boydell & Brewer Inc., 1994.

Czubiel, Lucjan. *Zamki Warmii i Mazur*. Olsztyn, Poland: Pojezierze, 1986.

Dagnan, M. Provins: *Guide touristique*. France.

de la Croix, Horst. *Military Considerations in City Planning: Fortifications*. New York: George Brazillier, 1972.

Delbruck, Hans. *The Barbarian Invasions*. Walter J. Renfroe (trans.). Lincoln, Nebraska: University of Nebraska Press, 1980. Vol. II of *The History of the Art of War*.

—. *Medieval Warfare*. Ed. Walter J. Renfroe. Lincoln, Nebraska: University of Nebraska Press, 1990. Vol. III of *History of the Art of Warfare*.

Deveze, Lily. *The City of Carcassonne*. France: Imprimerie J. Bardou.

Devries, Kelly. *Joan of Arc: A Military Leader*. Phoenix Mill, UK: Sutton Publishing, 1999.

Donnelly, Mark, and Daniel Diehl. *Siege: Castles at War*. Dallas: Taylor Pulbishing Company, 1998.

Duffy, Christopher. *Siege Warfare: The Fortress in the Early Modern World 1494-1660*. London: Routledge & Kegan Paul Ltd., 1979.

Dupuy, Ernest R. and Trevor N. Dupuy. *The Encyclopedia of Military History From 3500 b.c. to the Present*. New York: Harper and Row, Publishers, 1970.

Ebhard, Bodo. *Der Wehrbau Europas Im Mittelalter*. Wurzburg, Germany: Stütz Verlag GmbH, 1998.

Eggenberger, David. *A Dictionary of Battles From 1479 b.c. to the Present*. New York: Thomas Crowell Company, 1967.

Elton, Hugh. *Warfare in Roman Europe AD 350-425*. Oxford: Clarendon Press, 1997.

Enaud, Francois. *The Chateau of Vincennes*. Trans. John Seabourne. France: Caisse Natinale des Monuments Historiques, 1965.

Erlande-Brandenburg, Alain. *Cathedrals and Castles: Building in the Middle Ages*. Rosemary Stonehewer (trans.). New York: Harry N. Abrahms, Inc., 1995.

Estreicher, Karol. *Historia sztuki w zarysie*. Warsaw: Panstwowe Wydawnictwo Naukowe, 1988.

Etchéto, Pierre. "Le Caire: citadelle de Saladin." Toulouse, France, 1999. Unpublished.

—. "Méthoni: forteresse vénitienne de Grèce." Toulouse, France, 1999. Unpublished.

Fajt, Jiri, Jan Royt and Libor Gottfried. *The Sacred Halls of Karlstejn Castle*. Prague: Central Bohemia Cultural Heritage Institute, 1998.

Falkus, Malcolm and John Gillingham. *Historical Atlas of Britain*. New York: Crescent Books, 1987.

Forey, Alan. *The Military Orders: From the Twelfth to the Early Fourteenth Centuries*. Toronto, Canada: University of Toronto Press, 1992.

Forteresse de Largoet. Rennes, France: Imp. Simon.

Foss, Clive and David Winfield. *Byzantine Fortifications: An Introduction*. Pretoria, South Africa: University of South Africa, 1986.

France, John. *Western Warfare in the Age of the Crusades 1000-1300*. Ithaca, NY: Cornell University Press, 1999.

Frein, Kurt and Jan Miessner. *Burgen Am Rhein*. Norderstedt: Harksheider Verlagsgesellschaft, 1983.

Froidevaux, Yves Marie and Marie Geneviève. *Mont Saint-Michel from the Strand to the Spire*. Jean-Marie Clarke (trans.). Paris: Le Temps Apprivoisie, 1988.

Frombork: plan miasta. Poznan, Poland.

Garbaczewski, Zbigniew. *Szlakiem Zamkow Piastowskich w Sudetach*. Warsaw: Wydawnictwo PTTK Kraj, 1988.

Gardelles, Jacques. *Le château féodal dans l'histoire médiévale*. Milan: Publitotal, 1988.

Gaunt, Peter. *A Nation Under Siege: The Civil War in Wales 1642-48*. London: HMSO Publications, 1991.

Gies, Joseph & Frances. *Life in a Medieval Castle*. New York: Harper Colophon Books, 1979.

Gillard, F. *Revue historique du Chablais vaudois*. Aigle, Switz.: Imprimerie de la Plaine du Rhone, 1979.

Golawski, M. *Poland Through the Ages*. Paul Stevenson (trans.). London: Orbis Limited, 1971.

Grabois, Aryeh. *The Illustrated Encyclopedia of Medieval Civilization*. New York: Mayflower Books, 1980.

Gravett, Christopher. *Medieval Siege Warfare*. London: Osprey, 1996.

Griffith, Paddy. *The Viking Art of War*. London: Greenhill, 1995.

Guerquin, Bohdan. *Zamki w Polsce*. Warsaw: Arkady, 1984.

Guide to The Castle of the Counts of Flanders. Ghent, Belgium: Snoeck-Ducaju in Zoon, 1980.

Haftka, Mieczyslaw and Mariusz Mierzinski. *Malbork: Castle of the Teutonic Order*. Trans. Eliza Lewandowska. Milan, Italy: Master Fotolito, 1996.

Hamann, Bernard. *Hochkönigsburg. Die Geschichte einer Wiedererstehung*. Mulhouse: Edition L'Alsace, 1990.

Hammond, P.W. *Food and Feast in Medieval England*. Stroud, England: Sutton Publishing, 1998.

Harding, David. *Waffen Enzyklopädie*. Stuttgart: Motorbuch Verlag, 1993.

Haro, Elias. *Hame Castle*. Helsinki: National Board of Antiquities, 1980.

Harrison, Peter. "The Fortified Village of Ushguli in the Georgian Caucasus." *FORT* 25 (1997): 3-36.

Hawkes, Jacquetta, ed. *Atlas of Ancient Archaeology*. New York: McGraw, 1974.

Heath, Ian. *Armies of Feudal Europe 1066-1300*. Worthing, England: Wargames Research Group, 1978.

—. Byzantine Armies 1118-1461 AD. London: Osprey, 1995.

Hetherington, Paul. *Byzantine and Medieval Greece*. London: John Murray, 1991.

Hibbert, Christopher. *Agincourt*. New York: Dorset, 1979.

Higham, Robert and Philip Barker. *Timber Castles*. Mechanicsburg, PA: Stackpole Books, 1995.

Hill, David and Alexander Rumble, ed. *The Defence of Wessex: The Burghal Hidage and Anglo-Saxon Fortifications*. Manchester, England: Manchester University Press, 1996.

History of Gradara. Rimini, Italy: Foto Edizioni PAMA.

Hogg, Ian. *The History of Fortification*. New York: St. Martin's Press Inc., 1981.

Hogg, O.F.G. *Clubs to Cannon*. New York: Barnes & Noble, Inc., 1968.

Hooper, Nicholas and Matthew Bennett. *Cambridge Illustrated Atlas of Warfare: The Middle Ages 768-1487*. London: Cambridge University Press, 1996.

Hughes, Quentin. *Military Architecture*. London: Hugh Evelyn, 1974.

Härö, Elias. *Häme Castle Guide*. Trans. Helsinki The English Centre. Helsinki: National Board of Antiquities, 1980.

Jardillier, Armand. *Le château d'Harcourt*. Paris: L'Academie d'Agriculture de France, 1984.

Keen, Maurice (ed). *Medieval Warfare: A History*. Oxford: Oxford University Press, 1999.

Kemp, Anthony. *Castles in Color*. New York: Arco Publishing Co., 1978.

Koch, Wilfried. *Style w architekturze*. Warsaw: Bertelsmann Publishing, 1996.

Kohn, George Childs. *Dictionary of Wars*. New York: Facts on File, Inc., 1999.

Laffin, John. *Brassey's Dicitionary of Battles*. New York: Barnes, 1995.

LaMonte, John L. *The World of the Middle Ages*. New York: Appelton-Century-Crofts, 1949.

Lampl, Paul. *Cities and Planning in the Ancient Near East*. New York: George Braziller, Inc., 1968.

Lawrence, T.E. *Crusader Castles*. London: Michael Haag Ltd., 1986.

Le château du Grandson: guide du visiteur. Colmar, France: S.A.E.P. Ingersheim, 1980.

Lebedel, Claude. *Comprendre la tragédie des Cathares*. Tours: Editions Ouest - France, 1998.

Le Halle, Guy. *Précis de la fortification*. Paris: PCV Editions, 1983.

Leroy, Jules. *L'Éthiopie: archéologie et culture*. Bruges, France: Desclée De Brouwer, 1973.

Leroy, Marcel. *Bouillon et son château dans l'histoire*. Belgium.

Lewis, Archibald R. *Nomads and Crusaders 1000-1368*. Indiana University Press, 1988.

Libal, Dobroslav. *Castle of Britain and Europe*. Prague: Blitz Editions, 1999.

Loven, Christian. *Borgar Och Befästningar i Det Medeltida Sverige*. Stockhom: Uppsala University, 1996.

Lynn, John A., ed. *Feeding Wars*. San Franciscp: Westview, 1993.

Maestra, Francisco F., ed. *Contrahistoria gótica*. Barcelona: Okios-Tau, 1997.

Magnusson, Magnus. *Vikings!* New York: E.P. Dutton, 1980.

Malkowska-Holcerowa, Teresa. *Lipowiec: dawny zamek biskupow krakowskich*. Warsaw: Muzeum W Chrzanowie Wydawnictwo PTK "Kraj", 1989.

Marshall, Christopher. *Warfare in the Latin East 1192-1291*. London: Cambridge University Press, 1994.

Marshall, Robert. *Storm from the East.* Los Angeles: University of California Press, 1993.

Matteini, Nevio. *The Republic of San Marino: Historical and Artisitic Guide.* San Marino: Azienda Tipografica Editoriale, 1981.

McEvedy, Colin. *The New Penguin Atlas of Medieval History.* London: Penguin, 1992.

McEvedy, Colin and Richard Jones. *Atlas of World Population History.* Harmondsworth, England: Penguin Books Ltd., 1978.

McNamee, Colm. *The Wars of the Bruces: Scotland, England and Ireland 1306-1328.* East Lothian, Scotland: Tuckwell Press, 1997.

McNeill, Tom. *Castles in Ireland: Feudal Power in a Gaelic World.* New York: Routledge, 1997.

Melegari, Vezio. *The Great Military Sieges.* New York: Thomas Crowell Company, 1972.

Mertens, Charles. *Le château féodal de Beersel et ses seigneurs.* Bruselles, Belgium: Editions Historia.

Mesqui, Jean. *Châteaux forts et fortifications en France.* Paris: Flammarion, 1997.

—. *Les châteaux forts: de la guerre à la paix.* Italy: Gallimard, 1997.

Mierzwinski, Mariusz. *Malbork: The Castle in Close Up.* Trans. Enid Mayberry and Michael Senter. Warsaw: Terra Nostra S.C., 1996.

Migos, Athanassios. "Rhodes: The Knights' Battleground." *FORT* 18 (1990): 5-28.

Monreal y Tejada, Luis. *Medieval Castles of Spain.* Cologne: Konemann, 1999.

Montrottier Castle and Leon Mare's Collections. France: Imprimerie Typo-Offset Gardet Annecy-Seynod, 1987.

Morris, John E. *The Welsh Wars of Edward I.* Conshohocken, PA: Combined Books, 1996.

Morton, Catherine. *Bodiam Castle.* Plaistow, England: The Curwen Press, 1975.

Nadolski, Andrzej. *Polska technika wojskowa do 1500 roku.* Warsaw: Oficyna Naukowa, 1994.

Newark, Timothy. *Medieval Warfare.* London: Jupiter Books Ltd., 1979.

Nicolle, David. *Italian Medieval Armies 1300-1500.* London: Osprey Publishing Ltd., 1983.

—. *The Age of Charlemagne.* London: Osprey Publishing, 1985.

—. *Armies of the Ottoman Turks 1300-1774.* London: Osprey Publishing Ltd., 1986.

—. *The Armies of Islam 7th-11th Centuries.* London: Osprey Publishing Ltd., 1987.

—. *The Mongol Warlords.* London: Brockhampton Press, 1990.

Nobile, Marco. *A New Guide to Bracciano: The Odescalchi Castle and Its History.* Italy: Plurigraf, 1990.

Norman, A.V.B. and Don Pottinger. *English Weapons & Warfare 449-1660.* Englewood Cliffs, NJ: Prentice Hall, Inc., 1979.

Notice sur le château de Fougères. Fougères, France: Le Syndicat D'Initiative Fougères.

Oman, Charles. *A History of the Art of War in the Middle Ages.* Vol. 1 & 2. Mechianicsburg, PA: Stackpole Publishing, 1998.

Oman, Charles W.C. *Castles.* New York: Berkman House, 1978.

Ottendorff-Simrock, Walther. *Castles on the Rhine.* Barry Jones (trans.). Wurzburg, Germany: STV.

O'Neil, B.H. St. J. and G.C. Dunning. *Deal Castle.* London: HMSO, 1966.

Parment, Roger. *The Castle of Robert the Devil.* Rouen, France: Imp. A. Vallee.

Pépin, Eugène. *Chinon, son château, ses églises.* Paris: Successeur Henri Laurens.

Pepper, Simon and Nicholas Adams. *Firearms and Fortifications: Military Architecture and Siege Warfare in Sixteenth-Century Siena.* Chicago: University of Chicago Press, 1986.

Perrett, Bryan. *The Battle Book:Crucial Conflicts in History from 1469 BC to the Present.* London: Arms and Armour, 1992.

Platt, Colin. *The Castle in Medieval England & Wales.* New York: Barnes, 1981.

Polak, Tadeusz. *Zamki na kresach: Bialorus, Litwa, Ukraina.* Warsaw: Pagina, 1997.

Pratt, Colin. *The Atlas of Medieval Man.* New York: St. Martin's Press, 1979.

Prescott, William H., Albert D. McJoynt, ed., *The Art of War in Spain: The Conquest of Granada 1481-1492.* London: Greenhill Books, 1995.

Prestwich, Michael. *Armies and Warfare in the Middle Ages: The English Experience.* Hew Haven, CT: Yale University Press, 1996.

Quehen, René. *Peyrepertuse et San-Jordy.* Toulouse, France: La PHIM, 1979.

Raffa, Enzo. *San Gimignano: The Town with Beautiful Towers.* San Gimignano, Italy: Brunello Granelli's Edition, 1980.

Redman, Charles L., ed. *Medieval Archaeology.* Binghamton, New York: State University of New York, 1989.

Rees, William. *Caerphilly Castle and Its Place in the Annals of Glamorgan.* Caerphilly, Wales: D. Brown and Sons, Ltd., 1974.

Reynolds, Susan. *Fiefs and Vassals.* New York: Oxford University Press, 1994.

Rigold, S.E. *Temple Manor, Strood.* London: Her Majesty's Stationery Office, 1962.

Riley-Smith, Jonathan (ed). *The Atlas of the Crusades.* New York: Facts on File, Inc., 1991.

Robards, Brooks. *The Medieval Knight at War.* New York: Barnes, 1997.

Roberts, Peter. *Great Castles.* New York: Crescent Books, 1981.

Rodzinski, Witold. *The Walled Kingdom: A History of China from Antiquity to the Present.* New York: Free, 1984.

Roquebert, Michel and Christian Soula. *Citadelles du vertige.* Edouard Privat, 1972.

Ruaux, Jean-Yves. *Dinan.* Rennes, France: Imprimerie Raynard, 1983.

Runciman, Steven. *The Fall of Constantinople 1453.* London: Cambridge University Press, 1969.

Russell, Josiah C. "Population in Europe." *The Fontana Economic History of Europe.* Glasgow: Collins/Fontana, 1972. 25-71.

Saalman, Howard. *Medieval Cities.* New York: George Braziller, 1968.

Sailhan, Pierre. *La fortification: histoire et dictionnaire.* Paris: Tallandier, 1991.

Sainz de Robles, Federico Carlos. *Castillos en España.* Madrid: Aguilar S.A. de Ediciones, 1952.

Sancha, Sheila. *The Castle Story.* New York: Penguin, 1981.

Seward, Desmond. *The Hundred Years War: The English in France, 1337-1453.* New York: Atheneum, 1978.

—. *The Monks of War.* London: Penguin Books, 1995.

Seymour, William. *Battles in Britain 1066-1746.* London: Sidgwick & Jackson, 1975.

—. *Great Sieges of History.* London: Brassey's, 1991.

Sinisalo, Antero. *Olavinlinna Castle.* Sonja Tirkkonen and Stephen Condit (trans.). Painolinna: The Gild of St. Olof, 1997.

Smail, R.C. *Crusading Warfare 1097-1193.* London: Cambridge University Press, 1972.

Steinmetzer, Alfred and Jean Milmiester. *Château-palais de Vianden.* Trans. Roland Gaul. Diekirch, Lux.: Imprimere du Nord.

Stopar, Ivan. *Gradovina Slovenkem.* Ljubljana, Slovenia, 1987.

Sweetman, David. *The Medieval Castles of Ireland.* Woodbridge, UK: Boydell Press, 2000.

Sypek, Robert. *Zamki i obiekty warowne jury krakowsko-czestochowskiej.* Warsaw: Agencja Wydawincza.

The Fortress of Gradara. Italy: Litografia Marchia.

Tikhomirov, M. *The Towns of Ancient Rus.* Ed. D. Skvirsky. Trans. Y. Sdobnikov. Moscow: Foreign Languages Publishing House, 1959.

Toker, Franklin K. "Early Medieval Florence Between History and Archaeology." *Medieval Archaeology.* Charles L. Redman, ed. Binghamton, New York: State University of New York, 1989.

Toussaint-Samat, Maguelonne. *The History of Food.* Trans. Anthea Bell. New York: Barnes & Noble, 1992.

Toy, Sidney. *Castles: Their Construction and History.* New York: Dover, 1984.

Villena, Miguel Castello. *The Castle of Santa Barbara in Alicante.* Alicante, Spain: Sucesor de Such Serra y Compania, 1963.

Viollet-le-Duc, E.E. *Military Architecture.* Novato, CA: Presidio Press, 1990.

Vizcaino, Aureliano Gómez. *Castillos Y Fortalezas de Cartagena.* Cartagena, Spain: Aforca, 1998.

Wackerfuss, Winfried. *Burg Breuberg Im Odenwald.* Breuberg, Germany: Selbstverlag des Breuberg-Bundes, 1996.

Warner, Philip. *Sieges of the Middle Ages.* London: G. Bell and Sons, Ltd., 1968.

—. *The Medieval Castle.* New York: Barnes, 1993.

Watson, Bruce A. *Sieges: A Comparative Study.* Westport, CT: Praeger, 1979.

Wenger, Daniel and Jean-Marie Nick. *Randonnees Autour Des Chateaux Forts D'Alsace.* Mulhouse, France: Editions Du Rhin, 1996.

Wenzler, Claude. *Architecture du château fort.* Rennes: Editions Ouest-France, 1997.

Wezgowsl, Wladislawa. *Olsztyn, historie i legendy.* Poland.

Whitlock, Ralph. *The Warrior Kings of Saxon England.* Atlantic Highlands, N.J.: Humanities Press, 1977.

Wilson, David M., ed. *The Northern World: The History and Heritage of Northern Europe 400-1100.* New York: Abrams, 1980.

Wise, Terence. *Medieval Warfare.* New York: Hastings House, 1976.

Wood, Michael. *In Search of the Dark Ages.* New York: Facts on File Publications, 1987.

Zagrodzki, Tadeusz. *Czersk: zamek i miasto historyczne.* Warsaw: Biblioteka Towarzystwa Opieki Nad Zabytkami, 1996.

Index